A GUIDE TO O'CASEY'S PLAYS

A GUIDE TO O'CASEY'S PLAYS

From the Plough to the Stars

John O'Riordan

St. Martin's Press   New York

© John O'Riordan 1984

ISBN 0–312–35300–6

Library of Congress Cataloging in Publication Data

O'Riordan, John.
A guide to O'Casey's plays.
Includes index.
1. O'Casey, Sean, 1880–1964–Criticism and interpre-
tation. I. Title.
PR6029.C33Z783 1984   822 '.912   83–40587
ISBN 0–312–35300–6

To
KATE
with enduring love;
and to
JOHN TREWIN,
most amiable of drama critics,
whose inspiration has played its part
in the genesis of the present work

Contents

vii

Contents

* Full-length plays

Preface

One of the characters in Graham Greene's distinguished novel, *The Power and the Glory*, remarks that 'A poet is the soul of his country'. The same can be said equally of a great dramatist or true-born novelist.

Sean O'Casey (1880–1964) is not only an outstanding Irish dramatist but a world-venerated playwright of distinction. He was born of poor Protestant parents in Dublin (the youngest of a large family) and received little formal education, mainly because of a chronic, recurring, ulcerated cornea condition of both eyes (trachoma) – a condition common in malnourished families. Weak eyesight did not hamper his determination to write vigorous, poignant plays, which, throughout his active life, brought storms of controversy, even though all were opulently written in the finest traditions of Shakespearian and Biblical English. The mixture of conflicting moods and the kind of intrusion of comedy into tragedy, manifest in all his dramas, has its roots in the splendour of Shakespearian traditions, though O'Casey alone remains the supreme exponent among contemporary dramatists of this amazingly kaleidoscopic art.

His other great strength is his marvellous sense of character portrayal. Foremost among such, of course, is the inimitable 'Captain' Boyle – the 'Paycock' of the Dublin tenements and the closest approximation we have to Falstaff in contemporary literature. 'The Irishman', O'Casey once quipped, 'hasn't any sentimentality. He behaves when he is drunk as an Englishman does when he is sentimental'. In the later plays, where the setting is invariably modern Arcadian Ireland, rural 'paycocks' strut the stage, some of whose pronouncements and behaviour outclass even those of 'Captain' Boyle. All are gifted with golden-tongued oratory, thus illustrating there can be an air of fantasy to the utterances of all but the most rigidly sober of O'Casey's mythical creations in his fantastical but irresistable stage repertoire.

In Britain, O'Casey has been woefully undervalued, so that, for the most part, he is known principally as the author of two highly-acclaimed successes: *Juno and the Paycock* (1924) and *The Plough and the Stars* (1926). As the present analytical study reveals, he is the author of so much more. *The Silver Tassie* (1928) is now regarded by many as one of the finest anti-war testaments of the century. Fantasies such as *Purple Dust* (1940), *Red Roses for Me* (1942) and *Cock-a-Doodle Dandy* (1949) are also major works that deserve the stylish productions we reserve for the indirect-action drama of Strindberg and Chekhov. So far, the English theatre has done insufficient justice to these wayward, beribboned achievements. Abroad, they have won laurelled triumphs.

In 1937, O'Casey wrote that 'The beauty, fire and poetry of drama have perished in the storm of fake realism.' Subsequently, he, more than any other English-speaking dramatist of his day, has succeeded in blending genuine realism, the inner truth about people's lives and relationships, with *the beauty, fire and poetry of drama*. In the field of tragicomedy he remains unrivalled.

This analysis is the first complete study of all the playwright's dramatic works, spanning a forty-year cycle, from the period of the early twenties to the early sixties. Space is also given to O'Casey's very early apprentice-play, *The Harvest Festival* (1919), written long before the heyday of his Abbey renown and only recently published in America and Britain. The plays are viewed chronologically: each work has a theoretical introduction, an outline of plot and characterisation, plus considerations for staging, together with a brief history of important productions and an artistic evaluation intended to assist enterprising future directors, appreciative theatregoers and, indeed, all admirers of O'Casey's plays.

Comedy and catharsis suffused are keynotes of the dramas throughout. Humour – for O'Casey – lies in the disparity between human aspiration and performance, in the rare make-believe of theatre, as reflected in the mythical rainbow between fantasy and reality: the bridge between the plough and the stars, or 'the bridge of vision' suggested in his autobiographical play, *Red Roses for Me*.

Finally, there is O'Casey's own vision which sees beyond the mythological beings of his own indomitable characters into the dark and lovely impulses of the human heart, of which those superb dramatic creations are more than just an articulate record and reflection.

For allowing me to quote extensively from the text of the plays, I am immensely grateful to Eileen O'Casey for her help, affection and sustained interest.

I am also gratified by the persuasion and encouragement of drama historian J. C. Trewin – doyen, unchallengeably, among theatre critics – whose faith has been unwavering from the start. My appreciation, too, to Michael Foot, who once predicted to me in a letter that O'Casey would 'come back, with your assistance, again and again'.

Bibliographically, my debt to Professors Ron Ayling, David Krause and Edward Mikhail is apparent; also to Bob Lowery, editor of the *O'Casey Annual*. My thanks, additionally, to Bob Johns for his continuous and friendly advice; and to my publishers for their editorial perception and helpfulness.

J. O'R.

1 *The Harvest Festival* (1918–19): an Ironic Melodrama

O'Casey's earliest extant play – an ironic melodrama focusing on class struggles in the strife-ridden atmosphere of Dublin in 1913, the year of industrial turmoil – is of historic importance in that it established in the thirty-nine-year-old Irish labourer the unflinchable resolve to continue his repeated efforts to attain recognition as a major, universal dramatist in the well-sprung traditions of Shaw, Strindberg and O'Neill – and even no less a luminary than Shakespeare himself.

Written around 1918 or 1919, it was the second play O'Casey had offered the Abbey Theatre – home of Ireland's national drama. It was turned down, along with the first, *The Frost in the Flower* and the third, *The Crimson in the Tricolour* – both of which do not appear to have survived: in the opinion of Yeats and other Abbey directors, 'We don't think either [of the first two] would succeed on the stage'. About the third, there were mixed feelings: Lady Gregory favoured a production, Yeats was against. The undaunted workman-writer gritted his teeth and carried on. His fourth effort was his well-known two-acter, *The Shadow of a Gunman*, his first produced play. It was an immediate triumph; and along with *Juno and the Paycock* and *The Plough and the Stars* won him international acclaim.

With *The Harvest Festival* (an incomplete revised draft of the first act was retained among his papers, along with the original manuscript of the entire play), O'Casey became gradually disenchanted, not with the theme but its structure – 'interestingly conceived', declared the directorate, 'but not well executed'; though he himself was sufficiently enamoured of theme and purpose to have wished to have preserved it intact over the years. It was, of course, to become precursor of *Red Roses for Me* (with a near-identical theme treated instead in a phantasmagorical way) and,

1

characteristically and thematically, influences many of the later plays, such as *The Star Turns Red, Hall of Healing* and *The Bishop's Bonfire*. Its theme of mercy, towards the close, suggests pre-echoes of *Juno and the Paycock*. The play, therefore, merits consideration among the rich and capricious reserves of O'Casey's fertile repertoire.

Until recently, the playwright's earliest, surviving drama – like Shaw's final whimsicality entitled *Why She Would Not* – had remained altogether unpublished and unproduced. On the publication side, this has now been rectified. (A German translation is also available.) Pressures in the expanding field of research and O'Casey studies had prevailed upon the playwright's widow, Eileen, and trustees of the New York Public Library – which had purchased the manuscript of the play in 1969 for inclusion in its extensive O'Casey archive in the Berg Collection – to publish the text ten years later, in America in 1979, and in Britain and Ireland, as part of centenary celebrations of the playwright's birth, in March 1980.

The plot, in the wording of the dust-jacket to the English edition,

> deals with Irish workers' battles against economic oppression and religious hypocrisy, with that vital combination of passion, humour and pathos that distinguishes O'Casey's later plays.

A rich melodrama, involving representatives of Church, employers and labour, the play, O'Casey tells us, in his fourth autobiographical volume, *Inishfallen, Fare Thee Well*:

> dealt with the efforts of militant members of the unskilled unions to put more of the fibre of resistance to evil conditions of pay and life into the hearts and minds of the members of the craft unions whose gospel was that what was good enough for the fathers was good enough for the sons. The action took place in the busy preparations made by a church for holding the annual harvest festival, which the Anglo-Catholics sneeringly called the Feast of Saint Pumpkin and all Vegetables.

Although *The Harvest Festival* lays no claim to greatness, historical reasons dictate that it should be included in the corpus of O'Casey's works. The dramatist himself, in his meridian years, never strove to promote it. The play is a three-act drama set in contemporary Dublin, portraying industrial conflicts and internecine unrest. It is strongly autobiographical.

The cast includes Jack Rocliffe, a young radically-minded, socially aware unskilled labourer – a virile likeness of the playwright at the time – who leads his fellow-workers in a justifiably motivated strike, in the face of overwhelming odds, and dies for their cause; his widowed mother, heroically conceived, hard-working woman of the tenements, who bears a likeness to O'Casey's own mother, eulogised more fittingly in the early volumes of autobiography, such as *I Knock at the Door* and *Pictures in the Hallway* and, again, in *Inishfallen, Fare Thee Well*; the kindly and sympathetic clergyman, the Reverend J. Jennings, Rector of St Brendan's, where Mrs Rocliffe – despite infirmities of her age – still worships, even though Jack has become an infidel and pins his faith instead on a revolutionised society of the future; the Reverend W. Bishopson, Curate of St Brendan's, narrow-minded and sanctimonious; Melville Williamson, ignorant, protestantising Churchwarden, obsessed with tawdry self-importance and a tinkling symbol of human hypocrisy; his wife, sycophantic and shallow; their colourless daughter, Clarice, aspiring to the hand of the Curate; Sir Jocelyn Vane, arrogant, possessive, prosperous merchant and leading Synodsman – an intractable hard-liner, flaunting his influence as wealthiest parishioner; Mrs Duffy, a poor parishioner and neighbour to Jack's mother; Tom Nimmo, a bricklayer – conceived in the Irish romantic tradition and firmly against strike-action and employed in tasks at the Williamsons' home; Bill Conway, a docker on strike and comrade-in-arms with Jack (his name appears as Brophy in the *Dramatis Personae*); and Simon Waugh, prevaricating Sexton of St Brendan's.

The theme, basically, is the problem of conscience in a society that does not allow for conscience on one side of the great social divide; and the eventual triumph of conviction over intolerance, even though inequity and inhumanity prevail.

The scene in the first act is the lounge of the Williamsons, styled in the worst excesses of Victorian decor. As Tom Nimmo is engaged in restyling the hearth with decorative tiles, the Churchwarden's wife is hovering prominently in the foreground, watching over him as he works and sanctimoniously humming a hymn. Noticing his effective use of a craftsman's straight-edge, she remarks – before a ring at the

door-bell interrupts the flow of her mannered conversation – that
the Bible is 'The Christian's Straight-Edge . . . that makes us feel
the roughness and unevenness of sin'. While she is out of the room,
the workman relaxes for a moment with his pipe, soliloquising, from
a wry, Catholic standpoint, that 'Protestants is curious animals'.
(He repeats the catchphrase later.) When Mrs Williamson re-
enters, carrying huge home-grown vegetables handed in at the
front-door for display in the church – in readiness for the Harvest
Festival – the workman's reaction is one of caustic comment and
risible incredulity as he soliloquises yet again: '. . . I heard that
Cromwell turned churches into stables, but it beats all to think of
them turnin' churches into market gardens. God save us but
Protestants is curious animals'.

Discoursing on the dangers of strike-action spreading throughout
the capital, the workman is told by Mrs Williamson:

> When will the poor ignorant workmen get common-sense, and
> realise that God intended that they should be content to do the
> work that come to their hands. Oh, if they only knew the
> blessedness of content, & a quiet trust in God they would never
> trouble their heads about a strike. Oh, if they would only become
> converted and think only of that beautiful home that awaits all
> those that suffer patiently the few passing tribulations of this
> world . . .

ending on a sanctimonious note with a hymn: and interrupted again
by a ring at the door. In the short interval the workman soliloquises
again on the dangers of strike-breaking from his position as
conscience-stricken outlaw in an early, raw industrial society, where
acceptance of trade union principles and practice – in the face of
general incomprehension and prejudice – is as controversial as it is
today.

Before the return of Mrs Williamson, with the Curate and
Clarice, Jack Rocliffe has entered and mocks Nimmo for his passive
reluctance towards the impending strike, and for ever resenting, yet
accepting, the *status quo* of stagnation. His earnest plea is accompanied by a humorous cynicism:

> If this strike develops much more there will be a Harvest Festival
> in Dublin, in which the Labour Leaders will be the clergy, the
> strikers the congregation; in which curses will be prayers, hymns

will be lamentations, the choir will be police and soldiers, the seed will be the blood of the proletariat, and the crop will be the conception of the New Idea of Labour in Ireland.

With such a volatile climate prevailing in Ireland's capital at the time, one can imagine the reluctance of Yeats and other directors to stage such talk of wild insurrection and workers' bravado. The Harvest Festival ceremony itself (undertaken by the better-off parishioners in the community) is resented both by Jack and Nimmo, the poorer workers: it becomes the target for irony in the unpredictable atmosphere of stark melodrama as the play develops.

When Nimmo bemoans the strike, Jack quotes Emerson – and later Tennyson – in defence of emancipation of the workers' cause (the workers who, in Tennyson's phrase from *Locksley Hall*, were 'ever reaping something new'). Emerson's dimensions and self-reliant ordinances are Jack's: 'society everywhere', Emerson had foretold, 'is in conspiracy against the manhood of every one of its members'. Nothing great, nothing adventurous, Jack reminds his faint-hearted colleague – in the assimilation of Emerson's ideals – would ever be achieved without superhuman effort and enthusiasm. Emerson's view of poverty is also voiced by Jack (and later by Red Jim in *The Star Turns Red*) from the cold hand of personal experience – through the recollections of ineradicable scars of a poverty-stricken upbringing – though the Curate, Mrs Williamson and Clarice – confronted with the robust and studied 'insolence' of Jack, holding forth before them – are clearly sceptical.

Finally, when the Churchwarden makes his entrance, reminding his wife, in a fit of chauvinism, that she is also an oblate in his house as well as in church – demonstrating the fact by flinging the vegetables littering the table on to the floor – he reprimands Jack for his demagogic behaviour and disengaging radicalism in his own household (Jack's reply is that 'the Church teaches that it is a work of charity to instruct the ignorant'), amid sudden vociferous interruptions from an angry crowd, offstage, storming the house and stoning the windows. In the ensuing panic, Jack tells Mrs Williamson not to be alarmed: 'It's only the opening hymn', he affirms, 'of the workers' Harvest Festival'. (Just as in *The Silver Tassie*, later on, the twin themes of irony and mercy are exploited, in an unusual combination, within a melodramatic framework.)

Throughout the second act, the contrasting background in the poorly-furnished surroundings of the Rocliffes' upper tenement

home reflects the daily anguish and heartbreak which afflict Mrs
Rocliffe in her struggle to make ends meet for herself and Jack, even
though her son's intellectual pursuits and polemical sympathies are
beyond her simple though sincere understanding. In conversation
with Mrs Duffy, a humble parishioner, both are mystified by Jack's
crusading enthusiasm and avowed Gospel of Discontent, and regret
his recent, continued absence from church services, especially on
such occasions as the Harvest Festival. Both, who are incontrovertibly pious and planning to attend the Festival service, are
suddenly taken aback when Jack rushes in, aflame with expectation,
to tell them that his role as workers' tribune is now assuming an
urgent, embattled twist, as many hundreds of his fellow-strikers
have been arrested on the quaysides and streets and serious trouble
is expected.

While Jack is hurriedly taking his tea, the Rector and Curate pay
a surprise visit to persuade Jack to attend the Harvest Festival and
also to introduce, both to Jack and his mother, the new Curate,
who, of course, unbeknown to the Rector (in a neat, melodramatic
touch on the playwright's part), has already met Jack in a hostile
encounter at the Williamsons' during the first act. Because Jack
affirms his life's purpose is now the total overthrow of poverty and
industrial tyranny, he cannot promise to attend, even though he
acknowledges a debt of honour and gratitude to his kindly pastor
and former friend. The Rector respects his radical thinking –
admiring his messianic self-confidence – though his Curate roundly
condemns it and is noticeably aloof and antagonistic.

After Jack has departed to scenes of unrest and impending
violence, offstage – with armed police and scabs – the Rector
comforts Mrs Rocliffe in the belief that the leadership in Jack will
outshine and outstrip all danger. Jack's steadfast, as well as
headstrong qualities are the subject of admiration between the
Rector and Mrs Rocliffe, who both retain a reverential attitude to
the reforming zeal and passionate intensity that have replaced the
apostasy of her son. Like his dead father, during Jack's early
childhood, Mrs Rocliffe affirms, he belongs in a world not hers or
theirs.

From cosmic outposts, sounds of distant disturbances can be
heard. The Rector consoles Jack's mother but the Curate voices the
hope that the strength of law will be invoked and the strikers taught
a lesson. Suddenly, Mrs Duffy, who left earlier – when the Rector
paid his call – now dressed for attendance at the Harvest Festival,

rushes in to confirm that bloodshed and disorder are spreading, with crowds blocking the entrance to the church. After sounds of uproar have subsided, voices can be heard coming towards the house and upstairs, offstage, as Jack – in a seriously wounded state – is carried into the room, with the aid of Bill Conway, a fellow-striker, and another colleague. As he is laid gently on the sofa, Conway explains that in attacking a convoy of scabs, in the course of the conflict, Jack risked his life and was shot. In his last dying moments, he pleads forgiveness and asks both Bill and the Rector to take care of his aged mother and predicts that out of tribulations and woe will come industrial peace and stability and assured happiness in this transcendentalised ending, while Mrs Rocliffe laments the passing of her son. His plea of mercy ('Oh God, that it may please Thee to have mercy upon all men') is later echoed by the Rector in the ironic final conclusion to the play.

As preparations are being made for the burial of Jack, the setting, in the final act, is in the grounds of St Brendan's Church. Ravaging conflicts disturbing the peace of Dublin are symbolised by religious feuds which provoke contention among the Rector's own flock. The Rector is a ritualist determined to carry out the rites of faith, as he sees it, in the rubrics of tradition and order, which upsets the extreme Protestant viewpoint among his Select Vestry, who are determined to put a stop to such 'romanising' practices. They are motivated by an ignorant evangelism and hatred of the Rector's admiration for Jack, whom they look upon not as a former parishioner but as a scoundrel. They have a powerful ally in Sir Jocelyn Vane – local Citizen Kane – wealthy, dominant merchant and chief benefactor, and backed by Curate Bishopson. The Rector has only isolated support among the poorest of his parishioners, such as Mrs Rocliffe and Mrs Duffy; and, wedged in support of both sides, is the abject Sexton, the lugubrious Simon Waugh.

As a backcloth to the play, we should remember that Ireland's whole world was sharply divided against itself. England was on the verge of a fierce Continental war that was to conflagrate into world-wide catastrophe: at the same time, industrial warfare as well as nationalistic demands were wracking Dublin. When O'Casey wrote the play, in 1918–19, Anglo-Irish conflicts, leading to guerrilla war, were in full swing, following Sinn Fein's victories at the polls in Ireland in the General Election of 1918. As the Rector declines to listen to the dictates of his Vestrymen and ignores the counsel of Vane and Bishopson to disallow a church funeral for Jack – with a cortège supported by Republican working colleagues, whose spokesman is Conway – he reflects that he is isolated and alone. And he accepts, with weary though august resignation, that this is due, predominantly, to what he terms the 'terrible unrest of the lower-classes' in 'overthrowing all our long-settled ideas of peace and happiness'. His parish, he reflects, is also sharply divided and lacks, he regrets, charity.

In the face of such overwhelming opposition, the Rector backs down and tells Jack's mother that a funeral in his church is now impossible, reminding her that 'a priest-ridden laity was a terrible tyranny, but a laity-ridden priesthood is a more terrible one'. Mrs Rocliffe, in a bitter aside, exclaims: 'You are just as bad as the rest of them; you are afraid to go again' them . . . My poor, poor Jack was right – the Church is always again' the workin'-class'.

As the cortège approaches and a band playing The Dead March is heard in the distance, the Vestrymen mount guard outside the church, and the cortège is finally turned away (in the direction, instead, of Union Hall, more fittingly, for a workers' wake). When Sir Jocelyn enters the porch, he is taunted by Bill: 'Go on . . . and sing your psalms an' read your Bible, an' thump your craw . . . We'll stan' by the man that kep' himself down by fightin' the rich, again' them that lifted themselves up by fighting the poor'. Outside the church grounds Jack's work-mates, in true Socialist tradition, intone The Red Flag, while the church bell tolls, ironically, for the Harvest Festival. (The closing mood, as in most of O'Casey's early dramas, is one of bathos.) As the Rector sadly enters his church, to officiate instead at the planned service, he utters a prayer (similar to Jack's at the end of the second act) for all in danger and in tribulation. It is a prayer of mercy that God will have pity on *all* humanity, even families of renegade workers and those responsible, such as Vane, for offsetting their blacklegs against locked-out workers.

The ending foretells the conclusion to *The Star Turns Red* and Shaw's *Too True to be Good*: even though we may have outgrown our religion and our political system – is the inference – the preacher must preach the way of life; even the dawn of a new one.

As an early prefigurative effort, *The Harvest Festival* shows great potential. Its dialogue is original and racy in parts, its construction – as the Abbey directors had admitted – is commendable; and, though by no means a masterpiece, there is no naturalistic evidence to suggest that the Abbey Theatre, with its range of actors ideal for the leading parts, could not have staged a worthwhile production. It is, after all, a working-class play, written by a labourer, told from a labourer's standpoint.

The play is melodramatic in conception, but tragicomic in execution, presenting a panorama of social progress, not unlike Galsworthy's *Strife*. Its weakness is partly due to a lack of fully rounded, flesh-and-blood types of characterisation – well-marked in succeeding plays by the dramatist – as befits a naturalistic-styled play; and partly in the plot (the leading character dies at the end of the second act and is outwardly more of a trouble-making dissenter than a dramatic hero. The character of the Rector, in a conflict-torn situation, arouses our sympathy more). Sir Jocelyn Vane, the employer against whom the strike is directed, is not very much concerned with the main action, which is invested instead in the characters of the Churchwarden, Williamson, his wife and daughter who are fanatically devoted to the concept of Harvest Festival. Even so, the labourers themselves – as is to be expected – are more convincingly drawn.

Of the main characters, Jack Rocliffe is based on an idealised version of O'Casey himself, though a somewhat faceless, twenty-five-year-old revolutionary, who lacks the broad, humanistic vision of Ayamonn Breydon, the magnetic hero of *Red Roses for Me*. He is little more than a stock allegorical figure; though the raw youthfulness of his character is important. Mrs Rocliffe, the maternal mother-figure, in her seventy-sixth year, is also rather negative, compared to the firmness and indomitability of O'Casey's later characters, such as Juno, Bessie Burgess and Mrs Breydon. The fifty-five-year-old Rector, the Reverend Jennings, white-haired and white-bearded, with a handsome face and gentle smile, is in the same apostolic succession of Protestant pastors O'Casey knew personally from the days of his church-going youth. He is a less forceful prototype of the equally understanding and enlightened clergyman, the Reverend E. Clinton, portrayed in *Red Roses for Me*. Bill Conway is the earlier model for Brannigan in *The Star Turns Red*. He is based on O'Casey's former colleague, Barney Conway, and loyal assistant to Jim Larkin (model, in turn, for Red Jim in the same play). The remaining characters tend to be fixed, conventionalised representations.

Factions that occur between the Rector and his Select Vestry parallel those described by the playwright in the pages of his autobiography, *Pictures in the Hallway*, in the Chapter 'The Sword of Light'. There are traces, too, of O'Casey's friend of earlier days, the tram conductor, Ayamonn O'Farrel, in Tom Nimmo – with his nationalistic candour and humorous catchphrases, as well as abhorrence of an escalation of the class-struggle and workers' ideals of freedom and renunciation of poverty.

The flame of vision in *The Harvest Festival* is that which inspired Emerson, when addressing a gathering of mechanics' apprentices in Boston in 1841, to conclude:

> . . . the whole interest of history lies in the fortunes of the poor. Knowledge, Virtue, Power are the victories of man over his necessities, his march to the dominion of the world. Every man ought to have this opportunity to conquer the world for himself. Only such persons interest us . . . who have stood in the jaws of need, and have by their own wit and might extricated themselves, and made man victorious.

It is a recurring, as well as unifying theme throughout successive plays of O'Casey – a peerless Ploughman gazing, like Tennyson, at richer galaxies in the heavens – 'a swarm of fire-flies', in the poet's words, 'tangled in a silver braid'. Emerson, too, is a self-confessed transcendentalist. Jack – and, later, Ayamonn Breydon (though Ayamonn is a truer incarnation) – is modelled in the same transcendental mould: 'collectors', says Emerson, 'of the heavenly spark with power to convey the electricity to others'. As spokesman for the underprivileged, Jack Rocliffe is meant to be a more dynamic creation, in this early play, than the author intended; he is too rawly conceived and lacks poetic grace. He is an oratorical mouthpiece of Dublin's indestructible poor, portrayed in fuller panoply in the widely-accepted, later stage successes, for which O'Casey remains justifiably and uniquely renowned. (Before his established reputation as an international playwright, O'Casey himself – in his capacity of manual labourer – was a persuasive public speaker at workingmen's gatherings.)

Nevertheless, in comparison with most other characters in the play (the Rector and Mrs Rocliffe apart), Jack remains a bolder spirit, a more surrendered soul: a reformer, a herald of the future who embarks on seas of adventure and engages our interest throughout. As Emerson, in a *Lecture on the Times* (1841), epitomises:

For the origin of all reform is in that mysterious fountain of the moral sentiment in man, which amidst the natural, ever contains the supernatural for men.

The heaven as well as the earth. As the adolescent O'Casey, seen through a transmogrified vision in *Pictures in the Hallway*, reflects:

> . . . Look up, and they [the heaven and earth] don't seem to be so far away from each other. Anyhow, they were made together. In the beginning, God created heaven and earth . . . Yet, sometimes it seemed that they were a hell of a way asunder.

The next plays certainly reveal this widening, seemingly unbridgeable chasm, as Ireland – and especially Dublin – was becoming a place of stormy torment and fratricidal conflict. In Yeats's foretelling words from 'The Second Coming':

> Things fall apart; the centre cannot hold;
> Mere anarchy is loosed upon the world . . .

Irishmen everywhere, as Yeats and later O'Casey – in glorified stage triumphs – were to testify (in the poet's words from '1919'), 'were crack-pated when we dreamed'. The dream, worse than the actuality, was soon to turn sour. In Yeats's own poetic admonition from 'Two Songs from a Play':

> Whatever flames upon the night
> Man's own resinous heart has fed.

The drums of guerrilla war were beating; and already there was blood upon the drums.

2 *The Shadow of a Gunman* (1923): Kaleidoscope of the Troubles

O'Casey's next play, his familiar two-acter and first acknowledged triumph by the Abbey Theatre, bears witness to the ugly sphere of worsening Anglo-Irish relations and portrays his native Ireland, in support of Yeatsian metaphorical claims, as 'a fool-driven' and 'dragon-guarded land'.

Theatrically, it is an unnerving, as well as compassionately compounded experience: it is also a warmly lyrical, highly satiric, kaleidoscopic drama, set against the background struggle for Irish freedom involving terrorism at the hands of the gunmen. As Irish Republican Army activities – in pursuit of an independent Ireland – were reaching their climax in 1920, Dublin is seen as a bleak back-cloth of escalating violence, with daily ambushes and guerrilla house-raids (the occupants pulled out of bed, searched and, on the slightest pretext, hauled off to the nearest barracks), transforming the country into a 'Gunman's republic'.

The play triumphs with a history-on-one's-doorstep approach, and is a trenchant illustration of a scalding tragicomedy and prototype black comedy. A compound of anger and pity, and of laughter and sorrow, O'Casey's technique puzzles many critics used only to easy formulations and simplifications. To an interviewer in 1925 the playwright would confide: 'They tell me *The Shadow of a Gunman* breaks all the rules. If the characters live and the play holds the audience, that's enough'. Here, O'Casey's characterisation is already vivid and his dialogue passionately alive.

With this and succeeding plays, such as *Juno and the Paycock* and *The Plough and the Stars* – forming a triptych of Dublin in the troubled years of pre-independence – the author quickly won world-wide renown as a dramatist of New Born Ireland. Like its two mighty sequels, *The Shadow of a Gunman* is a testament of

12

working-class Dublin life during the Troubles. Almost all Sean O'Casey's great qualities as a dramatist are reflected in this, his first produced play.

As Allardyce Nicoll in *British Drama* has noted, O'Casey's dramatic kaleidoscope, along with *Juno and the Paycock* (subsequently published as *Two Plays*), is one of 'two brilliantly bitter studies of Irish life. These at once marked him out as among the most gifted of latter-day playwrights'. (The devastating sense of bitter irony is characteristic of most O'Casey plays.) *The Shadow of a Gunman*, claims Raymond Williams in *Drama from Ibsen to Brecht*, is 'a bitter postcript to Synge's *Playboy of the Western World*': a mythopoeic recreation of Synge's farcical portrayal of the image of false hero – so beloved by the Irish – and its even absurder heroism. 'The mantle of Synge', comments John Gassner, in his monumental *Masters of the Drama*, 'had at last found a shoulder that could wear it with honour'. O'Casey's taut drama has an outward semblance of 'realism' and yet a quality of inner-truth that is beyond realism, as well as an assured feeling for words and for their rhythms, and the extraordinary commingling of comedy and tragedy. The dramatic thrust continually changes.

O'Casey's two-act play is set in a tenement room in Dublin in 1920 when guerrilla warfare was at its most menacing. The whole country was under martial law. The Irish Volunteers, now known as the Irish Republican Army, harried the British at every opportunity, and the British Government sought to counter the threat through reprisals – as reinforcements for the already established Royal Irish Constabulary – by the Black and Tans (so-called because of their khaki coats and black trousers) who were, in turn, later reinforced by an Auxiliary Division of ex-British army officers, known as Auxiliaries – or the hated 'Auxies' – some of whom burst in to the tenement during the raid in the second act. Although these British ex-service men were cruel and brutal in their methods of search and tactics – the Auxiliary in the play is a typically representative exponent – the cowardice and callousness of the revolutionaries and gunmen-snipers are emphasised by the tortured degree of civilian suffering and murder.

The play is a troubled skein of tragedy with comic overtones – with victims but without heroes. It embodies a classic caprice of Irish awareness and human folly. Although relatively short, O'Casey's play already clearly shows his characteristically pungent form of artistry.

The lodging-room of the setting is cramped and squalid, surrounded by a towering blind alley of slum windows: and, of its two inmates, one, Seumas Shields, a slovenly, erratically-disposed pedlar (a daily communicant who, invariably and indolently, mistakes the sound of the midday Angelus bell for the sound of the early-morning Mass bell), sleeps in a bed, when conditions permit, and the other, his rooming-mate, under subleased circumstances, a self-styled, self-engrossed poet, Donal Davoren – whose 'efforts towards self-expression' (in the words of the direction) have overcome 'the struggle for existence' – sleeps on a couch, adjacent to a typing table. In the thickening fog of Irish politics and opacity of religious exaggeration, Davoren remains aloof and is both sceptic and wise-fool.

The poet speaks eloquently, in Shelleyan fashion, of his own views on Irish emancipation and is mistakenly assumed by his neighbours – and especially by the other residents of the tenement – to be a heroic revolutionary and member of the IRA. A young girl from the same lodging, the attractive Minnie Powell, is fired by his words, and he is sufficiently flattered by her flirtatious and romantic approach to encourage and accept the idea (for her sake, princi-pally, he decides to become the semblance of a revolutionary – the shadow of a gunman – as she, as well as others, have fallen in love with the heroic notion of gunman-poet), and consequently rank, in the eyes of the audience and playwright, as self-deceiving poetaster ('poet and poltroon'), on whom the tragic, ironic momentum of the play impinges, ineluctably and intumescently. His fellow room-mate, Shields, is an inveterate boaster and wind-bag, who prates about the follies of the Irish and the hopelessness of his country. He is lazy, as well as cowardly, though filled with a wry sense of humour.

The plot is simple and inexorable: Donal, who at first revels in the undue praise showered upon him, misbegottenly, by a romantic peasantry ('A pioneer in action as I am a pioneer in thought', he mythically asserts to Minnie), is later haunted by the figment of neighbourly imagination – a re-enactment of Synge's myth of mock hero-worship – because one of the pedlar's itinerant callers, an unknown man named Maguire, who quietly disappears to the mountainous outskirts of Dublin's Knocksedan ('to catch but-terflies') – turns out to be the real man of action by transplanting a bag of bombs under Seumas's bed. Before the rooming-tenants can dispose of the explosives, a British military raid on the premises, in the dead of night, surprises all the occupants, including the play's rich reserves of sardonically portrayed subsidiary characters (over-flowing with life and humour in this overcrowded Dublin tene-ment). The infatuated, unsuspecting Minnie, on learning of the plight of Davoren and Shields, insists on hiding the dynamite in her room, as the English Auxiliaries approach. ('. . . maybe they won't search it', she naively believes; 'if they do aself, they won't harm a girl'.) In the end, she is caught, dragged away and killed in ambush while trying to escape from the soldiers' lorry.

The irony of the play is that loud-mouthed romanticists, like the pedlar and poet, are the real ones who cause such tragic waste of life, by basking in their own self-esteem; their wanton words sending the girl to her unnecessary and inevitable death, in an ironic interpret-ation of poetic justice, inhumanly applied. O'Casey uses Irish characters and themes to provide a tragic and ironic commentary on mankind in general (a technique of Synge and Shaw).

In two short acts, O'Casey, in *The Shadow of a Gunman*, manages to contain much of the Irish dream and the Irish tragedy. No people need martyrs and heroes more than the Irish; and in Dublin in 1920 (just as in Belfast in 1970 or 1980) it was the gunmen who provided them with an endless stockade of plaster saints and stuccoed heroes. The philosophy of the play is mouthed by the droll, unshaven, layabout Shields, who is presented as the archetypal reprobate Irishman:

> I wish to God it was all over. The country is gone mad. Instead of counting their beads now they're countin' bullets; their Hail Marys and paternosters are burstin' bombs – burstin' bombs, an' the rattle of machine-guns; petrol is their holy water; their Mass is a burnin' buildin'; their De Profundis is 'The Soldiers' Song', an' their creed is, I believe in the gun almighty, maker of heaven an' earth – an' it's all for 'the glory o' God an' the honour o' Ireland.'
>
> (Act II)

Although Shields insists he is a Nationalist – believing in the freedom of Ireland and that the English presence is unwelcome – he carries the play's total conviction when he gives the lie to the belief about 'the gunmen blowin' about dyin' for the people, when it's the people that are dyin' for the gunmen!' (The relevance of which is not lost on contemporary audiences in the shadow of the Ulster Troubles.) The play is not only a lament for the future of a people.

O'Casey makes a great plea for tolerance which seems never to have been heard.

The cruel topicality of the play's final impact is now firmly established: bewilderment and horror at one section of the community trying to murder and kill the other; the play is clearly against war, against strife. An American interviewer in 1958 asked O'Casey why it was the women, mostly, in his plays, who always seemed to be the courageous ones. His reply was: 'Women must be more courageous than the men. Courage doesn't consist in just firing a pistol and killing you. I wouldn't call that courage at all, I'd call it stupidity'. And, when asked what a woman's courage consisted in, he suggested: 'Fortitude – and patience – and understanding'. In life, women are more courageous than men, he avowed, because they are much nearer to the earth than men are. 'Men are more idealistic, stupidly idealistic. They're not as realistic as women. The woman has to be nearer the earth than the man.'

Although rightly regarded as an authentic tragedy (the second act dramatises the raid and its tragic outcome), the first act is little more than a comic interlude, with the recurrent theme of the invasion of personal privacy within a tenement depicted with a vaudevillist flavour. (The technique is repeated in subsequent plays, from *Juno and the Paycock* to *The Silver Tassie*.) The second act is a web of intrigue, apprehension and search leading to the climactic shooting, in a climax of melodramatic tragedy, ending on a note of bathos. The power of the play lies in its oblique treatment of tragic events: the agony of Ireland is apprehended through a gallery of mostly unheroic people. O'Casey's group of raffishly comic Irish people and strong, manipulative women from the tenements has more vitality than most stage narratives and resembles the artfully feckless characters who invade John Ford films and the more powerful Hollywood Westerns.

Of the dozen characters depicted, at least ten are sharply observed and incisively drawn: the thirty-year-old poet and dreamer, Donal Davoren – eponymous anti-hero, whose efforts to compose inspirational verse are baulked by a succession of unwelcome interruptions, within the flimsy demarcations of tenement life, culminating in a Black and Tan raid; his companion and rooming-mate, the stocky, garrulous, thirty-five-year-old Seumas Shields – a man of little action and even untidier self-respect; Minnie Powell, pretty colleen from one of the upstairs rooms of the same tenement – in love with Davoren, whom she admires as a fugitive gunman; Tommy Owens, small, scrawny, simple-minded hero-worshipper – also from the same tenement – embued with nationalistic fervour and richly full-throated (a braggart and 'blower' when he has a sup taken); Adolphus Grigson, splendidly truculent as the drunken roaring Orangeman who lives downstairs (his reaction to the bomb is somewhat different from his reaction to the bottle); Mrs Grigson, as cowed as her braggart Protestant husband is bombastic – who subjects his wife to strict Ulster interpretations of the Bible over their married state; Mr Mulligan, comical landlord, a stage-Irish figure in the Dion Boucicault tradition (the nineteenth-century melodramas of Boucicault, along with the clowns of Shakespeare's richly-textured masterpieces, are among the emergent playwright's formative influences, we learn from *Pictures in the Hallway*); Mr Maguire, a pedlar who associates with Shields; Mrs Henderson, a large-hearted harridan and timid Mr Gallogher, residents of an adjoining tenement, who plague the writing life out of Davoren with futile, neighbourly requests for supposedly IRA protection, and are farcically drawn characters; and, finally, the stereotyped Auxiliary, one who, in the playwright's comments from his later, autobiographical *Inishfallen, Fare Thee Well*, is of a brutal band 'of sibilant and sinister raiders', akin to the hired thuggery of the British Black and Tans.

The stage opens, in the first act, on a May afternoon in 1920, with the embryonic poet typing his Shelleyian thoughts, in a hesitant haze of vision, on an old typewriter, in the gloomy untidiness of the all-purpose tenement room, with his room-mate, the congenial pedlar, still a-bed and fast asleep, in his congenital slovenliness, blissfully unaware that the streets have already been aired by the Kellys and the O'Kellys, parading the insurgent capital, in a country whose world, O'Casey would chronicle in *Inishfallen, Fare Thee Well*, was dominated by danger and fear, and where 'the angel of death is a biting bitch'; and where, in the subsequent words of the pedlar himself, with reference to the pitiful plight of Ireland caught up in the death-throes of bloodshed and insurrection, 'Kathleen ni Houlihan is very different now to the woman who used to play the harp an' sing . . . for she's a ragin' divil now', giving rise to the constant shibboleth and oft-repeated catchphrase of Shields, 'Oh, Kathleen ni Houlihan, your way's a thorny way!' in comic contrast to the equally mock-disturbing and repetitious maxim – derived from Shelley – mouthed by the budding poet by way of reply, 'Ah me! alas, pain, pain ever, for ever!'

The initial mood of non-glorification of hostilities is apparent from the casual words of Shields, soon after a tenement neighbour has come banging on his door to rouse him from slumber and to remind him it is long past the cold light of early, jocund day, in a post-Angelus realisation of after-noon reality, when the pedlar rouses himself, in the course of somnolent mystification, to exclaim: 'I'm beginnin' to believe that the Irish People are still in the stone age. If they could they'd throw a bomb at you'. The madness of the gun, the bomb and the bullet becomes a kind of touchstone and Rod of Jesse in subsequent O'Casey tragedies, from *Juno and the Paycock* to *The Plough and the Stars*, culminating in the world catastrophe and howitzer-madness which engulfs *The Silver Tassie*, where, in the climax of legal lawlessness, in the words of Shaw, 'the earth is still bursting with the dead bodies of the victors'. (Only those who have lived through a major world war as well as a succession of senseless national rebellions will fully comprehend the bitterness and wrath of O'Casey, adopting the artistic precedents of Shakespeare, Shaw and Swift.)

The tenement, in contrast, is an isolated world set in a chaotic and mad universe, even though it houses a gallery of splendidly exotic and raffish characters, who, in Dr Eric Bentley's words in *What is Theatre?*, are 'charming children'. Despite their deep flaws of human weakness, they are endearingly presented, and through them successive audiences are aware of sufferings which the hostilities cause on such slum portrayals as the Grigsons, Tommy Owens, Mrs Henderson and Mr Gallogher (precursors of the exuberantly-exaggerated, lusty species which inhabit *Under Milk Wood*, in a predisposition of poetic fantasy and voluptuousness anticipating Dylan Thomas), as well as, of course, on richly carved main characters, such as Donal, Seumas and Minnie.

As the act continues its medley of human interruptions – the poet having to endure incursions from callers, from the mysterious Maguire to the caricatured landlord, who is not only worried about non-payment from Shields of the arrears of his rent but who, avoiding the gaze of Davoren, also disapproves of the pedlar's subletting proclivities (crystalised in the notice-to-quit impositions); as well as the idiotic posturings of Tommy Owens, in a fit of tipsy topsyturviness, shouting 'God Save Ireland, ses the hayros'; and jejune demands by hallucinatory-minded neighbours, such as big-

framed and big-mouthed Mrs Henderson impelling the incongru-
ously taciturn and timid Mr Gallogher (a music-hall duo in
themselves) to seek Davoren's advice about imagined IRA protection under threat of neighbourly recriminations in the growing field
of hooliganism and lawlessness. Most significant of all interruptions
centre round the artless invasion of the poet's privacy by the
guileless, ingenuous Minnie, derisively termed by the sex-fearing
Shields as 'A Helen of Troy come to live in a tenement!' She is a
single, younger counterpart of Nora Clitheroe in *The Plough and the
Stars*.) As reward for her interest and affections, Donal is prepared to
romanticise himself as a gunman-poet, to satisfy the fabrication of
her false hero-worship. Only when the hero, in the second act,
proves to be a fictitious entity does Minnie's heroism become the
only heroic criterion in the play.

Minnie is a heroine by default, because the male counterparts, in
this and most O'Casey tragedies, are too full of blarney and
braggadocio to live up to any heroic expectations. In *The Shadow of a
Gunman*, Minnie is herald of a parade, in successive O'Casey
dramas, of women of intangible strength – in the least likely of
heroic circumstances – who outface and eclipse their menfolk and
male comrades. She possesses the twin attributes, necessary for
O'Casey bravery, of timidity and audacity. During the raid, in the
second act, while the men in the tenement cower in their beds, the
timorous Minnie, alone, assumes the initiative of courage. She dies
to save Davoren, and dies instead of him, thus accentuating the cold
cowardice of the imaginary hero and Shields and all the rest of the
boastful compatriots who flaunt their 'bravery' and 'heroism'. The
ending to the play has more than an implied touch of irony and
bitter bathos about it as Davoren, self-proclaimed and popularly
acclaimed gunman 'on the run' (the play's original title, incidentally), resolves to pack up his belongings and go in a fugitive search for
accommodation elsewhere; away from suspect premises altogether.

Circumstances of the play are largely autobiographical, though
details are conditional to the play's imaginary purpose. Late in
1920, shortly after his mother's death, O'Casey moved into a room
at Mountjoy Square (the scene in the play is Hilljoy Square), which
he shared with a Micheal O'Maolain (Michael Mullen), the
original inspiration for Seumas Shields; and although Davoren is in
part personification of the younger playwright, some of the attitudes
and wisecracks voiced by Shields reflect those of the playwright
himself.

Shortly before he died, O'Casey's former lodging associate published an article in Irish in *Feasta* (Bealtaine, 1955) describing his life with O'Casey and the Black and Tan raid that took place on their tenement on Good Friday, 1921. The English translation appears in a recent American edited anthology entitled: *Essays on Sean O'Casey's Autobiographies* by Robert G. Lowery. The circumstantial meeting of the two is described by O'Maolain thus:

> We had known each other for some years before Sean moved in to room with me. We were both active in the Irish language movement; however, we weren't in the same branch of the Gaelic League. We were both very involved with the 1913 labour strike and we participated in other movements as well. Occasionally, as we sat in our seats by the fire in that room, I would criticise those movements, and it was our difference of opinion – especially about movements and people – that caused our disagreements. It's fair to say each of us was stubborn about his own opinion!

O'Casey, we gather from this account, was an earlier riser than O'Maolain, having dressed, breakfasted and folded his bed, long before daylight would even have penetrated the morning gaze of his fellow-lodger, who would, he owned, often purposely linger in bed listening to O'Casey moving about, singing snatches of songs from Burns. 'He had a sweet, soft, singing voice that would remind you of a robin – low without being too remote, and as the little red-breasted bird has a sweetness of his own, it was so with O'Casey'. As O'Maolain remembers:

> One morning he called me to get up. As I recall, the morning was very cold, so I gave him this answer:
> Up in the morning's no for me,
> Up in the morning early;
> When a' the hills are covered wi' snow
> I'm sure it's winter fairly.
> 'Have you read Burns?' he said to me. 'Do you think', I replied, 'that I haven't read anything?' That started the sort of discussion we used to have about books and authors.

The ingredients and autobiographical framework are all incorporated into the scenario of Act One: tenement life is graphically depicted, with its constant stream of vermicular life and vernacular talk and tedious interruptions from plain people who speak with rich imagery and saloon-type disagreements over philosophical and political questions. Nightly, we are meant to visualise the colourful occupants roaring at each other in red-hot philosophical and literary dispute, within the limits of a single, spectacular scene, such as the one described in the first or second act, as Shields and Davoren rant away at each other, hammer and tongs. As the poet chidingly says to Shields: 'You know as little about truth as anybody else, and you care as little about the Church as the least of those that profess her faith; your religion is simply the state of being afraid that God will torture your soul in the next world as you are afraid the Black and Tans will torture your body in this'. Shields's counter-blasts are equally effective, too: 'That's right, that's right – make a joke about it! That's the Irish People all over – they treat a joke as a serious thing and a serious thing as a joke'. The disputatiousness, present in the morning's acrimony, as illustrated by the chequered portrayal of happenings in the first act, resumes in the evening, as indicated in the second act and continues into the night until the banterers fall asleep.

A few hours elapse between the two acts. At the beginning of Act Two it is after curfew and past midnight. Shields is in bed, and Davoren, after invoking Shelley and Shakespeare, is still writing his verses, which, later, O'Casey acknowledges as his own: they appear as 'Sunshadows' and 'A Walk with Eros' in his curiously-coloured miscellany, *Windfalls* (1934). Shields intercepts the poetic flow of Davoren's thoughts with bluster about the uncertainty of the political climate, with its indiscriminate and sudden outbursts of ambushes and explosions.

Indignant, too, about the death of his pedlar-friend, Maguire, who, as a furtive revolutionary, was ambushed outside Dublin (we learn from a stop-press report at the end of Act One), Shields rants on about the futility of guerrilla warfare and risks to civilian livelihood: '. . . With all due respect to the gunmen, I don't want them to die for me'. This is countered by Davoren's grimly ironic, 'Not likely; you object to any one of them deliberately dying for you for fear that one of these days you might accidentally die for one of them'. Dramatic irony, indeed, pointing to premonition of Minnie's plight. With veiled portentousness, Shields also remarks: 'An' as for bein' brave, it's easy to be that when you've no cause for cowardice'. Hardly have both proclaimed their fearlessness – Shields because of religion and Davoren because of his philosophy – when shots ring out from the wall of the back-yard behind the tenement. In the words of the direction, 'Religion and philosophy are forgotten in the violent fear of a nervous equality'.

As Shields and Davoren remain terrorised with fear, a bravura piece of black comedy erupts upon the scene; and, as the two brave exponents of fearlessness cower in their beds, steps are heard beyond their door. Presently, a knock reveals a worried neighbour from downstairs, Mrs Grigson, anxious about her absent husband, the braggardly temerarious Adolphus ('Dolphie') Grigson, who, despite curfew, hasn't returned from one of his regular nocturnal drinking-bouts. (His disarming catchphrase is always 'Here's the first to-day'.) In the suspense of the night, she is worried about his safety. To Davoren's exasperation and impatience, she keeps up a whining tirade of diatonics with Shields at the threshold:

MRS GRIGSON: Do the insurance companies pay if a man is shot after curfew?

SEUMAS: Well, now, that's thing I couldn't say, Mrs Grigson.

MRS GRIGSON (*plaintively*): Isn't he a terrible man to be takin' such risks, an' not knowin' what'll happen to him. He knows them Societies only want an excuse to do people out of their money – is it after one, now, Mr Shields?

SEUMAS: Aw, it must be after one, Mrs Grigson.

When the heavily top-coated figure of Grigson at last approaches and fumbles his way into the room, he is arrogantly unrepentant, and Orange Monarch of all he surveys: an unsmiling Trinculo of the tenements. Rounding on his wife and putting the furies of apprehension into Davoren and Shields, he drunkenly boasts: 'Mindin' me, is it, mindin' me?' And, shouting loudly, in the still of the night, he follows it up with : 'Is there any one wants to say anything to Dolphus Grigson? If there is, he's here – a man too – there's no blottin' it out – a man'. His timid wife exacerbates the situation with her own anxious interruption: 'You'll wake everybody in the house; can't you speak quiet'.

Then follows a classic piece of folly and clowning, as deft as any we encounter in Shakespeare:

ADOLPHUS GRIGSON (*more loudly still*): What do I care for anybody in the house? Are they keepin' me;

are they givin' me anthing? When they're
keepin' Grigson it'll be time enough for them
to talk. (*With a shout*) I can tell them
Adolphus Grigson wasn't born in a bottle!

MRS GRIGSON (*tearfully*): Why do you talk like that, dear; we all
know you weren't born in a bottle.

ADOLPHUS GRIGSON: There's some of them in this house think that
Grigson was born in a bottle.

DAVOREN (*to* SEUMAS): A most appropriate place for him to be
born in.

MRS GRIGSON: Come on down to bed, now, an' you can talk about
them in the mornin'.

ADOLPHUS: I'll talk about them, now; do you think I'm afraid of
them? Dolphus Grigson's afraid av nothin',
creepin' or walkin', – if there's any one in the
house thinks he's fit to take a fall out av
Adolphus Grigson, he's here – a man; they'll
find that Grigson's no soft thing.

DAVOREN: Ah me, alas! pain, pain ever, for ever.

MRS GRIGSON: Dolphie, dear, poor Mr Davoren wants to go to
bed.

DAVOREN: Oh, she's terribly anxious about poor Mr Davoren, all
of a sudden.

ADOLPHUS (*stumbling towards* DAVOREN, *and holding out his hand*):
Davoren! He's a man. Leave it there, mate.
You needn't be afraid av Dolphus Grigson;
there never was a drop av informer's blood in
the whole family av Grigson. I don't know
what you are or what you think, but you're a
man, an' not like some of the goughers in this
house, that ud hang you. Not referrin' to you,
Mr Shields.

MRS GRIGSON: Oh, you're not deludin' to Mr Shields.

SEUMAS: I know that, Mr Grigson; go on down, now, with Mrs
Grigson, an' have a sleep.

ADOLPHUS: I tie meself to no woman's apron strings, Mr Shields;
I know how to keep Mrs Grigson in her place;
I have the authority of the Bible for that. I
know the Bible from cover to cover, Mr
Davoren, an' that's more than some in this
house could say. And what does the Holy

Scripture say about woman? It says, "The woman shall be subject to her husband", an I'll see that Mrs Grigson keeps the teachin' av the Holy Book in the letter an' in the spirit. If you're ever in trouble, Mr Davoren, an' Grigson can help – I'm your man – have you me?

The image of imp in a bottle is no deterrent to further pantomimic farce, and, oblivious that the house is under surveillance – and surrounded by English soldiers – Grigson breaks out into a drunken dirge, proclaiming his Ulster loyalties by bellowing out, 'Erin's Orange Lily O'. (Davoren's terrified interjection, 'Holy God, isn't this terrible!' fails to halt the refrain, which is later only brought to an abrupt conclusion by the ominous sound of an approaching lorry and the imminent prospect of the house being alive with crawling soldiers, ready at an instant to smash and shoot.)

Thereafter, the play darkens to black tragedy. The action has the Elizabethan juxtaposition of tragedy and farce. With astounding blends of earthiness and wit, pathos and comedy conjoined reach their heightened conclusion. The dramatist moves from naturalism to fantasy with grace and ease – as only O'Casey can so enrich comedy with poignancy.

In the shock turn of events, Grigson, who has sobered considerably, offers phoney assurance that the Tans are not likely to invade the tenement at such an hour – unless, adds his wife, they have learnt something about Mr Davoren. In the immediate expectancy of the raid, the implications are lost on Davoren, too preoccupied in his frenzy, searching frantically for the foolish letter he kept from Mr Gallogher and Mrs Henderson, addressed to the IRA. More rifle-shots and military shouts from outside cause further, frenetic fear; and the Grigsons, at last, return to their own quarters downstairs. Davoren, in his panic, discovers the letter in his pocket and Shields cautions him to burn it. The silence is startled by sounds of a motor-engine warming up, getting ready to go; and Shields, with relief, remarks: 'There's the motor goin' away; we can sleep in peace now for the rest of the night'. (A moment of ironic bathos, of course, before danger intensifies.)

Before preparing himself for sleep, Shields suddenly remembers the bag under his bed left by Maguire. (He supposes it merely contains spoons and hairpins.) But Davoren, on checking, is horrified to discover it contains explosives. Unwittingly, the two have fallen into a trap, and are potentially subversive suspects. Their panic is frenzied. Whilst they are arguing what to do, Minnie rushes into the room, confirming the house is completely surrounded. Sensing they are in the middle of a raid, she seizes the suitcase filled with explosives and takes it to her room, believing, in her ingenuousness, that the military will not search her room – not realising the ruthless ruffianism of the Tan soldiers' smash-and-search methods and the ordeal of alien torches blinding the darkened household.

Presently, violent and continued hammering on the street door followed by breaking glass and the breaking-down of the front-door, indicates a swoop by English Auxiliaries. One of them, torch in one hand, revolver in the other, bursts into the room where Shields and Davoren remain petrified with fear. (In the revealing stage-direction 'Davoren reclines almost fainting on the bed; Seumas sits up in an attitude of agonized prayerfulness'.) In a short scene of macabre comedy, the Auxiliary, tossing the contents off the mantlepiece to the ground – including the statue of Christ and Shields's crucifix: ('You'd think you was in a bloomin' monastery') – remains sceptical when told by Shields that 'no one in the house has any connection with politics': in a flurry of military resourcefulness, he exclaims, 'We're a little bit too ikey now to be kidded with that sort of talk'.

Soldier's slang and tenement blarney skirmish, briefly, in a clash of claustrophobic humour, interrupted by the dishevelled appearance on scene of Mrs Grigson, horror-stricken at the degree of brutality of the search. She relates how the military discovered her husband's whisky under his pillow, and drank it while they forced him to sing a hymn – 'We shall Meet in the Sweet Bye an' Bye' (a favourite, we recall, of Mrs Williamson's, the Churchwarden's wife, in *The Harvest Festival*) – and then, under duress, offer a prayer of atonement for the Irish Republic! The Auxiliary quickly vanishes when he hears mention of whisky, leaving Davoren and Shields to bicker over their unyielding views on self-recrimination or exoneration. (Both are cowards, though Davoren alone remains repentant.)

The bag is discovered and Minnie is dragged off, shouting bravely, offstage: her hysterical cries of 'Up the Republic' can be heard in the distance as Mrs Grigson rushes in to tell them of the news, and adding maliciously: 'I hope they'll give that Minnie

Powell a coolin' ". The tenement woman blames her downfall on 'her fancy stockin's . . . an' her crepe de chine blouses!' Davoren and Shields know otherwise. 'God grant she'll keep her mouth shut!' is Shields's lame, pathetic response.

After the Auxiliaries have left, the braggarts resume their boasting. Grigson's braggadocio is equalled only by Shields's:

> MR GRIGSON: *(nonchalantly taking out his pipe, filling it, lighting it, and beginning to smoke)*: Excitin' few moments, Mr Davoren; Mrs G. lost her head completely – panic-stricken. But that's only natural, all women is very nervous. The only thing to do is to show them that they can't put the wind up you; show the least sign of fright an' they'd walk on you, simply walk on you. Two of them come down – 'Put them up' revolvers under your nose – you know, the usual way. 'What's all the bother about?' says I, quite calm. 'No bother at all', says one of them, 'only this gun might go off an' hit somebody – have you me?' says he. 'What if it does', says I, 'a man can only die once, an' you'll find Grigson won't squeal'. 'God, you're a cool one', says the other, 'there's no blottin' it out'.
>
> SEUMAS: That's the best way to take them; it only makes things worse to show that you've got the wind up. 'Any ammunition here?' says the fellow that come in here. 'I don't think so', says I, 'but you better have a look'. 'No back talk', says he, 'or you might get plugged'. 'I don't know of any clause', says I, 'in the British Constitution that makes it a crime for a man to speak in his own room', – with that, he just had a look round, an' off he went.

Suddenly, an explosion is heard, and word is brought that Minnie has been shot. Shields refuses to take any of the blame: 'She did it off her own bat – we didn't ask her to do it'. Davoren is consumed by remorse. Mrs Grigson, in an excited and semi-hysterical manner, tells them how Minnie met her death in ambush whilst attempting to escape from the lorry.

Finally, in a supreme but solemn outburst of agonised self-recrimination and penitency, the poet bemoans:

Ah me, alas! Pain, pain, pain ever, for ever! It's terrible to think that little Minnie is dead, but it's still more terrible to think that Davoren and Shields are alive! Oh, Donal Davoren, shame is your portion now till the silver cord is loosened and the golden bowl be broken. Oh, Davoren, Donal Davoren, poet and poltroon, poltroon and poet!

And, in the stunned silence, before curtain-fall, Shields interrupts bathetically with, 'I knew something ud come of the tappin' on the wall!'

More than just a foretaste of the playwright's finer things to come, *The Shadow of a Gunman* is a play in its own right, and one of the most impassioned of modern dramas. A naturalistic interpretation is called for, with undertones of farce and satire, culminating in black tragedy. The combination of riotous laughter and grimmest tragedy are concomitant throughout and it is a prominent feature of all the dramatist's subsequent plays. O'Casey is a master of the genre; and in the switchback ride from comic farce to tragic bathos, there is none to equal him; not even Shakespeare – in truest tragicomic mode or kaleidoscopic approach.

Although labelled 'A Tragedy in Two Acts', the play is not a tragedy in the traditional sense: its ribbon of technique represents a tapestry of constantly changing contrasts. Instability of human character and conduct is revealed in the satiric vision and wit of the author's essentially transcendental imagination. The theme is a blow at hypocrisy, idealism with low horizons, at big talk when matched by little courage. The edge of O'Casey's satire is Swiftian – extending to mankind in general. Human hypocrisy is satirised – sometimes bitterly, sometimes lovingly – with an extraordinary degree of dramatic poignancy.

For pretence of sheer grandiose heroicness, Shields and Grigson are hard to supplant; both are heralds of the renowed, hypocritical 'paycock' species – present in all major plays from *Juno and the Paycock* to *The Drums of Father Ned*. In the unconsciously ironic words of Grigson, all are poised to keep 'a stiff upper front' and are exploited as incomparable clowns of the taproom variety in typically O'Caseyean underworld territory; viewed, telescopically, as in the equally characteristically pungent world of Dickens. Such rich, cornucopean types are not only recognisable burlesques of the concept of stage Irishman but of the mercurial Pride and Fall of Man. Quicksilver changes in delineation of human character – from braggart to coward – represent the triumph of dramatic artistry and strength. One of O'Casey's strongest features – as Lady Gregory, in her *Journals*, has highlighted – is his characterisation; one American scholar, Professor Bernard Benstock, has devoted an entire study, appropriately entitled *Paycocks and others*, to the dramatist's memorable charactery, with its richly, comic assortment of low-life manifestations and eccentricities.

In his presentation of Minnie, O'Casey also emphasises the latent hypocrisy of his remaining characters. Believing she dies a heroic death, Minnie – in a classic instance of dramatic irony – dies for a false ideal: a shadow without substance; her shadow of a gunman is as delusive as Davoren's totemistic philosophy or Shields's crackbrained religion divorced from morals. Human foibles of the remaining subsidiaries – including gratuitous locals such as Mrs Henderson and Mr Gallogher, as well as Mrs Grigson, with their phoney philosophisings, adroit malapropisms and 'parrotoxes' (in Julia Henderson's view, the enhanced phraseology of Mr Gallogher's written circumlocutions is reflected in her voiced 'as good a letter as was decomposed by a scholar') – are basic butts of the author's satire; well exploited, too, in the rich interchange of ironic dialogue between Seumas and Donal.

Although Davoren is an ostensible representation of the poet-dreamer class, he remains only a manipulative manifestation of stage-poet: poltroon-poet, separated from people and reality – the antithesis of Whitman and Emerson, O'Casey's admired mentors. Shields, ironically, is a truer exponent of the dramatist's concept of where poetic truth resides: 'a poet's claim to greatness', says Seumas, 'depends upon his power to put passion in the common people' (which is ridiculed in Shelleyian fashion by Donal: 'Ay, passion to howl for his destruction'). Later, by contrast, in maturer plays, O'Casey's poet-figures grow in stature, when they become leaders and men of action rather than passive dream-fantasists, divorced from the aspirations and realities of ordinary people, linked, in a lesser degree of bathos, with the absurder follies and delusions of Grigson and others, who fulsomely declare: 'What do I care for anybody in the house? Are they keepin' me; are they givin' me anything?' (a variant on Melville Williamson's similar outburst to his wife in *The Harvest Festival*: 'The working men! What do I care for the working men. Am I depending on them? Did they ever give me anything. Damn them, and you, too').

Minnie, alone, subscribes to a consistent ideal, even though her ideal remains false. She resembles those like Juno and Bessie in successive plays, who accomplish deeds of courage, without prate or preposterous badinage. (The talkers of brave deeds, in O'Casey's plays, are rarely the doers.) O'Casey's notion of poetic heroism matches Whitman's – as expressed in the American Poet's line –

Always the procreant urge of the world –

from *Song of Myself*, crystallised, in O'Casey's own belief, in the expression in *The Green Crow* (his pungent, self-styled 'nest of Ids and Trends'): 'The artist's place is to be where life is, active life, found in neither ivory tower nor concrete shelter'. The plough, indeed, as well as the stars.

The Shadow of a Gunman is deceptively, marvellously, self-contained, with no loose ends and not a moment wasted. In the hands of a capable director, the play will not give the impression that the first act is too torpid for a drama about quicksilver people and events. In both acts, the pitch is varied in successive scenes, the gradations of which must be as carefully executed as the un-premeditated nature of the structure of the performance as a whole. The serious message of the play must not be overexposed at the expense of overlooking the tragicomic mixture, at which O'Casey excels.

The play is still valid, for its theme is universal: it has the lasting truth that in every revolution there is always the shadow of a gunman: the inert, passive revolutionary, secretly seduced by ideas of violence and heroism, but slow to act or condemn. Change the climate of circumstance and could this not be an incident anywhere in the world, featured in tomorrow's headlines?

So effective is the total dramatic picture painted by O'Casey's words and ceaseless tensions of offstage violence, that in some ways only a very bad production can harm the play. Full of serio-comic potential and pusillanimity, the play presumes a production of robust energy with attention to a myriad of tiny details such as the initial letter. This is presented in comic circumstances in the first act and with tragic overtones in the second. Similarly, the piece of paper Donal types for Minnie as a lighthearted, romantic keepsake in the comic events of the first act is found smeared with her blood when a bullet pierces her breast-bone in the irrevocable shooting amid the tragic happenings of the second.

The dramatist's rhetorical gifts and frank affection for Irish casting make for an expansive style which can be occasionally self-indulgent but mostly full of enormous vitality. Despite rich delineation of main roles, organised ensemble-playing is essential in the supporting cast. (These are more than one-note, one-gesture caricatures.) The vivid sense of comedy which O'Casey demands can best be served from the absolute cream of Irish acting: in any case, acting abilities must be well marked and chosen. Donal's final words are soul-searching and fraught with pathos and heightened self-condemnation. The finale, with deliberately-intended touches of bathos, must not appear to be crudely melodramatic.

The *dramatis personae* is a fine cross-section of vibrant, tenacious, tenement life: among the main representatives, Donal Davoren, desperado by repute and priggish outsider and onlooker who does all he can to ignore events and people around him so that he can get on with writing his imitations of Shelley, is thirty, with an expression that mirrors quixotry between activity and passivity. His only saving grace is his penitence and recognition of himself as he really is; Seumas Shields, pretentious boaster, tinker, republican and coward – droll and garrulous and splendidly slippery as the precursor of O'Casey's 'paycock' breed and Falstaffian figure in the later 'Captain' Boyle-Fluther Good mould; Minnie Powell, the brave, pretty-girl innocent, but with enough roguishness to ensnare a saint, let alone a sceptical poet such as Davoren, and with enough simplicity and independent-mindedness to make her way in the world; Tommy Owens, diffident, twenty-five-year-old adulator and illiterate drunk, braggart and saloon-bar poltroon as well as small-dimensional humbug, dreaming of false escapism and heroism; Adolphus Grigson, roaring Orangeman and martinet of the lower tenement – a splendid embellishment of Irish truculence and bombast.

Lesser subsidiaries – such as Julia Henderson, Mrs Grigson and Mr Gallogher – are also finely drawn. Mrs Henderson is representative of female dominancy (though her heart is in the right place), whereas Mrs Grigson and Mr Gallogher are either cowed or subdued. Residual characters, such as the landlord and the Auxiliary, are stock portrayals, in choicest Boucicault comic tradition. Maguire, with his code-catchword, 'good-by . . . ee', is a minor O'Casey vignette of vintage dye.

The play's *première* was in Dublin at the Abbey Theatre on 12 April 1923, directed by Lennox Robinson. Arthur Shields played Davoren, F. J. McCormick played Shields and Gertrude Murphy played Minnie. Packed houses in the finish ensured a re-run in August of the same year. Lady Gregory's judgement was that it was an 'immense success, beautifully acted, all the political points taken up with delight'. Thereafter, in the Irish capital, there were many presentations. Indeed, in the Abbey's historical repertoire, the play ranks with both *Juno and the Paycock* and *The Plough and the Stars* as one of the most frequently revived plays. By 1980, it had been revived more than three hundred times.

In London, it opened at the Court Theatre, under Sir Barry Jackson's management in 1927 and ran for two months. Directed by Arthur Sinclair, an affinitive cast included Sinclair himself (a notable comedy actor of former Abbey fame) as Shields, with Harry Hutchinson as Davoren and Sydney Morgan as Grigson. Eileen Carey (the playwright's future wife) played Minnie, and the cast included Sara Allgood and her celebrated sister, Maire O'Neill. Other revivals in London have included John Gibson's at the Lyric, Hammersmith in 1957 (with Desmond Jordan as the poet and Jack MacGowran as Shields); MacGowran's own outstanding Mermaid production in 1967 (with himself as Shields and the playwright's daughter, Shivaun, making her professional début on the London stage as Minnie); the Young Vic's production in 1972 (with Peter McEnery as Davoren and Niall Buggy as Shields), as well as the Royal Shakespeare Company's outstanding centenary commemoration (a successful transfer of Michael Bogdanov's highly-acclaimed Stratford-upon-Avon production), featuring Michael Pennington as the poet, Normal Rodway as Shields, and Dearbhla Molloy as Minnie. Elsewhere in Britain, Nottingham Playhouse's 1978 production focused on John Hurt as the poet. Cedric Messina's televised presentation for BBC-2 in 1973, under the directorship of Alvin Rakoff, won renewed honour, with Stephen Rea as the poet, Sinead Cusack as Minnie and Donal McCann as Shields.

In America, the Abbey Theatre Players, on tour, gave New York its *première* on 29 October 1932 (the cast included Barry Fitzgerald, Arthur Shields, F. J. McCormick, Michael J. Dolan and Eileen Crowe). Subsequent revivals have included Gloria Monty's at Long Island in 1950, the Cheryl Crawford-Joel Schenker run in 1958, and the 1972 Sheridan Square Playhouse New York presentation, with Philip Minor as director (all in sharp contrast to the cold reception of the play's early history in Chicago). In 1981, the Abbey featured the play, directed by Joe Dowling, at the Baltimore International Theatre Festival, with subsequent tours in Washington, Philadelphia and Boston.

On the Continent, the play has remained popular both in Communist countries and in the West. In France, there have been several successful post-war productions: beginning with Philippe Kellerson's of 1947 in Paris, and a staging at the Comédie de L'Est in 1951, as well as the spectacular Stephane Ariel run in 1964 for the Théâtre Gerard Philipe of Saint Denis (later visiting Berlin's Deutsches Theater). The 1972 Comédie de Saint-Etienne showing won further acclaim. In Germany, its *première* at East Berlin's Kammerspiele des Deutschen Theaters, in 1954, directed by Rudolf Wessely, struck instant response, even though its revival in West Berlin in 1962 was less successful. In Italy, Florentine audiences responded warmly in 1968, when the visiting Abbey Company, on its first Italian tour, staged a hit, with Vincent Dowling's production, at the city's Teatro della Pergola. In the centennial year, 1980, Siobhan McKenna directed at Vienna's English Theatre. East German radio broadcast a centennial dramatisation, directed by Helmut Hellstorff, as did the BBC, with Bryan Murray and Alan Devlin in the leads. The play has also been performed in cities as diverse as Warsaw (1955) and Teheran (1980). A Gaelic version appeared in 1940 at Galway's Taibhdhearc Theatre, directed by Walter Macken. Published translations are available in French, German, Italian, Japanese, Roumanian, Russian, Persian and Polish (details of which, and those referred to at the conclusion of each subsequent chapter, can be found in Ronald Ayling and Michael J. Durkan's comprehensive *Sean O'Casey: A Bibliography*).

3 *Kathleen Listens In* (1923): a Post-Civil War Whimsicality

Subtitled, 'A Political Phantasy in One Act', this quixotic caricature is described by the playwright, in his autobiographical volume, *Inishfallen, Fare Thee Well*, as 'a jovial, sardonic sketch on the various parties in conflict over Irish politics – Sinn Fein, Free State, and Labour'. By way of explanation, many years later, O'Casey has stated: 'it was written specifically to show what fools these mortals were in the quarreling factions soaking Ireland in anxiety and irritation after the Civil War'.

This short one-act piece is a forerunner of many bracing aperitifs and extravaganzas in the O'Casey repertoire (just as in Shaw), and anticipates the author's later fuller-length fantasies, such as *The Star Turns Red*, *Red Roses for Me*, *Cock-a-Doodle Dandy*, *The Bishop's Bonfire* and *The Drums of Father Ned*, as well as shorter, satiric effusions, such as *Time to Go* and *Figuro in the Night*.

Like Shaw, upsetting apple-carts has ever been one of O'Casey's main occupations, and, in this satirical little 'phantasy', he succeeded in upsetting the apple-cart of newly-won Irish political freedom.

The main theme is elaboration of Seumas Shields's recurring shibboleth in the author's first major play: 'Oh, Kathleen Ni Houlihan, your way's a thorny way'.

The play is mainly witty dialogue; no pretence of physical action is offered. The heroine is Kathleen, daughter of Miceawl Houlihan, symbolising newly-independent Ireland; and, among the twelve other representational characters are a Free Stater, a Republican, a Business man, a Farmer and a Labourer – all vying with each other for the hand of Kathleen and making a loud clamour in her house (another symbol representing the separate state of Ireland). The spectral Gaelic League is lampooned in the figure of a feeble old

33

man in kilts, who has been a long-standing lodger in the house and who insists that all visitors to its habitation should speak Irish. As Kathleen's father explains to an inquisitorial neighbour, Tomaus Thornton, the old lodger has, in his room, 'all the walls destroyed with comical figaries that he calls fibulas, turks an' crosses o' cong; an' he won't let Kathleen read anythin' but the Book o' Kells – he says anythin' else ud be bad for her morals'. The rest of the characters regard the enfeebled lodger as nothing but a quaint nuisance; and, once inside the house, pay only lip-service to his demands. (This is underscored nearly forty years later in the playwright's trenchant little satire, *Behind the Green Curtains*.)

Allegorical assumptions are couched in simplistic, sardonic dialogue, calculated to enlighten as well as entertain. As a political cartoon, some of the topicality has blunted, though factional comment, such as 'its nothin' now, but a nest o' jobbery', still rings true to be considered a ferocious target in much later satires, as in *Cock-a-Doodle Dandy* and *Time to Go*.

Like most representations of political groupings, the spokesmen-characters are badly informed, yet convinced that only their viewpoint counts. Here, they are political knights-errant in a quixotic whimsicality.

Kathleen herself wears a robe of indifference throughout, refusing to see any of her ill-assorted suitors; inaccessible, she is too busy 'listenin' in!' (in the golden heyday of recently discovered radio). 'Oh, for God's sake, go away', she ejaculates, at one stage, 'an' done be annoyin' me. I have to practice me Fox Trots and Jazzin' so as to be lady-like when I make me deboo into the League o' Nations'.

Hardly surprising, in the face of such wrangling and war-games (after the Civil War, Ireland took a long time to heal from her wounds), the symbolic heroine, in a fainting fit, takes to her sick-bed, as her doctor warns all those in the house: 'She's very weak, but she'll pull round after a bit, if she gets perfect quietness: A whisper may prove fatal – she'll need perfect peace and quietness for the rest of her National life'. To which, the nonchalant Thornton – 'dressed in working clothes, which bear no marks of work' (prototype of 'Captain' Boyle in *Juno and the Paycock*) – quips, with sly serenity: 'Oh, be heavens, she's sure to get it too! If peace came we'd all die a sudden death!' (An ironic contrast to Yeats's declared aspirations for 'peace' in 'Innisfree'.)

The satire ends with the archetypal Orangeman, who suddenly appears outside the garden, banging a big drum and bellowing loudly, in a flutter of newly-won sovereignty, adding his voice to the chorus of courtship, and with Kathleen's father lifting the window and shouting back in threatening tones; 'Holy God, are we not goin' to be let get even one night's sleep in peace!'

The play was originally performed at the Abbey Theatre, following the success of *The Shadow of a Gunman*, in the week beginning 1 October 1923. Under Lennox Robinson's direction, F. J. McCormick played Miceawl, with Maureen Delany as his wife, Eileen Crowe as Kathleen and Barry Fitzgerald as Thornton, in a glittering cast. Critics, as well as audiences, were nonplussed at first by the fantasy surrounding the satire. According to one critical source, 'it was a play to slightly puzzle a first-night audience', but, later, conceded: 'The play is hilarious throughout in the manner intended, marvellously acute in its irony'.

To judge from O'Casey's own bitter comments afterwards, the play was certainly greeted with a mixed response, particularly on the first night, which the playwright himself attended; and at the end of the performance, he avowed in *Inishfallen, Fare Thee Well*:

> The audience received the little play in dead silence, in a silence that seemed to have a point of shock in its centre. Not even a cold clap of a hand anywhere. They all got up from their seats, and silently filed out of the theatre. He was the one and only playwright to have had a play received in silence by an Abbey audience . . .

Discouraged by the disappointing response to an accredited showpiece of fantasy, for which he later was to become so internationally acclaimed (especially in Germany and America), though British and Irish audiences were to remain lukewarm and sometimes hostile, he immediately returned to the robust, natural-realistic style in tragicomedy – for which in Britain and Ireland he is more famously praised – beloved by a wider spectrum of audiences; the mould which produced his pinnacle-pathed achievements, his highly revered, tragicomic masterpieces *Juno and the Paycock* and *The Plough and the Stars*.

Although not included in the canon of *Collected Plays*, the text of *Kathleen Listens In* was published in *Feathers From The Green Crow* (1962), edited by Robert Hogan, who has rescued it from the mists of undeserved obscurity for posterity's closer (and more accurate) judgement. (A German translation exists.) It remains a shadow-spectre of the playwright's maturer, still controversial, kaleidoscopic fantasy-creations, which, we are only now beginning to realise, epically, are the equal of Strindberg's, Shaw's and O'Neill's.

4 *Juno and the Paycock* (1924): a Camouflage of the Irish Civil War

O'Casey's most popularly universal play, with its amazing plunges from wild comedy to black despair, retains all its dramatic potency and much of its social relevance a half century and more since it was written. Although, in the judgement of George Jean Nathan in his foreword to *Five Great Modern Irish Plays*, it is 'one of the richest tragicomedies', the final impression is one of a play steeped in poetic, humorous, baleful outrage, ringing with human compassion and condemnation. Lady Gregory, in her *Journals*, saw the play as 'A wonderful and terrible play of futility, of irony, humour, tragedy'. And James Stephens, in a whimsical aside, called it 'a dote' of a play. (The reference is included in his *Letters*, published in 1974.)

It is an orchestrated hymn against all poverty and hate. The play is deeply moving without being sentimental or sententious. The tragic background is the ominous, omnipresent Irish Civil War. The comic superstructure portrays the Irish as a race of fun-loving, feckless buffoons, summed up in the aphorism of Charles Lever as: 'Fightin' like divils for conciliation, an' hatin' each other for the love of God'.

The ruthless guerrilla war, known in Ireland as the Terror, which formed the foreground in *The Shadow of a Gunman* of brutal and senseless killings and ambushes in towns and countryside throughout Ireland, spilled over into an even greater terror, in its wake, in the horrendous shape of the Irish Civil War – influencing the lives of those in *Juno and the Paycock* – 'while the good catholics in the south', O'Casey was bitterly to relate afterwards, 'were at one another's throats, spraying death and disillusion in the minds of men'.

The folly of further insurrection and bloodshed is condemned in the autobiographical *Inishfallen, Fare Thee Well*:

37

Kelt was killing Kelt as expertly and as often as he could; catholic Kelts, too. Not a freethinker among them. As diligent as the Black and Tans themselves. And just as clever. Men were shot down while at business, on pleasure, even when they whispered to a girl. A young man was swung up to a beam; as much castor oil as he could hold was poured through a funnel into him, and he was left hanging there to mutter rosaries as best he could without being able to tell his beads. And that was a merciful method.

The sniping and in-fighting which had characterised the Anglo-Irish guerrilla war of 1919–1921 were brought to only a brief halt, when both sides agreed to a tenuous truce in midsummer 1921. And, following the precarious treaty signed between Britain and Ireland in London later that year, Ireland, in 1922, drifted into a dastardly civil uprising emanating from the factitious wording of the treaty, which did not concede an all-Ireland republic – as many had hoped – but established, instead, an Irish Free State with near-sovereign powers for all Ireland, with the exception of six Ulster counties and – most contentiously of all, in the eyes of dewy-eyed revolutionaries and gunmen – required an Oath of Allegiance to the British Crown from members of the Irish Parliament, or Dail, in virtue of an alleged common citizenship between the two countries and the new Free State's membership of the Commonwealth. The fury of Republicans at once erupted on those fellow-compatriots and soft-liners who were satisfied with compromise and appeared to have sold out to the British.

In Robert Kee's exacting words:

> This was the beginning of a savage Irish Civil War in which the Free State gradually gained the upper hand. The anti-Treaty forces who used the same sort of guerrilla tactics as they had used against the British, but with much less support from the Irish people, became known with some reason as "Irregulars". The Free State victory was not completed before Michael Collins [one of the Free State leaders and representatives of the Irish government] himself had been killed in an ambush and the first free Irish Government had shot by firing squad more than twice the number of I.R.A. men executed by the British.
>
> (*The Green Flag: A History of Irish Nationalism*)

In an essay written in 1957, included in *Blasts and Benedictions*, O'Casey sums up the play and his feelings about its traumas and

tribulations affecting the commonalty of citizens in Dub
elsewhere:

The play *Juno and the Paycock* concerns itself with the time of the
calamitous Civil War in Ireland, a fight between two parties over
a few words included within the Treaty made by one of them with
England. The difference between the two parties was trivial,
almost insignificant, not worth a fight with fists, much less
cannon, machine-gun and rifle . . . But they went to war about
it, and devastated Ireland between them. The members of the
contending parties, too, were all of the same faith, all good
Catholics, yet they tortured and slaughtered each other with
vigour and venom, in the way that Christians do, have done, and
will do again.

During the fight, father was against son, brother against
brother, girl against her lover; all fighting it out for a cause no one
understood, and for which very few cared; while the mothers,
alone sensible and suffering, bore the brunt of it all among the
workers, knowing, probably, that when it would be all over, they
and their families would be living in the same old way, denying
themselves things that the rent might be paid, and uncertain
where the food for the next day would come from.

In the play the impact is shown on two worker families, on two
mothers each of whom has lost a son; and, if there be a message in
the play, I imagine it to be that a Civil War should be waged only
for a deep and great cause, like the overthrow of tax paid without
representation that evoked the American War of Independence,
the overthrow of Feudalism as in the French Revolution, and the
establishment of political and economic rule and ownership by
the people as in the October Revolution of the Soviets. We
should, however, be careful of personal idealism; good as it may
be and well-meaning, its flame in a few hearts may not give new
life and new hope to the many, but dwindle into ghastly and futile
funeral pyres in which many are uselessly destroyed and
enormous damage done to all.

Although bloodshed and civil strife form the background against
which Sean O'Casey sets his play, it is, as Sean Kenny once
perceptively remarked, in a programme-note for the 1973 London
production, the author's 'razor sharp characters, who live in and

around the tenement room of the Boyles, with their violence, vanities, humour, and courage, that lifts the play into the world of universal drama – away from Dublin and its 'special' background'.

Set in 1922 in the two-room tenement home in Dublin of Juno Boyle and her husband, 'Captain' Jack, the strutting waster and pub-peacock of the title, the play is described by O'Casey as 'A Tragedy in Three Acts'. It was in the nature of O'Casey's brilliance to concede that neither Abbey audiences in Dublin, two years after the traumatic turn of events and turbulent Civil War, nor audiences elsewhere, in any decade for that matter, would accept a play on a theme of violence in the form of unremitting tragedy, as in the manner of Synge's *Riders to the Sea* (even though the mother-figures of both plays share an Irish Mother Courage affinity); and although *Juno and the Paycock* is described by its author as a tragedy, it is not tragedy in the authentic sense, but tragedy beyond tragedy: an ironic comedy – a comedy of Irish manners – that permeates the tragic underlay, one moment centred round the fraudulent 'Paycock' himself and his parasitical crony, 'Joxer' Daly, a Uriah Heep to Boyle's self-deluding Micawber and scapegoat of Boyle's own desperate muddledom, and yet another instant, focusing on the tragic and forceful predicament of Juno herself, struggling to keep the home together against impossible odds of fate and her husband.

In a letter of 1955, O'Casey says of *Juno*:

It is the tragedy of vanity, and of subservience to vanity. There is a touch of Boyle in all of us. We strut along thinking that our shadows shine. There's a touch of Joxer in a lot of us; saying yes where we ought to say no. And I hope there is some of Mrs Boyle in us all. To be brave even at the eleventh hour . . .

Poverty as well as the stark events of the Civil War help to explain Boyle's obsessive escapism and Joxer's sycophantic collaboration in it (in the same way that it nearly destroys but does not deflect or defeat the unquenchable spirit of Juno, even though the rest of the suffering women of the neighbouring tenements such as Mrs Tancred and others are bowed with grief). The fact that O'Casey's play mirrors poverty, and poverty seen at its drabbest in war, does not prevent it from being funny to the point of caricature, in the Hogarthian, Swiftian sense, though O'Casey's tragicomedy is uniquely, interwovenly his own (differing from Shakespeare's juxtapositioning of tragedy and comedy). More consonantly with the mood of the twentieth century and the atmosphere of civil strife of the time, O'Casey's tragedy is domestic and social drama, moulded supremely in comedy, and shot through, as in a mixed media of kaleidoscopic brilliance and intensity, with tragic overtones, to give superb, ineluctable tragicomedy.

The method of O'Casey's dramaturgy, at heart, is founded on Shaw's: the Shavian principle, underlined in *Man and Superman*, 'When a thing is funny, search it for a hidden truth', or again, the tragicomic maxim propounded in *The Doctor's Dilemma*, 'Yes. Life does not cease to be funny when people die any more than it ceases to be serious when people laugh'. Shaw himself might almost have been referring to O'Casey when he stated on another occasion: 'There is nothing that marks the born dramatist more unmistakably than this discovery of comedy in his own misfortunes almost in proportion to the pathos with which the ordinary man announces their tragedy'.

The duality of O'Casey's early plays, especially as exemplified in *Juno and the Paycock*, has led to extremes in shifts of critical opinion invoking both comical and tragic muses in the unusual synthesis of Melpomene and Thalia conjoined in surprising wedlock. For instance, James Agate, in 1925, saw the play 'as much a tragedy as *Macbeth*, but it is tragedy in the porter's family'. And George Jean Nathan, in 1940, influenced no doubt by what he termed 'the boozy low measures of parts of *Juno*', viewed the vivacious, gyratory comicality as being in traditions of the wittiest descendent of Congreve, Sheridan and Shaw: 'Moliere full of Irish whiskey, now and again Shaw off dietetic spinach and full of red meat, Flanagan and Allen (if such critics insist) in the classical garb of Falstaff and Dogberry'.

On the occasion of the Royal Shakespeare Company's O'Casey centenary production in London, in 1980, one contemporary critic, versed in the modern complexities of drama, could make us realise: 'the great thing about Trevor Nunn's magnificent Aldwych production is that instead of offering us two-and-half hours of gorgeous fooling and twenty minutes of tragedy (which is what James Agate said the play consisted of) it imbues the whole work with a measured sadness', recognising, perhaps, the playwright's later dictum: 'A laugh is the loud echo of a sigh; a sigh the faint echo of a laugh', in the belief that comedy and tragedy step together, as in life, arm in arm: Siamese twins of an inexorable, preordained fate.

Such is the kaleidoscopic factor of the play, another London critic, Sheridan Morley, saw it differently: a black comedy, the intention of the dramatist being (he considered) to give his audience the Agate assumption of ' "*Macbeth* as viewed from the Porter's lodge", and then gradually turn it back on the customers so that the laughs would freeze on their lips. And still, half a century later, those laughs freeze'.

The O'Casey enigma stems from specific insight into the Irish characters and their mixture of moods. In the play, 'life is seen as farce', observes Raymond Williams, 'with death cutting across it'. One moment we are laughing at an intrusive drunk and the next we are mourning a bereaved mother, keening over the death of her soldier son at the hands of revolutionaries. Yet it is this blend of farce and tragedy (which Chekhov, in his plays, effected so beguilingly) that gives O'Casey his enchanting flavour as a dramatist – and also makes him difficult to produce.

O'Casey's rousing masterpiece, *Juno and the Paycock*, is the play most audiences associate with him, and it is the one which, perhaps, most epitomises his extraordinary dramatic technique and style. The 'astonishing volatility of its emotional variations' impressed Laurence Olivier, who staged the play in 1966 as the National Theatre's tribute to O'Casey after his death. The production endeavoured to show O'Casey's 'switchback ride between hilarity and extreme pathos' (to quote Olivier's words from a programme-note to the production), but fell into the trap of accentuating the comedy at the expense of the tragedy. Basically, the play requires all the resources of an experienced tragedienne to extract the full poignancy from the part of the heroic Juno, the pitiable working-class mother, struggling to keep house and home together despite depredations of fate and the drinking habits of her wastrel husband, the 'Paycock', who is the living embodiment of the stage Irishman as he really is – all bounce and blarney. The climax of tragedy comes with Juno's mourning exit, the Ezekiel-inspired 'Sacred Heart o' Jesus, take away our hearts o' stone, and give us hearts o' flesh! Take away this murdherin' hate, an' give us Thine own eternal love!' The ending is supreme: in the midst of all the tragedy, the 'Paycock' and Joxer saunter in, roaring drunk, turning Ireland's misery, and their own family misfortunes to ridicule. The irony of it hits the audience like 'a bullet in the kisser' (to use Joxer's memorable phrase). It is the whole feeling of the play and the whole spirit of O'Casey.

In *Juno and the Paycock* the dominant action is the talk of Boyle and Joxer: idle, procrastinating talk, with a continual show of importance, in an effluent, engaging spin of fantasy:

JOXER: God be with the young days when you were steppin' the deck of a manly ship, with the win' blowin' a hurricane through the masts, an' the only sound you'd hear was, "Port your helm! " an' the only answer, "Port it is, sir!"

BOYLE: Them was days, Joxer, them was days. Nothin' was too hot or too heavy for me then. Sailin' from the Gulf o' Mexico to the Antanartic Ocean. I seen things, I seen things, Joxer, that no mortal man should speak about that knows his Catechism. Ofen, an' ofen, when I was fixed to the wheel with a marlinspike, an' the wins blowin' fierce an' the waves lashin' an' lashin', till you'd think every minute was goin' to be your last, an' it blowed, an' blowed—blew is the right word, Joxer, but blowed is what the sailors use . . .

JOXER: Aw, it's a darlin' word, a daarlin' word.

BOYLE: An', as it blowed an' blowed, I often looked up at the sky an' assed meself the question – what is the stars, what is the stars?

The formal plot is rooted in the continuous fount of words and endless, bibulous rhetoric. The Boyle family lives in a Dublin tenement during the Troubles. The work-shy 'Captain' and 'dryland sailor' – self-spoken 'procrastinator an' prognosticator' – spends his days idling with his crony, the fawning, foxy, 'shoulder-shruggin', mendacious Joxer, usually tucked up in one of Dublin's 'snugs', or tap-room sheltered retreats (the city's equivalent of Synge's country shebeens). While they engage in idle and fruitless posturings in a bar-haze of semi-transparent reality, Juno Boyle – so named because she was born in June, married in June and her son, Johnny, was born in June; and she is truly the living embodiment of the 'venerable ox-eyed' wife of Jupiter, of Greek mythological renown (as queen of the tenements, special protectress of marriage and of suffering womanhood) – she alone keeps temerarious hold on a tenuous household. (The women in the play, Juno herself, her daughter Mary and Mrs Tancred, a neighbour from the same tenement, are the ones who carry the eventual burden of reality,

while the men override and outface it in a defusion of prevarication
and talk.)

The spiritless fantasy surrounding the family remains unchanged,
though challenged for a time by the false expectation of a
phantasmagoric legacy. Family misfortunes multiply when the
daughter Mary, expecting a child, is abandoned by her lover, the
suave school-teacher Bentham; and the unfortunate war-crippled
son, Johnny, revealed as an informer, is killed by his former cowardly
comrades in an act of savage reprisal. (The action, though offstage,
reveals the killing from outside; the devastating shadow of Civil
War.) The bereaved Juno, following in the same footsteps that
befall Mrs Tancred, in the death of her die-hard son in a similar
ambush, echoes a cry of mercy and lament of forgiveness, transforming the stony-hearted, war-torn generation into one of more
civilised and meeker consideration of human compassion: 'What
was the pain I suffered, Johnny, bringin' you into the world to carry
you to your cradle to the pains I'll suffer carryin' you out o' the
world to bring you to your grave! Mother o' God, Mother o' God,
have pity on us all!' In a cynical postscript, with the same switch of
emphasis we find coincidentally in Shaw's *Saint Joan* (both plays
were presented to the world in 1924), the oblivious-hearted Boyle,
in company with his feckless jackal, rails on about the immorality
and insensitivity of the human race, always to him 'in a terrible state
o' chassis', his abiding catchphrase, while Juno, in her suffering and
composure, alone reveals her strength and fortitude. The bravery
and blathering talk are counterpointed and counterbalanced in the
twin colours of changing patterns in a rotating kaleidoscope and
camouflaging cameo of the Civil War.

In such a tapestry of sharp contrasts, O'Casey makes his
drunkard a comedian and his tragic heroine something of a shrew:
Boyle and his wife Juno, in their embattled exchanges, reflect
remarkably the tough realities of Dublin life; and in the new ironic
mixture of fantasy escaping from realism, which the play offers, is
pointed the extraordinary combination of hard-hearted zeal and
misplaced idealism, as qualified by the First and Second Irregulars,
who, in the final act, appear before Juno's son, the terrified Johnny,
and bear him off to his doom. These are the youths who were
engaged in the fighting between 1916 and 1923, and represent the
real tough, fighting Irish – cynically portrayed.

The atmosphere of a Dublin tenement is evoked with little more
than a kitchen-dresser and table, a couple of chairs and the

obligatory holy figures and candles. The setting is the same throughout all three acts: the living apartment of a two-roomed tenancy occupied by the Boyle family in a tenement house in Dublin in 1922. A few days elapse between Acts One and Two, and a couple of months between Acts Two and Three.

The Boyle family, in their shabby Dublin tenement, are a microcosm of Ireland – a family like a country, divided against itself: the picture of a nation at bitter war, mirrored in a few hearts and minds. The power of the play, and its enduring strength, are founded on cameo possibilities of each character part, however peripheral. Every character registers a distinctive personal mark.

As a dramatist, Sean O'Casey became a master of characterisation beginning with the Dublin 'types' he knew from the city's tenements and expanding as his perspectives broadened. Based on the triumphs of *Juno*, what O'Casey offers his audiences in successive plays is not simply an array of ineffectual but likeable 'poltroons' and vain egotists and believably blathering barflies exchanging curses, confidences and prayers, unable to see the irony of their words and actions – based on the inimitable duo of the archetypal 'Captain' and his 'butty' Joxer – but an infinite exploitation of the theme of 'paycockery' in Ireland and its unlimited range of possibilities. And offsetting the ineffectual males are the strong dominant women characters, of which Juno herself is the supreme prototype. (Bessie Burgess in *The Plough and the Stars* and Mrs Breydon in *Red Roses for Me* are later examples of this indomitable class of womanhood.) 'Irishwomen in Ireland', says Liam O'Flaherty, 'generally rule their families. Abroad, especially when they marry foreigners, they invariably do so. Humanity has never witnessed beings of stronger character than Irishwomen' (quoted in his autobiographical *Two Years*, Jonathan Cape, 1930).

With the later plays, too, there emerges a whole panoply of resolute young women (based on the self-determined, gay-hearted independence of outlook of Minnie Powell, Mary Boyle and others) and O'Casey frequently displays them with an outgoing sexuality which he applauds with delight (from Julia in *The Star Turns Red* and Avril in *Purple Dust* to Keelin in *The Bishop's Bonfire* and Bernadette in *The Drums of Father Ned*, though there are many other claimants in the O'Casey charactery). Although *Juno and the Paycock* is devoid of male heroes in what is predominantly a feminist work of inspiration (in the same way that *Measure for Measure*, *A Doll's House* and *Miss Julie* are), the young male hero or poetic lover – stemming from Donal Davoren to the Dreamer of *Within the Gates*, O'Killigain of *Purple Dust* and Robin of *Cock-a-Doodle Dandy* – is a creation prominent only in O'Casey's later idealistic plays, an evolvement activating from the personal life of the dramatist himself in his more inward, reflective moments of exiled tranquillity.

Ibsen's *The Wild Duck* (the subject of scornful riposte when 'Captain' Boyle picks up a book belonging to his daughter consisting of *A Doll's House* and other plays: 'buks only fit for chiselurs!') and O'Casey's own *Juno and the Paycock* have this much in common: each centres on a windbag's family kept more or less on the rails by a realistic, self-sacrificing wife; and each ends with the death of one of its members, sacrificed to somebody else's will-o'-the-wisp and whim of idealism. O'Casey's Johnny Boyle, caught up in the most brutal stage of the Irish struggle, is shot by former comrades masquerading as dauntless revolutionaries, while Ibsen's Hedrig Ekdal shoots herself because she imagines her father hates her.

Here, in *Juno and the Paycock*, the domestic atmosphere is maintained by the welding process of the disparate members of the Boyle family and tenement neighbours who co-exist in tragic circumstances. All the characters, save Juno, are romancers. The drunkards and patriots are never free from dozing and dreams, even if the dreams go by contraries: what Shaw, in *John Bull's Other Island* (which O'Casey reaffirms, in *Drums Under the Windows*, had such a profound effect on him), terms 'the torturing, heart-scalding, never satisfying dreaming'.

The dominance of Juno, in her moments of suffering and fixation of mothering tyranny, in her day-to-day existence of resisting and doing, instead of yielding and dreaming, is the play's fortitude and triumph. To a measure of some degree, the Shavian philosophy of *Heartbreak House*, whether consciously or unconsciously, has coloured and softened the skein of suffering and heartbreak, the sustained fantasies and ignorance breaking through O'Casey's play. Hesione Hushabye in Shaw's play might almost be speaking for Juno, when she exclaims:

What do men want? They have their food, their firesides, their clothes mended, and our love at the end of the day. Why are they not satisfied? Why do they envy us the pain with which we bring them into the world, and make strange dangers and torments for themselves to be even with us?

And, apart from Juno herself, martyr-figure of Ireland's sufferings, the play's cast offers superb opportunities for all-round golden performances. The characters are neither heroes nor villains, but some magical mix of both. Like those in *The Shadow of a Gunman*, they are of the same hardihood as American Westerners (tough of fibre and filled with the vigorous juice of life) whom they indigenously resemble. (After the Famine, a million Irish emigrated to America, where they joined the ranks of ranchers and city-bosses in the maelstrom of Western society.) Among the principals is 'Captain' Jack Boyle himself, 'infernal rogue an' damned liar!' as his butty and drinking companion, 'Joxer' Daly, one of the residents in his tenement, alludes to him in one of his more ungracious and sardonically malicious moments. And Joxer, too, who is no boon companion: shifty and cringing, a fawning crony and plausible rogue, 'gifted with tags of seedy culture' as Guy Boas, an equally gifted headmaster whom O'Casey held in the highest respect, once commented in his memorably useful annotated edition of the play (along with *The Plough and the Stars* – two plays, in his estimation, of 'infinite fascination and variety'). These three characters alone, Juno, Joxer and Boyle, says Boas, are likely to take their place among the immortals of the theatre.

Along with Juno's worthless husband, wrecked by his own folly, is their crippled son – an arm missing and a shattered hip which he incurred in street fighting in successive Irish rebellions – a prey to constant nervous and ambitious idealism and heroism shrouded in the butt of a gun, and finally killed by his own weakness; together with their attractive daughter, Mary, an impassioned, intelligent lass of twenty-two, on strike because of alleged 'victimisation' of a fellow working colleague. 'We couldn't let her walk the streets, could we?' she tells her mother, and Juno who, at forty-five, still shows traces of former good looks, though the harassed anxiety of tenement circumstances has bequeathed 'an expression of mechanical resistence', wryly counters, 'No, of course yous couldn't – yous wanted to keep her company. Wan victim wasn't enough. When the employers sacrifice wan victim, the Trades Unions go wan betther be sacrificin' a hundred'. But Mary Boyle, in her espousal of equal rights and social justice, sees the issue, instead, as a matter of 'principle'. Juno's sensible stoicism and family pride retaliate, more realistically, with the pragmatic warning: 'Yis; an' when I go into oul' Murphy's to-morrow, an' he gets to know that, instead o' payin' all, I'm goin' to borry more, what'll he say when I tell him a principle's a principle? What'll we do if he refuses to give us any more on tick? '

Juno's advice is similar when she tries to soften the hardened, irrational zeal of her son, who declares rashly, in an instant of foolish consistency, 'I'd do it agen, ma, I'd do it agen': 'Ah, you lost your best principle, me boy, when you lost your arm; them's the only sort o' principles that's any good to a workin' man'. Her mediatorial and maternal role are summed up in her own affidavit: 'Amn't I nicely handicapped with the whole o' yous! I don't know what any o' yous ud do without your ma'. Such practical well-springs serve her well when family fortunes flounder and plummet even more deeply into an unforeseen abyss of chaos and destruction when the vainglorious members of her family reap a bitter whirlwind of ill-fortune and self-induced fate, stemming from the paternal attribute of false pride. (Mary, whose romantic rapture quickly fades, is abandoned at the onset of pregnancy to single-parent sacrificial fortune and insecurity, even though, in Juno's comforting words, the future baby will have the added advantage, with Juno's help, of two mothers, when the 'dry-land' sailor and his sponging jackal are finally left to fend for themselves and sink beneath the waves of their own good-for-nothing grandeur.)

In addition to the sly antics and shifty demeanour of Joxer Daly, the babblative bachelor of the upstairs tenement whose shoulder-shrugging postures masquerade a foxy interior with an aptitude for surveillant survivorship, other occupants of the tenement are constantly intersecting the lives of the Boyles and transposing their vitality to O'Casey's stage. There is the magniloquently effusive and robustly extrovert Mrs Maisie Madigan, described by the playwright as 'a strong, dapper little woman of about forty-five', who, with a touch of Dickensian patter and pathos in similar circumstances, is a Mrs Fezziwig of the tenements, 'a widespread smile of complacency' (in O'Casey's words). She differs exceedingly from her longsuffering, grieving neighbour, Mrs Tancred, a much older woman, whose conventional conformity cracks under the shadow of personal grief – in sharp contrast to Juno – because her die-hard son, antagonistic to the compromising ardour of the Free Staters, was shot dead by opposing revolutionaries (betrayed by Johnny). His body, riddled with bullets, is discovered on a lonely Finglas road in the arresting opening of the play, based on tragic incidentals from the dramatist's own experiences – memories 'encumbering Ireland's way' (as he was to relate and foretell in another context later), whilst living in the corner tenement of 422 of Dublin's North Circular Road, where O'Casey wrote all three of his well-known Dublin trilogy of plays. Of the three tenement house-wives, Mrs Boyle, Mrs Tancred and Mrs Madigan, Juno is undoubtedly the heroine of unusual strength; the pathetic Mrs Tancred is thoroughly broken by the tragic event in her family.

Another tenement resident is Jerry Devine, jilted lover and half-baked socialist, who over-estimates his own narrow powers of forgiveness when the time is ripe, and his humanity, as Mary discovers, is firmly rooted in middle-class morality and gentility. 'Needle' Nugent, a tailor with a Joxerian eye to the main chance, even amid flimsy foundations of doubtfully worded legacies, who also hails from the Boyle tenement, is a peripheral character complementing Maisie Madigan, whose roots, like Joxer's, are part Dublin and part music-hall and reminiscent of the broad Boucicault comedies of the nineteenth century, which stirred the volatile workings of O'Casey's early imagination.

The only other minor character of proud distinction is the visiting teacher, Charles Bentham, the alien Englishman who cultivates Mary's love and overthrows the affections of her former lover, Jerry Devine. He aspires to a legal career in Dublin, possibly at the Boyles' expense, when expectations of the matured legacy, with which he has been incontinently concerned, are realised; and he is, as his overthrown rival complains, 'a thin, lanky strip of a Micky Dazzler, with a walkin'-stick an' gloves!' Later, in the ensuing confusion of events, mainly due to inconsiderate wording on this legal bull-calf's part, 'his majesty, Bentham' (as Boyle pejoratively alludes to him behind his back, in sly confidence with Joxer) escapes to England, leaving no forwarding address; thus confirming their darkest suspicions.

The unwarrantable, infuriating interruptions of tenement life, from outside as well as within, are here personified by inclusion within the cast of such street-hawkers as a coal-block vendor and a sewing-machine man. The unforeseen violence of the time also results in brief, menacing appearances on set – in pursuit of their own political aims and ends – of such ruthless revolutionaries as the two Irregulars, who gun down their intended victim, Johnny. Their actions are at the behest of the lone Irregular Mobiliser of their battalion, whose cold, admonitory tactics seek out such political ambushes (prefigured in the comical cachet of Boyle's, in an early scene in the first act, when he remarks: 'Is a man not to be allowed to leave his house for a minute without havin' a pack o' spies, pimps an' informers cantherin' at his heels?'). Other side-line characters include the two furniture removal men (one of whom has a salty Irish tongue) who come to reclaim their items of borrowed property when family fortunes collapse and nemesis sets in. In addition there are two neighbours (one of whom gives a religious seal of affection to Republican activities) who accompany Mrs Tancred from the house at the beginning of the funeral procession. Their voices can also be heard in the hall with Mrs Madigan's, when the chilling news of Johnny's death is known at the end.

Death's bright shadow surrounds the stage from the start – the living, as Maeterlinck once wryly remarked, are the dead on holiday. Mary Boyle, seated at the kitchen-table in the early forenoon, dawdling over her dressing because she is on strike, is peering into a small mirror, arranging her hair, at the same time glancing at the morning paper, which tells of the tragic news of Mrs Tancred's son shot in cold blood in one of the ever-frequent, terrifying ambushes waylaying the paths of Dubliners in the relentless Civil War rampaging the lives of everyday citizens. The play's initial line tells all: 'On a little bye-road, out beyant Finglas, he was found', Mary's intent inquisitiveness – in her reading aloud – proclaims. Her brother, Johnny Boyle, a wounded wreck – testifying to such outbreaks of soulless violence – is crouched nervously beside the fireside, tetchily interrupting his sister when she reads out the grisly details of Tancred's death: 'Oh, quit that readin', for God's sake! Are yous losin' all your feelin's? It'll soon be that none of yous'll read anythin' that's not about butcherin'!'

Juno, their mother, who has just returned from shopping before going to work, enquires whether their father, the mock-temerarious 'Captain', out on one of hs usual pub-crawls with his nefarious neighbour, the bold, artful, sponging 'Joxer', has come in for breakfast; for on this one occasion she is deliberately determined, if need be, to make herself late for work, in order to set up an ambush of her own to surprise her husband and his ingratiating companion. (In her absence, she knows only too well that the two of them will breakfast together in their apartment, while she slaves to provide the household's frugal necessities.) Exasperated, she exclaims: 'He wore out the Health Insurance long ago, he's afther wearin' out the unemployment dole, an' now he's thryin' to wear out me! An' constantly singin', no less, when he ought always to be on his knees offerin' up a Novena for a job!' When word of a construction job is

delivered by Jerry Devine, Juno is sure her wastrel-husband will
seize every opportunity to wriggle out of it: 'I killin' meself workin',
an' he sthruttin' about from mornin' till night like a paycock!' (The
directions, too, tell us that Boyle walks with 'a slow, consequential
strut'.)

   Almost immediately, Boyle is heard singing outside ('Sweet
Spirit, hear me prayer!') followed by Joxer Daly who is prepared to
saunter in and luxuriate over a relaxed breakfast in the Boyles'
apartment, while Juno, supposedly, is at work and, in Joxer's
characteristic idiom, 'when the cat's away, the mice can play!' The
singing duo are unaware that Juno is hiding behind the arras of an
adjacent bedroom overlooking the lounge, watching their foxy
movements:

> BOYLE (*with a commanding and complacent gesture*): Pull over to the
>   fire, Joxer, an' we'll have a cup o' tay in a minute.
> JOXER: Ah, a cup o' tay's a darlin' thing, a daarlin' thing – the
>   cup that cheers but doesn't . . .
> (JOXER's *rhapsody is cut short by the sight of* JUNO *coming forward and
>   confronting the two cronies. Both are stupefied.*)
> MRS BOYLE (*with sweet irony – poking the fire, and turning her head to
>   glare at* JOXER): Pull over to the fire, Joxer Daly, an' we'll
>   have a cup o' tay in a minute! Are you sure, now, you
>   wouldn't like an egg?
> JOXER: I can't stop, Mrs Boyle; I'm in a desperate hurry, a
>   desperate hurry.
> MRS BOYLE: Pull over to the fire, Joxer Daly; people is always far
>   more comfortabler here than they are in their own place.

After Joxer's hasty exit, in reply to Boyle's feigned eagerness for a
job, Juno informs him of the real opportunity of forthcoming
employment. Her irony and invective increase, when, predictably,
Boyle angrily rejects such a job, pleading 'the pains in me legs' (in
Joxer's later idiom, 'you can do nothin' while they're at you'), to a
deeper thrust of his wife's asperities – 'You can't climb a laddher,
but you can skip like a goat into a snug! . . . an' don't be actin' as if
you couldn't pull a wing out of a dead bee'. She threatens to stop
supporting him altogether, but offers to prepare his breakfast before
leaving for work. Boyle proudly refuses: 'it ud choke me afther all
that's been said. I've a little spirit left in me still' (a catchphrase to
countermatch Grigson's, in the shadow of alcoholic similarities!).

When she has gone out, he stealthily begins preparing it himself, not forgetting the 'sassige': a scene which offers myriad comic possibilities for a superb, self-contained performance. The frying-pan is switched from hearth to cupboard, backwards and forwards, in a frenzy of agitated expectancy (while its manipulator hums to himself 'When the robins nest agen'), intercepted continually by hawkers' knocks and loud persistent 'tatherarahs' (indicating not Juno's return but 'a fella in a thrench coat', who eventually walks away, getting no reply; an abortive quest in possible premeditated pursuit of Johnny).

The knocks inevitably bring Joxer back on scene and the vapourising at the breakfast table resumes. Joxer obsequiously sympathises, in the form of punctuations of tarnished clichés and tags of idiomatic misnomers and 'daarlin'' rejoinders, as Boyle complains about his wife ('' 'T isn't Juno should be her pet name . . . but Deirdre of the Sorras') as well as the priest who found the construction job for him:

BOYLE: . . . D'ye know, Joxer, I never like to be beholden to any o' the clergy.

JOXER: It's dangerous, right enough.

BOYLE: If they do anything for you, they'd want you to be livin' in the Chapel . . . I'm goin' to tell you somethin', Joxer, that I wouldn't tell to anybody else – the clergy always had too much power over the people in this unfortunate country.

JOXER: You could sing that if you had an air to it!

BOYLE (*becoming enthusiastic*): Didn't they prevent the people in ' '47' from seizin' the corn, an' they starvin'; didn't they down Parnell; didn't they say that hell wasn't hot enough nor eternity long enough to punish the Fenians? We don't forget, we don't forget them things, Joxer. If they've taken everything else from us, Joxer, they've left us our memory.

JOXER (*emotionally*): For mem'ry's the only friend that grief can call its own, that grief . . . can . . . call . . . its own!

BOYLE: Father Farrell's beginnin' to take a great intherest in Captain Boyle; because of what Johnny did for his country, says he to me wan day. It's a curious way to reward Johnny be makin' his poor oul' father work. But, that's what the clergy want, Joxer – work, work, work for

me an' you; havin' us mulin' from mornin' till night, so
that they may be in bether fettle when they come
hoppin' round for their dues! Job! Well, let him give his
job to wan of his hymn-singin', prayer-spoutin', craw-
thumpin' Confraternity men!

After nostalgic references to his period of phoney sea-captaincy –
having its origins in a single trip made on an old collier from Dublin
to Liverpool – with Joxer intent on swallowing the conversational
bait of sea-sovereignty, their thoughts are suddenly grounded, as
Boyle's maritime law is propounded, based on Anglo-Irish Treaty
declarations: 'To-day, Joxer, there's goin' to be issued a proclamation be me, establishin' an independent Republic, an' Juno 'll
have to take an oath of allegiance'.

But Juno's presence in the hall makes such a declaration short-
lived, and Joxer beats a hasty retreat out the back window on to the
roof of the return room, hiding himself while the emergency lasts.
Instead of the threat of a bout of renewed squabbling, Juno brings
fortuitous news: Mary's latest boyfriend, an English schoolteacher
by the name of Bentham, is introduced, and he tells Boyle of an
inheritance from a wealthy relative, Boyle's fervent reaction to
which is never to doubt 'the goodness o' God agen' and to renounce
his previous reprobate existence with Joxer in a firm resolve of
unexpected amendment, prior to pre-celebratory family expectations. This is cut short by angry machinations from a surprised
Joxer, suddenly appearing at the window and bounding into the
room: 'You're done with Joxer, are you? Maybe you thought I'd
stop on the roof all the night for you! Joxer out on the roof with the
win' blowin' through him was nothin' to you an' your friend with
the collar an' tie!'

Ridiculing Boyle's pretensions, he echoes, with malice, as
afterthought:

I was dhreamin' I was standin' on the bridge of a ship, an' she
sailin' the Antartic Ocean, an' it blowed, an' blowed, an' I
lookin' up at the sky an' sayin', what is the stars, what is the stars?

And, as he is shunted out of the room by Juno who declares to her
astonished company – unaware of maudlin fantasies of the Boyle-
Joxer duologue – that she always believed he 'had a slate off', he
flings back, with ironical mischief:

I have to laugh every time I look at the deep-sea sailor; an' a row on a river ud make him sea-sick! . . . Say aw rewaeawr, but not good-bye. Lookin' for work, an' prayin' to God he won't get it!

'He'll never blow the froth off a pint o' mine agen, that's a sure thing', vows Boyle after the jackal's departure. He promises to be 'a new man from this out', and amorously serenades his wife (with the parodied words, 'Oh, me darlin' Juno, I will be thrue to thee', substituting 'Juno' for 'Jennie') in a roundel of hope and eager anticipation that 'Springtime's sunny smile' will for him and his family 'banish all sorrow an' gloom'.

For a while, great expectations persist: two days after the announcement of the legacy, Boyle has borrowed heavily on the strength of the inheritance, reflected in the ampler furnishings and additional vulgar furniture which ostentatiously advertise, at the beginning of Act Two, a change in family circumstances. The 'boul'' Joxer is back in the fold, and he, as well as the rest of the tenement dwellers – albeit in a comical and reverential turn of outlook – rejoices with them in their new-found prosperity.

At the beginning of the scene, Boyle, who is voluptuously stretched on his newly acquired sofa, tells his erstwhile companion, the smiling toady, that being rich is 'a great responsibility, Joxer, a great responsibility. And when Joxer attempts to speak derisively of their local priest, Father Farrell, Boyle reprimands him for his arrant discourtesy: 'You're seldom astray, Joxer, but you're wrong shipped this time. What you're sayin' . . . is very near to blas-feemey'. The snidely quizzical and quick-silvered temperament of his sly associate quickly matches Boyle's present mood with his *ad hoc*: 'the heart o' the rowl, that's what he is; I always said he was a darlin' man, a daarlin' man', and to cement the sudden change of front he follows it up with the hackneyed substitute, 'Soggart Aroon?', a Gaelic term of endearment signifying darling priest (with or without the Joycean or Joxerian implications!).

With yet another switch of emphasis, the jackal, probing the new mood of family expectancy, echoes his belief that Bentham, Mary's new suitor, who has given up his job as a teacher to become a solicitor – doubtless riding on the backs of the Boyles for financial enhancement – belongs in his sphere of pinnacled hyperbole, 'a darlin' man'. Boyle disagrees, but asks Joxer, with their other upstairs neighbour, Mrs Madigan, to join them in their co-celebration later that evening. (Juno brings in a hired gramophone

– a period novelty, complete with horn – in preparation for their little soirée.)

Earlier, over tea, Bentham discusses, with a certain amount of swagger, his theosophist beliefs, with ghostly implications which in turn produce a nervous chain-reaction on the agitated Johnny – pent up in fear and foreboding – who suddenly screams out in a distraught outburst of agonised terror, as previsions of death convince him the reassuring light of the votive lamp in front of the statue of the Virgin has gone out and he imagines he sees the bullet-ridden corpse of young Robbie Tancred, his slain neighbour: 'Oh, why did he look at me like that? . . . it wasn't my fault that he was done in . . . Mother o' God, keep him away from me!'

Later, the Boyle family and their tenement neighbours celebrate with drink and songs as planned, and Juno and Mary join in the party-spirit with a plaintive duet, Maisie Madigan sings with near operatic flamboyance and Joxer forgets his lines. Outside, the funeral of their neighbour Mrs Tancred's son is about to begin, and the rejoicing subsides, while the grieving mother remains un-comforted either by political ideals or consolations of religion: neither, she sobs, will bring her beloved son back from the grave; and, in a threnody of grief, she accompanies the cortège. (From her lips, the universal maternal plea of mercy and an end to the fighting is first voiced; sadly echoed at the end by the bereaved, though braver, Juno herself, in what has since become a classic plea in the history of modern drama, for unrequited forgiveness, mercy and human compassion.)

Juno, who reminds her festive assembly that in the throes of civil war dependants of those living in the whole tenement block have been either butchered or 'massacreed', is answered by Boyle, who avows that such happenings are the Government's concern and need not affect them (in a touch of dramatic irony on the part of O'Casey). 'If they want a wake, well, let them have a wake', he shruggingly suggests. And, in blathering tones, he comments: 'When I was a sailor, I was always resigned to meet with a wathery grave; an', if they want to be soldiers, well, there's no use o' them squealin' when they meet a soldier's fate'. To which, the oily Joxer declaims: 'Let me like a soldier fall – me breast expandin' to th' ball!'

While the family entertainment is in full swing – and with it the novelty of the gramophone intimating that 'If you're Irish, Come into the Parlour' – the funeral procession of Mrs Tancred's son passes by; and another resident from the same tenement, a tailor – a brisk, bald-headed, little busybody, known as 'Needle' Nugent – interrupts the jollities with an open chastisement, based on what he terms 'the Irish people's National regard for the dead'. The hypocrisy of the rebuke angers Juno, who, after the gramophone has been switched off, counters with the O'Casey-approved: 'it's nearly time we had a little less respect for the dead, an' a little more regard for the livin''. In reinforcement to this, Maisie Madigan shows her mettle with the added rebuke: 'We don't want you, Mr Nugent, to teach us what we learned at our mother's knee. You don't look yourself as if you were dyin' of grief; if y'ass Maisie Madigan anything, I'd call you a real thrue Diehard an' live-soft Republican, attendin' Republican funerals in the day, an' stoppin' up half the night makin' suits for the Civic Guards!'

From the window they pause to watch the heavily-wreathed procession – Joxer ejaculating, 'it's a darlin' funeral, a daarlin' funeral!' – and then go down to the street to join the mass mourners.

The clouds of foreboding quickly gather: no sooner is Johnny left alone than a mysterious intruder appears at the doorway – the Mobiliser from his former battalion of Irregulars, who has tracked him down at last. (His comrades believe him to be the traitor who gave the Free Staters the signal that led to Tancred's death.) In sinister tones, he issues Boyle's son with clipped instructions to attend a meeting of their contingent at a later date. Johnny begs to be left alone: 'I've lost me arm, an' me hip's desthroyed so that I'll never be able to walk right agen! Good God, haven't I done enough for Ireland?' The hard-headed reply is delivered firmly and unemotionally: 'Boyle, no man can do enough for Ireland!', with the mourners in the background chanting their orisons of death below, in this sombre, prismatic conclusion to the second act. The piety and hate remain; and co-exist, side by side, like the wheat and the tares in Ireland's bitter harvest.

The cumulative misfortunes of the Boyles – like the undiminished sorrows afflicting their newly independent country – multiply in a downward course of misery and wretchedness in the play's final act, the events of which are centred on an early evening in November two months later. The Shakespearian emphasis in *Hamlet*:

> When sorrows come, they come not single spies,
> But in battalions

is buttressed to the full, reinforcing the play's darker side. Boyle's strutting pride has almost become the living embodiment of a national weakness.

The leaden lining of O'Casey's cloud unveils a series of piled-on disasters which escape the charge of melodrama because of the shrewd banter and hypocritical observation of his own comic tenement-folk caught in their web of poverty, meanness and self-awareness. Boyle and Joxer demonstrate, more forcefully than ever, that they are a superb pair of cross-talk rogues. And, throughout the macabre events of the drama, Johnny Boyle continues to rest uncomfortably on the bed at the side of the room behind the cretonned curtains – an unwilling listener and spectator to all the ironic irrelevancies that befall the hapless family – conveying the agony of the trapped son waiting for the fatal knock at the door.

His hysterical behaviour matches Boyle's angry outburst when he hears that his sister, who has been listless since her lover abandoned her and went off to England, now finds herself pregnant. And his splenetic reaction (itself a prefiguration on the dramatist's part) to the news that the inheritance proves a fantasy ('I wish to God a bullet or a bomb had whipped me ou' o' this long ago! Not one o' yous, not one o' yous, have any thought for me!') is almost beyond the assuaging powers of comfort from Juno, who declares:

> If you don't whisht, Johnny, you'll drive me mad. Who has kep th' home together for the past few years – only me. An' who'll have to bear th' biggest part o' this throuble but me – but whinin' an' whingin' isn't goin' to do any good.

At the beginning of the scene, the tragicomedy of the Boyles' downfall is presaged by the stigma of cunning displayed jointly by Nugent and Joxer, who, between them, give a brisk precipitatory nudge in their conversation to the teetering fortunes of the errant sea Captain: in Joxer's mocking tones, 'Gentleman Jack an' his frieze coat!' and Nugent's sardonic outburst, 'Maybe you think you're better able to owe it than pay it', punctuated by Joxer's reverberating jeers, 'Ah, him that goes a borrowin' goes a sorrowin'!' and, most trenchantly of all, 'man's inhumanity to man makes countless thousands mourn' (twisting Burns's ejaculation). The foxy jackal, sensing that Boyle is stony broke and hopelessly in debt, savours his motiveless revenge: 'Wasn't it a mercy o' God that I'd nothin' to give him! The softy I am, you know', he confides to

Nugent, 'I'd ha' lent him me last juice! I must have had somebody's good prayers. Ah, afther all, an honest man's the noblest work o' God!'

Events move to their inexorable conclusion: after Johnny's hysterical outburst over the hopeless situation, the 'Paycock' angrily warns Juno not to bring their daughter back to live in his respectable household (he waxes strong about the disgrace); he summons Joxer to accompany him on his last drinking binge and leaves Juno to face the ordeal of the movers repossessing the furniture. Chaos and confusion within the tenement signify turmoil outside, as a result of the selfishness of the Civil War.

Mary's plight is worsened when her former suitor, Jerry Devine, declines her hand when he hears of her 'fall'. (Distraught, she rushes out to follow Juno, who has gone to track down Boyle.) Alone, Johnny is visited by two Irregulars from his former battalion, belted and gruff, who drag him off to avenge the betrayal of their ambushed comrade. (While the removal-men are stripping the apartment, the oil in the votive lamp burns itself out, and Johnny cries out in super-woeful anguish: 'I'm afther feelin' a pain in me breast, like the tearin' by of a bullet'.) Soon, the military roughnecks, advising him to take with him his rosary beads, lead him off to an unknown rendezvous with death. His frenzied departure is in keeping with the haunting lines of verses Mary has just recited to Jerry before he finally rejects any reconciliation with her:

> Like the agonizing horror
> Of a violin out of tune . . .

(The verses, which are O'Casey's, are subsequently included in *Windfalls*.)

After an hour, Juno and her daughter are back in an empty flat, stripped of all vestige of habitation, and they wait in anxious foreboding. Tragedy strikes, and with the force of 'an eagle's tearin' claw'. Johnny's bullet-ridden corpse is found – a replica of Tancred's before him – in the spate of reprisal killings which disfigured the history of Ireland's independence. And, in the masterful finale, before Juno and Mary decide to quit their tenement for good, Juno repeats the self-same lament echoed by her neighbour – though not in the same anguished unconsolation – during which she reiterates the final message of the play: 'Take away this murdherin' hate, an' give us Thine own eternal love!' (together with the Ezekiel-inspired: 'take away our hearts o' stone, and give us hearts o' flesh') in a universal prayer of mercy and compassion, shutting the gates of vengeance on mankind. Mercy, O'Casey wishes to remind us, is the 'twice blest' Shakespearian attribute enunciated in *The Merchant of Venice*, although 'enthroned in the hearts of kings' and 'mightiest in the mightiest', which blesses not only him that gives as well as him who takes – in a compassionable society of the future, 'when mercy seasons justice' (in Shakespeare's earnest aspirations). O'Casey invokes traditions of the Prophets and the Bard in his equanimous view of a less warring and fairer society in which man can prosper.

Although Juno leaves in tragic dignity, the last glimpse of the play's earth-tragedienne is a reminder of Mother Ireland following the same downward path of sorrows, viewing the causes in a clarity of practical vision and wisdom, but unable to offer any salvation: 'Ah, what can God do agen the stupidity o' men!' is her tragic explanation. The tragic irony of the play's conceptualism is founded on ironic implications of Burns's ejaculation from 'Man was made to Mourn':

> Man's inhumanity to man
> Makes countless thousands mourn!

(voiced, first of all, in heightened comic circumstances during a bout of Boyle-Joxer tomfoolery and then, anticlimatically, applied in the latter half of the play, in the gulf of tragedy which lingers in a Stygian lake beneath).

The drama ends on two notes: first with Juno's highly emotional, impassioned lines, and then with the blindly drunken entrance of Joxer and Boyle (on to a completely empty and deserted stage). The final scene reflects the mosaic of O'Casey's command of total tragic and irreversible irony. Joxer sings:

> Put all . . . your throubles . . . in your oul' kit bag . . . an' smile . . . smile . . . smile!

to which Boyle counters:

> The counthry'll have to steady itself . . . Chairs'll . . . have to . . . steady themselves . . .

Boyle drops his last coin ('The last o' the Mohicans'); both wallow in patriotic slogans, and Boyle philosophises tipsily before collapsing on the floor:

> I'm telling you . . . Joxer . . . th' whole worl's . . . in a terr . . . ible state o' . . . chassis!

Tragedy and comedy, in this segment of true sensation of living – as based on a harrowing chapter of Ireland's immediate past – are but two sides of the same coin. Not only in his early naturalistic drama but also in his conceptualised theatre of his later years – moulded on phantasmagoric lines – does O'Casey aim at thrusting together laughter and tears in indivisible mixtures. In the mercurial mood of tragicomedy, his plays prompt a high degree of emotional response; and, cleverly and uniquely, display both the heightening of tragedy and the exaggerations of comedy. An artistic conjunction of these two modes – the one inviting us to share in the sufferings of a particular character and the other warning us through the delicious display of buffoonery and comicality to avoid his individual mistakes – can instil a mutative response. O'Casey's main concern is to show us that man is a jester as well as a paragon; a clown as well as a fool. And, in a realistic or even dangerous world, the truer world of exotic comedy (O'Casey reflects), familiar to us in forms of music-hall, pantomime and circus, lends an ever-present thread of fantasy, forming a rainbow from the plough to the stars – the earth to the heavens – in the glorious counterbalancing of joy and tragedy. This is the strength of O'Casey's mould of tragicomedy: its balancing of both the new and traditional; and, of course, its sheer vitality in an unforgettable portrayal of life as it really is, in the less determined aspects of vacuities and uncertainties of mundane existence.

Juno and the Paycock is not an easy play to produce. It is a delicate balance of comedy, tragedy and pathos which requires vast technical resources from its actors to be effective. If the comedy spills over into the tragedy, and if the pathos and poetry are lost, dramatic disaster ensues and audiences are unaware of the author's true purpose. The play is basically a tragedy highlighted with humour: it should be played as stark tragedy, with many shifts of irony and humour. The successful director will be faced with the task of smoothly orchestrating the bewildering shifts of mood that sweep like emotional waves through this play. A naturalistic interpretation is called for, with side-lights of fantasy. The temptation to romanticise O'Casey must be resisted; to play him merely for charm and blarney and outright comedy.

The infinite moulding and studying of character should not stop the progress and momentum of the play: timing and pace in the shifting moods of scene and character are important. The harrowing tragicomic power should be skilfully handled and never descend to grotesquerie. The sound of O'Casey's dialogue comes through and it is a marvel to the ear as well as the mind in the variety of its measure. Periods of precognition in the plot are underscored by use of dramatic irony which should be duly emphasised.

In *Juno and the Paycock* there is an Irish undercurrent which runs powerfully counter to O'Casey's surface anti-clericalism, the Catholic pathos for all womanhood illustrated by the grieving scenes of Mrs Tancred and Juno. Yet the party scene must have the necessary boozy exuberance if the break-up caused by the Tancred funeral is to have its full impact.

The play's supreme sense of hyperbole must not be dislocated by clumsy acting or interpretation. Exceptional convergence of deep talent among casting is essential, illuminating matchless ensemble playing, showing the deep artistry of O'Casey's play. Each actor has a powerful contribution to make in the play's development.

Foremost, of course, are the roles of Juno, Boyle and Joxer. An inappropriate choice in any of these roles will impair the final tantalising effect.

The sterling Juno, ten or fifteen years younger than her husband, should be played with infinite courage, emphasising her rock-like steadfastness – watchful, rueful (by turns), eager for hope, realistic, but continually crushed by circumstances – so that even in the final breakdown, no doubt is left of her will to survive and to salvage what is left of her wrecked life and family. Her role needs to be played straight, actuating both her humour and bravery, as well as the anguish in her soul as her life is crushed about her. On her performance will devolve the basic qualities and spirit of the play, giving that ennobling enactment which fortifies O'Casey's sincerity and sense of outrage in what transpires to be utmost purity of feeling.

Her husband, the shiftless Jack Boyle, who at sixty is an idle wastrel – bluff and ebullient; stout and stocky in appearance – needs to be played with Falstaffian gusto. He is a self-dramatising egotist. His portrayer must move from the realms of comedy to bluster, and finally to selfish, stupid cruelty, with convincing skill. His bravado is enshrined in the faded seaman's cap he continually wears.

Joxer Daly is his prodigal crony and has a wizened cunning appearance, crowned with roguish impishness encapsulated in his own catchphrase, 'It's better to be a coward than a corpse!' He compliments Boyle, and both are 'paycocks' in their own rite – Joxer all the while playing foil to the greater 'Paycock'. Boyle's mannerism is his strut; Joxer's is his shoulder-shrugging. Their complementary comic roles are contributory factors towards a tragedy of death and destruction – even though they are unaware of it. Their indolent, garrulous, useless lives mirror much of the pathos of Ireland's manhood. The extended possibilities of their tragicomic interdependence are exploited on numerous occasions in successive O'Casey plays (from Simon and Sylvester in *The Silver Tassie* to Binnington and McGilligan in *The Drums of Father Ned*).

Mary Boyle, as a promising, good-looking colleen of twenty-two, should convey the essence of an eager, confused girl, whose self-acquired sophistication is of little help when the full impact of her own tragedy engulfs her.

Her brother, Johnny, whose confused actions, too, have led to his physical and psychological break-up (ultimately leading to his death in the wretched struggle for Irish independence), is a test of real acting strength: his political guilt lies behind the whole momentum of the play, and manifests itself in the form of hallucinations, fits of temper, bitterness and whining self-pity. (As one of life's fugitives, he is maddened as much by an obsessive preoccupation with escape, as by jollity in the house or horror outside.)

Maisie Madigan is a typical, vulgar tenement woman, with a gay heart and a sharp tongue. Her wit is endless and her moods are as changeable as the Four Winds of Eireann.

Jerry Devine, at twenty-five, is an earnest activist within the Labour movement – a prototype of today's shop steward – able to convince his fellow-workers, but lacking the broader vision to convince the rest of his countrymen and mankind.

Charles Bentham, the fortune-hunting theosophist who has his way with Mary, should be caddishly portrayed, with comedy underlying his ambitions. 'Needle' Nugent, the seemingly propitious tailor, is as cunningly motivated as his rural kinsman, the wily tinker. Like Joxer, he is a gimlet-eyed imp. Deferential, at first, to Boyle, he later reclaims his unpaid-for suit with Joxerian vengeance, adding smiling malice with the rejoinder: 'What do I care what you dhress yourself in! You can put yourself in a bolsther cover, if you like'. Mrs Tancred, whose die-hard son has been killed in ambush, is an elderly neighbour broken by grief, displaying none of Juno's humanity or courage to circumvent her personal tragedy. By refusing even a cup of tea from the Boyles before she follows her son's coffin, she shows a dominant life-weariness in her attitude, totally at variance with Juno's outlook. The Irregular Mobiliser, who appears at the end of the second act, is a subtle, ruthless shadow of a gunman, knowing that Juno's son is poised on the brink of certain death and whose fate is squarely in his hands. His agents, the two Irregulars, who later apprehend Johnny and take him away to be shot, are coldly callous in the same revolutionary vein. Remaining characters, though supportive, are interestingly and poignantly conceived.

The play's Dublin *première*, at the Abbey Theatre on 3 March 1924, was a resounding success. Under Michael J. Dolan's direction, Barry Fitzgerald played Boyle definitively, Sara Allgood played Juno and F. J. McCormick played Joxer. Eager audiences thronged the theatre, thus ensuring frequent revivals, so that up till 1980 well over four hundred performances had been recorded in the whole of the Company's history. 'A great play and a great playwright has come' declared James Stephens.

In London, opening on 16 November 1925, the play was directed by J. B. Fagan, at the Royalty Theatre, later transferring in March 1926 to the Fortune, as the total run exceeded over two hundred performances – the longest for any O Casey professional run in Britain. Arthur Sinclair played Boyle, Sara Allgood played Juno, Sydney Morgan played Joxer and Maire O'Neill played Maisie Madigan. The acting won hyperboles of praise and the play itself the Hawthornden Prize in 1926. After the triumphant success, Sinclair's company toured the Midlands with performances in Liverpool, Birmingham (and later in the Irish provinces).

In America, the 1926 Augustin Duncan version at New York's Mayfair lacked impact with no luminaries among the cast. Tours in the thirties by the Abbey Company and Irish Players gave American audiences a truer insight, though the 1940 Ambassador production, directed by Arthur Shields, partnering Fitzgerald and Allgood in their original roles (with Shields himself playing Joxer), gained unstinted praise, thus ensuring permanent success with a run of 105 performances. Frequent revivals thereafter were, inevitably, paler comparisons, though the 1954 and 1955 Greenwich Mews and New York ventures were moderately successful. The 1974 Los Angeles revival, with Walter Matthau as Boyle and Jack Lemmon as Joxer, was warmly received. In Britain, Sinclair's revivals continued till 1937. Post-war London revivals have included Peter Daubeny's 1964 presentation for the World Theatre Season, with a visiting troupe from the Abbey in Frank Dermody's disappointing interpretation; Laurence Olivier's 1966 National Theatre's tribute, with Colin Blakely, Frank Finlay and Joyce Redman in the leads; Denis Carey's at Dublin's Gaiety, with Peter O'Toole as Boyle and Jack MacGowran as Joxer, redeemed by the Bernard Miles 1973 presentation at the Mermaid, focusing on Siobhan McKenna's Juno. The Royal Shakespeare Company's homage in 1980 achieved the crowning glory in Trevor Nunn's stunning revival, with Judi Dench as Juno, Norman Rodway as Boyle and John Rogan as Joxer, with a matchless ensemble playing all round. A filmed version by Alfred Hitchcock in 1930 featured Edward Chapman as Boyle and Allgood as Juno. A musical version by Glickman and Stein on Broadway in 1959 was a failure. There have been numerous television transmissions and a record by EMI featuring Siobhan McKenna as Juno, Seamus Kavanagh as Boyle and Cyril Cusack as Joxer.

In Europe, revivals have been numerous. The Kellerson Paris version in 1950 made a strong impact, as did the 1961 Jean Goubert staging. The 1953 Munich *première* precipitated revivals in West Berlin in 1964 and 1974, though the Adolf Dresen East Berlin presentation of 1972 won greater favour, as did the 1955 version at Madrid's National. Extensive translations have included those in Arabic, Chinese, Danish, Dutch, French, German, Hungarian, Italian, Japanese, Portuguese and Spanish, as well as Russian, Roumanian, Swedish and Turkish.

5 *Nannie's Night Out* (1924): a One-Act Vignette

This little diversion, after the glorification of *Juno*, was something of an anti-climax; though, within its short compass, such a one-act vignette bubbles with undertones of rich tragicomic farce and vivid, realistic characterisation, carved, of course, in firm naturalistic mould: an etching of slum-life in Northern Dublin suburbs, in a stratification of comicality, suffering and heartbreak, personified by the street Ballad Singers' cry, forming a chorus to the general action within the play:

> For Ireland is Ireland thro' joy an' thro' tears.
> Hope never dies thro' the long weary years.
> Each age has seen countless, brave hearts pass away,
> But their spirit still lives on in the men of today!

The main character, Irish Nannie, a methylated spirits drinker of the streets, a boisterous, once good-looking spunker – widowed early, and left with a fragile, sickly boy of twelve to rear, who is hunchbacked and cunning; a street loafer, in the disorientated society around him – is a vortex of raw emotions and human reactions within circumstances imposed upon her. She is described by the playwright as 'recklessly merry' and 'very near to hysterical tears'. She has her counterpart in Mild Millie, the street spunker, symbolically and sympathetically portrayed in *Drums Under the Windows*. Traces of her character can be seen in Bessie Burgess, the volatile widow with heroic determination in *The Plough and the Stars*. But she is best seen as a prototype of Jannice, the Young Whore, in O'Casey's first full-length, expressionist play, *Within the Gates*.

As O'Casey has indicated in a letter dated 27 December 1925 to the *New York Times*, he felt, on reconsideration, the character of

65

Nannie 'deserved the richer picture of a three-act play'. So, requesting leave to withdraw the work from the Abbey Theatre's repertoire, he seemed dissatisfied with the play's loose-knit style and insubstantiality. Subsequently, the play was never included in the main corpus of his work. Robert Hogan, however, included it, with the playwright's sanction, in his miscellany, *Feathers From the Green Crow*. Dramaturgically, at least (though whether this judgement is purely arbitrary may be questionable), *Nannie's Night Out* was to be regarded as just another episode; an interlude in the playwright's main output.

O'Casey labels his farce 'A Comedy in One Act'. A reviewer in the *Irish Statesman* describes it quintessentially as:

> a rocking, roaring comedy – Dublin accents; queer "characters"; window-smashing; burlesque love-making. Our sides ache, we laugh; we roar; we gasp – and then – a sudden feeling of discomfort, a queer, stupid feeling as if we wanted to cry . . . He brings us to his plays and then he heaves life at us, with its sharp corners and its untidy jumble of laughter and tears . . . And the worst of it is, that if we go on allowing him to make us laugh and cry together in this hysterical manner, we may end by insisting that he is a genius.

The scene is a small dairy and provisions shop in a Dublin working-class district of the twenties. (Gabriel Fallon, in his *Sean O'Casey: the Man I Knew*, tells us it was a shop O'Casey knew well in Dorset Street.) The store owner, Polly Pender, is a shrewd, frisky-minded, fifty-year-old widow, who is regularly courted by a trio of disproportionately idle old boasters – Oul Johnny, Oul Jimmy and Oul Joe – inadequate as well as unchivalrous in their dissymmetry. The Street Singer, 'who has all the cuteness of his class', is a harbinger in the shop, too, and belongs to the same triptych of useless expectation, harbouring a perpetual grudge against humanity and society, reflected in his repetitive slogan-cry: 'it's cruel, it's cruel!' (which also identifies him as a prototype of Green Muffler, in the later sketch, *Hall of Healing*).

The ostensible theme of the play, like that of *The Shadow of a Gunman* and also *Juno and the Paycock*, is the cavity between cowardice and self-deception of men and courage and compulsive endurance of women. Environmental contrast between Nannie and Mrs Pender is stressed in the conflicting factors of daily slum life.

The widow has her health, her store and her assortment of suitors. The crazed methylated spirits drinker, on the other hand, is destitute and utterly alone and has only her tragic vision to counteract her beleaguered circumstances (even if it leads to battles with the police, whom she regards as a 'gang o' silver button'd bouseys', and spells in jail). Her tormented philosophy is perpetually summed up as: 'we'll be long enough dead . . . A short life an' a merry wan, ay, oul' cock'.

Although dying on her feet from 'th' spunk' that 'has me nearly done for', like Jannice, the Young Whore, in *Within the Gates*, she vows to 'die game'. Nannie dramatises chaos as well as happiness in a pungent, highly original manner. When replete with methylated spirits, she causes havoc by smashing windows and engaging in brawls around her. To the outside world, she bawls:

> Nannie doesn't care a curse for anybody . . . Let them send down their Foot, an' their Calvary – Nannie's waitin' for them; she'll give them somethin' better than cuttin' down th' Oul' Age Pensions . . . Republicans an' Free Staters – a lot of rubbidge, th' whole o' yous! Th' poor Tommies was men!

Her bravery is demonstrated – in contrast to the buffoonery of the three suitors cowering behind their self-imagined fearlessness – when an armed burglar holds the store-owner to ransom (the bold suitors suggesting capitulation), but is foiled by the unexpected re-arrival on scene of Nannie, on a drunken spree, rampaging her way into the shop and scaring the burglar away, singing and roaring, in her deranged path of destruction, the acclaimed antiphon:

> Tho' she wears no fine clothes, nor no rich silken hose,
> Still there's something that makes her divine,
> For th' angels above, taught th' way how to love
> To that oul' fashion'd mother o' mine!

The play's perspective is seen through the eyes of Nannie: a slum world where everything seems hopeless and distorted and irrationally connected – a theme that has its roots in many of the dramatist's later full-length fantasies and one-act imprecations. In the force of tragicomic factors afflicting her, Nannie's suffering is the more intense, precisely because she discerns, so passionately and defiantly, the hopelessness of such sordid and soul-destroying conditions

associated with a slum-ridden existence. As the playwright proclaims, in *Drums Under the Windows*, when speaking of the bravery
and intrepidity of Millie, aflame with red poteen: 'Righteousness
isn't a badge on the breast, but a living glow in the heart, like the
core of flame in a smoking fire'.

In one ending to the play, Nannie dies from a heart attack after
the robbery; while in another, the police drag her to jail for 'Th'
hundhred an' second time' for being her normal, gesticulating,
dancing, demented self, on the verge of drunken, tattered collapse:
a huddled mass of torn clothes and mud. As O'Casey, in *Drums
Under the Windows*, with characteristic benevolence and heartfelt
sympathy, eulogises on behalf of Millie's hopeless plight:

> She loves Cathleen ni Houlihan . . . in her own reckless way. In
> a way, she is Cathleen ni Houlihan – a Cathleen with the flame
> out of her eyes turned downwards. The feet of this Cathleen, the
> daughter of Houlihan, are quiet now, but none have bent low
> and low to kiss them.

Of such is the salvaged hope of humanity: irreverence one of its vital
links in the chain of wisdom and human understanding.

Although Nannie remains the centralised character, most of the
other characters, as in the author's naturalistic dramas, are liberally
endowed with absurd and likeable foibles: the same characters
appear in other guises and inspirations in the dramatist's later
fantasied plays. Oul Johnny, a 'stout, rubicund visaged man
approaching sixty', is a recognisable example of the 'Paycockian'
species, whilst his rival Jimmy, of similar age, is a Joxerian
prototype. Being painfully near-sighted, and peering closely at
everything, he is a visible reminder, too, of Barry Derrill in *The End
of the Beginning*. Oul Joe, though bent in body, but dressed up to kill,
as signalled by the fancy muffler he wears, is an inveterate boaster,
in the style of Shields and Fluther (whom we meet in *The Plough and
the Stars*). All belong to O'Casey's armory of self-deceivers; and,
being vulnerable to their superhuman failings, cannot see themselves for what they are or understand the plight of others. Polly
Pender escapes from their clutches by resolving to remain, in the
words of the playwright, 'a bird alone'.

Only Nannie is aware of the essential spark in life: the bright face
of danger, with its troubled dreams and endless 'sound and fury' (to

quote Macbeth). As the Ballad Singer, at the end, in mournful tones apostrophises:

> Yous gang o' hypocrites! . . . It was only when she was dhrunk an' mad that anywan took any notice of her! What can th' like o' them do, only live any way they can? Th' Poorhouse, th' Prison, an' th' morgue – them is our palaces! . . . D'ye think th' blasted kips o' tenement houses we live in'll breed Saints an' Scholars?

Neither saint nor scholar is she, but, in the image of her own choral commentary, a distinctive 'Mother Macree'; an indomitable woman of the tenements, and, in the wider inspiration of the playwright, a representation of Cathleen Ni Houlihan herself.

The play's only production at the Abbey Theatre was on 29 September 1924. The director was Michael J. Dolan. Sara Allgood played Nannie with Maureen Delany as Polly Pender and F. J. McCormick as the Ballad Singer, whilst Barry Fitzgerald played Oul Johnny, Michael J. Dolan played Oul Jimmy and Gabriel Fallon played Oul Joe. The play, although equally infused with pathos as with ironic comedy, suffered in production from being juxtaposed between *Juno* and *The Plough and the Stars* – plays that have the undeniable stamp of genius on them. Later, O'Casey came to have little regard for his early one-act invocation and did not include it in the canon of his collected plays, though Lady Gregory, in a letter to the playwright, considered it 'a fine and witty piece of ironical comedy'.

Although, in Dublin, there were no further revivals, the playlet was revived, with the author's permission, by Robert Hogan in America in 1961. He directed it at the Little Theatre, Lafayette, Indiana. 'The whole play', the director afterwards wrote, 'is eminently alive. It is packed with the song, the dancing, the wild rhetoric, and the verve that have become O'Casey's trademarks' (*Feathers from The Green Crow*). The conjunction of Nannie's wild exit against the Ballad Singer's closing song on a darkened stage, says Hogan, is as memorable and kaleidoscopic as the renowned prismatic endings of both *Juno and the Paycock* and *The Plough and the Stars*. Translations exist in French and German.

6 *The Plough and the Stars* (1926): Evocation of the Irish Easter Rising

O'Casey's next full-length play, dealing with the insurgence of Easter Week in Dublin in 1916, 'A Tragedy in Four Acts', cemented his reputation as undoubtedly the greatest and most successful playwright the Abbey Theatre has produced; and, in the opinion of the directorate themselves, *The Plough and the Stars* is 'a fine play, possibly the best work I have yet done', he wrote enthusiastically to Macmillan and Company, his publishers.

'This piece contains that greatness which is something different from the sum of small perfections', James Agate was to remark after seeing the first London production in 1926. 'Mr O'Casey has done what Balzac and Dickens did – he has created an entirely new gallery of living men and women'. Eugene O'Neill, the American playwright, on a rare occasion in a letter to O'Casey in 1943, had confided: '. . . don't you know I want to bite off one of your ears in jealous fury every time I think of – Well, of *The Plough and the Stars*, to mention only one of several'. And, in the opinion of Nathan, O'Casey's latest play is 'one of the finest dramas in the modern theatre'. Nowhere, in Nathan's view, in the drama of living Irishmen is there 'greater and more genuine dramatic poetry' to be found than in the mighty sweep of *The Plough and the Stars*.

Several years later, O'Casey was asked what 'significance' the play would have for theatregoers of today and he replied:

> If it has any 'significance', it is that a small number – or even one fine mind – may initiate a movement, but cannot bring it to success without the cooperation of what is called 'the common people'. The gallant men who rose in 1916 to strike for Ireland's independence were defeated, and what they stood for only succeeded, when, years later, the people, as a whole, swung round

from opposition to support. It was so with Christianity. It is so with every movement, whether idealistic or materialistic . . . Life depends on cooperative and collective energy.

(O'Casey, *Letters*, vol. 2)

'Not Revolutions, but men', O'Casey had told Lady Gregory in 1925, 'must bring about the Brotherhood of Man'.

Of the ill-fated and abortive Easter Rising, J. Hampden Jackson, the English historian, tabulated some twenty years afterwards the main events which led to its failure:

> The plan of rising in arms against the might of England seemed desperate, but there was the ghost of a chance that it would succeed. It was timed for Easter, 1916, and that spring England had her hands more than full on the Continent. Sir Roger Casement's job was to run arms in from Germany. At the last moment he was caught and his cargo captured. The official leader of the Nationalist Movement, Eoin MacNeill, called the rising off, but Patrick Pearse was determined to go on with it. He and his six friends called themselves the Provisional Government of the Irish Republic. 'We declare the right of the people of Ireland to the ownership of Ireland . . .'
>
> Dublin still bears the marks of that rising, physically in the bullet-scarred walls of her public buildings and morally in her mourning of the men who suffered in it. 58 Irishmen were killed in the fighting. The British held a court-martial and sentenced 97 others to death as rebels. The sentence was actually carried out in the case of 16 men. Only one leader was reprieved, and that was because he had been born in America and the English were anxious not to offend the United States just when there was a chance that they would come in to the World War on the English side. The name of the reprieved man was Eamonn de Valera.
>
> (*England Since the Industrial Revolution*, Victor Gollancz, 1936)

The reprisal killings instituted by the British Government swayed popular Republican sympathies among the Irish electorate, and in the General Election of 1918, the former Irish Nationalist party, under Redmond and Dillon, was heavily defeated, and, instead, Sinn Fein swept the board. The new leaders were Griffiths, Collins and De Valera. The watchword of newly elected representatives to the British Parliament was 'Ourselves Alone'. Their intention was not to take up their seats at Westminster, but to establish an undercover parliament, or secret Dail, which met in Dublin. The upshot was guerrilla fighting with British soldiery on a nation-wide scale in the prolonged wars of independence which rampaged Ireland. The country, as background events in *The Shadow of a Gunman* starkly testify, rapidly became a terrifying 'Gunman's Republic', and the revolutionary aspiration of Pearse, which motivated the short-lived Easter Rebellion – 'The old earth of the battlefields is thirsty for the wine of our blood' – was activated less than three years afterwards.

Yeats's prophecy in *Cathleen Ni Houlihan* (1902) was realised in awesome national catastrophe, foretold in his play: 'They that have red cheeks will have pale cheeks for my sake and for all that they will think themselves well paid'. But Yeats could romanticise the fight between Ireland and England, never having seen blood flow, whereas O'Casey, a more fervent lover of his fellow men than Yeats, found it necessary in the name of truth to take the anti-romantic view. Hence *The Plough and the Stars*, the climax of his Dublin trilogy: in the eyes of some, his most enduring gift to the world's drama.

During the interval between the first production of *Juno and the Paycock* (1924) and *The Plough and the Stars* (1926), O'Casey, in a letter to the *Irish Statesman*, in its issue of 7 February 1925, reaffirms what most audiences outside Dublin firmly believed from the outset – that here was a Prometheus of the drama, a Phoenix from the slums of Dublin, with deeply-entrenched Socialist convictions and beliefs. 'My sympathies', he says, 'were always with the rags and tatters that sheltered the tenement-living Temples of the Holy Ghost'. Almost forty years later, in *Under a Colored Cap* (1963), the last book he wrote before his death in 1964, in a shrewd and witty article entitled 'Purple Dust in their Eyes', he answers the gibes and taunts of a group of persistently hostile London critics with the rejoining reminder, 'As for me, I abandoned the romantic cult of Nationalism sixty years ago, and saw the real Ireland when I read the cheap edition of Shaw's *John Bull's Other Island*; hating only poverty, hunger and disease'.

After the terrible class-hatred experienced in the great Dublin strike and lock-out of 1913 and its unprecedented misery for thousands of Dublin working-class families driven to the verge of starvation in the face of the employers' intransigent attitude backed by police brutality (a telescoping of these events is conjured in *Red*

Roses for Me), O'Casey, who himself had faced near-starvation at this particular time, was thoroughly and irrevocably disillusioned with talk of Nationalist ideals and principles. In the course of an article, written for the *Irish Worker* in 1914, and included in *Feathers from the Green Crow*, we find him saying, 'Nationalism [for the workers] is a gospel without hope; it does not signify life to them'. The deeply-held conviction of Sean O'Casey that the workers should 'keep clear of politicians', who would use the workers for their own purpose, is apparent in his declaration of this time that 'not in the shouts of deluded wage-slave Volunteers but in the hunger cry of the nation's poor is heard the voice of Ireland'. His prime interest in economic freedom (paving the way for socialism) is reflected in Rosie Redmond's outburst in Act Two of *The Plough and the Stars*:

'A lot o' thricksters', says I, 'that wouldn't know what freedom was if they got it from their mother . . . ' Well, 'flash in th' pan, or no flash in th' pan', says I, 'they're not goin' to get Rosie Redmond', says I, 'to fight for freedom that wouldn't be worth winnin' in a raffle!'

O'Casey's true ideal of freedom is expressed by Ayamonn Breydon, the hero of his symbolic play, *Red Roses for Me:*

Let us bring freedom here, not with sounding brass an' tinkling cymbal, but with silver trumpets blowing, with a song all men can sing, with a palm branch in our hand, rather than with a whip at our belt, and a headsman's axe on our shoulders.

O'Casey's quarrel with the Nationalists was that for most of them the Labour movement in their eyes seemed to be 'a decrescent force'. After the failure of the Easter Rising, James Stephens, the poet, in *The Insurrection in Dublin*, remarked with some truth, 'The reputation of all the leaders of the insurrection, not excepting Connolly, is that they were intensely patriotic Irishmen, and also, but this time with the exception of Connolly, that they were not particularly interested in the problems of labour'. O'Casey was particularly incensed that against the awful, catastrophic background of World War I, these narrow patriots could think nothing of the world's unparalleled dangers except their own sterile little republicanism. In his own biographies and, in particular, his *The Story of the Irish Citizen Army* (1919) included in *Feathers From The Green Crow*, the flag of whose army the plough and stars symbolise workers' ideals and reality, O'Casey gives the lie to republican aspirations. He was very bitter that men like James Connolly, theorist of the Irish Socialist movement and to many the father-figure of Irish Socialism, should have appeared to have abandoned Socialism for Republicanism. Of Connolly, he wrote: 'The high creed of Irish Nationalism became his daily rosary, while the higher creed of international humanity that had so long bubbled from his eloquent lips was silent for ever, and Irish Labour lost a Leader'. James Stephens was more magnanimous in his appraisal: 'James Connolly had his heart in both the national and the economic camp, but he was a great-hearted man, and could afford to extend his affections where others could only dissipate them'. But O'Casey disagreed: 'Connolly was no more an Irish Socialist martyr than Robert Emmet, P. H. Pearse, or Theobald Wolfe Tone'. Under Connolly, the Citizen Army linked up with the Irish Volunteers and was determined on armed rebellion. Genuine Socialists, such as O'Casey, viewed such a spectacle with horror and disaffection, and kept aloof from the struggle.

A fuller realisation of the implications behind the events which led to the abortive Easter Rising, and which inspired the writing of O'Casey's play, *The Plough and the Stars*, can be gleaned from certain passages in his autobiographical volume, *Drums Under the Windows*, which treats in a phantasmagoric way the chequered course of Irish history at this time. In the chapter, 'Under the Plough and the Stars', O'Casey tells us:

> Now there were two Cathleen ni Houlihans running round Dublin: one, like the traditional, in green dress, shamrocks in her hair, a little brian-boru harp under her oxster, chanting her share of song, for the rights and liberties common to all Irishmen; they who fight for me shall be rulers in the land; they shall be settled for ever, in good jobs shall they be, for ever, for ever; the other Cathleen coarsely dressed, hair a little tousled, caught roughly together by a pin, barefooted, sometimes with a whiff of whiskey off her breath; brave and brawny; at ease in the smell of sweat and the sound of bad language, vital, and asurge with immortality. Those who had any tinge of gentility in them left the Citizen Army for the refeenianed Volunteers.

The magnetic centre of the Irish Labour movement, O'C
tells us elsewhere, its 'banner and beacon-fire', was James La
'In this man's burning words were the want, the desire, the
resolution of the world's workers. Here . . . was the symbol of the
revolting proletariat. The personal manifestation of "Each for all,
and all for each". The symbol of a march forward . . . a march
forward *en masse* for what the workers never had, but for what they
will win and hold for ever'. In the same article, O'Casey informs us
that the men who formed Larkin's Citizen Army at its foundation
were 'an ill-fed, ill-clad, largely inarticulate army'. They comprised
solely working-class trade unionists – those of the Transport and
General Worker's Union – arming themselves in readiness for any
future combats in the class-struggle. O'Casey himself was one of
their number. James Stephens, himself reared in the Dublin slums,
pin-points the reasons for armed resistance in the case of these
workers:

> The great strike of two years ago [the 1913 lock-out] remained
> undoubtedly as a bitter and lasting memory with Dublin labour –
> perhaps, even, it was not so much a memory as a hatred. Still, it
> was not hatred of England which was evoked at the time, nor can
> the stress of their conflict be traced to an English source. It was
> hatred of local traders, and, particularly hatred of the local
> police, and the local powers and tribunals, which were arrayed
> against them. One can without trouble discover reasons why they
> should go on strike again, but by no reasoning can I understand
> why they should go into rebellion against England, unless it was
> that they were patriots first and trade unionists a very long way
> afterwards.

'Jim Larkin it was', says O'Casey, in *Drums Under the Windows*,
'who first said that the Citizen Army should have a banner all on its
own, its pattern and sign away from the commonplace ones of other
national and labour bodies, its symbols showing labour's near and
higher ideals; symbols, too, of the great Irish playwright's constant
and cherished ideals. And he goes on to say:

> It was queer that such a lovely thing should spread itself so
> proudly in such a lowly place before a crowd of hardy, rough-
> handed, dusty-skinned, ignorant men, tempting them to look at
> it, and seeming to say, Be worthy, men, of following such a

banner, for this is your flag of the future. Whatever may happen to me; though I should mingle with the dust, or fall to ashes in a flame, the plough will always remain to furrow the earth, the stars will always be there to unveil the beauty of the night, and a newer people, living a newer life, will sing like the sons of the morning.

(The plough, after all, is the instrument which, above all else, made civilisation possible, and, therefore, is closely associated with earthly existence. Throughout its long history it has spearheaded development of new ideas.)

Significantly, the Labour flag was not the one chosen to emblem the Irish Revolution or the Irish Republic in the years later. The Covey echoes O'Casey's sentiments of disgust when he remarks, sardonically: 'They're bringin' nice disgrace on that banner now'. And, when Jack Clitheroe (a Commandant in the Irish Citizen Army) asks how they are bringing disgrace on it, the Covey snappily retorts (again, echoing O'Casey):

> Because it's a Labour flag, an' was never meant for politics . . . What does th' design of th' field plough, bearin' on it th' stars of th' heavenly plough, mean, if it's not Communism? It's a flag that should only be used when we're buildin' th' barricades to fight for a Workers' Republic!

Instead, the adopted flag was that of the Irish Tricolour of orange, green and white, proclaiming the more popularly-accepted union of Labour and militant Nationalism. At a mass meeting in front of Liberty Hall, the Trade Union headquarters of the Citizen Army, the flag was hoisted in front of a cheering crowd. Says Fluther, in *The Plough and the Stars*:

> Jammed as I was in th' crowd, I listened to th' speeches pattherin' on th' people's head, like rain fallin' on th' corn; every derogatory thought went out o' me mind, an' I said to meself, 'You can die now, Fluther, for you've seen th' shadow-dhreams of th' past leppin' to life in th' bodies of livin' men that show, if we were without a titther o' courage for centuries, we're vice versa now!'

'Labour', commented O'Casey bitterly, in his chronicle of the Citizen Army, 'had laid its precious gift of Independence on the altar of Irish Nationalism'.

The revolutionaries lost no time in striking, though, apparently, oblivious of the senseless slaughter in the face of England's mightier strength while England (and all Europe) was fighting desperately for its very existence, and the irony of the timing (in O'Casey's eyes) is fiercely exposed at the conclusion to Act One in *The Plough*: while the hundreds of Dublin men march their way through the city's streets to the tune of 'It's a long way to Tipperary', to enlist in the British Army on their way to the fighting on the Continent, a handful of revolutionaries are biding their time to strike a blow for an independent Ireland, and, this time, Bessie Burgess, the indomitably-minded woman from one of the upstairs tenements, echoes O'Casey's feelings, when she shouts:

> There's th' men marchin' out into th' dhread dimness o' danger, while th' lice is crawlin' about feedin' on th' fatness o' the land! But yous'll not escape from th' arrow that flieth be night, or th' sickness that wasteth be day . . . An' ladyship an' all, as some o' them may be, they'll be scatthered abroad like th' dust in th' darkness!

Although O'Casey exiled himself for ever from Ireland shortly after the stormy reception which Dublin gave to *The Plough and the Stars* in February 1926, it is clear from his autobiographical account in *Drums Under the Windows* that he was already a voluntary and theoretical exile in his own land even while the traumatic events were happening in Ireland from 1916 onwards. Ireland's patriot-political go-boys were cruelly summed up in O'Casey's words thus:

> These aren't internationalists; they aren't even republicans. They aren't able to see over the head of England out to the world beyond. They would be lost among Desmoulins, Danton, Couthon, St Just, and Robespierre, and Marat would frighten the life out of them. Their eyes can see no further than their feet can cover. A frail few would stand at ease under the workers' banner. They would be the heralds of the new power, having time but to sound the reveille, and then sink suddenly down into sleep themselves.

Eight years later, in an article in *The Bell* (summer 1953), Sean O'Faolain reveals how prophetically true O'Casey's assumptions were:

We must, finally, understand that the class that thus came to power and influence was not a labouring class; the most able among them changed their nature by changing their place in life – they graduated rapidly into petit bourgeois, middlemen, importers, small manufacturers, thus forming a new middle class to fill the vacuum formed by the departure or depression of the alien middle class. These men, naturally, had had very little education, and could have only a slight interest in the intellectuals' fight for liberty of expression. They were ordinary, decent, kindly, self-seeking men who had no intention of jeopardizing their mushroom-prosperity by gratuitous displays of moral courage. In any case, since they were rising to sudden wealth behind protective tariff-walls, they had a vested interest in nationalism and even in isolationism. The upshot of it was a holy alliance between the Church, the new businessmen, and the politicians.

No wonder the Irish Rising, fiercely satirised in *The Plough*, is dismissed later in the autobiographies in searing phrases such as: 'a fiery-tale, a die-dream showing a false dawn that no soul saw', and 'naked foolishness – a child's patthern of war!' O'Casey knew in his innermost heart that the plight of Dublin's working-class would be no better under Sinn Fein than it was under John Bull. The Civil War that followed the treaty with England in 1922 politically broke his heart, and De Valera's Ireland disgusted him. 'A discordant symphony in green', he termed it in *Inishfallen, Fare Thee Well*. And, of De Valera himself, in a letter to Lady Gregory in 1924, he wrote: 'I wish he would read *Back to Methuselah*, and long a little less earnestly for the salvation of his countrymen'. Life behind the clerical curtain had become unbearable and Cathleen ni Houlihan was (to him) no more than 'a whimpering figure in a darkened doorway'. It was more than time for Sean to go.

As an Irish Englander in exile, he remained a world-betterer in the strongest Shavian sense; an unremitting combatant for the spread of world socialism. In an article in *The Green Crow* bearing the significant title, 'Always the Plow and the Stars', he stresses that 'the artist's place is to be where life is, active life, found in neither ivory tower nor concrete shelter'. To an interviewer, he once confessed: 'There must be blood in all things that are written, in all pictures that are painted, in all songs that are sung. There must be the cry of humanity; it may be a ferocious cry, a bitter cry, an angry cry; but if it isn't a human cry it isn't Art. For life is the primary fact'. In another article, 'Art is the Song of Life', reprinted in *Blasts and Benedictions*, O'Casey, the peerless artistic ploughman is the compassionate sower who goes out to sow, singing his Whitman-like song:

> What is called Culture isn't just the theatre here, the other arts there, music yonder: Culture is the life we live . . . Culture is expressed, shown, in the schools where we are taught, the homes where we live, the factories and fields where we work, the streets we walk through, the simple things we use when we eat and drink, and the packages that carry them safely into our homes, the very bindings on the books we read, the clothes we wear, the way we live and move and have our being. It is far more than books on our shelves and pictures in our galleries. It is all that is within us, all without, colouring all our activities.

Within the combination of revolutionist and drama-maker, his foreign critics, especially, have chided him for being too emotional in style and for portraying characters which were, in their view, exaggeratedly anti-heroic and contrary to the spirit of post-revolutionary theories; whilst his English and Irish and a few of his American critics failed to see how such a revolutionary playwright could become so deep-rooted in humanity and seemingly so attached to its foibles and eccentricities. Many Soviet admirers, including Boris Izakov, who corresponded regularly with O'Casey, as well as English critics such as Kenneth Tynan, who were always openly hostile, were apparently irreconciled to the constant and cumulative anti-heroic attitudes and character-portrayal in plays such as *The Shadow of a Gunman*, *The Plough and the Stars*, and others. Izakov and other critics were doubtless puzzled by the apparent condoning on O'Casey's part of the looting which took place by tenement-dwellers during the Easter Week Rebellion. Deaf, it would seem, to the world's drumming under their windows and ignorant at the same time of the porcelain clay of humankind, these critics had evidently forgotten the playwright's earlier impassioned defence of his fellow tenement workers:

> Sean watched their wonderful activity, and couldn't desecrate their disorder with dishonour. All these are they who go to Mass every Sunday and holy day of obligation; whose noses are ground

down by the clergy on the grindstone of eternal destiny; who go in mortal fear of the threat of a priest, he thought; but now he was glad to see they hadn't lost their taste for things material. In spite of the clergy's fifing and drumming about venial and mortal sin, they were stretching out their hands for food, for raiment, for colour, and for life. If the lilies of the field, that neither toiled nor spun, could be lovely, how much more that these whose lives were a ceaseless labour should be lovely too? The time would come when they would no longer need to take their kingdom of heaven by violence, for they would build it themselves, and warmth, adornment, and satisfaction in the midst of fair sounds and bright colours would be their own.

(*Drums Under the Windows*)

Again, O'Casey returns to the defence of these Dublin civilians in a hard-hitting attack, aimed mainly at Tynan and others who shared his view-point, in that pungent essay of his, 'Purple Dust in their Eyes':

Now the looters gambled before they went looting, and to go looting was a brave thing to do, for the streets sang songs of menace from bullets flying about everywhere; and the play [*The Plough and the Stars*] explicitly states and shows the courage of Bessie Burgess who risked her life for her neighbour, as did the bold Fluther, too; more, the sons, fathers, and husbands of thousands of these 'cowards', thousands of them, were fighting in Flanders, Mesopotamia, and on the death-swept Gallipoli peninsula. Mr Tynan, too, should remember that the progenitors of these tenement people everywhere fought for, and created, the powerful Labour Unions which made the Labour Movement possible, of which, I believe, Mr Tynan is himself a member; and these great Unions still form the spearhead of Labour. I can tell him, too, that more civilians than combatants were killed and wounded in the general fighting of the famous week. Roses don't grow around tenement doors; pianos are rare in rooms; but brave people are there, and many have wider visions and more original chatter than others who come from dignified college or glossier high school.

O'Casey, the renowned ploughman-playwright of the twentieth century, had evolved his own prophetic vision (the 'Bridge of

Vision' as he alludes to it in *Red Roses for Me*), like the vision of old of Piers Plowman in Chaucer's time. Characteristically, and significantly, we find it expressed at the end of the chapter, 'Under the Plough and the Stars', in the volume, *Drums Under the Windows*. The substance of that vision is translated into this simple message:

> To plough is to pray, to plant is to prophesy. Again, as in an age gone by, the plough will with a wreath be crowned, and wise men will twine the garland; and the stars will last, and those who have loved them fondly will never be fearful of the night.

Every dream is a prophecy, says Shaw, in *John Bull's Other Island*; and some may protest that O'Casey's dream, like the Shavian dream of Keegan, is but the dream of a madman. The Shavian dream transformed itself into the O'Casey prophecy – the O'Casey philosophy, really – the dream wherein 'the State is the Church and the Church the people: three in one and one in three. It is a commonwealth in which work is play and play is life: three in one and one in three. It is a temple in which the priest is the worshipper and the worshipper the worshipped: three in one and one in three. It is a godhead in which all life is human and all humanity divine: three in one and one in three'. O'Casey's epiphany, like Shaw's, in his own words, 'was the showing forth of man to man'.

Like all rebellions, the time of the Easter Rising, as O'Casey, afterwards avowed, was

> A rare time for death in Ireland; and in the battle's prologue many a common man, woman, and child had said goodbye to work and love and play . . . There they are, lying so quiet – a child surprised in the doorway; an old man stretched in the street . . . an old woman on the floor of her tenement room, alone, her blood seeping through the ceiling below; all the goodly company of the dead who died for Ireland . . . Many will die like that before Ireland can go free.

Ireland's 'chains . . .an' . . . slaveree' (to echo Joxer's procrastinating words of drunken nemesis) were intertwined with death and tragedy – interwoven in the tragicomic fabric of O'Casey's play. The play manifestly declares that all revolutionaries or independently-minded citizens may not be as dedicated or even as pure-minded as some of their leaders, such as

Pearse and Connolly. Many, on their own admission, did not want to die, unless they had to. Doubtless, many of similar disposition and frame of mind as 'Captain' Boyle were there in the streetways of Dublin, 'doing their bit' for Ireland 'in Easther Week', but not wishing to die: many wanted glamour and glory – but not bloodshed. 'Whoever expects a 'pure' social revolution will *never* live to see it', Lenin once declared, apropos of the Irish Rising. 'Such a person', he added, 'pays lip service to revolution without understanding what revolution really is'.

One of the controversies engendered by the play was the author's apparent condonement of the looting which went on while Dublin's main street – then known as Sackville Street but now known as O'Connell Street – was in ruins. According to one Nationalist viewpoint:

> Pubs and bars were particularly attractive, of course, but soon many other stores had been broken into; and James Connolly was in a quandary. These were the poor and starving of Ireland, the people he had pawned his life for; but he could not stand by and see them bring disgrace on the rising. He ordered his men to fire over the heads of the looters, and when that was ineffective they were forced to fire into the crowd.
>
> (Redmond Fitzgerald, *Cry Blood, Cry Erin*
> Barrie and Rockliff, 1966)

O'Casey's standpoint is different, as he subsequently explained when discussing his play to an American Company, the Hudson Guild Players, when they staged *The Plough and the Stars* in 1950:

> [The looting] is usually condemned as 'a dastardly insult to the unselfish men who were risking all for Ireland'. I don't look at it this way. When they got a chance, they 'illegally' seized the brighter goods of life which, with all others, they, too, had the right to have. Here people were usually called 'the rats of the slums'; but I, who lived among them for so long, knew they had their own intelligence; they had courage, humour, and, very often, a great zest for life.
>
> (O'Casey, *Letters*, vol. 2)

Some were irresponsible, he maintained, but no more than in all walks of life, well-to-do as well as socially deprived.

Like his previous masterpieces, *The Shadow of a Gunman* a
and the Paycock, *The Plough and the Stars*, O'Casey's rich, turbulent
and eloquent play, synthesises the very hearts and souls of his people
driven into a hollow of indigence and insurrection, uniting the
conflicts into a majestic whole in an emotional drive reminiscent of
the technique of O'Neill and Strindberg.

In a series of lightning flashes of episodic brilliance, at once
combining gargantuanly authentic and marvellously evoked
characterisation and penetrative dialogue – forming a broad, heroic
canvas – O'Casey, against a welter of fire and bloodshed, shows a
deep compassion for human suffering as well as an ironic contempt
for human stupidity (as in his previous plays) unmatched in the
sweep of its emotional range and complexity.

Guy Boas, in his skilfully annotated edition of the play,
summarises the extraordinary range of O'Casey's international
representation:

> The play, less concentrated in plot and personalities than *Juno*,
> sweeps spaciously in chronicle form through Acts I and II, where,
> in the home of the Clitheroes and the public bar of *The Plough and
> the Stars*, the storm is heard brewing beneath an unflagging
> vitality of conversation: in Act III it flames into insurrection, and
> in the final Act knits itself into a tragic tension unsurpassed by the
> author or by any other dramatist of our day.

The text moves with astonishing harmony from laughter to tears.
The play is dedicated, quixotically 'To the Gay Laugh of My
Mother at the gate of the grave' – symbolising, how, when her son
was out, Mrs Casside (O'Casey's mother) rose from her deathbed to
do the washing, and joked with neighbours while she hung it out to
dry.

The title of the play refers to the flag which was the pennon and
symbol-mast of the Irish Citizen Army, O'Casey becoming the first
Honorary Secretary in 1914 in its early stages as a peaceful non-
violent movement, formed to protect strikers and men of the
tenements from future police attack in times of economic and
militant crisis. By the time it had become an army in the full military
sense, and resorted to rifles and drilling, O'Casey, Francis Sheehy-
Skeffington and others had broken their association with it. The
plough and the stars which are emblemised in its picturesque design

(rolled up prior to the Uprising and never since seen 'the light of other days', in Tom Moore's familiar words) symbolise both the workers' ideal and reality. Ironic contrast between the two permeates the play. The setting is Dublin in November 1915; and later, Easter Week 1916.

O'Casey's scene, in most of the acts, is a decayed Georgian residence, transformed by ill-fortune into rooming tenements, some of whose wide, spacious rooms are subject to endeavoured improvements (as in the case of the Clitheroe family's) whilst others (most noticeable in Bessie Burgess's attic-flat), in the playwright's assertive self-description, flaunt 'the more savage assaults of the tenants'.

The plot concerns Commandant Jack Clitheroe, a military idealist, who hearing the siren sound of Connolly's call to arms and freedom, re-enlists in the Citizen Army, fighting alongside the wider contingent of Irish Volunteers, to overthrow British rule in Ireland, while England was heavily engaged in the grim toll of World War I. Fearful for his safety and tragic destiny is his pretty wife, the dark, red-lipped Nora, who yearns, exclusively, for their future untortured happiness (as well as escape from drabber surroundings), only to be driven, in the end, to a demented insanity, in a tragic conclusion which culminates not only in the tragic death of her husband, in a clash of bitter street fighting, but the unforeseen deaths of those who live in the same tenement.

Alongside, stand a lusty assortment of neighbours – razor-sharp in their evocation and delineation – who gradually steal the limelight in an aureole of comedy woven into the tragic saga of suffering and death. Nora Clitheroe and Bessie Burgess, a good-hearted neighbour with a rough tongue, are the main tragic figures, those spiritually assaulted in this woeful tale of irredeemable vanity and grief. The patriots – Jack Clitheroe, Captain Brennan and Lieutenant Langon – are minors; heralds from the bloodied realities of surging, self-centred madness and folly which end in tragedy. Once again, O'Casey's women are drawn in lines that reveal chivalry and respect; the men diminish into farcical leprechauns which belie the heroic circumstances of their false idealism.

In a former programme-note, written by the playwright, the play's spectrum is reflected:

The first scene of the play shows Captain Clitheroe called to an assembly of both organisations [the Irish Volunteers – inspired by the Fenians – and Irish Citizen Army], held to inspire the members for the fight that was soon to come. He leaves his wife to join the meeting and procession.

The second act shows the meeting in progress outside a public-house; the Volunteer Leader speaking to his men, and the effect of his words on the civilians present. The third act shows the rebellion in full swing, with three Irish soldiers – including Captain Clitheroe – falling back on their Headquarters – one of them wounded. It shows, too, the civilians – who were hostile to the fighting – taking advantage of the confusion, to loot all they can lay their hands on.

The fourth act shows the city of Dublin – a lot of it in flames – in the hands of the British troops, who are closing in on the Volunteers, making their last stand together in the Headquarters of the Irish Army, and the happenings in the tenement home during the fighting.

A rich gallimaufry from the earth-board of Dublin – those from the teeming tenements of the city's northern regions – are indelibly and endearingly portrayed. Each comes to picturesque and picaresque life. There are cameo-roles for even the most marginally conceived; and the play offers spectral opportunities for gorgeous ensemble playing. The antagonists, male and female, are well counter-balanced. Among principal roles, the most human and most masterly conceived is Fluther Good, the shrewd carpenter, one of the residents in the tenement occupied by the Clitheroes. He is one of O'Casey's finest comic creations and a quintessential Irishman-labourer, earth-born and celestially inspired. Although he has many characteristics of the 'paycock' prototype, as a more isolated representative he is more substantial and self-contained – less egotistical than Seumas Shields, his near-counterpart in *The Shadow of a Gunman*. And he embodies much of the fighting Irish as well as of the drunken, gambling paddy-whack: although a liar and boaster, he is earth-spun in his dogmatism, magnanimous as well as vainglorious in his dealings with his fellow man. His favourite word is 'derogatory', which is more often overstated than misapplied, and he sees everything in a 'vice versa' context. 'Arrogant courage' and 'jovial determination' are attributes O'Casey underlines elsewhere in his make-up.

Concomitant with Fluther are a pair of clowning combatants from the same tenement who exchange thrusts and parries of argumentative banter with each other in bouts of verbal fencing and shadow-boxing (as only the Irish know how), refereed, not always impartially, by the ubiquitous carpenter himself: Nora's uncle, Peter Flynn, who is crabbed and cocky in his vaingloriousness, a labourer, who is seen as a 'paycock', both preening and 'foostherin', dressed up in his peacock feathers of the national Foresters' uniform, which occasions the disrespectful jibe from Fluther: 'Ah, sure, when you'd look at him, you'd wondher whether th' man was makin' fun o' th' costume, or th' costume was makin' fun o' th' man!' The chief source of Peter's tetchiness is the jibes and jeers he has to endure from Nora's cousin, Willie (known as the Young Covey), among whom he brackets with 'all th' scorners, tormenters, an' twarters' that are forever goading him into 'prayin' for their blindin' an' blastin' an' burnin' in th' world to come!' (Covey is a diminutive we come across in low society from Dickens's time onwards. In *Oliver Twist* there is the expression, 'Hullo, my covey! what's the row?' which nicely epitomises The Covey's character in *The Plough and the Stars*.)

Although the Young Covey's chief role in O'Casey's play is irritant to the foolish old uncle, he is a sardonic mouthpiece of the playwright's contempt for swaddling Socialists who aridly voice Marxian platitudes, with neither a glint nor gleam of respect for gaiety, colour and song in their estimation of values of life, paying only lip-service to revolutionary ideas without being able to relate them actively in the course of their interactions with others. The Covey is ridiculed for his cocksure aridity, first by Fluther, and then by one of his opposite number, Corporal Stoddart of the British Army. O'Casey, although a Socialist himself, has with subtle partiality, humour and understanding created a memorable carica-ture in the Covey's portrayal, and to his amazing credit has exalted the humanity of earthier characters, such as Fluther Good or Bessie Burgess: these, centrally, invoke the playwright's sympathies.

The heroine as hero, as in so many of O'Casey's plays, is the hallmark of *The Plough and the Stars*. Bessie, the Protestant loyalist (the rough-tongued fruit-seller who occupies the attic tenement) whose soldier-son is serving in Flanders, is boisterous and aggressive flaunting her shouts of 'Rule Britannia' in the faces of her fellow Catholic patriots, but with a deep reserve of stoicism and compas-sion within her withal. '. . . as for law an' ordher', she maintains 'puttin' aside th' harp an' shamrock, Bessie Burgess'll have as much respect as she wants for th' lion an' unicorn!' She is perpetually a loggerheads with the hot-tempered, vituperative but warm-hearted charwoman from the same housing-block, Mrs (Jennie) Gogan, whose mind runs constantly on scenes of death when she is not involved in verbal or physical violence with Bessie. 'Sure, she's in her element', says Fluther, 'mixin' earth to earth, an' ashes t'ashes an' dust to dust, an' revellin' in plumes an' hearses, last days an' judgements!' Her consumptive child, Mollser, is sweetly wise and coolly-courageous, among the play's vociferous minor characters.

Nora Clitheroe, the most complex of O'Casey's young females, 'alert . . . and full of nervous energy' (we gather from the dramatist's textual description), reflects the heartbreak a proud, enlightened, domestically happy young housewife experiences while her patriot-husband feels the greater tug of military promotion and the lure of the barricades and abandons her to the companionship 'of th' loneliness of th' night' (in her words). Nora voices the playwright's acute understanding that bravery and fear are but two sides of the same coin, and arouse (in her own case) tormenting moments of agonising perception. She tries to dissuade her husband Jack from going off to fight, but without avail. The terrible self-conflict this dissuasion produces and its eventual despair – leading, in the finish, to pathetic madness – are totally absorbing. O'Casey makes it all the more painfully explicit when Nora tries to impede Jack's departure in the presence of his fellow rebels. Later, in her incipient insanity she is unaware of the impact of full tragedy when one of her husband's colleagues brings the news, in the final act, of Jack's death – 'in a gleam of glory' – whilst in combat.

Her domestic determination and 'mothering tyranny' – as Shaw, in *Heartbreak House*, through Hector, has already prejudged – bring fury and humiliation to her patriotically-inclined husband who, in common with his fighting colleagues, Lieutenant Langon of the Irish Volunteers, and Captain Brennan of the Irish Citizen Army, is fired fanatically with the Pearse-Connolly motivated expressions, enunciated by the Voice of the Speaker – the Figure in the Window – on a parodic level (in tragicomic synthesis), in the fervour of the mass-organised political meeting outside the pub, in the powerful second act:

CAPT. BRENNAN: We won't have long to wait now.
LIEUT. LANGON: Th' time is rotten ripe for revolution.
CLITHEROE: You have a mother, Langon.
LIEUT. LANGON: Ireland is greater than a mother.

CAPT. BRENNAN: You have a wife, Clitheroe.
CLITHEROE: Ireland is greater than a wife.
LIEUT. LANGON: Th' time for Ireland's battle is now – th' place for Ireland's battle is here.

Further convincing oratory occasions a greater litany, expressionistically styled:

CAPT. BRENNAN (*catching up* The Plough and the Stars): Imprisonment for th' Independence of Ireland!
LIEUT. LANGON (*catching up the* Tri-colour): Wounds for th' Independence of Ireland!
CLITHEROE: Death for th' Independence of Ireland!

Their actualistic chorus turns out to be prefigurative in this glimpse of foolhardy glory on which the mood of the play focuses a jaundiced beam.

When the lurid flames of the Easter Rebellion end in failure, and the British troops quell the insurrection, Corporal Stoddart of the Wiltshire Regiment – as tragicomedy gradually predominates – remarks: 'we're clowsing in on the bloighters. Ow, it was only a little bit of a dawg foight'. Although both Stoddart and Sergeant Tinley are cynical about 'plugging' and giving snipers 'the cold steel', as regular soldiers, they are less brutal than the Tans or Auxies, the hired mercenaries who were ruthless in their soulless reprisal killing; the Tommies, as personified by Stoddart and Tinley, are even 'jocular in their funny English way', as O'Casey underlines in his chapter, 'The Raid', in *Inishfallen, Fare Thee Well*.

Jocular, in an altogether different and delightful way, is the professional prostitute, Rosie Redmond, who appears in the pub of the second act. To the barman she confesses:

. . . They're all in a holy mood. Th' solemn-lookin' dials on th' whole o' them an' they marchin' to th' meetin'. You'd think they were th' glorious company of th' saints, an' th' noble army of martyrs thrampin' through th' sthreets of paradise. They're all thinkin' of higher things than a girl's garthers . . .

She is both flaunting and mocking when she sees her trade impaired by the men's preoccupation with patriotic enthusiasms and deadly attempts at playing soldiers. When she attempts to give the Covey the glad-eye, but he fails to respond, Rosie, realising the Covey's Marxism will not pay her rent, shoots a baroque line of abuse at the undersized revolutionary: 'Jasus, it's in a monasthery some of us ought to be, spendin' our holidays kneelin' on our adorers, tellin' our beads, an' knockin' hell out of our buzzums!'

The Barman is as studiously noncommittal, subjectively, as any Irishman can be in the circumstantial likelihood of a crazed fight 'smirchin' ' (in Fluther's expression) the night and in the avoidance of bloodshed within the perimeters of his own saloon. The short episode of the Woman from Rathmines in the third act, during the bombardment and looting, is usually missing from most productions of the play – certainly in Abbey productions – at the author's request (although she has never been erased from the text). She may not be relevant to the plot, any more than are the two old crones in the first scene of *Behind the Green Curtains*, but she adds, dramatically, to the atmosphere of sardonic configuration in the tragicomic atmosphere created. Hence, her reappearance in the National Theatre's production of 1977–8.

In the first act, we meet the various residents in the Clitheroe tenement, before the Uprising of Easter Week has taken place. The time-scale is November 1915. Before we are introduced to either Nora or her husband Jack (who is a bricklayer), Mrs Gogan, the fussy charwoman, overladen with curiosity, is talking to Fluther, who is repairing a lock on the inner door from the hallway – to keep the interlopers at bay. (The neighbours, including Bessie from upstairs, resent the new air of gentility and 'notions of upperosity' – in Mrs Gogan's words – that are creeping into the life-style of the Clitheroes at Nora's instigation.) Nora, we gather from Mrs Gogan, is averse to living in a tenement whose social evils are denounced in the course of the conclusion to *Nannie's Night Out*, in O'Casey's previous play. 'Vaults', Nora is quoted as saying, 'that are hidin' th' dead instead of homes that are sheltherin' th' livin' '.

Intimations of armed, national revolt are already being spoken of, whilst Fluther and Mrs Gogan, in Mrs Boyle's previous words, are 'colloguin' ' with one another; whilst, at the same time, old Peter Flynn, Nora's uncle, in readiness for an important open-air demonstration and meeting to be held the same evening at Parnell Square – whence an oath of fealty to the new concept of an all-Irish

Republic is expected – is pottering about dressing himself in the elaborate costume of the national order of Foresters – his 'green an' glory uniform' and Brian Boru sword – as Fluther derisively describes them later in the play – cursing and swearing because the collar is too stiff and the stud too tight. (The cursing continues as the Young Covey, the dedicated young socialist who has just entered, continues to tease and thwart him for his outward show of Nationalist aspirations.) The Covey is annoyed because he believes nationalism to be irrelevant. He succeeds in upsetting both Peter and Fluther (he has a long-standing family feud with the former), because, although Fluther is relatively indifferent to the Cause and has renounced his former proclivity for drink, the Covey argues politics and religion with him, and takes the opportunity of enlarging on the scientist's view of man's origins and functions, as opposed to that of the church (in the same spirit of dissent practised by Mullcanny in *Red Roses for Me*). Although not a devout believer, Fluther, like Feelim in *Oak Leaves and Lavender*, is basically a religious man, and is goaded into shouting at the pipsqueak revolutionary:

> You'll be kickin' an' yellin' for th' priest yet, me boyo. I'm not goin' to stand silent an' simple listenin' to a thick like you makin' a maddenin' mockery o' God Almighty. It 'ud be a nice derogatory thing on me conscience, an' me dyin', to look back in rememberin' shame of talkin' to a word-weavin' little ignorant yahoo of a red flag Socialist!

The jibes of the tormenting nephew also goad the old Forester into grabbing his sword, and pursuing him round the room with it: the Covey enjoys the chase and slams the door in his face and then continues to tease him through the keyhole, with shouts of 'cuckoo!'

The Covey's teasing is interrupted by Nora, whose appearance, speech and actions confirm the assumption of Mrs Gogan and others that she is longing to improve her condition and station in life (by escaping from a tenement environment). She reprimands both her relatives, who are also her sub-tenants, for acting like 'a pair o' fightin' cocks!' The Covey who has called his old relative 'a lemon-whiskered oul' swine', rushes back, declaring to Nora that if she doesn't exercise some measured control over the septuagenarian old fool, 'there'll be a funeral, an' it won't be me that'll be in th' hearse!' (Earlier, the charwoman, digressing to Fluther on her favourite topic – death – had expressed 'a kind o' thresspassin' joy' to be inside 'a mournin' coach', particularly if it were somebody else's funeral.) And now Bessie Burgess, a vigorously built woman from upstairs – herself a hardened widow and partial to a drink – rasps her whole-hearted disapproval of Nora's attempts at self-betterment in threateningly truculent tones (reminiscent of Irish Nannie) but is prevented from translating it into a brawl through the timely intervention of Fluther, running to Nora's aid. At that precise moment, Clitheroe arrives and hustles Bessie out. (Fluther then departs with Bessie.)

Nora prepares tea, and the four – herself, Jack, Peter Flynn and the Covey – sit down to the semblance of a respectable meal, marred by further outbreaks of controversy (in the style of altercations over the Christmas dinner table in Joyce's *Portrait of the Artist as a Young Man*), instigated by animosities between the Covey and Flynn: Covey (in a quarrelling bout) makes fun of Peter in his uniform, 'Lookin' like th' illegitimate son of an illegitimate child of a corporal in th' Mexican army!' and denounces the Irish Citizen Army for supporting the cause of the Nationalists rather than the workers. Clitheroe's resentment against the Citizen Army is reflected in his jealousy of Captain Brennan and his own supposed disqualification for promotion. (We remember O'Casey's stage indication that 'His face has none of the strength of Nora's. It is a face in which is the desire for authority, without the power to attain it'.)

After the bickering has ceased and the combatants have been hustled out, Nora and Jack, for a temporary while, enjoy a quiet interlude together and seem romantically inclined, Nora beseech-ing her husband to sing her one of their sentimental, honeymoon songs, 'Th' violets were scenting th' woods, Nora' (to the tune of 'When You and I were young, Maggie'). Their romantic scene ends abruptly when a knock at the door reveals Captain Brennan, in full uniform of the Irish Citizen Army, who addresses Jack as 'Commandant' (to the disquiet of Nora) and gives Clitheroe a dispatch from General Connolly, to the surprise of the newly enlisted recruit. Nora, who had destroyed the notification of his appointment without telling him about it, now implores Jack to stay home:

Is General Connolly an' th' Citizen Army goin' to be your only care? Is your home goin' to be only a place to rest in? . . . Your vanity'll be th' ruin of you an' me yet . . . That's what's movin' you: because they've made an officer of you . . .

But Clitheroe abandons his now-bitter wife. As Nora remains disconsolate (all have gone to the meeting), she is approached by Mollser, Mrs Gogan's daughter. The young consumptive is lonely too (her mother has also gone to the parade) and seeks the company of Nora, whose happiness and imagined security (in a manifestation of extraordinary dramatic irony on the playwright's part) she envies compared with her own fragile and uncertain future prospects. Fears of death for her are real, too. While she is speaking, a contingent of the Dublin Fusiliers passes the house to the accompaniment of 'It's a long way to Tipperary', on their way to the British Front in France. Bessie, in a bitter declamation at the doorway (her own son is in Flanders), predicts ruin and destruction, in Biblical undertones, for those who shirk their duty and whose minds are set on military treachery. The scene ends on a bathetic note as Mollser conjures: 'Is there anybody goin', Mrs Clitheroe, with a titther o' sense?'

The theme in the various episodes of the first act is a related one of conflict, prefiguring death and destruction, albeit on a domestic and comic level; later, to be magnified into a wide-scale political tragedy, involving killings of innocent citizens. As the play develops, smaller conflicts affecting those within the tenement are set against the greater backcloth of the Great War itself, which transcends even national evils on an hitherto unenvisaged international scale, portrayed, overwhelmingly, in O'Casey's next play, *The Silver Tassie*.

The second act is centred in a bar of a public house in Parnell Square, the northern end of O'Connell Street. (It is one hour later and the meeting is in progress.) The scene, again, is one of mock-conflict (whether in verbal provocations leading to, at times, near physical assaults inside the pub, or bold declarations from without, from the speaker addressing the meeting, in the form of pledges extolling militant patriotic fervour – 'without the shedding of blood there is no redemption!') in preparation for the forthcoming battle of Easter Week. '. . . the finest act Mr O'Casey has written', acclaimed Desmond MacCarthy – echoing the praise of Yeats – on seeing the play in 1926. 'In the scene in the pub he has expressed his theme perfectly.' Previously, Yeats had remarked (in a letter to one of the directors): 'The scene as a whole is admirable': 'of excellent and mordant comedy', avowed MacCarthy.

Rosie is standing at the bar talking to the barman, Tom, bemoaning the poor state of her trade. Outside, adjacent to the pub, is a fiery meeting of the patriots and Independents. (The address includes snatches from Pearse's speeches before the eventual proclamation of the Irish Republic.) Through the large window to the left of the bar come shafts of idealistic rebel oratory, glorifying bloodshed and war, in the manner of Pearse's patriotic rhetoric: 'When war comes to Ireland she must welcome it as she would . . . the Angel of God!' (During the speeches, Fluther, the Covey, Flynn and others fortify themselves with drinks at the bar, even though words are the alcohol of the Irish!)

Activities inside the pub provide ironic counterpoint and commentary. Bar heroism and alcoholic encouragement give an added spurt (apart from the revolutionary words of the Figure in the Window) to heightened crescendos of comic invective and a 'pitch of gloriously virulent verbosity' (to echo MacCarthy's words); the women (Mrs Gogan and Bessie) outvoicing the men (Fluther, Flynn and the Covey) and 'vice versa' (to use the pet expression of Fluther). Echoes of vituperation reach the fantastic height of Synge's characters; the mood is the resplendently mocking one of *The Playboy of the Western World*:

BESSIE: Bessie Burgess doesn't put up to know much, never havin' a swaggerin' mind, thanks be to God, but goin' on packin' up knowledge accordin' to her conscience: precept upon precept, line upon line; here a little, an' there a little. But [*with a passionate swing of her shawl*], thanks be to Christ, she knows when she was got, where she was got, an' how she was got; while there's some she knows, decoratin' their finger with a well-polished weddin' ring, would be hard put to it if they were assed to show their weddin' lines!

MRS GOGAN (*plunging out into the centre of the floor in a wild tempest of hysterical rage*): Y' oul' rip of a blasted liar, me weddin' ring's been well earned be twenty years be th' side o' me husband, now takin' his rest in heaven, married to me be Father Dempsey, in th' Chapel o' Saint Jude's, in th' Christmas Week of eighteen hundhred an' ninety-five; an' any kid, livin' or dead, that Jinnie Gogan's had since, was got between th' bordhers of th' ten Commandments! . . . An' that's more than some o' you can say that are kep' from th' dhread o' desthruction be a few drowsy virtues, that th' first whisper of temptation lulls into a sleep, that'll know one sin from another only on th' day of their last anointin', an' that use th' innocent light o' th' shinin' stars to dip into th' sins of a night's diversion!

BESSIE (*jumping out to face Mrs Gogan, and bringing the palms of her hands together in sharp claps to emphasize her remarks*): Liar to you, too, ma'am, y' oul' hardened thresspasser on other people's good nature, wizenin' up your soul in th' arts o'dodgeries, till every dhrop of respectability in a female is dhried up in her lookin' at your ready-made man-oeuverin' with th' menkind!

The argument – a minor war in itself – between the two women intensifies, in spite of the efforts of Fluther and Peter to calm them down. (Bessie, who in romping truculence, had at the start of the quarrel advised Mrs Gogan to mind her own business, 'an' stupify your foolishness be gettin' dhrunk', now vents her scorn at Flynn: 'G'way, you little sermonizing, little yella-faced, little consequential, little pudgy, little bum you!')The two women square up to one another, Peter victimised, yet again, by being handed Mrs Gogan's baby – the shawled mite accompanying its mother to the tavern in times of crisis and emergency (Mollser the elder child being left at home) – as Mrs Gogan takes up a defiant stand in front of the rasping Bessie. The scene magnifies into rich farce as the barman ejects the two women and Peter is left literally 'holding the baby.' He tries to call the mother back, and involve the Covey and Fluther ('D'ye think Fluther's like yourself, destitute of a tither of undherstandin'?') in his efforts to get rid of the baby; but, in the end, when he is told by the barman to remove the child and search for its mother, he self-exits with the swaddling infant in his arms on a note of censure and defiance, cursing all 'tormentors an' twarters' who are for ever assailing him and making every nerve in his body 'quiverin' to do somethin' desperate!' (Earlier, Fluther had richly cautioned indifference. To Flynn, he advised: 'I wouldn't be everlastin' cockin' me ear to hear every little whisper that was floatin' around me! It's my rule never to loose me temper till it would be dethrimental to keep it. There's nothin' derogatory in th' use o'th' word "cuckoo", is there?' – outcapping even his own flutherism, in the previous act: 'There's no reason to bring religion into it. I think we ought to have as great a regard for religion as we can, so as to keep it out of as many things as possible'.)

In an alcoholic and patriotic haze of fervour, each endeavours to outstrip the other in flights of argumentative fancy; but Fluther has the comic edge, for his speech is racy and more high-flown, even if he stumbles through a minefield of malapropisms. The would-be patriots heed the speaker's words of adulation on the sanctity of bloodshed, and are more than inclined to take his words to heart within the inner reaches of the pub. The barman, who had to forcibly restrain Mrs Gogan and Bessie, is driven to the same lengths, again, because the Covey, disagreeing violently with the words of the spokesman, remarks that Irish patriotism is merely 'dope' for 'th' Boorzwawzee', at which the hackles of Fluther begin to rise.

Now, it is the turn of the menfolk to outstrip the pugnacity of the women. After arguing with the Covey on the merits and demerits of nationalism, Fluther admonishes him that 'It would take something more than a thing like you to flutther a feather o' Fluther'; the cock-fighting begins in earnest, especially when the Covey insults Rosie, who has slipped back in quest of further trade. Fluther defends the humiliated prostitute and accuses the Covey of being 'a tittherin' chancer' and tells him he is 'temptin' Providence' when he is 'temptin' Fluther!' The two, with irreconcilable sound and fury, embark on a classic 'no-holds-barred' confrontation. 'Sing a little less on th' high note', threatens Fluther, 'or, when I'm done with you, you'll put a Christianable consthruction on things, I'm tellin' you!'

After the landlord has ordered the Covey, by the scruff of his neck, to leave, Fluther and Rosie retire to one of the corners of a snug for a drink, and Fluther is in triumphant mood. When Rosie remarks, ' "Men like Fluther", says I to meself, "is gettin' scarce nowadays" ', Fluther retorts: 'I wasn't goin' to let meself be malignified by a chancer . . . He got a little bit too derogatory for Fluther . . . Be God, to think of a cur like that comin' to talk to a man like me!' And, swelling visibly with transparent pride, he swaggers: 'I hit a man last week, Rosie, an' he's fallin' yet!'

The rest of the scene with overcast swiftness plunges to its darkling conclusion: the military representatives – Langon, Brennan and Clitheroe – their faces aflame with patriotic fervour, hurry into the bar in a flush of excited enthusiasm. They vow to give their all for Ireland, thus repudiating Bessie Burgess, whose son and sympathies are with the Crown; and Fluther leaves happily and tipsily in the company of Rosie, their arms around each other as she sings a lusty amorous ditty, 'I once had a lover . . . as strong an' as wild as th' sea' (which was considered too bawdy by certain members of the Abbey cast and directorate; in deference to whom and for fear of possible public repercussion, the song was deleted from productions, though retained in the printed text). Outside, as the act draws to its close, Clitheroe's voice can be heard, commanding units of his battle-inspired men.

Act Three centres on Easter Week itself, at the time of the actual fighting in April 1916. It is Easter Monday and the rebellion has begun. In front of the Clitheroes' home, Mrs Gogan is settling Mollser in the sunshine and enquiring half-heartedly and perfunctorily how she feels. Her replies are hardly reassuring to the tubercular child, for her conversational fancy wafts off again into flights of death, first of Jack's, in a coincidental foreboding, and then, in an inspired vision, of Nora's, in ironical prefiguration on the dramatist's part. Kept awake all night with the shooting, Mrs Gogan declares:

> An' thinkin' o' that madman, Fluther, runnin' about through th' night lookin' for Nora Clitheroe to bring her back when he heard she'd gone to folly her husband, an' in dhread any minute he might come staggerin' in covered with bandages, splashed all over with th' red of his own blood, an' givin' us barely time to bring th' priest to hear th' last whisper of his final confession, as his soul was passin' through th' dark doorway o' death into th' way o' th' wondherin' dead . . .

The various disputants from the pub (having temporarily forgotten their differences) are discussing events of the rebellion, when Fluther carries in Nora. (The pregnant young wife, who unsuccessfully sought her husband amidst the battle lines, is thoroughly exhausted and has been saved only by Fluther's courage.) 'They told me I shamed my husband an' th' women of Ireland be carryin' on as I was . . . there's no woman gives a son or a husband to be killed – if they say it, they're lyin', lyin', against God, Nature, an' against themselves!' At the barricades, she tells that she read fear in the faces of the men. 'They're afraid to say they're afraid' are the romantic realities she discerns – conveying O'Casey's own message, which upset the trenchant beliefs of many fervent Nationalists. (The playwright must have realised he was skidding on thin ice: no wonder there was rioting in the theatre during the play's first week's performance. It was more than the patriots of the newly formed independent Republic or Free State could stomach.) Hysterical with worry about her husband and deploring the insurrection for overshadowing their family happiness, she is now prey to the complete mock-wisdom of fools and leprechauns around her (just as Shaw's Saint Joan, in the Epilogue, is surrounded by the stock advice of platitudes from earthly presbyters, elders and rulers):

PETER: You'll have to have patience, Nora. We all have to put up with twarthers an' tormentors in this world.

THE COVEY: If they were fightin' for anything worth while, I wouldn't mind.

FLUTHER (*to Nora*): Nothin' derogatory'll happen to Mr Clitheroe. You'll find, now, in th' finish up it'll be vice versa.

Bessie, viewing the traumatic scene from her top window, angers the others with her harangue, complaining of disloyalty against the English as well as the cowardice of the Irish who are not fighting. (Conscription in Ireland during World War I was voluntary, as Home Rule was to be implemented immediately after the European war.) When she harasses them with shouts of 'Rule, Britannia', Mrs Gogan comments: 'She's th' right oul' Orange bitch!' Presently, as Nora is led into the house with the help of Mrs Gogan, Bessie passes them with her head in the air. But as she leaves the front steps and passes by the railings that enclose the front of the house from the street she pauses to give a mug of milk to Mollser (as a neighbour, she has some of O'Casey's own mother's instincts) and, discounting danger, makes her way into the streets, bypassing the wastrels ('Why aren't yous in th' G.P.O. if yous are men?') who are playing pitch-and-toss in the streets, whom she mockingly calls 'sham-battle soldiers', and scornfully shouts back at them: 'A lot o' vipers, that's what th' Irish people is!'

While the game continues and the coins are tossed, the boom of distant gunfire obtrudes. The heroes are less confident. 'What would happen if a shell landed here now?' enquires Peter with trepidation. 'You'd be off to heaven in a fiery chariot', the Covey twitters. As the game is resumed, Bessie returns armed with loot and tells of the people plundering the shops as the fighting intensifies. The men decide to join the looters, but Peter is too fearful:

PETER: Supposin' I happened to be potted?

FLUTHER: We'd give you a Christian burial, anyhow.

THE COVEY: (*ironically*): Dhressed up in your regimentals.

PETER (*to the Covey, passionately*): May th' all-lovin' God give you a hot knock one o' these days, me young Covey, tuthorin' Fluther up now to be tiltin' at me, an' crossin' me with his mockeries an' jibin'!

The farce continues as a fashionably-dressed, middle-class woman, from one of the city's suburbs, asks the way to Rathmines. Fluther is not helpful: 'I have to go away, ma'am, to thry an' save a few things from th' burnin' buildin's', and he and the Covey rush off in the direction of the shops. Peter is even less obliging and takes a Joxerian stand: 'D'ye think I'm goin' to risk me life throttin' in front of you? An' maybe get a bullet that would gimme a lame leg or something that would leave me a jibe an' a jeer to Fluther an' the young Covey for th' rest o' me days!' And, indignantly, he retires into the house.

When the woman leaves and the firing continues, Bessie and Mrs Gogan emerge from the house, arguing fiercely over the right of access to a pram which belongs to one of the residents who is away for the Easter holiday and which the charwoman is pushing with the intention of hauling as much loot as possible. She is stopped in her tracks by Bessie, but Mrs Gogan argues richly in self-defence (Peter has re-appeared at the door, looking on in amusement):

MRS GOGAN (*taking no notice of Peter, and pushing the pram on another step*): Take your rovin' lumps o' hands from pattin' th' bassinette, if you please, ma'am; an', steppin' from th' threshold of good manners, let me tell you, Mrs Burgess, that's it's a fat wondher to Jennie Gogan that a lady-like singer o' hymns like yourself would lower her thoughts from sky-thinkin' to sthretch out her arm in a sly-seekin' way to pinch anything dhriven asthray in th' confusion of th' battle our boys is makin' for th' freedom of their counthry!

PETER (*laughing and rubbing his hands together*): Hee, hee, hee, hee, hee! I'll go with th' pair o' yous an' give yous a hand.

MRS GOGAN (*with a rapid turn of her head as she shoves the pram forward*): Get up in th' prambulator an' we'll wheel you down.

BESSIE (*to Mrs Gogan*): Poverty an' hardship has sent Bessie Burgess
to abide with sthrange company, but she always
knew them she had to live with from backside to
breakfast time; an' she can tell them, always havin'
had a Christian kinch on her conscience, that a
passion for thievin' an' pinchin' would find her soul a
foreign place to live in, an' that her present intention
is quite th' lofty-hearted one of pickin' up anything
shaken up an' scatthered about in th' loose confusion
of a general plundher!

Peter changes his mind when the gunfire becomes noisier, quickly
looks down the street, runs up the steps and shuts the hall-door, sits
sucking his pipe in the chair that Mollser (after feeling unwell) has
vacated, and looks imperturbable as the Young Covey comes
staggering in with a heavy sack of flour on his back plus a ham.
Ignoring Peter and trying to push open the door, which he finds he
cannot open, he angrily declaims:

THE COVEY (*to Peter*): Who shut th' door? . . . [*He kicks at it*] Here,
come on an' open it, will you? This isn't a mot's
hand-bag I've got on me back.
PETER: Now, me young Covey, d'ye think I'm goin' to be your
lackey?
THE COVEY (*angrily*): Will you open th' door, y'oul' –
PETER (*shouting*): Don't be assin' me to open any door, don't be
assin' me to open any door for you . . . Makin' a
shame an' a sin o' th' cause that good men are fightin'
for . . . Oh, God, forgive th' people that, instead o'
burnishin' th' work th' boys is doin' to-day with quiet
honesty an' patience, is revilin' their sacrifices with a
riot of lootin' an' roguery!
THE COVEY: Isn't your own eyes leppin' out o' your head with
envy that you haven't th' guts to ketch a few o'
th' things that God is givin' to His chosen
people? . . . Y 'oul' hypocrite, if everyone was blind
you'd steal a cross off an ass's back!

The two women return with their pram laden with an odd
assortment of plunder, mainly clothing (in the excitement of their
haul they forget their differences). As a single shot is heard, Peter

bolts for the house and is on the point of slamming the door, when the women decide to enter as well.

In the street, outside the house, suddenly appear Brennan, Clitheroe and Langon – the latter badly wounded in the stomach – and they pause for rest, as Langon's condition gives cause for alarm: Brennan is also reprehensive of Clitheroe for not firing on the slum dwellers and looters 'mobbin' th' men riskin' their lives for them'.

Nora rushes from the house and embraces her husband, in an agonised appeal, begging him to stay with her and leave the madness outside. But he is determined to fight on and not make himself look ridiculous in front of his colleagues. His decision is helped by the cries of Langon, writhing on the pavement and strengthened by the abusive Bessie, shouting obscenities from the upstairs window. Finally, he releases Nora's grip and flings her from him, and she is left weakly calling after him. In her distraught condition, her screams indicate that her labour pains have intensified. Presently, Bessie, her mocking anger subsided, runs to Nora's assistance and drags her into the house. Then Fluther returns, alone and roaring drunk, carrying a half-gallon jar of whisky. (He is too drunk to be of any help, and the others remain too scared.) Fortifying herself with a prayer, Bessie dashes swiftly through the gunfire in search of a doctor.

After an interval of a few days, the final act is cast in the compressed little attic living-room of Bessie Burgess. (The room is one of the poorer ones in the tenement.) It is furnished sparsely and shabbily. British troops in the street have been machine-gunning the downstairs apartments in an effort to flush out snipers, who have been receiving the added protection of sympathisers. Fluther, Peter and the Covey are now all huddled in the small room sheltering from the street-barrage below. It is dusk and there is no light save from the red sky showing the glare of distant burning buildings, and two lighted candles placed on a rough stool surrounding a coffin housing both the bodies of Mollser and Nora's premature baby. (The shadow of death reflects bitter ones to come.) Fluther is peeping out of the window and is urged by the others to come away in case he is mistaken for a sniper. The men while away the time playing cards, whilst Bessie who has been looking after the demented Nora, night and day, is exhausted and drained of sleep. Periodic moans and ramblings can be heard coming from Nora in the adjacent small bedroom. Bessie tells of her struggle to calm Nora at great personal self-sacrifice. The deranged woman imagines, says

Bessie, that 'dead things are livin', an' livin' things are dead'.

The bitter irony of this remark is soon reflected in a visit from Captain Brennan, who has shed his Citizen Army uniform, and weary from the fighting brings doleful news that Jack is dead – killed in the collapse of the defence at the Imperial Hotel. With mordant irony, he exclaims: 'Mrs Clitheroe's grief will be a joy when she realises that she has had a hero for a husband'. Bessie is on the point of disillusioning the escaped officer, when the disordered figure of Nora in her nightdress wanders into the room, and her actions speak for themselves, as she babbles about former trysting-places she imagines she and Jack are reliving, her conversation tinged with irrationality, and then crying out in delirium for her baby and her husband. Screaming at them, she shouts: 'Murderers, that's what yous are; murderers, murderers!' Bessie leads her into the other room and quietens her by promising to sing to her. Characteristically, her large Protestant heart dictates her to choose – with significance – 'Lead, kindly Light'.

Brennan, although he speaks of heroism, is reluctant to return to the hopeless battle. The military are everywhere. He has no choice but to remain, which disturbs both the Covey and Peter. Fluther, taking the lead and displaying some of the courage he showed when looking for Nora, earlier, urges them to resume their card-playing. A Tommie, Corporal Stoddart of the Wiltshire Regiment, appears at the doorway and orders the men to carry out the coffin. He enquires the cause of Mollser's death: when he learns that she hasn't been shot but died of consumption, he is relieved; but the Covey uses the opportunity to underline social evils and promote Socialism. He is delivered a military rebuff: 'Oi knaow. Oi'm a Sowcialist moiself . . . ow, cheese it, Paddy, cheese it!'

Mrs Gogan, in her bereavement, thanks both Fluther and Bessie for their considerations, and, in particular, refers to Bessie's kindness to Mollser as she accompanies the four men with the coffin. Alone with the tired and weary Bessie, the corporal checks on the number of men the house contains. He voices the opinion that conscription should be enforced in Ireland but assumes all in the room are 'Shinners', little realising Bessie is a faithful supporter of the Crown. When the hearse-bearers return they are told by Stoddart that they will have to be rounded up and detained in a church until the fighting is over. Fluther is aghast when he is told it will be a Protestant church, but the corporal suggests they bring a pack of cards with them. Amid further shooting relays and ambulance sirens, Sergeant Tinley enters, worried that stray bullets from snipers are still effective: 'Gang of Hassassins potting at us from behind roofs. That's not ploying the goime: why down't they come into the howpen and foight fair!' Fluther's Nationalist hackles rise and he suddenly explodes:

> Fight fair! a few hundhred scrawls o'chaps with a couple o' guns an' Rosary beads, again' a hundhred thousand thrained men with horse, fut, an' artillery . . . an' he wants us to fight fair! [*To Sergeant*] D'ye want us to come out in our skins an' throw stones?·

(The inequalities of the situation remind us of Shaw's words, through Sergius, in *Arms and the Man*: 'That is the whole secret of successful fighting. Get your enemy at a disadvantage; and never, on any account, fight him on equal terms'.) Tinley then roughly forces them from the room. Fluther's last words on stage are: 'Jasus, you an' your guns! Leave them down, an' I'd beat th' two o' yous without sweatin'!' They sum up, perhaps, that mixture of tragedy and humour, bravery and bravado, sentimentality and stoicism that are hallmarks of the irrepressible, unconquerable Fluther: embodiment of the everlasting, fighting, pugnacious Irishman.

In the play's last poignant moments, the demented Nora, while Bessie is asleep in the chair, enters the room and starts preparing tea (thinking she is in her own apartment). Ophelia-like, she sings plaintively (her favourite song – and Jack's – that we heard in the first act), while she lays the table and waits for the kettle to boil. Suddenly, she rushes to the window calling for her baby and her husband. Soldiers from below shout to her to get away. Bessie, roused by the disturbance, tries to drag her away, but in the struggle is herself shot at the window. Her final words – and warring passions – are ones of stunned vituperation and pleas for help. Charity, for her, has become the soured milk of human kindness: nursing a mad woman, day and night, who thinks only of a dead man. And her own reward is nothing less than an unwarranted death. The irony of fate matches the dramatic irony of the play. Bessie's final consolation lies in the hymn she struggles to finish ('I do believe . . . that Jesus died for me'). Her stiff, rigid body is found first by Mrs Gogan and then by the two soldiers, taken aback at first by the error of shooting in mistake for a marauding sniper, but conceding they could not have taken risks. Nora screams and begs Mrs Gogan to cover up the body; Mrs Gogan then leads her away to her own apartment before they 'give th' last friendly touches to Bessie in th' lonely layin' of her out' while the soldiers forage out a cup of tea from the pot Nora has just brewed ('Pour it hout, Stoddart, pour it hout. Oi could scoff hanything just naow').

As the city continues to burn and the glare of the sky flares into a fiercer glow outside, as the general attack on the Post Office begins, the play ends, as the English soldiers, with unconscious irony, sing: 'Keep the 'owme fires burning' – recalling similar ironies of the fatalistic ending of *Heartbreak House*, where, in Shaw's characteristic stage direction, 'Randall at last succeeds in keeping the home fires burning on his flute'.

The Plough and the Stars shows O'Casey as a dramatist of the first rank. He is, indeed, the Ibsen of early twentieth-century Dublin, and, assuredly, the Ibsen of the tenements. And O'Casey knows the tenements as O'Neill knows the waterfront. In this mighty play, he gives us, to a superlative degree, the scalding humour of the tenements, as well as its sorrows and sadness in the midst of privations and bitter hardships. Of the play's impact, Lady Gregory once stated (in her *Journals*): 'An overpowering play. I felt at the end of it as if I should never care to look at another; all others would seem so shadowy to the mind after this'.

The play needs a gala production of the type reserved for Chekhov, Ibsen or Shaw. It is clearly the masterpiece it is because of an exhilarating fusion of sombre tragedy and boisterous comedy (interladen with buoyant farce); its unique range of memorable characters; and its unquenchable vitality of language (O'Casey's words tread a narrow tightrope between comedy and tragedy). His Irish characters have the right pathos and obstinacy, flashes of rage and wit; and wonderful, elaborate insults flowing with true spontaneity.

Although the play is usually played in a naturalistic key, a keen director should not attempt to mingle too much documentary with drama (even in television adaptations) – the play, after all, is but an evocation of the Easter Rising, and there are distinct expressionistic undertones throughout. The full O'Casey rhetoric must be given its head, not only in the stylised words and effect from the Voice in the Window, reflected in the chorus of adulation and oaths of fealty among the revolutionary soldiers, but in the delicious harangue and heady argumentation among the slum characters themselves, surging into peaks of gloriously inventive prose. O'Casey is not really a true realist (Sean O'Faolain described him, more properly, as 'the biggest old romantic we ever produced'). Theatre for him is for the artist, whom he sees as master of make-believe who hides his ingrained truth in the ingredients of fiction and fantasy. (Peter Flynn is a beplumed creation that might well have originated from a Christmas tree.) The lyrical note must never be missing; and the sustained abuse that O'Casey puts into the mouths of his characters is nothing short of picturesque.

The scope and depth all the way through is Shakespearian: onstage, his sculkers and scavengers are boozing and bickering, swearing and boasting, very much like those we come across in *Henry IV*; while, offstage, great battles are being prepared and fought. O'Casey, only two years away from the definitive denunciation of war in *The Silver Tassie*, here offers an anti-romantic view of the Easter Rising.

The emotional flames which set the play alight engulf the audience, too, in one of the rare moving tragedies of the twentieth century. In the turmoil of deaths and hysteria in the finish, the author's grimmest melodrama is given its fullest range, which gives the inner tragedy a fierce and terrible emphasis.

The play's outrageous scepticism and irony keep it afloat. Burlesque of nationalist oratory – the driving force behind the rebellion – the play suggests the whole of Easter Week may have been based on sham-rhetoric, and that bloodshed is not glorious red wine but unnecessary human sacrifice. No wonder the patriotically-minded among original audiences rioted when the play was first staged, ten years after the event. (The heroes of Easter Week, to the vast majority, were sacrosanct.)

Song and speech are more varied than in previous O'Casey plays. The Irish brogue, which is particularly thick in this play, is full of dialect and colloquialisms and racy low speech characteristic of the northern suburbs of Dublin in the working-class areas of the period with which O'Casey was familiar. It is racy in terms of image, cliché and vivid slang, with a curious interjection of proverbial wisdom, learning and Biblical phraseology. And, as always, a powerful vein of humour runs through the whole play. The persuasive, repugnant oratory of fiery nationalism – reflected in fragments of oration from the speaker – are well captured and conveyed, in pilloried form. This political jargon, in an Irish context, anticipates the slanted stunted fascist invocations of the Nazi period, some of whose imprecations are caricatured in *The Star Turns Red*. Communistic jargon as mouthed by the Covey is also given a wry, satiric twist. The characters are as exaggeratedly defined as those we come across in the novels of Dickens. 'Chancers' and 'picaroons' they may be, but in their exquisite childishness ('a dream world of sublime infantility', as Dr Eric Bentley once declared), they are sketched with a great artist's fine endeavour and will endure forever. They remain disarmingly charming. All are victims of national self-delusion. They string out across the stage like a Hogarthian frieze; absurd, kindly, craven, brave and soaked in the marvellous compassion of the slum poor. Drinkers and boasters, but neighbours in the truest humanitarian sense. There are few small parts in *The Plough and the Stars*: all require big and proven actors.

The play's chief comic delight and special rarity is the bold, jaunty Fluther. He is no mere stage Irishman, but flesh-and-blood impersonation of the good-hearted slum workman, who is also a wayward argufier and has 'a vice versa' opinion on anything. He is forty, fistic and imperturbable: in short, a whole man and completely acceptable. The veteran Peter Flynn, elf-like in his green-accoutred uniform, is a peacetime-brave but a little defeatist as a war-hero. He considers himself a patriot 'par excellence' because of his yearly visits to Tone's grave at Bodenstown in County Kildare. In the words of critic John Barber, apropos of the National's 1977 production, he is 'half bantam-cock and half chicken-heart'. He is almost a pixie character. The Young Covey, a thin slip of a revolutionary, in his mid-twenties, is indefatigably keen to convert everyone, even the Tommies, to Communism. His biggest spare-time pastime is tormenting the life-force out of old Peter, whom he regards as a nationalist sham. Bessie Burgess, the loud-mouthed harridan who turns heroine, is a good-hearted termagant, avenging angel as well as squabbling street-trader. Her character constantly surprises by its shifts from bigotry to compassion. She is forty and her face is coarsened by drink as well as toil. The playwright, we feel, admires her slum determination. Mrs Gogan, the vituperative charwoman with bubbling talk and colourful objurgations – Bessie's sparring partner – is a slum survivalist with a sovereign heart. Death and misfortune are her main topics of interest.

Nora, the warm-blooded, persuasively attractive young wife of Jack Clitheroe, is sensually motivated as the war-hating, bliss-loving mother-to-be, in her early twenties, whose life ends in delirium. Her role is a difficult one to achieve; she can be sentimentally or embarrassingly overplayed. Her husband Jack has a comparatively smaller role: initially, he is a simple working man, domestically viable; subsequently, when the Citizen Army intervenes, he remains an iron-faced patriot, convinced that his own blood is a cheap price to pay for a free Ireland. His fellow officers, such as Brennan and Langon, also plunge into the emotional flames, spurred on by the same repellent patriot philosophy. Later, when the rebellion misfires and Jack is killed, Brennan loses his valiance and does not return to the fighting. The voice of the speaker is that of a mob orator, evoked in stylised oratory, based on the burningly corrosive rhetoric of one of the poet leaders of the Uprising who was afterwards executed – Patrick Pearse. His words expound the fearful ethos of 'Ireland is greater than a wife', which motivated most of the hardened patriot-fighters during the wars for independence in the early twenties. Rosie Redmond is convincingly down-to-earth, as the portrayed prostitute: she is humorous and cynical by turns, and has her own share of rich idiom. Mollser, the pitifully drawn tubercular daughter of Mrs Gogan, is fifteen, but looks only about ten. In Goldsmith's words from 'The Deserted Village', she

> Bends to the grave with unperceiv'd decay,
> While resignation gently slopes the way.

The Woman from Rathmines is a cartoon character: a lampoon of middle-aged respectability who has strayed, indecorously, into the danger-zones of poverty and insurrection. The two British soldiers from the Wiltshires are also etched in caricatured form. By a nice stretch of dramatic licence on O'Casey's part they are provided with cockney accents. Both Shaw and O'Casey, as stage Irishmen, are fascinated by Cockney dialogue and wit. (Doolittle is a master of the species.) O'Casey, too, realises their music-hall potential and linguistic gusto. Even as an overpowerfully Irish dramatist, he cannot resist the dramatic temptation to 'shove his oar' in the racy idiom of Cockney acquisitiveness; and, later, in his play with a London setting, *Within the Gates*, he tries to capture the spirit of Cockney speech which usually shocks genteel observers. And O'Casey realises all too well that the Cockney vocabulary enables him to add to his established range of the witty and humorous, the blatantly cynical and enthusiastic as well as the primarily materialistic. He knows, too, basically, it is a vocabulary natural to townspeople living in poverty. (In London – as in Dublin – slang is used extensively only in slum areas and among the poorest people.)

The play's Dublin *première* at the Abbey, which opened on 8 February 1926, provoked riots within the theatre during its first week, upsetting patriot sympathisers. Under Lennox Robinson's direction, F. J. McCormick played Clitheroe, Shelah Richards played Nora, Barry Fitzgerald played Fluther and Maureen Delany played Bessie; others included Eric Gorman, Michael J. Dolan, May Craig and Ria Mooney. Howls of protest in the Irish press suggested the play was meant to be a slur on the nation. Fortunes, however, quickly reversed, and after the success of the 1928 and 1930 revivals, the play triumphed, and at present holds the record as being the Company's most revived play, with well over 500 performances by 1980.

The London *première*, flush on the heels of *Juno*, opening on 12 May 1926 at the Fortune, was an outstanding success. Later transferring to the New Theatre, it finished its West End run in September. In J. B. Fagan's production, Arthur Sinclair played Fluther, Sara Allgood played Bessie, Eileen Carey (later Eileen O'Casey) played Nora, with strong affinitive support from Sydney Morgan and Maire O'Neill. Sinclair and his players, whilst touring America, gave New York its *première* in 1927, where its reception at first was mixed, but was replaced by euphoria over the years. (In Cork and Limerick there was also widespread opposition and postwar reaction in the south of Ireland persisted even in the fifties.) After 1930 there were few significant revivals in London until the 1964 Peter Daubeny presentation for the World Theatre Season, with a visiting troupe from the Abbey which did scant justice to the play. (Joss Ackland's 1962 Mermaid production, despite the inclusion of Katherine Blake and Donal Donnelly, was also not well received.) Revivals in 1970 and 1977 at Belfast's Lyric provoked the National Theatre's important staging in their season of 1977/8, in the large auditorium of the Olivier Theatre: by far the most ambitious London production of recent years, even though there were flaws of interpretation in Bill Bryden's direction, recompensed by Susan Fleetwood's Nora, Cyril Cusack's Fluther, Anna Manahan's Bessie and J. G. Devlin's Peter Flynn (Geoffrey Scott's settings were admirable and realistic).

In America, the Hudson Guild Players staged their robust revival in 1950, and there were off-Broadway revivals in 1953 and 1960 at Cherry Lane and Phoenix. The run at the Vivian Beaumont, in New York's Lincoln Centre in 1973, was by far the most significant (Jack MacGowran excelling as Fluther). Toronto Arts revived the play for Canadian audiences in 1975, and a highly successful American tour the following year by the Abbey resulted in definitive performances by Cyril Cusack and Siobhan McKenna.

Abroad, in 1954, Cusack, with a visiting Abbey troupe, won over French audiences, establishing the playwright as a major figure on the French scene, with revivals in Paris in 1962 by the Comédie de Saint-Etienne, and ten years later by the Théâtre de Bourgogne. In Germany, ovation has been slower, with only moderately successful productions in outer cities in 1931, 1963 and 1972 at Osnabruck, Recklinghausen and Celle. A filmed adaptation for French television, featuring Francoise Rosay among the cast, was transmitted in 1963. Apart from numerous English-speaking televised versions, Leila Doolan's for RTE and BBC in 1966–7, with Marie Kean as Bessie, has been the most outstanding. John Ford's filmed version for the cinema in 1937, featuring Barbara Stanwyck, Barry Fitzgerald, Eileen Crowe, among others, was a deeply flawed venture. Liberties were taken with the playwright's plot and scenario. More successful was Elie Siegmeister's transposition as opera, premiered in 1969 at Louisiana and performed soon afterwards at Bordeaux. Translations include those in French, German, Italian, Spanish, Roumanian, Russian, Arabic and Japanese. A Gaelic version was staged at Galway's Irish Theatre (An Taibhdhearc), in 1942, directed by Walter Macken.

7 *The Silver Tassie* (1928): Testament of World War I

In his monumental play, *The Silver Tassie*, which several critics claim is the finest anti-war play in the English language, O'Casey creates a symbolic second act depicting the inhumanity of war; and despite the play's mixture of styles, combining naturalistic as well as expressionistic, it is undoubtedly one of the most powerful tragic dramas of our time.

The Silver Tassie is described by its author as 'A Tragicomedy in Four Acts'. It is a searching testimony as well as serious experiment in a new form; 'an extension of naturalism', says Professor Raymond Williams, 'to what is presented as an expressionistic crisis'. (The second act is one of the most remarkable in the history of drama in English this century.) The entire play is a theatrical experience of great and moving magnitude.

Although all three Abbey plays – *The Shadow of a Gunman, Juno and the Paycock, The Plough and the Stars* – are outstanding and substantial achievements in themselves (forming a trilogy of Dublin in her crucible years prior to independence), they are far surpassed by *The Silver Tassie*, which, in its sweep from laughter to tragedy, from tragedy to farce, and even from the riches of vaudeville to symbolism, reveals to the fullest extent the dramatist's outreaching powers. In February 1928, O'Casey had confided by correspondence to Lady Gregory: 'Personally, I think the play is the best work I have yet done . . . and have written the work solely because of love & a deep feeling that what I have written should have been written.'

The Silver Tassie is a poetic, ritualised vision of war; a passion play, a war requiem, in which all humanity suffers, dies and lives again in the form of crippled survivors, which war, in all its inexhaustible chaos and suffering, hurls back at the mindless superfluities of

109

mankind; in Wilfred Owen's own words (from his poem, 'Mental Cases'), 'purgatorial shadows', whose minds and bodies, 'the Dead have ravished'. It is a searing testament of World War I.

The play is far more compelling than the stiff-upper-lip heroics of *Journey's End* – Sherriff's widely-acclaimed play about World War I – which London audiences had seen for the first time in 1929. (*The Silver Tassie* was also staged in London that year.)

With the completion of *The Silver Tassie*, written at the beginning of the dramatist's exile, whilst in London, between the end of 1926 and the beginning of 1928, an entirely new dimension is felt. Here, observes J. C. Trewin in his Introduction to O'Casey's *Three More Plays* (1965), O'Casey works in a medium that seems 'to wed flame and ice'. Harley Granville-Barker, in his Romanes Lecture, *On Poetry in Drama* (1937), makes reference to the 'remarkable Second act' – unnaturalistic in design – in which O'Casey employs 'symbolism of scene and character, choric rhythms of speech and movement, the insistence of rhyme, the dignity of ritual, every transcendental means available in his endeavour to give us, seated in our comfortable little theatre, some sense of the chaos of war'.

Although Dublin scenes, at first, recall *Juno and the Paycock*, O'Casey, in *Rose and Crown*, defends his metamorphosis of style, as the play develops:

> There was no importance in trying to do the same thing again, letting the second play imitate the first, and the third the second. He [Sean] wanted a change from what the Irish critics had called burlesque, photographic realism, or slices of life . . .

The play has been criticised because it combines two methods: realistic presentation with impersonal expression of character and entity (purists seem to object, for some reason, to the mixing of two techniques), but the skill with which the playwright has allowed the one to merge into the other ought to have silenced such objections. In this, as in all his subsequent dramas, O'Casey establishes that fantasy and reality can be handled together with noted sureness of touch and rare delicacy. Nothing finer or more moving in modern theatre has been done than the bitter incantation to the gun, at the end of the powerful second act, in this irreverent portrayal of war. 'Without question', says Allardyce Nicoll, *The Silver Tassie* is 'one of the truly arresting plays of our generation'.

O'Casey was never very interested in narrative, but always cared passionately about people. He rages against war, deploring, like Ruskin and Shaw, its waste of humanity. His message is explicit: 'The Lord hath given and Man hath taken away' (Act Four). It was, as we shall witness, more than his disapproving critics could withstand, forgetting that Tennyson, in *Ulysses*, had voiced similar unflinching emotions amid unvanquished ideals:

> Tho' much is taken, much abides: and tho'
> We are not now that strength which in old days
> Moved earth and heaven; that which we are, we are;
> One equal temper of heroic hearts
> Made weak by time and fate, but strong in will
> To strive, to seek, to find, and not to yield.

It was over this play that O'Casey broke with the Abbey Theatre – for whom the play was written – refusing to temper either its bitterness or its expressionism. Prompted by Yeats – and with a culpable lack of foresight – the Abbey directorate, in 1928, rejected the play, which blazoned forth a fierce international row. The folly and cack-handedness of the decision were characteristically exposed by Shaw, who, in a letter to Lady Gregory, came out overwhelmingly in O'Casey's favour:

> It is literally a hell of a play: but it will clearly force its way on to the stage and Yeats should have submitted to it as a calamity imposed on him by the Act of God, if he could not welcome it as another *Juno*.

And, to O'Casey himself, he afterwards wrote:

> Of course the Abbey should have produced it . . . A good realistic first act, like Juno, an incongruously phantastic second act, trailing off into a vague and unreal sequel: could anything be wronger: What *I* see is a deliberately unrealistic phantasmo-poetic first act, intensifying in exactly the same mode into a climax of war imagery in the second act, and then two acts of almost unbearable realism bringing down all the Voodoo war poetry with an ironic crash to earth in ruins. There is certainly no falling-off or loss of grip: the hitting gets harder and harder right through to the end . . .

The rejection of a major work by one of its most powerful dramatists is still largely incomprehensible and inexplicable: Yeats's letter to O'Casey of 20 April 1928, upholding the decision, is unconvincing. So, also, is George Russell (AE)'s explanation that the rejection was made to save O'Casey's reputation. As James Stephens had already declared, when he wrote to O'Casey in 1925, long before the rumpus over *The Plough and the Stars* or the bigger row which ensued over *The Silver Tassie*:

> 'Tis all rubbish what people say – that an author isn't a good judge of his own work. Given that he is a writer he knows better than anyone else will ever know, and if the rest of the world is against him then the rest of the world is an ass.

This did not prevent Yeats and the rest of the Abbey directorate from making asses of themselves in rejecting O'Casey's epic and uncompromising play. 'The tragedy', said Yeats, in a letter to Lady Gregory afterwards, 'is that O'Casey is now out of our saga'.

The Silver Tassie must, therefore, rank as one of O'Casey's most crucial plays since it severed his connections with the Abbey Theatre, and left him, in the chasmy fortunes of serious drama, a playwright in isolation and without a theatre. Henceforward, as the playwright underscores in *Sunset and Evening Star*:

> There was the perennial difficulty of getting a play produced, and worse still, the poverty of producer and of production that inhibited any performance given.

The struggle to go on writing future plays on his own incomparable and unfettered terms became an artistic blight which plagued the rest of his professional career. Comments Dr David Krause, in the first volume of *The Letters of Sean O'Casey* (1975):

> As an innovative playwright determined to experiment with symbolic and nonrealistic techniques, he was a generation ahead of his time and ironically had to suffer for his creative insight since the theatre of London was not ready for him and the theatre of Dublin had disowned him.

Yet, anyone who had closely charted O'Casey's cometary career as far as *The Plough and the Stars* ought not to have been totally surprised at the apparent transition – transubstantiation even – of subject and style in his next play, as befits treatment of the European war in O'Casey's wider contextual sympathies, and with altogether greater emphasis on choreography welded into the dramatic scene.

The pro-British outbursts of Bessie Burgess in *The Plough and the Stars* (Act One), as well as the dominating presence of British soldiery at the close of the play (to the chilling chorus of the familiar First World War chant, 'Keep the 'owme fires Burning'), would have suggested, sooner or later, treatment of a broader canvas, such as the Great War, on a subsequent broader dramatic scale. So when Yeats, in his letter of rejection to O'Casey, summarily declared, 'You have no subject . . . you are not interested in the great war; you never stood on its battlefields or walked its hospitals', Yeats was talking umbrageous nonsense. He must have known that many Dubliners, including the playwright's elder brothers, had enlisted for service in the British Army, which meant that Dublin, during the war, had become an arsenal for the sick and wounded returning from the battlefields of Flanders and the Somme. When O'Casey himself was in St Vincent's hospital in Dublin in 1916, he saw sufficient sickening evidence of injured and disabled flooding into the hospital wards from European battle-lines. And, indeed, in the chapter, 'St. Vincent Provides a Bed', in *Drums Under the Windows*, he reflects:

The war was singeing England badly . . . and the English stood now with their backs to the wall. The black, white, and red banner of the Germans was cocking a snoot even at the naval forces of her foe, and Got Mit Uns looked forward to being the enforced motto of the world.

O'Casey clearly saw the wider menace of German domination than the alternative threats to Britain from sporadic Irish Republicans or Sinn Fein. Bessie's sentiments, in *The Plough* (Act Two), match those of O'Casey's:

There's a storm of anger tossin' in me heart, thinkin' of all th' poor Tommies . . . dhrenched in water an' soaked in blood, gropin' their way to a shatterin' death, in a shower o'shells! Young men with th' sunny lust o' life beamin' in them, layin' down their white bodies, shredded into torn an' bloody pieces, on th' althar that God Himself has built for th' sacrifice of heroes!

In his reply to Yeats, in defence of his play, O'Casey stresses:

> It happens that I was and am passionately and intensely interested in the Great War. Throughout its duration I felt and talked of nothing else; brooded, wondered, and was amazed. In Dublin I talked of the Great War with friends who came to see me, and with friends when I went to see them.

And, later, in his own reminiscences, O'Casey mentions 'the dreary madrigal of moaning' he heard from the hospital beds. In *Drums Under the Windows*, there are some poignant recollections and reflections upon the War, which show how uppermost it was in his thoughts at the time:

> Half the Christian world had just discovered that the other half no longer deserved to live. The slime, the bloodied mud, the crater, and the shell-hole had become God's Kingdom here on earth. Deep trenches led to the delectable mountains; and a never-ending line of duckboards led to where they could see Him even as they themselves were seen . . . In every ravine, on every hill, through every golden cornfield tens of thousands of Irish wriggled and twisted to death, their dimming eyes dazzled by the flame from a scarlet poppy, their dulling ears shocked by the lilting notes from a rising lark. The ghosts of them who fell at Dettingen, Fontenoy, and Waterloo were clasping their colder arms around the newer dead . . .

O'Casey, with these memories still vividly before him, plus inspiration from Burns ('My Bonnie Mary'), which influenced the title of his play:

> Go, fetch to me a pint o'wine,
> And fill it in a silver tassie,
> That I may drink, before I go,
> A service to my bonnie lassie

sets out to write a lacerating drama around what he calls 'the odious figure of war'; a war-tragedy so deeply moving and overpowering, beside which most others would pale into insignificance by comparison. His aim, as he tells us in *Rose and Crown*, is to 'silently show the garlanded horror of war'. In an exceptionally moving, antiphonal second act, he provides an excoriating war-zone scene, set 'somewhere in France'; a black Golgotha of suffering and death, which produced such an effect on T. E. Lawrence that he later acknowledged, in a letter to Lady Astor, this act to be his 'greatest theatre experience'; the experience, he again confessed, 'which came rawly upon those new from the war'.

The play, specifically, is the story of Harry Heegan – athletic hero and champion football player and winner of the silver tassie trophy for the local Avondale Football Club in Dublin – who, as a Volunteer in the British Army, loses the use of his legs in the battlefield during World War I, and becomes an unwanted reminder of the War. His plight, like all disabled, is to spend the remainder of his life, as Wilfred Owen so poignantly reminds us in 'Disabled',

> a few sick years in Institutes,
> And do what things the rules consider wise,
> And take whatever pity they may dole.

Likewise, his case is paralleled by that of his tenement-neighbour and fellow-soldier, Teddy Foran, who loses his sight; whose fate is to suffer the perennial taunts of civilian unease and complacency, reflected in the mock-response of Sassoon's bitter war poem:

> Does it matter? – losing your sight? . . .
> There's such splendid work for the blind;
> And people will always be kind . . .

Throughout the bitterness and dramatic irony, O'Casey provides, as usual, a comic contrast to the tragic and cosmic situation he has created. Laughter, he always recognises, is a potent weapon against evil ('Comedy and tragedy step through life together', he reminds us in *The Green Crow*). Tragicomedy is his special style, as his Dublin plays effectively demonstrate. And tragicomedy impregnates *The Silver Tassie*, too.

Written before and after his marriage to Eileen Carey in London in 1927, the dedication is to his young actress-wife, who, in her much later book, *Sean*, published seven years after O'Casey's death, explains the context behind the dedication:

In the spring I always filled a large green vase with daffodils. Sean, who looked forward to this, dedicated the book of the *Tassie* to 'Eileen, with the yellow daffodils in the green vase'.

Although production was delayed until October 1929, because of the Abbey Theatre's rejection, the text of the play was first published, as intended, in June 1928. Some alterations, following the London production, were later made by the playwright, which were subsequently incorporated in *Collected Plays*, vol. 2, where the text is described as a 'Stage Version', and is now regarded as definitive. Although twenty-three characters are listed in both versions, there are, in fact, more: the Third Stretcher-Bearer and Third Casualty are not listed in the *Dramatis Personae* in either version; crowd-sets, endemic in production, are also not mentioned.

'One of Mr Yeats's objections to the play', O'Casey told a London interviewer, in 1929, 'was that it contained no dominating character . . . In the *Tassie* the tragedy dominates the characters'. In another words, the playwright's imagination is no longer focused, abundantly, on character: the universal theme is over-riding. In her *Journals*, Lady Gregory regrets that naturalistic presentation of character is missing, unlike *The Plough and the Stars*, where 'every character [is] so clean-cut, an etching of life caught up in tragedy'. In *The Silver Tassie*, she complains, 'the characters, equally vivid in the first act, become lay figures, lantern slides, showing the horror of war'. Yet, only by so impersonalising – as the progress of the play is seen and the extent of suffering orchestrated – can the play's original purpose be achieved in extremes of chilling and burning synthesis. One of the War's generals, Sir Ian Hamilton, stated in 1917 (his statement has a bearing on the drama's subject and treatment) that: 'in war no soldier is free to say what he thinks: after the war no one cares what a soldier thinks'. Humankind is reduced, therefore, to a cipher: impersonality an imposition of war.

Transcendence of the tragic theme is masterly and overwhelming, completely eclipsing characterisation, plot, and kaleidoscopic changes of mood. The effect on stage is extraordinarily successful and scalding: a tragicomic masterpiece of stirring proportions, which later occasioned a change of heart in both Lady Gregory and in Yeats; Lady Gregory recording in her *Journals*, after seeing the London production: 'I am troubled because having seen the play I believe we ought to have accepted it'. The Abbey, eventually, made amends by staging it in 1935 amid howls of critical and clerical protests from the Irish press; even though its run was tragically short.

Along with athlete-protagonist, Harry Heegan, whose sporting prowess and physical behaviour in the opening act contrast starkly with the travestied, tormented shell in a wheel-chair he becomes in the last two acts (an incisive study, indeed, of the 'maimed' hero, sharing in some ways the anguished affinities of O'Casey's other spiritually maimed character, Manus Moanroe of *The Bishop's Bonfire*), is the exacerbated role of Barney Bagnal – soldier mate of Harry's – goaded into unmitigatory revenge after demobilisation, on being confronted by Harry, who cannot forgive his traitorous behaviour. Barney's quieter, though less sensitive nature, turns suddenly 'savage and wild' (to quote the playwright) when thus enraged. And, as the drama unfolds, their contrasting natures are accentuated, reaching fever-heat in the final act.

Jessie Taite, Harry's girl-friend, who defects to Barney – overthrowing the injured form of Harry for the more virile and battle-heroic survivor – is as much a study in feminine fickleness (unable to hide her discomfort in the presence of a cripple who has once been her lover) as any exaltation on the playwright's part of animal spirits inherent in her shallow nature, though O'Casey's women, for the most part, are appreciably lustier than their male counterparts. She is matched by Susie Monican, the attractive, sexually repressed young woman we meet in the opening scenes of the first act. Religiously inhibited, like Foorawn in *The Bishop's Bonfire*, she assumes the role of lay theologian, while polishing Harry's rifle during the last moments of his leave-taking shortly before his embarkation for France, administering unwanted spiritual advice to those around her, such as Harry's father, Sylvester Heegan, and his crony Simon Norton, two typically outspoken 'paycockian "butties" ' locked in mock-conversational combat, whose presence represents a recurring hallmark in many O'Casey plays and who resent her tantalising attempts at over-evangelising – 'Heaven', says Simon, 'is all the better for being a long way off ', and remarks Sylvester, 'Susie'll have to be told to disintensify her soul-huntin' ', adding, 'You only succeed in distempering piety when you try to mangle it into a man's emotions'. A sensualist at heart, the War's effect on Susie, while helping as a Voluntary Aid Detachment nurse attending the wounded, brings about a sudden and violent transformation in her character, leading eventually, in the third and fourth acts, to extremes of sexual abandonment. 'The peculiar bend in Susie's nature', to quote Simon's observation during Act One, is due, as Sylvester also explains, to a natural fondness for Harry in the face of Harry's adoration of Jessie; the result being 'she hides her rage an' loss in the love of a scorchin' Gospel'.

In addition to plaintively drawn, unheroic Mrs Heegan, we are given, contrastingly, different impressions of Teddy Foran, also serving, like Harry, in the front-line in France, and his wife (occupants of the upper rooms in the same tenement-house where the Heegans live). Foran, whom the playwright describes as 'big and powerful, rough and hardy' – a man, we learn, 'who would be dominant in a public-house, and whose opinions would be listened to with great respect' – is a braggart in the style of Shields and Fluther; he resents his wife's carefree attitude while he is away at the Front, reflected in the recurring ditty she joyfully hums, 'I'll be single again!', to which her husband, later, tauntingly, refers: 'Blowin' her sighin' in me face all day, an' she sufferin' the tortures of hell for fear I'd miss the boat!' Rewarding his wife's inconstancy by flinging his dinner into the fire, and starting to smash the crockery on the dresser – the noise of which can be heard downstairs by the Heegans – the rough-and-tumble occasions the wry comment from Harry's mother: 'You'd imagine now, the trenches would have given him some idea of the sacredness of life!'

The play's remaining characters, including Surgeon Forby Maxwell, a philandering physician we are introduced to, sardonically, in the third act, while he is tending the sick and wounded (he is also President of the Avondale Football Club), are expressionistically drawn: caricatures inhabiting the visionary, or dreamlike scenes to accord with the transubstantiating purpose of the dramatist. (Joyce, in *Ulysses*, we remember, had perfected the technique. 'The tempestuous writings of James Joyce', alluded to in *Inishfallen, Fare Thee Well*, had made a deep and lasting impression on O'Casey, and proved a bond of communication between himself and Doctor Joseph Cummins, the Bohemian-styled eye surgeon, who was responsible for treating O'Casey's recurrent ulcerated eye-condition (trachoma) which had nearly blinded him during childhood. Cummins had shown a personal interest in O'Casey's ideas and ambitions for future play-styles, following the meteoric and spectacular success in Dublin of *Juno and the Paycock* and *The Shadow of a Gunman*. O'Casey had later dedicated *Red Roses for Me* to his one-time friend as a memento of those emergent years in Dublin in the early and mid-twenties. Possibly, a little of Cummins is reflected in Maxwell's portrait.)

Fourteen of the demonstratively drawn, expressionistically-styled characterisations are soldiers, lugubriously depicted, with emotionally charged lines which swing dramatically from the depths of human despair to ribald, unforeseen laughter in the heightened war-zone scene, representing the core of European battle-front-lines making such a crater in men's lives, during the insane slaughter of 1916–18, and where mock-heroics of militarism are ruthlessly and savagely exposed. The terrible message from the Preface to Shaw's own *Heartbreak House* is underlined: namely, 'If men will not learn until their lessons are written in blood, why, blood they must have, their own for preference'.

In O'Casey's resolute parable, his rank-and-file men are portrayed as representative types behind the battle-front, in a rest-camp stationed near an adjoining improvised Red Cross station in the shattered remains of a shelled monastery commandeered by a British Army unit. In addition to Barney Bagnal – undergoing field punishment for thieving poultry – who alone, of the soldiers portrayed in the second act, remains a separate identity (turning the spotlight on him so that audiences, later, can realise the symbolic significance of this particular act of misdemeanour, in relation to Barney's stealing his friend's girl), are four unnamed, unknown soldiers – listed simply as First, Second, Third and Fourth Soldiers – grimed and battle-scarred and huddled round a brazier in the face of a cold, biting wind and steadily falling rain. Crouching above them, on a ramp, is a soldier, nicknamed 'the Croucher', a skeletal figure, with a death's head appearance, whose clothes are covered with mud and splashed with blood. He intones his lines like an Old Testament Prophet of doom. (His colleagues, too, chant their war-weariness, in stentorian tones of boredom and fatigue.) The playwright, in his letter of 28 February 1928 to Lady Gregory, had indicated that 'Most of the Second Act is to be sung. A good deal to Gregorian chant, & some to the airs of songs & a hymn'.

Other military personnel, in this travestied scene, include a routine corporal accompanying a pastiche-figure of an inanely foppish outsider, or visitor, dressed in a semi-civilian, military manner, intent on irrelevant psychological reconnaissance, in the course of mock-diplomatic manoeuvres, plus a prim platoon-officer, dressed in immaculate khaki, dubbed the Staff-Wallah (in the jocularly-styled military jargon of the period), who issues clipped, disciplinary orders, even in the heat of battle, 'with a gasping importance'. In the translocation of this harrowing scene, as the act progresses, three soldiers acting as stretcher-bearers (the third is not mentioned in the casting, but is an essential participant, in the litany of soldiers' slang, accompanying the slow-moving procession, winding its way into the Red Cross station), carrying with them three stretcher-case casualties (the third, again, is not listed) weave their way past the remaining tired soldiers, whose presence has dominated the stage in this vale of desolation. The Visitor's function, in the words of the Third Stretcher-Bearer, is to keep up, albeit with varying degrees of hopefulness, 'the morale of the awmy'.

One other remaining character – a cameo of cold authority – appearing briefly at the end of an almost unbearably tragic ending to the third act, in the hospital scene, in the wake of war's aftermath, is the nun who is depicted as Ward Sister. She is ostensibly modelled on the ward sister at St Vincent's Hospital, Dublin, where O'Casey, in *Drums Under the Windows*, describes his stay as a patient. The coldness of her composure and religious exterior contrast, startlingly, with bitter incantations from the injured Harry, broken both in body and spirit, and about to undergo intensive surgery, to reinvigorate his lifeless limbs and legs, reflected in his impassioned cry:

> I'll say to the pine, 'Give me the grace and beauty of the beech'; I'll say to the beech, 'Give me the strength and stature of the pine'. In a net I'll catch butterflies in bunches; twist and mangle them between my fingers and fix them wriggling on to mercy's banner. I'll make my chair a Juggernaut, and wheel it over the neck and spine of every daffodil that looks at me, and strew them dead to manifest the mercy of God and the justice of man!

(Another piece of dramatic irony, for, in the final act, the symbolical club trophy – the silver tassie itself – gets twisted and mangled at the hands of the dispirited hero, signifying his empty and battered post war existence.)

The sets comprise, in the first act, the main room in the Heegans home; later, in the stylised second act, an outdoor rest-camp immediately behind the Front, 'somewhere in France'; while, late on, in the third act, the interior of a hospital ward (we are back again in Dublin, where the wounded from European battlefield have arrived in an unending stream of desolation); and later still, in the fourth act, the setting is the club-room of the Avondale Football Club premises in Dublin, the occasion being a dance to celebrate past victories and triumphs. Irony is implicit throughout. The silver tassie itself which, earlier, had represented the Grail that would hold wine holy enough to redeem all suffering, becomes an emblem of empty celebration and wanton, irretrievable sacrifice.

The futility of World War I is given a mocking, bitter twist, symbolised in the words of Susie, at the end of the last act: 'we, who have come through the fire unharmed, must go on living'. Those who can must participate, whole-heartedly, in the dance of life: the future belongs to those who are sound in limb and have their health intact, the disabled and war-injured fighting a lost fight against the infirmities of their state. As the couples waltz on the dance-floor – Jessie in the arms of Barney, Susie dancing with Surgeon Maxwell – in the final, agonising spectacle of those who are able to enjoy themselves, as opposed to those who are unable to participate, the callous and casual words on the lips of the doctor, in the song that he chants, reaffirm the irreversible axiom of the play:

> Swing into the dance,
> Take joy when it comes, ere it go;
> For the full flavour of life
> Is either a kiss or a blow.
> He to whom joy is a foe,
> Let him wrap himself up in his woe;
> For he is a life on the ebb,
> We a full life on the flow!

As Shaw, indeed, had predicted when he wrote to O'Casey in 1928:

Now if Yeats had said 'It's too savage: I can't stand it' he would have been in order. You really are a ruthless ironfisted blaster and blighter of your species; and in this play there is none righteous – no, not one.

In a letter to the playwright, Barry Jackson, adventurous London producer and founder of the Malvern Festival which pioneered many of Shaw's own plays, after an initial reading of *The Silver Tassie*, pronounced the play 'one of the greatest of post-war plays', but felt he himself could not stage it, as its possible effect on an audience, in his opinion, would be too frightening and harrowing.

Bravest of managers, C. B. Cochran – flamboyant impressario – came to its rescue and produced it in London the following year, which earned him the especial gratitude and jubilation of Shaw, who wrote to him, in ecstatic applause:

> I really must congratulate you on *The Silver Tassie* before it passes into the classical repertory. It is a magnificent play; and it was a magnificent gesture of yours to produce it. The highbrows should have produced it; you, the unpretentious showman, did, as you have done so many other noble and rash things on your Sundays. This, I think, will rank as the best of them . . . There is a new drama rising from unplumbed depths to sweep the nice little bourgeois efforts of myself and my contemporaries into the dustbin; and your name will live as that of the man who didn't run away.

The Silver Tassie provoked so much controversy that 'some', declared Cochran, 'thought I ought to be canonised, for it, while others thought I ought to be burned at the stake'. Yet he himself regarded the play as the finest work yet accomplished by 'one of the century's greatest living playwrights' (Sam Heppner, '*Cockie*', 1969).

The opening scenes of the first act give no unusual indications of candour or savagery in which the remaining acts are cast. The stage opens, in naturalistic style, with the two typical 'butties' – Sylvester Heegan and Simon Norton – embroiled in a friendly fray of argumentation in the sleazy atmosphere of the ground-floor tenement living-room of the Heegans' house. In the background lingers Sylvester's wife, stiff and attentive, watching anxiously through the curtains for a sign of Harry's arrival, in the full flush of sporting celebrations, and concerned, lest he overstay his allotted leave-span before returning to the trenches, together with Susie Monican standing at the table diligently polishing Harry's rifle, in readiness for his departure to the battle-front.

Such is the conversational field-works between the two sparring partners – the subject at stake being the sporting exploits of Harry – that the two combatants are oblivious to what is happening around them. Sylvester, we learn from O'Casey's stage remark, who has 'one arm outstretched crooked at the elbow, is talking with subdued intensity to Simon'. The mock-contentiousness of their conversation is continually interrupted by pious philanderings of Susie – ridiculed by Sylvester as 'persecutin' . . . tambourine theology' ('People ought to be forcibly restrained', says Simon, 'from constantly cannonadin' you with the name of the Deity') – as well as by frequent comings and goings of tenement life. Mrs Foran, from upstairs, interrupts the conversational flow with a rhetorical request to put a frying pan, containing a piece of steak, on the fire of the Heegans' lounge, because, as she puts it, 'A pot of clothes is boilin' on the fire above, an' I knew yous wouldn't mind me slappin' a bit of steak on here for a second to show him, when he comes in before he goes away' (in oblique reference to her husband), 'that we're mindful of his needs, an' I'm hopeful of a dream that the sea's between us, not lookin' very haggard in the mornin' to find the dream a true one'.

As Susie fails to heed Simon's plea to 'defer the dosing of your friends with canticles till the time is ripe with rest for them to listen quietly', exhorting them both 'Not to live leg-staggering an' belly-creeping among the pain-spotted and sin-splashed desires of the flesh', the two contestants, in their moral uneasiness, look for a means of quick escape, making Mrs Heegan (now outside in the cold and still on the alert for Harry) a lame excuse for leaving the room, only to be forestalled by Mrs Foran herself racing to the door instead, flinging back the retort, before leaving, that both can relax, allowing Susie 'to take the sin out of your bones an' put you both in first-class form for the kingdom of heaven'.

While Susie continues her evangelising with protestations from Simon that 'Religion is love, but that sort of thing is simply a nullification', Mrs Heegan, pale and shivering with cold, re-enters with Mrs Foran; the latter immediately suspicious of a smell of burning, as she confronts her pan with its contents burnt to a frazzle. Susie, as well as the 'argufiers', are lambasted for having failed to rescue the sacrificial steak: 'Even the gospel-gunner couldn't do a little target practice by helpin' the necessity of a neighbour'. The whole room reels from the smoke of unneighbourly recriminations as Mrs Foran exits, smoulderingly, fanning the accusation: 'I can hear the love for your neighbours almost fizzlin' in your hearts', preluding deeper unrest among those in the tenement, before the close of the act, when delf, dinner and self-respect will have been flung to the wall, indicating, in a domestic way, how war's inflammable barbarities can obliviate, on a national, or even international scale, all traces of human dignity and universally accepted codes of human rights and behaviour.

When Harry eventually appears outside with a concertina, followed by a crowd of admirers, with Barney and Jessie hitching on to him, it is on the crest of a sporting triumph. Joyously and excitedly, he proclaims to everyone: 'Won, won, won, be-God; by the odd goal in five', and hoisting up the silver cup – the silver tassie won by himself, for the honour and glory of the Club – he shouts out, unaware of undertones of later irony, 'Lift it up, lift it up, Jessie, sign of youth, sign of strength, sign of victory!'

The courage, gaiety and astringent cynicism – touchstones of these Irish Volunteers who have found themselves, unwittingly, at the centre of the front-line – are reflected in the earnestly sentimental, ribald and military-styled behaviour and conversation of Harry and Barney, with a true authentic ring of the trenches:

HARRY (*to Barney*): The song that the little Jock used to sing, Barney, what was it? The little Jock we left shrivellin' on the wire after the last push.

BARNEY: 'Will ye no come back again?'

HARRY: No, no, the one we all used to sing with him. 'The Silver Tassie'.

The nub of war phraseology is skilfully embedded in O'Casey's rich and highly diversified dialogue: 'push', 'napoo', 'estaminet' being emotive and accepted soldiers' slang expressions of the period, personifying vicissitudes and verisimilitudes of the War. 'The big push' was the general name, at that time, for British assaults on the Somme in 1916. In this campaign, a way had been cut through British barbed wire defences but thousands died because the German wire had not been destroyed by bombardment; 'push', tragicomically, indicates a desired ideal rather than actuality.

In the last precious moments of their civilian leave, the 'mucking-in-pals' (to use the slang of the day) – Harry, Barney and Teddy – gather up their kit and informally bid their farewells, humming the words, derived from Burns, of the 'Tassie' song, Harry emphasising:

> It's not the roar of sea or shore,
> That makes me longer wish to tarry,
> Nor shouts of war that's heard afar –
> It's leaving thee, my bonnie lassie!

Jessie, in the aura of adulation, reflects universal attention of the nation focusing on the 'Khaki heroes', as they were regarded. (Bronze-faced soldiers, home on leave, everywhere, had their attendant group of admirers and girl-worshippers.) In the well-springs of emotion, resulting from leave-taking, the families in the play and the phalanx of sporting admirers protest that the heroes must not linger, that they must return to the trenches (in Heegan's phrase, 'before we set out to kiss the guns!'), the crowd chanting, expressionistically, 'You must go back' – an ironical twist to the familiar words of 'Will ye no come back again?' mentioned earlier – as the sound of the troop-ship's siren is heard blowing from the quayside, beckoning the return of the soldiers to the scene of battle.

And, in the 'humid seal of soft affections' – to echo Burns's metaphor from 'To a kiss' – the act closes amid scenes of mingled sorrow and joy, as lingering lips are parted in 'adieu's last action', in face of symbolic intrusions from the chanting crowd, offstage, and soldiers in the distance marching towards the boat, to a subdued chorus of 'The Silver Tassie' accompanied by strains of a con-certina, the sounds growing fainter till they cease. Through the window of the set, the light on the ship's masthead moves slowly away, the shouts of the crowd dying with it, the act's vivid realism (with concluding, expressionistic touches) ending with Mrs Heegan's ironic sigh of relief as the three soldiers embark for the front: 'Thanks be to Christ that we're after managin' to get them away safely'. (Mrs Heegan, like Shaw's Mrs O'Flaherty, is thinking of the security of her war pension.)

The presence of the chanting crowd at the end of the first act prepares audiences for the outright expressionism of the awe-inspiring second act – recreating the front-line atmosphere of World War I, enunciated by the soldiers themselves participating in liturgical chant, in order to indicate the blasphemy of war. In striking contrast to the brawling vitality of the first act – where texture is the same rich mixture as in *The Plough and the Stars* – the ice-cold abstractions, centred in a corner of a military camp, somewhere behind the trenches in France, its locale is unspecified, are wrenching in their naked futility and despair.

The setting shows a ruined monastery with a figure of the Virgin in stained glass and a broken life-sized Crucifix, also a gunwheel (to which the figure of Barney is tied for military misdemeanour) and a gun. On the broken wall, a crouching Tommy, made up to suggest a skeleton, voices the curse of an Old Testament Prophet, while other soldiers and stretcher-bearers pass in and out to the accompaniment of choral chanting, plainsong-fashion. This interlude effectively demonstrates the drab chaos and sterility of war.

The war-scene is a deliberately distanced episode – a battlefield black mass, based on laments of Ezekiel (used also by T. S. Eliot, in *The Waste Land*; and later in *Ash Wednesday*) to convey a total, tragic and depraved picture and universal canvas of 'a valley of dry bones'. The earth is barren, the sea salt, as in Eliot's poem. Intoned, initially, by the Croucher, the theme is taken up by the remaining soldiers – anonymously portrayed – in a scene of utter desolation and lamentation, punctuated with tragicomic cynicism; indicating a universal voice crying in a woe-filled wilderness of human misery and unmitigated despair.

The second act employs stylised, formal and ultimately self-mocking devices to make its hideous point. The soldiers express themselves in a litany, symbolising pain and brutality, ritualising the raw horrors of the trenches. In song and licentious laughter, they express emotions, stressed by T. E. Lawrence in *Seven Pillars of Wisdom*:

> The everlasting battle stripped from us care of our own lives or of others' . . . The weak envied those tired enough to die; for success looked so remote, and failure a near and certain, if sharp, release from toil. We lived always in the stretch or sag of nerves, either on the crest or in the trough of waves of feeling . . .

Stylistically, O'Casey's scene conveys the abject horrors of the front-line, without the turmoil: fire, smoke, din, screams, stench, mud, blood and death, in an abstract way (the dramatist's aim is to present the spirit and essence of those terrible events); and, in and out of the brutalising chaos – the infernal 'chassis' of war – move dim crouching shapes of horror-filled stretcher-bearers hovering in the background.

The foundations of war are astonishingly evoked in this stylised dramatisation, which David Jones, who directed the play for the Royal Shakespeare Company's revival in London in 1969, described 'as a piece of effective theatrical engineering'. Although the whole scene takes place behind trenches in a war zone ('The ground is dotted with rayed and shattered shell-holes', we learn from montage-descriptions in stage instructions accompanying the text), the horrors of trench-warfare are starkly conveyed, emphasising the painful warning of one prognostic comment, long after the campaign: 'No it couldn't be done again. Even if man were so foolish, modern arms – aerial, nuclear, mechanical – would make it impossible, and it is certain that trench-warfare will only be experienced once in the whole history of the world' (Col. Howard Green in Masefield's *The Old Front Line*). The Battle of the Somme was one of the most terrible in British history. It killed or maimed over one million two hundred thousand men, over half of them British. For the men who fought there, it was never the same afterwards. In the grim toll of the war, the songs, the writing, the poetry, became cynical, after the Somme. The mud of the Somme, suggests John Masefield, will be remembered long after the shelling; roads and villages were turned into vast horrendous quagmires. Tanks plunged and stuck fast, stricken 'dead' in the wake of mud.

And tanks were not alone in not being able to 'plunge'. In a monumental passage of supra-military-styled burlesque, the dramatist introduces into the rest-camp scene, accompanied by a unit corporal, a foppish figure – a reconnoitring, visiting supremo – who wishes (in his own phraseology) to 'Penetrate a little deeper into danger', but bemoans the fact that 'military authorities are damned strict – won't let a . . . man . . . plunge!' His arrival coincides with the soldiers' chanting, in tired and bored tones, words of a popular army marching song, to the tune of 'Auld Lang Syne':

> We're here because we're here
> Because we're here
> Because we're here . . .

The acutely conscious and purposeful visitor is embarrassed by such a display of *ennui*, instead of *esprit de corps*; the purpose of his visit being to instil confidence and even 'Heroism in the Abstract' into the band of war-weary soldiers. Military satire momentarily relieves the gloom:

VISITOR: . . . not too much rest, corporal. Dangerous. Keep 'em moving much as possible. Too much rest – bad. Sap, sap, sap.

CORPORAL (*pointing to the left*): Bit of monastery left intact. Hold services there; troops off to front line. Little organ plays.

VISITOR: Splendid. Bucks 'em up. Gives 'em peace.

Clipped dialogue accentuates the irony, just as it does in Joyce's *Ulysses*. We recall the asides of Leopold Bloom, satirising traditional beliefs and customs: 'Blind faith. Safe in the arms of kingdom come. Lulls all pain. Wake this time next year'. (Always laughter in the tragedy. We encounter it, too, in O'Casey's autobiographies: for instance, in the hospital-scene of suffering at St Vincent's, in the ward occupied by shell-shocked soldiers, in *Drums Under the Windows*. The parody sets the tone of the bored recital of prayers in the hospital-ward: 'Holmarmotherogoprayfrusmisrablesinnrs nowana thourofhoudeath'.)

Crudities of trench-warfare are in sharp contrast to Joxer's mock-heroics, on a more natural plane, mouthed in the course of *Juno and the Paycock* (or Simon's, even, in the next act): 'Let me like a soldier fall – me breast expandin' to th' ball!' Those offended critics who rage about O'Casey's 'raw torso' and blasphemous language are, in the context of such a play, those who have been reared on a diet of *Oh, What a Lovely War!* or Sherriff's *Journey's End*, contemptuously described by O'Casey as 'a demure echo, told under candlelight, at a gentle fireside, of a fight informal . . . the stench of blood hid in a mist of soft-sprayed perfume'. O'Casey's more savage treatment of war bears out Oscar Wilde's belief that 'as long as war is regarded as wicked, it will always have its fascination. When it is looked upon as vulgar, it will cease to be popular'.

Hazards and fatigues of trench-life are epitomised by litany-led resignation from the soldiers, who intone in unison:

1ST SOLDIER: If the blighters at the front would tame their grousing.
THE REST: Tame their grousing.
2ND SOLDIER: And the wounded cease to stare their silent scorning.
THE REST: Passing by us, carried cushy on the stretchers.
3RD SOLDIER: We have beaten out the time upon the duckboard.
4TH SOLDIER: Stiff standing watch'd the sunrise from the firestep.
2ND SOLDIER: Stiff standing from the firestep watch'd the sunset.
3RD SOLDIER: Have bless'd the dark wiring of the top with curses.
2ND SOLDIER: And never a ray of leave.
3RD SOLDIER: To have a quiet drunk.
1ST SOLDIER: Or a mad mowment to rustle a judy.

In such scenes, O'Casey captures the raw life of the trenches with frequent lapses into strong gusts of pungent humour and language. In the episode of the Tommies 'brassing off', their grousing is contrasted, ironically, with tab remedies and brass-hat injunctions: 'Must stick it. There's a war on' (where everything is couched in unnatural and imperative mood).

Throughout the military rough and tumble, the soldiers instinctively share the anguish and anxieties of Shakespeare's Hamlet, echoing his beliefs:

> There's a divinity that shapes our ends,
> Rough-hew them how we will.

As the visiting brass-hat lights a cigarette by striking a match on the arm of the life-size Crucifix – leaning against the window of the shell of the ruined monastery – he is reproved by a soldier: 'Blarst you, man, keep your peace-white paws from that!' And, another reminds him: 'The image of the Son of God'. The brass-hat is told: 'There's a Gawd knocking abaht somewhere', and a fourth soldier adds, sardonically, 'Wants Him to be sending us over a chit in the shape of a bursting shell'. In the litany to the Gun, which follows, all join in the terrifying and terrible refrain: 'We believe in God and we believe in thee'.

In the shadow of an enormous howitzer, which is swung round and points horrifyingly to the horizon (in the RSC production of 1969, it was pointed, even more terrifyingly, at the audience; whereas, in the original 1929 production, the gun grew, menacingly, in size throughout the act), the soldiers chant a savage parody of the litany to the symbol which has crucified them – 'the cool-harden'd tower of steel'. The act closes with the loud, moving cry, 'To the guns!' No gunfire or gunpeel is heard; only flashes are seen – an expressionistic device (the silent flame is an angry expression itself against the carnage of the trenches) – with searchlights moving towards the red glare of the sky. The flashes increase as the soldiers load and fire with rhythmical intensity, while the scene darkens to a vivid close. In tumult, darkness and presence of death, the Tommies are ready to resume the attack before the massacre begins. We can almost picture Sassoon's 'Lines of grey, muttering faces, masked with fear', as the footlights fade.

In the switch-back emotions engendered by war, the theme of the third and fourth acts is a lament of the demobilised and disabled, with additional ironies that survivors can find no readjustment or rehabilitation in post-war civilian life. Heroes are lauded when they are healthy, but cast off and forgotten when they are wounded and permanently disabled. Although the remaining acts return to prevailing naturalistic moulds, O'Casey uses fixed-character group- ings and stylised speech habits to throw into relief the extreme changes of relationship that occur, when, as a result of the terrible ravages of the War, a bullying husband – the former hectoring Teddy Foran – returns home blind, to be bullied instead by his wife (in an excess of overweening sympathy and pride) and, more tragically still, a football hero – the remarkably athletic Harry – whose home-coming reveals him permanently paralysed from the waist downwards, finds his girl turning away from him in disgust. Anti-climaxes in public attitudes after the War are cynically portrayed. Camaraderie and *entente cordiale* have given place, wantonly, to human outrage and disillusion. Indifference and revulsion have conquered former admiration and respect. (Similar attitudes prevailed after the Second World War, underscored in *Oak Leaves and Lavender* where physical suffering and mental collapse were equally degrading.)

Amid extravagant touches of comedy and farce, in the skilled switch from grim humour to bathos, occasioned by the hospital scene (immediately after the campaign), the setting is again Dublin, though not specified as such, but accents are unmistakable. Harry and many of the wounded are undergoing severe treatment, ending up, ironically, in the same hospital run by nuns as the two old cronies, Simon and Sylvester, who are being treated for relatively minor ailments. The third act's main concern is the indifference of society to its crippled. Against a background of tragicomedy, O'Casey tempers his message with heightened effect: like Shaw and Shakespeare, he is vaudevillist and wiseacre combined.

Holding sway are the amusing antics and drolleries of O'Casey's clowns, who proceed to turn the hospital ward into a veritable state of comic 'chassis'. On being told by Susie, now Nurse Monican, a transformed hospital harridan acutely conscious of her new role as VAD, to take 'a bawth', Sylvester, in characteristic sally, retorts: 'Can't they be content with an honest to God cleanliness an' not be tryin' to gild a man with soap and water', followed by other choice examples of richly unexpected cachinnations involving the two buffoons, excelled only in the final act, when in an isolated scene of protracted knockabout the two comic 'Irregulars' struggle to manipulate (and manhandle) a telephone call at the football club dance in which they demonstrate their bemused bewilderment at humanity's latest example of telecommunication – generally regarded as indispensable in big cities after 1920 – tangling themselves in a tirade of cross-talk with the talking-stem and shouting hysterical histrionics into the ear-piece, in moments of mangled manipulation – ending with Simon's ejaculation: 'I can see no magnificent meaning jumping out of that!' (preceded by Sylvester's 'Holy God, what are you yessin' and noin' and cheerioin' out of you for then?').

Interwoven, throughout, is an instilled atmosphere of quickly changing contrasts, though verve of comedy does not impair the scene's serious undertones – expressed by Harry when he rages, with futile indignation, on behalf of the dead and maimed, as if with corkscrew-emphasis on the dramatist's part, reinforcing the grim message of the scorching second act, showing the 'exceeding great army' finishing as a cemetery of dry or rotting bones.

Expressionistic touches are inherent too: hospital patients have become medical ciphers – Sylvester is in a bed numbered '26', Simon an up-patient beside him numbered '27', while Harry, restless in a wheelchair, is referred to by hospital staff as '28', Tragicomedy strikes poignantly when, with the arrival of Harry's well-meaning family and friends, each, in turn, inflames his despair with a marathon tactlessness, summarised in vain hopelessness by the quoted cliche, 'while there's life there's hope' (what he really needs, he confides later, is a 'miracle', not an operation). Infused irony is apparent when Simon, whilst attempting to reassure Sylvester on the eve of a minor operation, colloquially recalls the old song, 'Let Me like a Soldier Fall!' (Sylvester's response to which is couched in the nonsensically-inspired, 'Look! If you can't think sensibly, then thry to think without talkin'!'). Nothing can kill or stay laughter, O'Casey implies, not even war with all its apparatus of in-built hate and lingering suffering. In the hospital scene, the hurt and wounded are not pacified with a soothing hand but subjected, instead – more realistically – to intermittent, barracking laughter. Tragicomedy is seen as a flexible corrective between ideal and real; comedy in crisis, a truer reflection of mercy and compassion in the face of adversity and suffering.

In the eviscerating short span of the third act, where, following the empty desolations of war, we are shown the even greater desolations of peace, amid unsurenesses of readjustment and rehabilitation; we are reminded, too, that illusion and pity are

horrifying emotions discernible in rest-camps, hospitals and other
centres, in the wake of war; that human 'miracles' are scarce; and
supernatural love and mercy even scarcer. Hospital wards are
transformed into sepulchral and oppressive nightmares, where men
suddenly cry out from their sleep with excruciating pain and
submerged dreams of military fantasies. At the end of the act,
against a background of nuns chanting the *Salve Regina* prayer, we
experience the hopeless, impassioned cry of Harry – his dreams
haunted by memories of hostilities and shell-shock – shouting out
from his hospital bed: 'God of the miracles, give a poor devil a
chance, give a poor devil a chance!' (Compression, alone, matches
compassion, in this uncompromising, tormenting conclusion.)

In the fourth act – scene of the later football-club dance celebrations – we witness a head-on verbal assault on war and the false
pity aroused by it. Enacted to the full is the playwright's original
intention, as outlined in *Rose and Crown*, to

> set down without malice or platitude the shattered enterprise of
> life to be endured by many of those, who, not understanding the
> bloodied melody of war, went forth to fight, to die, or to return
> again with tarnished bodies and complaining minds . . .

The spectre of two maimed veterans – Harry and Teddy – the halt
and the blind, wandering like living dead among the party guests
foregathered at the dance, affords a glimpse of the play's underlying
vehemence and the final act's unforgiving recriminations, foreshadowing the uncertainties of peace as well as the post-war
political and social hazards ahead, mirrored, to a greater extent, in
O'Casey's next play, *Within the Gates* – a panorama of unsettled and
squandered peace.

Former hero Heegan, footballing playboy of the Dublin world
and incarnation of the joys of living – paralysed both in body and
spirit as a result of the universal carnage of the Great War, in
contrast to the rarer fortunes of his former friend, Barney Bagnal,
who has not only come through totally unscathed but has even been
awarded the Victoria Cross for bravery (for carrying Harry off the
battlefield under fire, and winning the attentions of Jessie in the
afterglory) – refuses to stand by with stoical endurance and rages
bitterly against the continuing pride of human hypocrisy, reminding his dissimulators – the treacherous Barney and unfaithful Jessie

– that 'even creeping things can praise the Lord!'

In a world of prevailing 'chassis', Harry's is the ultimate nemesis: tarnished in body as well as outlook. The bitter, tragic joke which life has played on him cannot be shrugged off in an irresolute sally, such as Sylvester's (in the previous act): 'Oh, it's not a fair trial for a sensible man to be struck down in a world like this!' Resentful of his degenerate condition, he can only exclaim:

And legs were made to dance, to run, to jump, to carry you from one place to another; but mine can neither walk, nor run, nor jump, nor feel the merry motion of a dance. But stretch me on the floor fair on my belly, and I will turn over on my back, then wriggle back again on to my belly; and that's more than a dead, dead man can do!

Hounding the consciences of the traitorous Barney and Jessie, Harry, in a series of embittered encounters with both, vents his jealous rage, ending with a brawl between Barney and himself (within the confines of his wheelchair), with the club trophy, the silver tassie, later, deliberately mangled by himself and thrown to the floor (an empty symbol disowned by a dispirited castaway).

The episode underlines that back in civilian life, the limbo of everyday existence is worse than the hell of the battlefields. The final act is one of the most powerful lessons in the whole universe of pity: the inevitable conflict between healthy and maimed, who must now dwell 'in another world'. Here, in this act, O'Casey piles bitterness and irony upon misery and suffering in such a way that we dare not detach ourselves from it or pass judgement. Echoing Wilfred Owen in his bitterly ironic poem, 'Disabled', the horrible conflict between illusion and pity is stressed to an even greater and unbearable degree, and the callous destiny we reserve for the plight of the disabled: a limbo of destitution and inhumanity.

Suffering degrades; and, as we are reminded at the end, 'As long as wars are waged, we shall be vexed by woe'. (Susie's reinforcement makes it nonetheless telling.) Such is the only possible conclusion; no dramatic victory is scored. Illusion is all around us: on the battlefields, in rest-camps, at home in civilian life. We cannot escape from its deleterious harm; in the words of Emerson from his essay, 'Illusions', in *Conduct of Life*, and echoed throughout by O'Casey:

Like sick men in hospitals, we change only from bed to bed, from
one folly to another . . . from the nothing of life to the nothing of
death.

Inescapably, 'we, who have come through the fire unharmed, must
go on living' is O'Casey's final Chekhovian message; the ebbed life
must give place to the 'full life on the flow'.

What lingers from this play is the poignancy of the second act; the
pity and pathos of the final act; and choric voices of the disabled,
reciting their litany of deprivation:

HARRY: The rising sap in trees I'll never feel.
TEDDY: The hues of branch or leaf I'll never see . . .
HARRY: I never felt the hand that made me helpless.
TEDDY: I never saw the hand that made me blind . . .
HARRY: The Lord hath given and the Lord hath taken away.
TEDDY: Blessed be the name of the Lord.

'O'Casey', said Robert Speaight, 'has seen into the heart of the
horror of war, and wrenched out its dreadful secret; that the co-heirs
with Christ destroy one another in the sight of the Son of Man'
(quoted in *Rose and Crown*).

The final scene, as the tenement community ostracise the cripple
at the club reunion dance, remains one of the most pitiable,
uncomfortable and harrowing in all modern drama. As Harry sits
singing to his ukulele, in his wheelchair (a poignant rendering of
'Swing low, sweet chariot, comin' for to carry me home'), the
balloons descend and everyone rushes away, glad to forget him. It is
a truly heart-rending theatrical moment, and, like the ending to the
equally moving second act, its impact is both scathing and
lacerating.

In his use of tragic farce to convey painful material, O'Casey
originates a technique which has since become one of the main
spearheads of modern drama. As Dr Katharine Worth, in a
perceptive analysis contained in her *Revolutions in Modern English
Drama*, has commented: 'Perhaps the Great War could only be fully
realized in this way, as a great grim joke, the kind of bad joke it is in
the war songs, those haunting expressions of the ordinary soldier's
stoicism and irony'. The spirit of those songs – 'There's a long, long

trail' and 'Carry me home to Blighty' – as well as the savage war poetry of Owen and Sassoon – as the soldiers 'blunder through the splashing mirk' of the mud and mire of the trenches – is a powerful element in the play, and the dialogue constantly stems towards a musical direction.

In addition to musical analysis of songs and chants employed throughout, the dramatist, in the 'stage version', provides a set of 'Notes' preceding the text of the play, doubtlessly inspired by his collaboration with Raymond Massey, director of the London *première*. (Such 'Notes' were not appended to first editions of the published text.) The 'Notes' in themselves contain useful hints and pragmatic considerations towards realisation of the fullest kaleidoscopic interpretation, giving that 'phantasmo-poetic' quality which Shaw so rightly observed and admired. Transitions from sublime to derision, and from absurd to heroic, must figure in any successful combination, illustrating how the ludicrous can verge upon the tragic.

When it is realised that the play is not in the naturalistic tradition (scenes are movements rather than acts – movements in a sombre, darkly changing symphony) but is suggestive, instead, of an apologue or parable, the successful director will endeavour to stage the play, making amplest use of the author's pseudo-liturgical chants in the allegorical second act, to suggest ritual-celebration in a dream-like presentation, though fantasy and reality are concomitant throughout. The difficulty for the astute director is to reveal the great naturalness and spontaneity inherent in the play, and yet, at the same time, lift the action from a plane of total realism. Whilst, of course, extreme stylisation is indicated in Act Two (here the author's 'Notes' are of useful importance), the director should aim throughout at an unnaturalistic aproach, with just the right note of realism to keep alive touches of the grimmest farce contextual to this unusual tragicomedy.

Indications of hysteria, in the football celebrations during the first act, are stylistic prerequisites for the nightmarish distortions of the second act. Crowd characterisation (a feature of expressionist plays), which concludes the ebullient first act – and which is present in intermittent touches during the final act – takes over almost exclusively in the second antiphonal act. Austere anguish of the play's theme and treatment is best served by an expressionistic approach, even though such-styled plays are not easy to interpret for English actors accustomed, for the most part, to realism.

At the root of expressionism, as the word itself suggests, lies the idea of distilled quintessence. Expressionism is a heightened form of the incarnation of 'super-natural': in the psychological climate stemming from a conceptual impression of the Great War, a distilled impression or undistorted view by means of radical technique is called for, which an expressionistic approach (shorn of the cinctures of realism and romantic naturalism) can substantively achieve. Such an approach can best cope with the chaotic flux of thought, feeling and experiences inherent in the elemental crucible of war.

Pace, timing, and, above all, orchestration, are essential in an inspired production. In choral passages of the important second act, correct inflexions of voices, with appropriate dove-tailing, are necessary, so that in waves of speech nothing is lost. In the 'Notes' O'Casey tells us chanting is based on simple plain-song – the traditional, recitative-like music of Roman Catholic Ritual (a purified form of singing, in itself). 'The first chant', he indicates, 'is given in full as an example of the way in which they are sung'. By way of explanation, he tells us that 'There are three parts in each chant: the Intonation; the Meditation; and the Ending. After a little practice, they will be found easy to sing'. Soldiers having the most musical voices, he suggests, should be selected to intone the chants, irrespective of numbers allotted to them as characters in the text. Music should modulate through military accents, as if wedded together in a passionate outcry of wild grief and fear, in this sustained protest against doom and Providence (as irrational and self-pitying and uncompromising as many passages we encounter in the plays of Aeschylus).

War-weariness is the unifying theme of the whole play. Use of poetry lifts the play from earth to dream, the chants of the soldiers giving added poignancy and reinforcement to the theme:

> Cold and wet and tir'd.
> Wet and tir'd and cold . . .
> Lifting shells.
> Carrying shells.
> Piling shells . . .
> And the shirkers sife at home coil'd up at ease.
> Fur coats for them and winding-sheets for us . . .

The characters – distanced for the most part – speak for all the dead and maimed and maddened of our century, and all the more convincingly because they speak in simple selfishness and without a trace of tawdry uplift.

Method, rather than technique, of character is dominant. Pragmatically interpreted, the remarkable feat is that such splendidly conceived impersonalisations (despite Lady Gregory's earlier reservations) are firm tests of actors' true abilities: in production, the roles are seen to be eminently actable.

Harry Heegan, at twenty-three, passes with remarkable skill from footballer to poet – resulting from war's cataclysm – becoming, finally, in the words of one commentator, 'a pursuing conscience in a wheeled chair'. He is described by the playwright as a typical young worker from the tenements, 'enthusiastic, very often boisterous, sensible by instinct rather than by reason. He has gone to the trenches as unthinkingly as he would go to the polling booth. He isn't naturally stupid; it is the stupidity of persons in high places that has stupefied him'. In the first act, we see him in soldier's khaki as well as sporting an orange-coloured football jersey when he makes his first breathless appearance. In the second act, he does not appear: his personality is submerged in the suffering abyss of the battlefields. In the third act, we see him as a pathetic figure 'crouched in a self-propelled invalid chair'. And, in the final act, though he might seem an embittered castaway, raging against his crippledom, hounding the consciences of those who are able to live life to the full, his portrayal offers a searching, agonised desperation which lingers in the mind long after the play's profound impact. His companion, Barney Bagnal, of the same age, is his exact antithesis: the soldier who has survived, having escaped injuries and successfully come through with fighting honours: the image of a lauded hero – in contrast to the pathetic presentation of tormented one – gratifying both to civilian and military minds, and one whose aura of attraction endears itself to the selfish emotions and ambitions of Jessie Taite.

Jessie, at twenty-two, is a brassy opportunist. In the recorded comment of the playwright, 'she gives her favour to the prominent and popular'. Harry's sporting triumph before his war injury, together with his DCM award, make Harry her favourite. Later, her natural vivaciousness recoils at the thought of Harry's permanent disablement and induces her to switch attentions, instead, to Barney, who emerges not only unharmed but the heroic possessor of the VC. For her actions she is not castigated by the playwright so much as shown as the unconscious though ebullient instrument of the doctrine of natural selection.

Jessie's contemporary, in age and ambition, Susie Monican – attractive Bible-quoter who finds new life tending the wounded and blossoming out as a flighty VAD nurse – is a complex portraiture of religious inhibitions and repressed sexuality. At the beginning of the play she is unconscionably pious, redeemed only by her good looks. Disappointed in love (Jessie has supplanted her in Harry's affections), she grimly proclaims the wrath of God. Later, when she turns nurse, she flowers in the service of man and is more than a match for the amorous, thirty-year-old Surgeon Maxwell. Some of the most arduous war work was performed by thousands of Voluntary Aid Detachment nurses, in hospitals, at home, and in all the major theatres of war. Many young girls, brought up in a world of sheltered security, endured the severe fatigues of hospital routine. The general need to relax from the rigours of war nursing had led to a wave of self-conscious pleasure-seeking and the growth, in 1917, of a dancing mania. Even the religious zealot turned flirt and the ineluctably seductive surgeon are more than aware that uniformed skirts, raised for once above the ankles (in convenience of carrying out war work), cannot, in the observations of one social commentator, prevent 'sex from breaking through in bright eyes, shapely ankles and ripe, red lips'. So when the dapper 'medico' plays the beau, Susie responds by playing coquette. The saucy Susie, the play suggests, is far more fetching than the tambourine evangelist.

In the sharp end of war and the tragic situation which predominates, the two old-timers – Sylvester Heegan, stockily-built, sixty-five year old docker, with a gift for droll repartee, and his taller crony, the more refined Simon Norton – provide the essential comic relief: they are a pair of eloquent poltroons who readily lapse into farce, undeterred by the stark, unmanageable woe of men at war, or the more savage spectacle of men who have returned from the battlefront destroyed by war. The nexus of their relationship stems from their more plausible blood-ties with Boyle and Joxer, in transposed circumstances. Their foolery is a 'paycockian' jollity belonging to the misarray of pantomime in a macabre variety show: in the midst of overwhelming tribulations their laughter is a golden thread linking audiences with actors; for even in direst tragedy we become unconscious humourists. (Nothing seems too severe, for the humourist is the underlying mood of the play, preserving sanctity as well as sanity in suffering and life.)

Sylvester's wife, designated simply as Mrs Heegan (older-looking than her braggart-poltroon husband, and stiffened with rheumatism), bears the hallmarks of a constricted resignation as housewife bound by tenement environment and ground into a baffled meanness (her caricature is a cruel vignette), exuding a thin-lipped anxiety not in keeping with O'Casey's usual mother figures. She is deliberately not given the same stature as Juno or Bessie, showing that in the final test of adversity and by not allowing herself to come to terms with Harry's permanent disablement she hasn't the heroism for noble self-sacrifice.

Contrastingly, Mrs Foran, the wife of Teddy, described by the playwright as 'one of the many gay, careworn women of the working-class', is less mean-spirited than her tight-lipped neighbour, Mrs Heegan (who remains unconcerned about the vagaries of menfolk in her life). Comely Mrs Foran wins our initial sympathies, being bullied by her hectoring husband, the subsequently blinded Teddy. In the post-war scenes, however, she undergoes a change and loses our affections, bullying her husband, in his helpless condition, instead. (Her unwitting remark in the first act, 'Nice thing if I lose the sight of my eye with the cut you gave me!' is ominous irony on the part of the dramatist.) She exchanges roles with Susie: philandering woman of the tenements in the first act, who turns peevish prude and scold in the final act, illustrating how suffering and adversity can bring about unheroic, as well as unexpected, changes in human temperaments.

Remaining character-types function symbiotically as part of a Greek chorus in O'Casey's drama-oracle of the War. Especially moving, in its Ezekiel-like conception, is the dramatist's delineation of the Croucher, a symbol of the soul-piercing horror of trench-warfare, figure of the shell-shocked soldier, whose make-up, as indicated in the dramatist's 'Notes' appended to *Collected Plays*, vol. 2, reveals a face resembling a death's head or skull. In the dim yellow light of nightmarish landscape adjoining the trenches, his appearance is skeletal, macabre and drained of life. The group of soldiers who appear huddled together in the regions of this anonymous battlefront are utterly exhausted and war-weary. They personify pain and brutality in a terrible amphitheatre of suffering, yet their militarised plain-song transcendentalises and heightens their languid, pitiful state. Their chanting is also humanly tragicomic, like those references that appear in popular war-songs and catchphrases of the period, such as:

Hi-ti-doley-hi-tee,
Carry me home to Blighty!

or,

Napoo! toodle-oo! Good-bye-ee!;

and perhaps even the morbidly jocular, 'You'd be far better off in a home'.

Raw horrors of the trenches are encapsulated in ironic, fatalistic chanting of the wounded from their stretchers:

And we show man's wonderful work, well done,
To the image God hath made!

(echoing Sassoon's poeticised war-cry in 'Dreamers' that soldiers, who are sworn to action, 'must win some flaming, fatal climax with their lives').

The War is portrayed from the soldiers' point of view, stressing their outraged protests. O'Casey's ritualistic presentation of trench-warfare produces a haunting requiem, a mocking *Dies Irae*, in tonal splendour, not far removed from a commemorative portrayal of macabre ballet in sound. Although the cameo-effect of the soldiers' crucifixion is captured quintessentially in the harrowing second act, the remainder of the play reinforces the cruellest stages of war's aftermath, which is the real crunch. As Shaw rightly observed, there is no trailing off and the hitting gets harder and harder. The end is not victory, so much as paying the price, or reaping a bitter whirlwind instead. The play is not a *cause célèbre*, but a lacerating reminder – a timeless post-mortem – of cataclysmic folly imposed by man on man.

The characters represented by the Visitor and Staff-Wallah are satiric figures, seen through the eyes of the average private. Although military discipline was not new in history some of its 1914-styled characteristics were fairly modern and probably stemmed from late nineteenth-century regard for success of Prussian methods in this field: significantly, it was after 1870 that parade-drill adopted by the British Army was jerky and noisy. This, indeed, was the process through which first a hundred thousand, then a million, eventually several million civilians were hurriedly trained and 'transformed' into soldiers. The play stresses the fact that the Army rarely allowed a private soldier to be an individual: he was a name and regimental number. The same applied also in militarised hospitals.

The Visitor in the war scene is a caricature of the stiff-upper-lip attitude and *esprit de corps*. (So too are Stoke and Poges later in *Purple Dust*). The Staff-Wallah is also a cartoon of clipped military authority, administered in the hardly less flexible or humane spirit and letter of King's Regulations themselves, personified by the soul-destroying catchphrase 'soldiering-on'. The harrowing appeal of the second act's savage assault on the emotions is effectively crystallised in the playwright's suggestion, in his production 'Notes', that 'The Soldiers' last response to the Staff-Wallah's declaration, namely, "To the Guns!" should have, in these three words, the last high notes of "The Last Post", thereby recreating, in that evocative call, the herald of death, and indication on the battleground of final sacrifice. If the author's stage directions and 'Notes' are closely followed, the second act should transform itself into a director's dream, with design and lighting blending into the wounding pathos of its poetry and appeal. In some respects, the domestic scenes which hem in the extraordinary sequence are more difficult to produce successfully as they are less immediately impressive. As David Jones, who directed the RSC production in 1969, realised: '*The Silver Tassie* is not a piece of anti-war propaganda but much more a play about the results of war, the aftermath when the fittest survive and the weakened, like Harry, go to the wall while others push on'.

So, we who take our 'peaceful share of Time, with joy to spare', should ponder the play's perennial message, poeticised in the awesome words of Sassoon in 'Aftermath':

. . . *the past is just the same – and War's a bloody game* . . .
Have you forgotten yet? . . .
Look down, and swear by the slain of the War that you'll never forget.

The play received its world *première* in Charles B. Cochran's accomplished production, directed by Raymond Massey, at London's Apollo Theatre, on 11 October 1929. The special set for the memorable second act was designed, at the request of the playwright, by Augustus John; sets for remaining acts were by Gladys Calthrop; music and chants by Martin Shaw. The author and Bernard Shaw were present at the first night. The play ran for two months: successful at first, audiences later dwindled as world recession began to bite. In an extensive cast, Charles Laughton played Harry, with persuasive support from Barry Fitzgerald, Sydney Morgan, Binnie Barnes and Beatrix Lehmann. Forty years later, in London, there was a major revival by the Royal Shakespeare Company. Trevor Nunn's praiseworthy production, directed by David Jones, drew widespread acclaim (likewise John Bury's remarkable sets and design). An imaginative cast included Richard Moore, Helen Mirren, Sara Kestelman, Frances Cuka, Patience Collier and Ben Kingsley. Elsewhere in Britain revivals have been at Nottingham Playhouse in John Neville's 1967 production, in 1971 at Belfast's Lyric by Mary McCracken, and in 1977 at Stratford East by Claire Venables. Patrick Troughton featured in a BBC radio transmission in 1957, and there was a more successful adaptation by R. D. Smith for the BBC in 1966 with Jim Norton and Barry Keegan among the cast. A joint BBC/RTE televised version was broadcast on BBC-2 in centenary year, with Stephen Brennan in the lead.

Abroad, the play's history has been chequered. In New York, its brief run at the city's Irish Theater, also in 1929, was undistinguished. (The 1949 Interplayers's New York interpretation, with Jack Palance as Harry, made a greater impact.) In Dublin, after Yeats had relented, its first Abbey production in 1935, directed by Arthur Shields, featured F. J. McCormick as Harry with a notable cast. It ran in face of extreme religious hostility though its theatricality was never questioned. The Abbey's 1951 revival, as a follow-up to the Gaiety's in 1947, was a failure, but its third revival in 1972 was splendidly redemptive (the director was Hugh Hunt), later touring Helsinki and Brussels with further renown. Performances in Zurich and Vienna in 1952 led to its West Berlin *première* at the Schiller, in 1953, where rioting, reflecting the mood of revolt in the city's Eastern sector, erupted in an overtly pacifist play. The 1968 version in the city failed to make amends, and Guy Retore's Paris version was only partially successful; but Roberto Guicciardini's Florentine staging was fully justified. Translations have appeared in French, German, Italian and Slovak.

8 *Within the Gates* (1933): an Epiphany of Peace

Rarely performed, O'Casey's epic epiphany – least familiar of his major plays – is, ironically, his most ambitious drama, being regarded by the discerning few as his most comprehensive as well as, perhaps, his most crowning theatrical achievement. Certainly, it is the most English inspired of his plays.

The theme of spiritual paralysis in the post-war world of the thirties, when it was written, may be compared to T. S. Eliot's earlier poem, *The Waste Land* (1922), where a combination of mythical, Christian and mammonist symbolic imagery, in a series of dramatic episodes, linked to each other by profound emotional patterns (conveying a sense of unifying consciousness), is representative of European civilisation at the nadir of its development: an unchanging panorama of unsettled peace; in Eliot's words, 'A heap of broken images'.

In the view of Hugh MacDiarmid, Scotland's national poet, O'Casey's artistry, in this apocalyptic drama, is infinitely deeper and broader than Eliot's, as he soars correspondingly higher, like the legendary lark in the Irish clear air. But O'Casey's admiration for Eliot was never in question. 'Eliot's integrity is undoubted', he told an interviewer. 'I always had a great respect for him . . . He admits to being an old Tory and a churchman'. The return of poetry to the stage, as effectively achieved by Eliot, was one of the few revolutions taking place in England at this time of which O'Casey approved. And, of *Murder in the Cathedral*, when it was first produced, in a tiny theatre in London in 1935, O'Casey afterwards wrote: 'This play is on the frontier, forming an outpost of the drama that will one day attack and subdue the theatrical harlotry of London's core'.

In form, *Within the Gates* is something between a masque, a tragedy, a pageant and musical-comedy farce: a dream-transmutation of contemporary elements of London life, as exemplified in the adaptation of the nursery rhyme, 'London Bridge is Falling Down', sung half way through the play and epitomising evils of the Depression and condemning peacetime disorders and social injustices. In the first published version (London, 1933) O'Casey offers, by way of sub-title, the simple description: 'A Play of Four Seasons in a London Park'. (Hyde Park, its inspiration, is seen as a microcosm of modern Britain.) Later, he would expand (in *Blasts and Benedictions*): 'If we are to confine drama to a sober and exact imitation of life, then the drama is dead, for life itself is much more interesting than its sober and actual imitation'.

T. E. Lawrence, after a first reading, remarked in a letter to Lady Astor: 'It will play better than it reads'. Even so, the poet's eye of MacDiarmid could discern from the play's context that the masterly blending of transitions from colloquialism to plain prose, from plain prose to intoned rhythms, and from those rhythms to declared lyric were sufficient justifications in themselves of the flexibilities of O'Casey's later technique. 'The second act of *The Silver Tassie*', wrote Lawrence, was my greatest theatre experience, and here is a whole play in that manner'. Professor Wilson Knight, in his fine testament, *The Golden Labyrinth*, confesses to an even greater reverence for *Within the Gates* than his admiration of *The Silver Tassie*: 'O'Casey's experience as a war dramatist enables him to master the far harder task of dramatizing peace through a number of *ritual conflicts*; and the interest never flags'.

George Jean Nathan, America's celebrated drama critic, had written to O'Casey in 1933 saying, 'I believe that your play, *Within the Gates*, is one of the true masterpieces of the modern theatre', and, in a subsequent dramatic notice, went on to elaborate:

It is a play that lays hold of silver poetry and gross low humour, of music and song and dancing, of the hot coals of drama and the cold ashes of romance, and out of them fashions a symphony that plays its deep melody in the mind for days afterward . . . One feels that here at last is the true masterpiece that all of us have been certain, since *The Plough and the Stars* (that profound and splendid achievement), O'Casey would someday surely give us.

Eugene O'Neill, admiring the play's 'rare and sensitive poetic beauty', wrote to O'Casey, congratulating him on 'a splendid piece of work'.

The play was highly regarded by Shaw, who advanced the opinion that

> Sean O'Casey is all right now that his shift from Dublin slums to Hyde Park has shewn that his genius is not limited by frontiers. His plays are wonderfully impressive and *reproachful* without being irritating like mine. People fall crying into one another's arms saying God forgive us all! instead of refusing to speak and going to their solicitors for a divorce.
>
> (Quoted in Hesketh Pearson: *Bernard Shaw: His Life and Personality*, Collins, 1942.)

What no one can doubt is that in this play, even more than in *The Silver Tassie*, O'Casey has given a new direction to the English theatre, as important as that given by Strindberg and Chekhov in their symbolic plays, as well as an instinct for drama of the future, with a more universal appeal than either playwright could have imagined or achieved. Belonging to the theatre of spiritual magnificence, it captures all the glories of stage art, and its long cast of twenty-seven characters (reduced to twenty in the revised 'stage version' incorporated in the *Collected Plays*) requires every single actor to measure up to his part in the synthesis.

Some of the practical problems presented by the play's complexity and richness of detail can be seen from the comment the playwright later made to his American agent, Miss Jane Rubin, in a letter of 8 November 1959:

> This play is the most difficult I have written from every point of view: the number of characters, the music, the acting . . . it needs a fine chorus of singers, a large stage, and a variety of costumes.

The music to the play, attributed in the original published version to Herbert Hughes, is basically the work of the playwright: 'Of the airs of the songs in *Within the Gates*', he later confessed in a letter to Nathan, 'they are modifications, done by myself, from Irish folk tunes'.

The action of the play centres round the Dreamer, the Bishop, the Young Woman, known as Jannice (described in the original version as the Young Whore), and her mother, the Old Woman. The theme, like life itself, is less a saga than a network of human relationships warring against each other in cosmopolitan frenzy and then drifting apart. Passion informs it, and it has, as another playwright, St John Ervine, has observed in a written review, 'the passion of the prophets. It burns away insincerity and all flippancy. It is a cry of sorrow for a beaten world, but it is not a cry of utter despair'.

Within the Gates is a symbolic drama in both setting and characterisation. Symbolism was never wholly absent even in O'Casey's earlier naturalistic plays. In *Juno and the Paycock* the red votive light before the statue of the Virgin flickers, burns brightly and finally goes out before Johnny is shot. In *The Plough and the Stars* the dark figure of the Speaker is silhouetted against the window and his revolutionary words can be symbolically interpreted. In the second act of *The Silver Tassie*, the characters, as Lady Gregory had noticed, become 'lay figures, lantern slides, showing the horror of war'. But not until *Within the Gates* does O'Casey exploit symbolism to its fullest capacity.

In his defence of the play, later printed in *Blasts and Benedictions* (1967), he declares: 'All fresh and imaginatively minded dramatists are out to release drama from the pillory of naturalism and send her dancing through the streets'. Notwithstanding, there are broad sweeps into naturalism and some of the dialogues, especially between the Bishop and the Young Whore, the Old Woman and the Bishop's Sister, are essentially earthily naturalistic rather than consciously stylistic:

> YOUNG WHORE: . . . You cross crown and anchor boys would expect the very nightingales to warble Onward Christian Soldiers during their off-time.
>
> BISHOP (*shocked, but trying to take it good humouredly*): Shush, now, no excitement, please.
>
> YOUNG WHORE (*vehemently*): I have to get a little farther away from the devil before I try to get a little nearer to God. I've a long way to travel before the white and holy candles are lit, and the golden incense scattered.
>
> BISHOP: My child, the sinner is always nearer to God than the sinner dares to think.
>
> (Scene III)

Pre-echoes, we recognise, of Graham Greene. Elsewhere are saline touches reminding us of Joyce: '. . . grant us grace to have faith in thy dignity en' importance, per benedicite pax hugger muggery ora pro puggery rigmarolum!' (Scene IV).

The long list of characters comprises: the Dreamer, Older Chair Attendant, Younger Chair Attendant, the Bishop, the Bishop's Sister, the Atheist, the Policewoman, First Nursemaid, Second Nursemaid, a Guardsman, a Gardener, First Evangelist, Second Evangelist, the Young Whore, a Young Salvation Army Officer, the Old Woman, a Man Wearing a Bowler Hat, a Man Wearing Plus-Fours, the Man with the Stick (*afterwards, an umbrella*), Man Wearing a Trilby Hat, Man Wearing a Straw One (*afterwards, a cap*), a Crowd of Down-and-Outs, and a Chorus of Men and Maidens. The significance of all these, and their place in the tapestry of the play, is explained by O'Casey in *Blasts and Benedictions*, to which we shall later refer.

After his exile in 1926, when he had settled in London (albeit briefly), O'Casey had spent many hours in Hyde Park, especially at Speakers' Corner, where he stood, he confessed, enraptured. 'I felt almost drunk at the end of it', he related, 'the characters are so rich in comedy . . . There was every sort of religious mania, dietetic mania, political mania, personal mania. And there it all goes on, night after night, under the trees'. Plenty of these abortive discussions, typical of Hyde Park Corner, and enlivened with O'Casey's wit and sense of comic argument, are to be found in the extraordinary fibrilating fabric of the play. Here, for instance, we come across such an interlude:

MAN IN BOWLER HAT (*interrupting*): Wait, hold on a second. Don't question me, yet. Listen carefully; let your mind follow what I say, and you'll get the idea.

MAN WITH THE STICK (*from behind*): Listen cautiously to wot the gentleman's a-saying: 'e knows wot 'e's torking abaht.

MAN IN THE BOWLER HAT: Now try to remember that all the old ideas of the cosmos are buried with Copernicus, Kepler, Newton, 'en all that crew.

MAN WITH THE STICK: Ay, en' buried deep, too.

MAN WITH THE BOWLER HAT: Now we all know that the clock created time, and the measuring-rod created spice, so that there is really neither spice nor time; but there is such a thing as spice-time. Get that?

MAN IN THE TRILBY HAT (*with confidence*): Quite; that much is perfectly clear.

MAN IN THE BOWLER HAT: Right. Now supposing that one night while we all slept, the universe sank down to the size of a football, 'en all the clocks began to move a thousand times slower, it wouldn't make the slightest difference to us, for we wouldn't realise that any change had taken place, though each of us would live a thousand times longer, and man couldn't be seen, even under a microscope.

VOICE FROM THE GROUP: Could a woman be seen under a microscope?

MAN WITH THE STICK (*with angry impatience at the interruption*): Aw!

MAN IN THE BOWLER HAT (*remonstratively*): Levity's out of place, friend, when men are trying to think out the truth of things.

VOICE FROM THE GROUP: Yes, but 'ow could the universe suddenly shrink dahn to the size of a football?

MAN IN THE BOWLER HAT: I said *if* it did, friend.

VOICE FROM THE GROUP: Oh, ay, if – a big if, I'd say!

MAN WITH THE STICK (*impatiently turning, and tapping the ground with his stick*): Aw!

MAN IN THE TRILBY (*patronisingly to the* VOICE): Our friend's just raising an hypothenuse, just an hypothenuse, nothing more.

MAN IN THE BOWLER HAT (*to the* MAN IN THE TRILBY): Well, friend, do you get the synoptic idea?

MAN IN THE TRILBY (*dubiously*): It's a presumptuous postulatum, en' requires quite a lot of thinking out.

MAN WITH THE STICK (*dogmatically*): It's as simple, man, as ABC said backwards. You've got your mind crahded with the dialectics of Genesis, en' all that sort of stuff. We're dealing now with a spice-time problem; not time en' spice, but spice-time; see?

(Scene IV)

O'Casey excels in such hyperbolic farce. Numerous other instances are to be found in most of his major plays; even, too, in his short one-act plays.

In essence, *Within the Gates* is a fantasy of the seasons in Hyde Park, though locale is not specified: seasonal changes are shown by the changing of the colours of flowers and trees. In the background to the set is a war memorial figure of a soldier, a statuesque reminder of human folly and a sinister recollection of war, with its possible foreboding of yet another one. The four stylised scenes or tableaux are set successively in the four seasons but at a different hour. O'Casey suggests, in a preliminary note to the printed text: 'If possible, the Curtain intervening between the opening of the play and the scenes following, should be one showing the Park Gates, stiff and formal, dignified and insolent . . . This curtain, when it is pulled back, represents the opening of the gates; and, when it falls back into its place, represents the closing of the gates: or, the outline of the gates may be suggested on the curtain'. (The idea of a front curtain was used by O'Neill in his impressive *Mourning Becomes Electra*, which O'Casey greatly admired.)

In his *Notes for Production*, appended only to the play's book form in 1933, O'Casey advises that 'scenic effects should be as simple as possible, suggesting, rather than emphasising, the features of the Park; and colours should be the prime way of indicating the different seasons'. (Colour and song are the demonstrating motifs throughout.) Stage directions riot in colour; the memorial figure changes in appearance according to season and light. From the opening spring chorus of Young Boys and Girls, 'representing trees and flowers', chanting 'Our Mother the Earth is a Maiden Again', the Gardener's Song, 'I'm Not Thinking of Blossoms at All' (with its refrain, 'Desire for a Woman's Both Worship and Play'), to Jannice's Air, as sung by the Dreamer, and to the final note of sadness, as epitomised by winter at the close, when, following Jannice's act of attrition, the Dreamer exclaims: 'You fought the good fight, Jannice; and you kept the faith' – O'Casey's faith – the whole emphasis is on fertility of nature and life.

Nature is associated with sexual energies in contrast to contemporary religion. The crucial theme – we find it also in Blake – is the conflict between sex, love and the Christian Church. O'Casey's thrust is against the gloom and joy-killing qualities of orthodox pragmatic Christianity, the self-righteous evangelisation of pain, woe and suffering (in the words of the Atheist, 'The hell en' red-fire-forever talk of the nuns! Framing the world en' filling life with it till we eat, sleep, work, play 'en go awhoring in the smoke of hell!'), satirised also in the first act of *The Silver Tassie*, as 'persecutin' tambourine theology', and constantly mocked in most of O'Casey's later dramas, where he would substitute, in Blake's phrase, 'a Heaven for Hell's despair'. O'Casey's exuberant, joyous philosophy is expounded by the Dreamer (counterpart of Davoren, in *The Shadow of a Gunman*, and personification of poetic wisdom): 'Offer not as incense to God the dust of your sighing, but dance to His glory, and come before His presence with a song!' Again, it is a reiteration of the antinomian ideas we meet in Blake; as, for instance, in the quaint, simply-styled 'The Little Vagabond' poem, from *The Songs of Experience*:

> . . . if at the Church they would give us some ale,
> And a pleasant fire our souls to regale,
> We'd sing and we'd pray all the livelong day,
> Nor ever once wish from the Church to stray.

Translated, in terms of O'Casey's superb sense of tragicomedy, we encounter a scene, such as the following:

SALVATION ARMY OFFICER: God is your only friend.

YOUNG WHORE: I've not called upon Him for years, and He will not hasten to hear me now.

S. A. OFFICER (*putting his hand gently on her knee*): God would empty heaven of His angels rather than let the humblest penitent perish.

YOUNG WHORE (*in low tones*): If I ask for help, will He hear?

S. A. OFFICER: He will hear.

YOUNG WHORE: And hearing, will He listen?

S. A. OFFICER: Hearing, He will listen.

YOUNG WHORE (*grasping his arm appealingly*): And listening, will He grant what the sinner asks, to save the sinner from a life of sin?

S. A. OFFICER (*fervently, as he caresses her knee*): God is able to save to the uttermost all them that come to Him.

YOUNG WHORE (*earnestly, after a few moments' thought*): I'll pray and pray and pray till all that's done's annulled, and all that is to do is blessed by God's agreement.

S. A. OFFICER (*softly*): Praise the Lord!

YOUNG WHORE (*becoming conscious that he is caressing her knee*): Oh God, don't do that, please! You'll make a ladder, and silk stockings aren't easy to get.

No matter what attitudes one may adopt to questions with which the dramatist deals, one must admit their overwhelming importance and urgency. Negative aspects of civilisation, as O'Casey sees them, still have the same relevance today: the majority of mankind

who are spiritually dead, whose chief concern, by what they read, is
the sadistic and sensational; the increasing numbers of 'drop-outs'
from society, the down-trodden, who correspond to the Down-and-
Outs of the play (an echo here, perhaps, of Eliot's *The Hollow Men*,
'Shape without form . . . gesture without motion'), whom life, with
her flaming colours and 'noisy laugh', has passed by: these
'challenge life no more' and have 'but a sigh for a song and a deep
sigh for a drum-beat'.

'This nightmare group', says Wilson Knight, 'is a stage conception of uncanny power', representing the dead army of the defeated,
who always make their entrance to the roll on a muffled drum and to
the accompaniment of mournful chanting. (The birds also cease
their singing and the scene darkens.) They make their entrance,
'chanting their miserere to the monotonous tap, tap, tap of the drum-
beat' (Scene III), though they are forebodingly introduced to the
attention of the audience in the first scene when the two chair
attendants, talking amongst themselves and reminiscing on the days
of England's greatness and thrilling to 'the sahnd of Drike's drum'
(a symbol, in this context), are suddenly brought to jolt by faint,
distant sounds of sombre music, offstage, 'saddened with the
intermingled beats of a muffled drum'. We are reminded of drums
in O'Neill's *The Emperor Jones*, conveying the power of tom-toms,
beating slowly at first then quickening as scene follows scene,
culminating in a headlong *prestissimo*, to convey the effect of
primitive terror on the face of the negro in O'Neill's evocation of the
noble savage. O'Casey, in *Within the Gates*, employs a similar
expressionist device – with muffled drum-beats and chanting as
ground-bass – equally haunting and conveying, at the end, an effect
both memorable and cumulative.

A number of theological, political, social and scientific issues are
also aired by a wide range of semi-stylised yet humorous characters
representing the main flotsam of humanity passing through
London's parkland (in this multi-stratified society of the Park, the
flippant gossip of the nursemaids and their guardsman-admirers
contrasts with those elements of alienation and protest, as represented by the Down-and-Outs and soap-opera speakers), some of
whom are an amalgam of cockney wit and Dublin jargon, coupled
with the usual O'Casey flair for certain notable catchphrases. For
instance, at the beginning of the play, the Bishop, his Sister and the
Policewoman, together with the chair attendants, are watching the
birds on an invigorating spring morning, and the Younger Chair

Attendant, in the ensuing cross-talk, exclaims fervently, 'Gord watches even over the fall of the sparrer! Dideray, dideree, diderum', repeating this last catchphrase several times, which O'Casey, in *I Knock at the Door*, tells us he heard from the lips of one of the hearse-drivers at his father's funeral. And, says one of the platform speakers: 'there isn't a clime that Christianity mikes that can be substanteeyted. Mark contradicting Matthew, Luke doing the same to Mark, 'en John on his own, contradicting all the others. Any scholar'll tell you it all comes aht of the Egyptian Book of the Dead. If I was to dive deep into things en' tell you the original meaning of so-called Christian symbols, I'd be arrested in double-quick time'.

The Old Woman, Jannice's mother, a cross between the hag of Beare (of traditional Irish fame) and a cockney soothsayer, frequently interrupts the speakers – the soapbox orators so richly characterised – with her auguries of national disaster and despair (reminiscent of 'Captain' Boyle's prognostications of 'chassis' in *Juno and the Paycock* and imagery in Ansky's play *The Dybbuk*):

> OLD WOMAN (*speaking tonelessly up to the* SPEAKER): There can be no rest nor work nor play where there is no life, and the golden infancy of England's life is tarnishing now in the bellies of the worms.
>
> 2ND PLATFORM SPEAKER (*bending down towards her*): Beg pawdn, mad'm?
>
> OLD WOMAN (*murmuringly*): Your politics are husks that only swine will eat; your power's behind a battlement of hunger; your religion's as holy as a coloured garter round a whore's thigh; truth's bent in two, and hope is broken. (*She begins to wander away.*) O Jesus, is there no wisdom to be found anywhere! All gone with the golden life of England into the bellies of the worms!
>
> (Scene IV)

Human interest, as the play unfolds, focuses on the pretty young prostitute, Jannice, whose shapely figure, according to the stage-directions, 'would make most young men immediately forget the seventh commandment', even though we are told, 'her heart is no in the business', having drifted into the profession because of a repressive, religious upbringing. Medically, too, she is aware tha her heart may give out at any time, but if she has to die, she pronounces to her step-father, the Atheist, 'I'll die game; I'll die dancing!' (Scene I). For differing reasons, the Dreamer, the Gardener, the Salvation Army Officer all compete for her favours, but she becomes the object of increased attention by the Bishop, whose modern pastoral attitudinising is summed up by the glib slogan he mouths, 'Get amongst the people; get them to talk with us, joke with us, then we may expect them to pray with us'. He is the antithesis of his Sister, who is symptomatic of a harsher Christianity. Both, of course, are objects, on the playwright's part, of a laughing satire on widely-held beliefs among respectable church-mindedness, a form of religion that is shown to be entirely out of touch with real life.

The false note of the thirties is, indeed, the chief target of scorn throughout the play; O'Casey would seem to have endorsed Byron's deeply-engrained cynicism, reflected in the lines:

> This is the patent age of new inventions
> For killing bodies, and for saving souls,
> All propagated with the best intentions.

Even in his final book, *Under a Colored Cap* ('Articles Merry and Mournful with Comments and a Song'), O'Casey never shows any shred of latterday respect for orthodox Anglicanism, or church leadership of any kind, treating the Archbishop of Canterbury as a contemporary figure of fun, along with the Prime Minister of the day and other 'clay figures in the national shop window'. ('Not in the coo-coo of the Archbishop . . . would I find God, if I troubled to search; rather, in Whitman's barbaric yawp sounding over the roofs of the world'.) O'Casey would seem to have agreed with the sentiment of Shaw's Captain Shotover: 'The Church is on the rocks, breaking up'.

The Bishop is alluded to, variously, as a 'purple-button'd deadman, whose name is absent from the book of life', by the Dreamer and by one of the chair attendants, in an astringent aside, as an 'ecclesiastical Mickey Mouse'. He whom the Old Woman refers to as 'a big jack-a-dandy in the church now', is, it is revealed, father of the Young Whore – in a youthful indiscretion from his seminarian days. (Interesting to note that Shaw's Mrs Warren's illegitimate daughter was also fathered by a clergyman.) Thus the relationship between the Bishop and Young Whore is personalised, which intensifies his struggle to reclaim her soul.

In the Dreamer's contrasting appeal, he alone offers the Young Whore the magic of song and the 'clutch of love', in an application of the philosophy the playwright commends in a long allegorical poem, 'Gold and Silver will Not Do', which appears in *Windfalls* ('Stories, Poems, and Plays'): 'I gathered her close to my love in a song that dulled, as I sang, the gleaming of silver and gold': variations on Blake's 'joys impregnate' and 'The soul of sweet delight can never be defil'd', couched in the style of the Song of Solomon. (Biblical influences are strong in O'Casey, dating from the church-going days of his boyhood and youth, recounted in *I Knock at the Door* and *Pictures in the Hallway*.) The Dreamer makes his bid in the following playfully ironic exchange with the Young Whore:

YOUNG WHORE (*slyly*): Tuck me up and sing me to sleep with one of your songs.

DREAMER (*eagerly*): I'd love to. He brought me home to his house of wine, and his banner over me was love. (*Getting up, and catching her arm*). Come on, dear, come on.

YOUNG WHORE (*pulling her arm free and speaking a little sharply*): Not so quick, please. Men are always ready to rush a pretty woman into bed looking for joy and behold trouble. (*A pause.*) Supposing I go and give, what do I get?

DREAMER: I'll pay your merry kindness with a song.

YOUNG WHORE (*scornfully*): A song! A puff of scented air! You're out on the hunt for bargains, young man. Goods reduced to the lowest possible figure; – actually given away. Go with a priest for a prayer, and with a poet for a song! It's hardly likely, as the soldier said to the lady.

(Scene II)

The Dreamer remonstrates that 'queens most lovely have been snared in the golden meshes of a poet's song'. In reply, the Young Whore mocks: 'I'm afraid you'll have to give me a greater encouragement than a song to get me to go with you', and then adds, with disdain, 'Go to bed and wake up to find a song under the clock! Can't you add something to the song, dear?'

Meanwhile, the Young Man in Plus-Fours, a self-parody of men's apparel in the thirties, has sat down on a bench eyeing the Young Whore, closely watched, as well, by the Gardener. Hesitatingly, the Dreamer tells the Young Whore who has revealed her name to him as Jannice, he could manage a pound. In an apparent ironic ending to the scene, significant of mid-summer, midday madness, the sort of mad inspiration that could only happen in a park, the Young Whore takes the pound and puts the offering in her handbag, humming as she does so to the tune of the Blue Danube Waltz, played by the open-air band, and disappears up the slope with the Young Man in Plus-Fours. Just before doing so, she has remarked to the Dreamer, at the close of the scene, 'The exchange isn't good enough'. The bewildered Dreamer remarks, when she has gone, 'A thief, be God, as well as a whore!' (O'Casey's characters, unlike Shaw's, are not naturalised Englishmen; they are only too ready to betray their Irish accents and mannerisms in moments of crisis!) Incidentally, those who are familiar with O'Casey's one-act burlesque, *Bedtime Story (Collected Plays*, vol. 4), will remember a slight variation on the theme of comic betrayal, to the detriment of the male, when the pretty lass, Angela Nightingale, does a similar walk-out on John Jo Mulligan, in his flat. Perhaps, because of similarities of situation, a different slant on this particular episode is imposed by the playwright in the revised text of the 'stage version', reference to which will again be made when considering practical suggestions for production.

On stage, a twilit wistfulness descends in the second half of the play; Scene 3, in this park-scape on an autumn evening, opens with ironic chanting by the crowd of 'Land of Hope and Glory', in the presence of the newspaper readers, 'the oblate brothers', in the scornful words of the Young Whore, 'busy reading the gospel for the day, sucking in holy thoughts of holy wisdom'. In a derisive prayer, over their heads, she intones: 'Oh Lucifer, Lucifer, who has caused all newspapers, stars of the morning and stars of the evening, to be written for our learning, grant that we may so read that we may always find punch in them, hot stuff in them, and sound tips in them, so that both outwardly in our bodies, and inwardly in our souls, we may get closer and closer to Thee!' Indignantly, as they fail to look up from over their newspapers, she shouts: 'Why the Hell don't you all say Amen?'

The Bishop, still prowling round the Park in his quest for the capture of Jannice's soul, is again repulsed: 'Go away . . . and leave

me in peace. Let me run my race in my own way. Don't be mousing
after me . . . I want no God's grenadier fooling around me'. In a
wild, hysterical frenzy, she soliloquises to the crowd of newspaper
readers, calling them a 'bunch of high-minded toads', entertaining
in their hearts 'only venom for a woman in the things ye think of
her'. She shouts at them, 'Jannice's going to die dancing'.
Attracting no notice, she vehemently calls out, 'Are all of you damn
perishers deaf and dumb?'

The newspaper readers then read out extracts from their papers
in the wording of familiar journalese associated with 'murder',
'suicide', 'racing' and 'divorce', punctuated with choric Gilbert-
and-Sullivan styled verse-responses satirising the banality of the
popular press. A voice from behind the words *'Great Cricketer talks
about God'* admonishes, expressionistically: 'God won't let the
English people down – you may take that from me! He'll keep our
wicket up, and the bat of faith'll drive the ball of unbelief and
communism far and away beyond the fair boundary of Britain!'
(Shaw's influence, recognisably.) Behind the cynicism is the
philosophy expressed in *Heartbreak House* (1919):

> HECTOR: And this ship that we are all in? This soul's prison we
> call England?
> CAPTAIN SHOTOVER: The captain is in his bunk, drinking bottled
> ditch-water; and the crew is gambling in the forecastle.
> She will strike and sink and split. Do you think the laws
> of God will be suspended in favor of England because
> you were born in it?
>
> (Act III)

Jannice, as the play develops, reveals herself more and more as an
indomitably-minded, Shavian-typed heroine in The Maid of
Orleans mould, gay-witted, but a true-born Protestant, both by
nature and determination. Wishing to turn aside from prostitution,
she implores the Bishop to help her. But his offer of a place in a
hostel, run by a pious Sisterhood and reliving her life 'with
becoming circumspection', is eventually spurned, as one that is too
freedom-restricting and self-imprisoning. She is contemptuous of
the thought, as she terms it, of being 'chained fast to prayer and firm to
fasting'; and stirred by the glitter in her eyes, partly the results of her
recent drinking-habits and partly due to her natural exuberance

and courage and wild joy, she shouts scathingly at the Bishop that she will have none of his Christianity (the 'crosstianity' that Shaw also declaims). There is no doubt that her portraiture derives, in many ways, from a combination of an earlier heroine, Irish Nannie, from O'Casey's one-act *Nannie's Night Out* and Mild Millie, the methylated spirits drinker from the Dublin tenements so graphically yet so sympathetically described in his autobiography, *Drums Under the Windows*.

Nor, too, will she accept the self-abasing, penitential attitude to Christianity, as practised by the Salvation Army. Here, in this respect, the influence of *Major Barbara* is strong. Just as in *The Silver Tassie* – with the powerfully effective invocation to the gun at the end of the impressive second act, together with the equally impressive voices of the disabled chanting their special litany of deprivation in the final act of that drama – the same choric effects employing litany technique are skilfully put to use in *Within the Gates*. Witness the ritualistic responses of the Salvationists towards the close of Scene III when their bid is being made for the soul of the Young Whore, ending, of course, in the usual O'Casey anti-climatic, comic-pathetic way:

YOUNG SALVATION ARMY OFFICER: Lord God Almighty, stretch out Thine arms and save those who are lost in trespasses and sins!

SALVATIONISTS (*in chorus*): Save them, great and most merciful Redeemer.

Y.S.A.O: That the trumpets of the angels may have a new and joyful note in their sounding!

SALVATIONISTS (*in chorus*): Save them, great and most merciful Redeemer.

Y.S.A.O: That the crown of thorns on the head of the crucified one may shine as the sun on a noon in the season of Summer!

SALVATIONISTS (*in chorus*): Save them, great and most merciful Redeemer . . .

YOUNG WHORE (*brokenly*): Great and most merciful Redeemer, save me!

SALVATIONISTS (*in chorus*): Save her, great and most merciful Redeemer . . .

MAN WITH THE STICK (*mockingly – from among the crowd*): I thought she said she'd die darncing!

(Scene III)

Then, without warning, and on a defiant whim of her own – like Shaw's Saint Joan – she suddenly recants her own recantation, brandishing in the face of the Bishop her own lively credo: 'Faith in God, old purple buttons, faith in God! Be merry, man, for a minute, for you'll be a long time dead, and it must be years and years since God heard you singing a song!' The words invite comparison with *Major Barbara's* jest: 'Many a sinner has played himself into heaven on the trombone'. In the grim mood of Depression, and tendency to capitulate to national despair, joy and happiness were palliatives understressed. (In the 1930s, the slump meant genuine suffering and hardship; and even moral degradation for those faced with long-term unemployment.) Alluding to the Salvationist's notion of joy in the 'stage version' of the play, the Dreamer tells Jannice: 'There's no peace or joy for you where he is. To him, peace may bring joy; to such as you, only joy can give you peace' (Scene III). The Dreamer also affirms: 'No one has a right to life who doesn't fight to make it greater'; a central tenet in O'Casey's own basic humanistic beliefs, reiterated, as well, by Shaw.

Shavianism even influenced, to some extent, the dramatic beliefs of O'Casey, who believed, like his fellow-dramatist, that 'the drama was born of old from the union of two desires: the desire to have a dance and the desire to hear a story' (with emphasis on narrative taking second place). Like his mentor, he was not, principally, a story-teller: things occurred to him as scenes, with action and dialogue. Exclaiming in *The Flying Wasp* (1937), his controversial book of theatre criticism, that 'realism in the theatre has been picked pretty clean', O'Casey agrees with Allardyce Nicoll that

> we do not want merely an excerpt from reality; it is the imaginative transformation of reality . . . we desire. The great art of the theatre is to suggest, not to tell openly; to dilate the mind by symbols, not by actual things.

Drama, O'Casey is firmly convinced, has grown out of dancing quite as much as from out of song and words. His ambition in *Within the Gates*, as he tells us in *Blasts and Benedictions*, is to

> put dancing and song back again where they belong and make the movements of the body express something quite as well as the sound of the voice.

At the close of the play, dancing is in fact used as a ritualistic affirmation of the creed which the Young Whore has learned from the Dreamer, that 'man can study man, or worship God, in dance and song and story' (Scene I). Jannice's dance, like that of Jessie Taite's in the final act of *The Silver Tassie*, is symbolic of a declaration of life, joy and defiance, in which some participate and others do not, either through inclination or tragic circumstances beyond their control.

O'Casey's park-drama, though set in the heart of depressed London, has throughout an atmosphere of Arcadian loveliness: its opening chorus heralds the 'lovely confusion of singing of birds and of blossom and bud'. There are more than hints of Eden's garden. Politically, there is the inference that post-war capitalism and organised religion have peopled this particular Eden with misery and crippled humanity, just as in Blake's trenchant little poem, 'London', from *Songs of Experience*,

> the youthful harlot's curse
> Blasts the new-born infant's tear;

and O'Casey's Garden of Love is synonymous with Blake's: he, too, shares the eighteenth-century poet's grief at 'tombstones where flowers should be' and 'priests in black gowns . . . binding with briars' the artist's joys and desires. Like Shaw, O'Casey regards poverty as a crime (the influence of *Major Barbara* again) and prostitution, as pointed out in *Mrs Warren's Profession*, another form of exploitation. It is in this light that O'Casey's sympathy for the exploited Jannice is so characteristic and so pervading in *Within the Gates*.

Similarly, the traditional Christian concept of the poor, voiced by the Bishop as 'the sacred aristocracy of God' (Scene III) – a variant on the poor-in-spirit principle – is also anathema to the playwright, speaking through his life-affirming characters, the Dreamer and Jannice. In her last moments, Jannice rejects the Bishop's assertion that her song should be identified with the sighing of the Down-and-Outs – a spiritual form of inanition worse than the death-in-life suffering of the crippled and maimed, resulting from World War I, so vividly portrayed in the final act of *The Silver Tassie*. Signalling fear and increasing hopelessness, the chant of the Down-and-Outs, to the accompaniment of menacing drum-beats, grows louder, engulfing all those who do not seek to strive and make a stand for a gay, intrepid and independent life. In a fit of premonition of palpitating heart-beats, and realising her death is near, Jannice (like Irish Nannie) reiterates her determination to 'go game' and 'die dancing'. In reckless abandon to all those around her, she dances with the Dreamer, responding to his invitation to 'sing them silent, dance them still and laugh them into an open shame!' Just before her final collapse, before the final curtain, the Dreamer encourages her with a defiant message of hope, which O'Casey himself has often since repeated, in Isaiah fashion, and reaffirmed: 'Fear nothing: courage in the hearts of men and women is what God needs most'. 'Courage', remarks Captain Shotover, 'will not save you, but it will show that your souls are still alive'.

Although O'Casey's Young Whore dies making the sign of the cross, the Dreamer's influence on her has remained. For he, too, we are reminded in *Windfalls*, worships God in his own way through the universe, just as the young woman of *Heartbreak House*, Ellie Dunn, tells Captain Shotover, 'we know now that the soul is the body, and the body the soul. They [the preachers of Christianity] tell us different because they want to persuade us that we can keep our souls if we let them make slaves of our bodies'. Jannice, too, in the end, has kept the faith, the Dreamer's faith, O'Casey's faith and Shaw's, too: faith in God through faith in Man. 'Let God's work be done for its own sake', says Major Barbara after her temporal conversion from the work of the Salvation Army, 'the work he had to create us to do because it cannot be done except by living men and women. When I die, let him be in my debt, not I in him'. And, as O'Casey underlines in *Sunset and Evening Star*: 'Advice from God was within ourselves, and nowhere else. Social sense and social development was the fulfilment of the law and the prophets. A happy people made happy by themselves. There is no other name given among men by which we can be saved, but by the mighty name of Man'.

Of all O'Casey's plays, *Within the Gates* may be the most difficult with which to come to terms.

While Jannice stands out as the principal character who undergoes a genuine religious or spiritual crisis, her indomitability and courage in the face of death so affect 'the Bishop that he begins to doubt his own ideals and actions. She has convinced him she is a better Christian than himself. At the end, all he can do is pray for

God's forgiveness and rebuke those like his Sister who are consumed with self-righteousness. Graham Greene's Father Rank, in *The Heart of the Matter*, following the death of Scobie, adopts a similar pattern: 'For goodness' sake . . . don't imagine you – or I – know a thing about God's mercy. The Church knows all the rules. But it doesn't know what goes on in a single human heart'.

Within the Gates is even more a 'conflict' play than O'Casey's previous drama, *The Silver Tassie*: it is a version of a modern morality, clothed in expressionist terms. Common to both morality and expressionistic plays is a perceptive central character, in this case Jannice, who reacts on a higher plane of consciousness than the other figures involved. Her role in this play is both long and strenuous. Her search for a spiritual goal or life-enriching process to resolve inner conflicts is paramount. Such conflicts are externalised through type or stock characters: the park attendants, evangelists, and members of the crowd. The speakers or religious controversialists are differentiated by the different hats they wear. Expounding the same stock opinions and shibboleths, they are intended to be absurdly comic and argumentative, in characteristic O'Casey comic-pathos style, in much the same way as his previous slum characters, etched in firm naturalistic mould, argue animatedly and uproariously among themselves. Important as it is from the producer's angle to get the correct slant on such improvisational episodes, it must be borne in mind that they do not constitute the essence of central experience embodied in this complex drama. The success of the play lies firmly on the shoulders of whoever is chosen for the part of the Young Whore.

The whole aim and direction of this play demand a bold, magnanimous and visionary approach. Emphasis, in O'Casey's words, must be on 'simple austerity, its swinging merriment, its beauty in music of word and colour of scene, and its tragedy too deep for tears'. The Dreamer is O'Casey's first attempt to create a positive hero of a new type. But it must be stated that a drawback for director and actor lies in the fact that his conception is too purely rhetorical and he is often too distanced from the significant action. On the other hand, all O'Casey's consummate skill has gone into the magnificent evocation of his heroine, the Young Whore, and O'Casey obviously sympathises with her.

The sixty-year-old Bishop is, in the playwright's words, 'anxious to show to all he meets that he is an up-to-the-present-minute clergyman, and that those who wear the stole are on the whole, a lusty, natural, broad-minded, cheery crowd'. He is good-natured, but his Sister, a few years younger, is sterner and more aloof from the creed-coveting crowd. Both the Bishop and the Young Whore are costumed in black throughout the play. The Bishop wears a black cassock with purple buttons and a pectoral cross, with a purple stock around his neck, in ecclesiastical style, and a purple biretta on his head, signifying his bishopric. The Young Whore is dressed in a black tailored suit, topped by a scarlet hat; on the hat is a black ornament of a crescent; and the hip of her dress is decorated, too, like Loreleen's in *Cock-a-Doodle Dandy*, with a scarlet ornament. The Dreamer is a lithely-built young man, but with rugged features and the appearance of a poet. He wears 'a tightly-belted trench mackintosh' and 'a light, vivid orange scarf' and a black, broad-brimmed hat. The Bishop's Sister is dressed in grey. The Atheist ('Ned') is a lean, wiry man of fifty. He wears a well-worn tweed top-coat with black muffler, and faded grey trilby hat. The Old Woman is white-haired and haggard-looking, though 'her face still shelters traces of what were once very good looks'. On stage she wears broken boots.

O'Casey's own guidance to social and symbolic significance of the extensive casting should not be overlooked. It is included in *Blasts and Benedictions*, in expressionistic prose, like a parable:

'The Young Whore', symbol of those young women full of life and a fine energy, gracious and kind, to whom life fails to respond, and who are determined to be wicked rather than virtuous out of conformity or fear.

'The Old Woman', symbol of those who stand still, think the little world was born to serve them, and that when they die, life dies too.

'The Gardener', symbol of the multitude mind moving on head down, shrinking from thought, and finding inspiration in all things cheap and everything easy. Seeking the things that present no risk and leave no risk behind them.

'The Young Man in Plus Fours', symbol of those young and old men whose whole life is an interest in the surface of women . . .

'The Evangelists', symbol of those preachers who daub the glories of God with mockeries.

'The Chair Attendants', symbols of life's wreckage who, with the Evangelists, are wasting life by living it.

'The Atheist', symbol of those who, trying to get rid of God, plant Him more firmly on His throne.

'Nursemaids and Guardsmen', symbols of those simple souls who take life as they find it, and, without much effort, make the best of it.

'The Disputants', symbols of those who hear and give great arguments, but are none the wiser for it all.

'The Young Salvation Army Officer', symbol of the coloured sob-stuff in organised religion that reflects no gleam from the mind of God, and brings no gleam to the mind of man.

'The Policewoman', symbol of woman dressed in a little brief authority.

'The Dreamer', symbol of a noble restlessness and discontent; of the stir in life that brings to birth new things and greater things than those that were before; of the power realizing that the urge of life is above the level of conventional morality; of ruthlessness to get near to the things that matter, and sanctify them with intelligence, energy, gracefulness and song; of rebellion against stupidity; and of the rising intelligence in man that will no longer stand, nor venerate, nor shelter those whom poverty of spirit has emptied of all that is worth while in life.

'The Down and Out', symbols of all who are dead to courage, fortitude, and the will to power; of those to whom a new thought or a new idea brings terror and dismay; of those who turn the struggle of life into a whine; of those, young or old, rich or poor, who in thought, word and deed, give nothing to life, and so are outcasts from life even as they live; even so.

It is important to discern, moreover, that *Within the Gates*, in the author's words, is 'a play written round life not from the outside looking in, but from the inside looking out'. It is a kaleidoscope of flamboyant colours, 'a patch of flame-coloured taffeta', singing and dancing its way into the sunlight. As O'Casey joyously proclaims in his other book of theatre recollections, *The Greeen Crow*: 'The flags are out. Come to the Fair! Life isn't La Danza, neither is she La Dirge. Though the dirge may be heard through the whirl of the dance, the dance is always stronger than the dirge'.

This conception of drama: 'a blend', says O'Casey, 'of classical, romantic and expressionist plays', must needs give rise to different forms of acting, production and audience-response. There is no gulf between real and symbolic, or between poetry and farce, in this play, and it must be recognised that this is a new element in drama. O'Casey's superb sense of a heightened vein of tragicomedy – more interlaced and pronounced, on occasions, than even Shaw's or Shakespeare's – shines through and never wavers. The same characters who are sketched in high relief at one moment stand out in tragic significance in the next and there is nothing false or incongruous about the change. Actors, schooled in the naturalistic trend and used to desporting themselves as central objects of such plays, could easily and without imaginative guidance from a sympathetic director, make of the play a meaningless impression. Vigour and sonority are merits of O'Casey's writing, and despite the use of cockney dialect on the lips of his subsidiary and 'driftwood' characters, the main rhythmic flow of dialogue spoken by principal characters lies in cadences of Irish speech.

One problem facing any director is choice of play texts: whether to opt for the original version of 1933, or the 'stage version' as printed in *Collected Plays*, vol. 2, which incorporates changes made by the playwright after the London and New York productions; changes which are quite substantially different in parts: mainly rewritten dialogue and some elimination of speeches and songs and a few minor characters; changes, some directors may feel, not always necessarily for the better, in which case compromise may well be the productive answer.

In comparing the two versions, consideration can be made, for instance, of the following episode – as previously quoted – from the end of Scene II, with that of the 'stage version': after the Dreamer's song, Jannice does not spurn his advances so abruptly as hitherto; her reaction is to tell the Dreamer, 'A pretty song, young singer, but its grace and meaning are hardly fit for me. I cannot live, or even hope, on the sweet sound of a song . . . Keep the little you have for yourself, young singer, for your life seems as uncertain as my own'. And instead of waltzing out with the Man in Plus-Fours, who, in the original, had been following her, she now encounters the Salvation Army Officer, while the Dreamer sits sadly on the bench opposite The air of 'Jannice', the revised directions tell us, is heard softly either on flute or violin. The scene concludes with the Salvation Army Officer and the Young Whore going slowly up the park slope and Jannice turning to the Dreamer with encouraging words, 'I have not quite forgotten your sweet song!'

Within the Gates had its *première* in London at the Royalty Theatre (in the same theatre where *Juno and the Paycock* was staged eight year previously) on 7 February 1934; 'hearsed within an atrocious production', O'Casey was to complain bitterly in *Rose and Crown*. It was a singular tragedy for the English theatre that the London production did not take place in a larger theatre instead of in a small one with impressions of a 'high-brow' atmosphere. Directed by Norman McDermott (who also designed; the music was by Herbert Hughes), the play ran for only twenty-eight performances. Present on the first night was the author with Shaw and Augustus John. Marjorie Mars played the part of the Young Whore, Sir Basil Bartlett played the Dreamer, Douglas Jefferies played the Bishop and Marie Ault played The Old Woman (Patrick Barr and Alan Wheatley were also among the cast). Notices were perceptibly cool. James Agate referred, contemptuously, to the play as 'pretentious rubbish', which angered the playwright, who later retaliated with a vitriolic article, 'The Cutting of an Agate', embodied in his controversial book of English theatre criticism, *The Flying Wasp*. Critics, by and large, measured the play by its furtive, timid production; though, in addition to poisoned chalices spilled, heart-warming toasts were raised. Martin Shaw, who directed the chanting in *The Silver Tassie*, wrote elatedly to the playwright: 'I saw the play . . . took T. S. Eliot. We both thought it rare'. T. E. Lawrence, in a second letter to Lady Astor, declared:

> I was right in feeling that this play would be bigger seen and heard, than merely read . . . Bless him again. He is a great man, still in movement . . . I have learned a great deal from him. When a rare Irishman does go on growing, you see, he surpasses most men. Alas, that they are so rare.

The New York production, at the National Theatre, on 22 October of the same year, in a fanfare of advance publicity heralded by Nathan and O'Neill, triumphed in its long run of a total of 141 performances. The production by George Bushar Markell and John Tuerk interpreted the true spirit of the play. Directed by Melvyn Douglas, the part of the Young Whore was played by Lillian Gish; Bramwell Fletcher played the Dreamer, Moffat Johnston played the Bishop and Mary Morris played the Old Woman. The huge cast – including chorus-singers, men and maidens – numbered seventy. Incidental music was by Milton Lusk and A. Lehman Engel, and dance arrangements were by Elsa Findlay. (Settings were by James Reynolds.) O'Casey himself visited America for rehearsals and performances, and, in *Rose and Crown*, pays due tribute thus: 'It was a beautiful production in every way, and any fault shown on the stage was in the play itself'. Brooks Atkinson, Broadway's esteemed critic, wrote enthusiastically, in the *New York Times*: 'Nothing so grand has risen in our impoverished theatre', and, in the opinion of Richard Watts of the *Herald-Tribune*, the play was declared 'theatre's most thrilling adventure'. On the success of the New York run, a tour of several American cities was planned, but in Boston several leading church organisations, headed by the Jesuits, succeeded in publicly banning the play. In form and theme, *Within the Gates* had proved too revolutionary for its time, even for America.

In an eloquent plea in his play's defence, O'Casey, in the closing section of *Rose and Crown*, reaffirms that the drama is neither offensive nor immoral:

> There is no more of venomous vice in the young woman of the play than there was in the young woman, Katerina Maslova, of Tolstoy's *Resurrection*; a book which, probably, the Jesuits never read, though a reading of it would do them more good than the reading of their Breviariums.

O'Casey's brave and beautiful play – a cry in itself, in the author's own words, 'for courage, decency and vitality in life' – was thus effectively swept from the boards for generations to come and has not been heard of or seen since, in either Broadway or the West End (though, in Ireland, there was a production at Belfast's Lyric in 1974). But it will find its actors and audience in the end, for it is the voice of a new and very real feeling about life. With its music and chanting and colour it gives visible form to our world today: it is a ritual symbolising of the very essence of life as we experience it. Its theme and mood remain undated.

Ideally, *Within the Gates* should be performed with all the panoply and magic which a large arena of a national theatre can bestow. Today, we are fortunate in possessing, especially in London, at the National and Royal Shakespeare Company's re-endowed premises such lavish and wideranging facilities in the shape of new and specially designed complexes. In the thirties, which witnessed the only two professional productions of O'Casey's play, no such resources were nationally available. A modern definitive production is, therefore, long overdue. A German translation is available.

9 *The End of the Beginning* (1934): a *Jeu-d'Esprit*

This one-act comedy is a well-flavoured, preposterous farce, one of two such sketches (the other being *A Pound on Demand*) included in the author's collection of *Windfalls*, revealing a welter of comicality within the confines of the shorter play form. Although brief in compass, they are remarkable instances of sustained, orgiastic comedy, aligning their coat-tails unmistakably in the seamless direction of *Juno and the Paycock* and the dramatist's other related and finely established masterpieces of Irish comedy.

Samuel Beckett, in an early critical notice, was quick to determine 'the principle of disintegration' inherent in O'Casey's superb classical clowning, explosively poised. O'Casey's unrestrained degree of incandescent comedy (whose natural outlet is farce) represents, for Beckett, 'the energy of his theatre', as well as what he discerns as 'the triumph of knockabout in situation, in all its elements – and in all its planes, from the furniture to the higher centres'.

Admiring *Juno and the Paycock* for its unique ability to release this quality of explosive laughter, where, in Beckett's expression, 'mind and world come asunder in irreparable dissociation', Beckett draws our attention to a furtherance of this eruptive technique, in these two delightfully executed miniatures: in particular, *The End of the Beginning*, where in natural progression 'the entire set comes to pieces and the chief character, in a final spasm of dislocation, leaves the scene by the chimney'.

Besides being a jaunty *jeu-d'esprit* in the rollicking traditions of farce, *The End of the Beginning* is a proliferation of talk and slapstick, carried along on its own tidal wave of richly inspired tomfoolery. Its subject is the inherent stupidity of man at odds with his environment, at the expense of probability, generating its own exorbitant fun. In origins, it belongs to the great submerged stream of folk-drama adorning the realms of widely-revered, universal farce.

167

Nathan was right to predict (in *The Entertainment of a Nation*, Alfred A. Knopf, 1942) that O'Casey's zany interlude 'would prove to be as hilarious a one-acter as our theatre has ever seen'.

The plot involves Darry Berrill – inveterate boaster in the style of 'Captain' Boyle – and his revengeful wife, Lizzie, who exchange jobs for a few brief hours to prove the alleged hardihood of man's perennial toil in relation to the supposed lighter chores of feminine domesticity. No sooner has his wife gone out to mow the fields than Darry is joined by his feckless friend, Barry Derrill, whose near-sightedness is such that 'he can't see the sky, unless the moon's shining in it!' The two butties are O'Casey's version of a music-hall duo, with twisted apron-strings, who proceed to wreak unimaginable havoc in the house, in the manner of Mutt and Jeff or Laurel and Hardy at their craziest. The obstinate Darry and near-sighted Barry fumble their way about, breaking almost everything within reach. It is irrational, rollicking fun.

Confrontation with such rude adversity not only provokes unadulterated, barracking laughter, but this is also caused by the psychological make-up of the characters O'Casey has deliberately created. His clowns are not ordinary clowns, or even man's *alter-ego*. They are variants of the unquenchable, arrogant 'paycockian' breed.

The main character, Darry Berrill, is a stocky, paunchy fifty-five-year-old and a domineering husband of uncontrollable vanity, who readily accepts his wife's challenge of exchange of domestic roles. His forty-five year old wife is domestically efficient but far from happily complacent. Her assumed natural commonsense hides a detectable vanity. Darry's friend and neighbour, Barry, in comparison with himself, is an easy-going pip-squeak but just as inanely self-confident. He is thin and ingratiating as well as suffering from the grave defects of bad vision; he is of the same age as Barry. They are as comical and well-matched as Boyle and Joxer in different circumstances.

It is Darry's pride which brings about the total fiasco, by encouraging his dimwitted, extremely near-sighted friend to make a hash of the chores. (The house is soon transformed into a near-wreck, preluding similar, hardly less sophisticated disasters, reserved for choicer moments in *Purple Dust*, *Cock-a-Doodle Dandy* and *The Bishop's Bonfire*.) His friend's vanity largely contributes because he insists upon showing off his illusory powers of self-imagined efficiency. Less patently, but apparent at the end, is his wife's vanity in thinking she can cure her husband of his folly by getting her own back and playing his own game. But she fails to realise the brow-beating husband (like the 'Paycock' in *Juno*) devises his own rules, and in wishing to humiliate her braggart-partner she is only thinly disguising her own vanity.

In the finish, Darry, like Boyle, overturns the blame onto her, so that it is he who is actually triumphant:

> DARRY (*to* LIZZIE): Now you see the result of havin' your own way! Why the hell didn't you hold on to the rope when you took it off the heifer, so that I wouldn't come down with a bump?
> LIZZIE: How'd I know you were hangin' on the other end?
> DARRY (*indignantly*): You didn't know – my God, woman, can you do nothin' right!

(And, ironically, all she can do is to repair the damage she has inadvertently helped to cause.)

The play was first produced at the Abbey Theatre, Dublin, on 8 February 1937. Arthur Shields directed, P. J. Carolan played Darry, Maureen Delany played Lizzie, F. J. McCormick played Barry. (It was revived in 1972 at the Company's Peacock Theatre, in John Lynch's production, along with the *première* of *Bedtime Story*.) Beatrix Lehmann directed the London *première* at the 'Q' Theatre on 16 October 1939. (Edgar K. Bruce played the husband, Beatrix Fielden-Kaye played his wife, John Laurie played the besotted neighbour, with huge success.) In America, Eddie Dowling presented the playlet, none too successfully, at Massachusetts in 1942, expunging the realism. There was also a London revival, at the Unity, directed by Ivor Pinkus in 1953.

Among foreign performances, the comic one-acter has been successfully staged in Paris, at the Théâtre de L'Oeuvre in 1939 and at the Théâtre de Bourgogne in 1968. In Germany, it remains an established favourite: it had its *première* in Berlin in 1966 by Moritz Milar; there were revivals there both in 1967 and 1975, and it was also featured, with *Bedtime Story*, in Gerhard Wruck's presentation at Neustrelitz in East Germany. Translations have appeared in French, German, Spanish, Russian, Persian and Roumanian.

Thurber's aphorism that 'humour is emotional chaos remembered in tranquility', may be one reason why, directorially, the

broad potentials of O'Casey's hilarious one-act interludes have
lodged themselves so successfully and repeatedly in comic rep-
ertoires that have been instant hits with audiences of all temperaments and tongues.

10 *A Pound on Demand* (1934): a Farcical Sketch

This little interlude is a rumbustious revue-sketch, which, as Philip Hope-Wallace in a pithy notice once acutely observed, 'is as nippy as a Charlie Chaplin prewar short'. Providing twenty exhilarating minutes of irrational, inexhaustible fun, it offers cornucopean farce, laden with tipsy extravagance; as rollicking as the drunken disintegration which finalises *Juno and the Paycock*. The same dehiscent touches light the fuse of devastating slapstick in the shorter play.

O'Casey chooses for his hero a workman whom he describes as 'in a state of maudlin drunkenness', one who is little more than 'a human bottle on shuddering legs' (to reinvoke Alan Brien's apt critical description), and transplants him, together with his wheedling companion, into the comparatively sedate quiet of a small, suburban sub-post office. The plot hinges on interpolations of indulgent, extravagant farce.

In the course of the sketch, the drunkenly paralytic Sammy, coerced by his parasitic friend, the feckless Jerry, into going through the official rigmarole of withdrawing a pound from his 'posht-offish' book, so as to ensure them another drink, is bedevilled by his own singularly unadaptable state of intoxication. Although unable to make the necessary signature on the form for withdrawal, despite frantic posturings from his mate (flaunting an aggressive tweed-cap, and acting, vicariously, as his civil rights defender), the irreparable Sammy is sufficiently alert to quarrel with an indignant, stoutish lady in an adjoining cubicle, who is mailing a letter to remote Tarraringapatam, to the perplexity of the girl-in-charge of the post office. ('Nex' parish but one t' ourish', interjects Sammy; 'Bus stop in the jungle', quips his mate, but is reproved sharply by the indignant lady, representing outraged public opinion.)

171

Amid maundering hilarity and efforts of topsyturvydom, a shadow of a signature is extracted from the wobbly applicant, with the over-assistance of his mate. As it bears no resemblance to the signature in the post office book, the girl decides to telephone for a policeman, which provokes a series of braggingly inflated responses, ending in: 'Poleeish to the right of me, 'n to the left of me, 'n nothing left of them in the end but silver buttons for souvenirs'.

Eventually, after more inestimable heroics, the two rascals find themselves flung out; and, in a classic moment of bathos, in the finish, the soberer of the two shouts through the door, with muddled malevolence: 'That's the last penny of our money the Government 'll ever get from us!'

In the unbridgeable clash between drunkenness and civil authority, national as well as professional foibles are exploited for the sake of riproaring, ubiquitous farce.

The sketch, which is included in *Collected Plays*, vol. 1 (along with *The End of the Beginning*), has great entertainment value, and, because of its absurd and robust buoyancy, has been produced many times, especially abroad. For the sketch to retain its savour, the drunkard's performance needs to be overwhelming. He and his mate are compounded on the broad-comic techniques of Boyle and Joxer, and bear the marks and transparencies of that incomparable duo. In supreme argumentativeness, they befuddle their way throughout.

The English *première* coincided with the outbreak of war. It was performed, in a triple bill, at London's 'Q' Theatre on 16 October 1939 (along with *The End of the Beginning* and Strindberg's *Pariah*). In Beatrix Lehmann's presentation, Edgar K. Bruce played the drunken Sammy, with John Laurie as his mate, Beatrix Fielden-Kaye as the Woman, Irene Handl as the Post Office Girl, and Alan Wheatley as the Policeman. *The Times* drama critic noted well enough that O'Casey 'shares with Mr Shaw a relish for knockabout farce. Its farcical situation is adroitly transformed into comedy'. In later revivals in London expert clowning triumphed. In Deni Carey's production at the Mercury Theatre in 1947, Fred Johnson and Liam Redmond clowned their way through the debacle. But it was not until its introduction in the Mermaid's celebrated presentation of *The Shadow of a Gunman*, with Jack MacGowran in the wobbly role of Sammy (assisted by Barry Keegan as Jerry, and

Shivaun O'Casey as the Post Office Girl), that the full force of slapstick resounded resplendently in Abraham David's presentation, establishing the play assertively in its own right.

The American *première* in 1946 at New York's International, as a prelude to Victor Jory's *Androcles and the Lion*, resulted in a lame direction, but the imbalance was redressed in 1959 in David Hay's presentation (*Bedtime Story* was featured in the four-part programme), when the Cronyns decked it with high comedy. In Ireland, the play has been curiously neglected (the amateur Irish Festival Players staged it in 1957 at Wexford).

Abroad, it has been done several times in Germany. Adolf Dresen's 1965 Berlin *première* was a hit (in a triple bill with *Hall of Healing* and *The Moon Shines on Kylenamoe*) and there was a revival by Gerhard Wruck in the city in 1968. Other revivals in 1968 and 1969 were at Cottbus and Leipzig. In France, it was staged in 1972 at Nevers, though Jean-Pierre Vincent's splendid 1978 revival in Strasbourg finally established its place in the French comic repertoire. Translations exist in Afrikaans, French, German, Irish, Russian and Spanish.

11 *The Star Turns Red* (1940): a Futuristic Extravaganza

O'Casey's next full-length play is a significant plunge into the field of serio-comic fantasy: an anti-fascist parable that is more than just a political extravaganza or 'fancied page of history'; a future warning whose urgency is even more pressing than Shaw's in *Heartbreak House* or *Geneva*; in design and texture, differently styled, and though lacking, ultimately, the epic strength of Shaw's fantasias, it more than compensates for the piquancy of its full-blooded onslaught on national complacency and its vision of a magical Armageddon.

In this play, O'Casey has nailed his colours firmly to the mast of symbolism and romantic melodrama, and the flag he is flying is the flag with the bright ray of socialism on its banner in the face of an upsurging fascism under Hitler which threatens to undermine the moral fabric of East and West alike. Fresh in his mind, when he wrote the play in 1937–8, was the Franco victory, aided by Hitler and Mussolini, in the Spanish Civil War of 1936. In addition, Mosley's Fascists, in black-shirted defiance, were parading through London streets, trotting their way, as they believed, to brighter pavilions, as likewise were General O'Duffy's Blue Shirts in Ireland. Peeping into the political future, O'Casey wrote this apocalyptic play before the swirling flood-waters of international war had broken loose, and, as he later told a correspondent, 'to awaken all to the menace of Nazism'. Soon afterwards, as he was able to relate in retrospect in *Sunset and Evening Star*: 'a great part of the world was about to do a ballet-dance in ruin'. The moment of holocaust had arrived.

Even in Britain, and elsewhere, today, there is no cause for adversarial complacency, with the emergence on political horizons of such menacing circlets as the National Front or Ku Klux Klan: fascist dominated and inspired. 'The neo-Nazism flaunted by some of these extremists is deeply offensive to the vast majority of the public and is a challenge to all the cherished values of our society', remarked the chairman of the British Commission for Racial Equality, Sir David Lane, when surveying the state of race relations in Britain at the beginning of 1981. We should never forget that fascism has more than once provided the Governments of Italy, Germany, Argentina, Greece and Spain; and its ugly resurgence remains a constant threat to peace and international stability.

The Star Turns Red is immensely topical and will be while democratic harassment remains socially intolerable and as long as opposing ideologies continue to confront each other 'here as on a darkling plain', in Matthew Arnold's vivid phrase, and where 'ignorant armies clash by night'. An impassioned fiery call, therefore, on the playwright's part, to the barricades in the day of reckoning: a view indeed of Armageddon; savage also in its swipes at Church and State in pre-war, purblind, Georgian England, and yet tender and rollicking by turns in its kaleidoscopic humour. (Equally purblind critics have labelled this play 'a political tract' – which adroitly it is not – and the author's most humourless as well; which, again, it is not: the one, I suppose, necessarily following from the other, in the view of certain misplaced, axiomatic minds.) In fact, both to read and see performed, the play is electrifying in the cadence of its Shakespearian English, making the revolutionary plays of Brecht and Arden, by comparison, pallid. O'Casey's cataclysmally conceived play is a theatrical broadside levelled at the 'No-brotherhood-in-our-boat' kind of philosophy, associated, in particular, with the declining civilisation of the mid-thirties, with its overriding 'only-who-can-cut-the-biggest-dash-and-who-can-swim' type of solutions, inherent in ugly reality in Graham Greene's *England Made Me* and also in Evelyn Waugh's *A Handful of Dust*.

The fierce social criticism which was first given explicit expression in *The Silver Tassie* in the form of 'opinions' which so soul-shocked Yeats and which deepened in intensity in *Within the Gates* (over-balancing the mental equilibrium of Agate) has found its honest and courageous answer in *The Star Turns Red*; the Red Star being O'Casey's symbol of signifying 'the herald . . . of man's ascent, bettering all things done; a badge on the people's banner'; an extension of the political faith propounded so nobly in *The Plough and the Stars*. Although O'Casey glorifies the goals and ideals which stem from communism, the play is not, as some leading London dramatic critics had believed, a pamphlet for the stage or communist tract, which, in the opinion of A. V. Cookman, at least, 'could not hope that its vehement drama would live down the unpopularity of the subject'. There is no degree of dogma as such in the play, and O'Casey has reiterated as much, both in interviews and in letters; though, assuredly, the play represents a confession of faith. The flame that keeps it burning is, as Shaw recognised, the spirit and prophecy of the English Bible.

Shaw was eulogistic enough: to O'Casey, he wrote, playful as ever: 'It shewed up the illiteracy of the critics who didn't know that like a good Protestant you had brought the language of the Authorized Version back to life. Splendid!' Shaw was acquainted with only the text published in 1940, a month before the advent of the London wartime production, which, because of his age, the black-out and other considerations, Shaw was unable to attend.

Ivor Brown's was one of few voices who discerned the playwright's essential purpose: 'The play is one of battle', he rightly surmised from the published version, 'and its trumpet calls are magnificently written in a series of unscanned poetry which raids both the Irish vernacular and the scriptures for its riches'.

An unexpected rhapsody came from the lips of James Agate, anxious on this occasion to make critical amends and to declare to the implacable and commercial theatrical world of the West End, with whom O'Casey was wholly at odds, that 'Mr O'Casey's play is a masterpiece . . . The passion, pathos, humour, and, above all, poetry with which this great play is hung, are there for all the world to see and hear'. The playwright later confided to a friend, in May 1942: '[Agate] calling *The Star Turns Red* a masterpiece shows him down; it isn't anything like one; I wish it were. It has a fine third scene, and good bits, here and there; but a masterpiece – no'.

O'Casey sent a copy of the play, before publication, to Nathan, in America, for his critical comments, adding:

It is, I think, much more compact than *Within the Gates*, though I don't yet know how much of the verse form ought to go to a play dealing with present-day life. There was too much singing in *Within the Gates*, or, maybe, as is most probable, the singing was in the wrong place; or the chanting, or whatever we can call it. The action takes place during the last few hours of a Christmas Eve; and by this means, I've managed, I think, to give an ironical twist here and there. And I've tried to give a symbolism in the coloring of the four scenes, as you will see.

Nathan did not share Agate's enthusiasm (he never saw the work in performance as there was no American production). Judged from his comments in print, he was inclined to derogate O'Casey's latest political will-o'-the-wisp as 'incontrovertibly poor', though 'peculiarly invested with a poet's prophetic vision'. Never a lover of propagandist plays, Nathan had written in *Encyclopedia of the Theatre* (1940):

> The fault of the proletarian boys is that they believe the only way you can make an argument impressive is to put it into a sandbag and hit the other fellow over the head with it. As a result, the plays they write and the plays they endorse are largely indistinguishable from so many holdups. To persuade an audience fully, the weapons must be equally distributed between the play and the audience.

The Star Turns Red, however, is no 'sandbag' drama. Tensions between the two sides: Saffron Shirts representing the fascists on the one hand, with their allies the repressive church leaders of the Christian Front, supported by most of their congregationalists and poorest neighbours of the community; and Communists on the other, very much isolated in their embattled support and lacking the bulk of trade union backing, presages uncertainty and maintains suspense all the way through. Victory for the freedom-fighters is only assured in the course of the final act.

What in the hands of a less-gifted playwright could so easily have become a hackneyed, proprietary theme is seen in this transcendentally conceived opus as a shining Aaron's rod, resplendent with an armoury of heroics and blossoming into a stage extravaganza of stirring proportions, uplifting in both language and convictions. Agate was right to observe: 'I see in it a flame of propaganda tempered to the conditions of dramatic art, as an Elizabethan understood that art'.

In one sense, *The Star Turns Red* is a parable about the role of forces of world socialism; in another, a stylised fantasy propounding the destiny of humanist heritage and man's future; in the voice and spirit of Yeats, in the manner of his play, *The King's Threshold*:

> Oh, silver trumpets be you lifted up,
> And cry to the great race that is to come.

O'Casey stresses fellowship of man in the wake of the Second World War and world nemesis. The underlying message is simply: who at such a turning-point in the world's upheaval (most of O'Casey's dramas are about upheaval or 'chassis') inherits the mantle of Christ in avowed overthrow of obsolescent Christian ideals? Who, in tomorrow's world, speaks with divine authority and hope? A Christmas play, indeed, with a twist; and one with a futuristic slant. A play, once again, that is religious in form and significance in its code of ethical values.

O'Casey once modestly declared in a letter dated 21 March 1940:

> There is little more in [the content] than there is in the American Constitution or in Lincoln's declaration of 'Government of the people, by the people, for the people'; or, in the prophecy by the prophet Amos, accepted as canonical by all the Anglican Communions – which they have conveniently forgotten; as they have forgotten many other things.

(Publication never went ahead in America at the time; America was implacably anti-communist: the Nazi-Soviet Pact and Russo-Finnish War proved political stumbling-blocks as well.)

In many respects the most committed of all O'Casey's plays, reflecting confrontation between Right and Left, whether it be seen in a historical context or present-day or future connotation, or, merely as an allegory, the play demonstrates the assured political and artistic maturity of its author and his theatrical expertise in carrying it through with pyrotechnic brilliance on stage and with the same flamboyant panache which accompanies *Within the Gates*. In this play, the mixture of Irish and English elements, of language – both poetry and prose – of realism and symbolism, presents a formidable challenge to the talents of any professional production at its highest.

The huge cast of twenty-nine characters or *personae*, typed rather than individually presented (though in performance actors may imbue some of these types with individuality), is further augmented with battalions of Red Guards, Saffron Shirts, soldiers and sailors, and others representing a crowd-scene endemic to the general action in this four-act play. In all, the resources of a protean company are needed, as for *Within the Gates*.

The Old Man and Old Woman are, up to a point, Boyle and Juno types in a transformed situation, where locality is not specified.

though accents are unmistakably Dublin. The author dedicates his play 'To the Men and Women Who fought through the Great Dublin Lockout in nineteen hundred and thirteen', whom O'Casey regards as precursors of revolution: flame-throwers symbolising the rising of Red Army soldiers in the Russian Revolution of 1917; prototypes not so much of the international struggle between labour and capital (treated in his later play, *Red Roses for Me*) but of the perpetual struggle between communism and fascism. It is in that setting with which the play opens; in what many would see as a typical O'Casey Dublin setting, in one of the city's rundown old Georgian houses or tenements.

Acts One and Three have such a dwelling, occupied by the old couple on an upper floor, for the location; Act Two is staged at the headquarters of the General Workers' Union; whilst Act Four is set in the lounge of the Lord Mayor's residence. The action takes place late on a Christmas Eve: time is deliberately overshadowed as 'tomorrow, or the next day'.

The main protagonists are the sons of the Old Man and Old Woman: Jack, a communist sympathiser and activist; his brother Kian, a fascist supporter and member of the fictional Saffron Shirt movement in league with the imaginary Christian Front; the Purple Priest, the chief spokesman for the Church, in sympathy with the fascists; and Red Jim, leader of the communists, poet and political leader, based on – and a tribute to – Jim Larkin of Dublin (1876–1947), whose sympathies, ideals and friendship are shared by the playwright, as illustrated in *Drums Under the Windows*; and whose inspirational and agitational role in the Dublin Lockout sparked off scenes of realism as graphic as those portrayed in *Juno and the Paycock*.

In *The Star Turns Red* character is attitude; message and theme are all important. Yet, because of its humour, directness and simplicity, as well as its tremendous drive and sense of theatricality and constant ability to sustain surprise with the effective use of symbolism, it is a work more easily appreciated and easier to stage than *Within the Gates*, with which, nevertheless, it has close affinities in style and technique.

The extensive cast-list comprises: the Old Man and Old Woman; Jack and Kian, their sons; Julia, Jack's sweetheart, and Michael, her father; Joybell, 'a Catholic flagwagger' – O'Casey's phrase – and confraternity man; the Purple Priest (named 'Red Priest' in the first edition), a servant of fascism; Brown Priest of the poor, lukewarm at first in support for the workers' cause, but later shows himself a man of the people as well as a man of God; the Lord Mayor and Lady Mayoress, official representatives of the local establishment; the collaborationist section of the trade union leadership, represented by Messrs Sheasker, Brallain, Caheer, Eglish and their pale shadow of a Union Secretary; Red Jim, socialist warrior and leader of the workers; Brannigan, his brawny accomplice; neighbours of the old couple, a cross-section of the local poor including, Man with Crutch, Blind Man, Young Man with Cough, Woman with Withered Baby, a Hunchback, and a Well-Dressed Man; First and Second Workmen at Lord Mayor's Residence, together with Worker at telephone (in the final insurrection scene); plus a score of Red Guards, Saffron Shirts and a Crowd.

Although there is much individual incident involving sharply drawn characters, most of these are not fully developed in the naturalistic sense: they are merely passengers on O'Casey's battle-train to revolution. Interest never flags, and there are moments of sparkling heroics, and a conclusion that is reached is moving melodrama. The play is intended to be both romantic and confrontational; rhetorical and resplendent, melodramatic and tragicomic at the same time. In its blending of realism and symbolism – scenes of naturalism rise to poetry and choral speech and converge into a ritual of pageantry – it whirls across the stage in a splurge of sound and colour. The ending is unashamedly Boucicaultian, the climax essentially Shakespearian: two formative influences we learn, from *Pictures in the Hallway*, that were to remain with the dramatist throughout his theatrical years of wisdom and experience.

When the play begins it is Christmas time and the Star of Bethlehem is in the east. This is signified by the large 'shining silver star' silhouetting the church spire, seen through one of the windows of the house of the Old Man and Woman. Through the other window are silhouettes of two smoke-filled factory chimneys. As the curtain rises, the significance of the expressionist star in the background foreshadows a widening of the kitchen-set into the greater political arena of conflict and ceremonial to come, as domestic dissensions set the pace for deeper and more divisive action later. The two sons, in their brief foregathering on stage, sneer at each other's political persuasions, while the Old Man and Old Woman are preoccupied with a sparring-match of their own about an impending strike, following the Old Man's pronouncement that 'The workers are getting like the tides now – always either coming in or going out, with their lightning strikes, stay-in strikes, stay-out strikes, sit-down strikes, and go-easy strikes . . . till the whole land's quivering with the rush around of revolution'. The sparring sparks off a scene of racy comedy, reminiscent of the cut-and-thrust between Juno and Boyle:

OLD WOMAN (*sorrowfully*): And the peace of Christmas, too, nearly down on top of us.

OLD MAN (*peevishly*): Oh, what has Christmas got to do with a stay-in strike or men arming? (*with his nose in his football coupons.*) Two away and three at home. (*Raising his head again.*) There's no use of bringing in mistletoe to stop a stay-in strike.

OLD WOMAN: I never once mentioned the word mistletoe.

OLD MAN: Oh, do try to keep your ears open so that you may hear what you're saying yourself. Why don't you be honest, and admit saying the saying that's still hot on your tongue?

OLD WOMAN: I never once mentioned mistletoe; never once.

OLD MAN (*furiously*): Don't be so positive, woman! The minute you mentioned the stay-in strike, you smothered it in mistletoe.

OLD WOMAN: Don't you be so positive.

OLD MAN: I'm not a bit positive. I simply said that it was you and not me who mentioned the word mistletoe. And, if I hadn't checked you, you'd have brought in bunches of holly and ivy too!

OLD WOMAN: I was just trying to think of something to stem the disorder that's sowing itself everywhere.

OLD MAN: Well, a barrage of holly and ivy won't avail much.

This is underlined later in the same act, when Jack, after the Old Woman's incantations on the peace of Christmas, as symbolised by its silver star, vehemently declaims: 'So it shone when it led the kings; so shall it not shine when it leads the people. It leads no more, and never shall till its silver turns to red'. In short-sighted dismissals of derision, the Old Man brings the dissensions to an abrupt end with his 'Oh, let's think of serious things, and not be disturbing our heads about stars and kings and never-present princes of peace! 'A domestic squabble is therefore skilfully presented in O'Casey's classic bathos-style, and given a kaleidoscopic twist later signifying allegorical allusions of more important divergencies of opinion on an international scale. It prepares us for the moving threnody at the end of the third act – with its choral chanting, accompanied by a steady drum-roll – when followers of Red Jim, after the death of their comrade Michael, reaffirm their determination to fight on for their cause, chanting: 'Aha, Red Star, arise the wide world over!'

The Red Star – implicit in the overall message of the play and explicit in the playwright's later volumes of autobiography – is identified here with the evening star; as, again, by its choice of title, the concluding volume of autobiography, *Sunset and Evening Star* – which derives from Tennyson's poem, 'Crossing the Bar' – is associated with noble aspirations in the dramatist's evening walk of life. In the play, the star that turns red is the Star of Christmas; and its social change symbolises a religious transformation, just as transition on a universal basis is also symbolically suggested in *Sunset and Evening Star:* 'In the uprising of the peoples, the spirit of God is once more moving over the face of the waters'. This was O'Casey's own road to communism, through the spirit of early Christianity to its modern-day equivalent, international socialism. 'In a storm of curses, God can bless', is the Brown Priest's message, at the end of the play:

> The star turned red is still the star
> Of him who came as man's pure prince of peace;
> And so I serve him here.

(The deep feeling for violence which Carlyle, in *The French Revolution,* declared to be religious in origin has obviously influenced O'Casey.)

As we have seen, in the context of *Within the Gates*, it is an extension of Shavian philosophy, voiced by Major Barbara herself and Lavinia (the good-looking young Christian woman of *Androcles and the Lion*) who vows, in clear tones, the new faith: 'I'll strive for the coming of the God who is not yet', and echoed somewhat elliptically by the elphin Androcles: 'Whilst we stand together, no cage for you: no slavery for me'. It is the core of O'Casey's own philosophy as well. For him, such is the true significance of Emily Brontë's 'steadfast rock of Immortality' and Yeats's 'red flare of dreams'. Heaven's glories shining in earthly satisfaction, as spelt out in the closing chapter of *Sunset and Evening Star:*

Work is the reveille and the last post of life now, providing for man, making leisure safe, enjoyable, and longer, profiting body, soul, and spirit, having a song in itself, even when the sun sets on old age, and the evening star shines a warning of the end.

Warning-notes which come from the logic of the calendar and passage of seasons are present, too, in the life-tapestry of the play. And, when *The Star Turns Red* was refused publication in America, O'Casey gently chided:

> I agree that war is a stupid and bloody business. I have seen a lot of it in my day. But intelligent and fair men must begin to bring about a condition of things in which the bounty of the earth will be possessed by all. If this war spreads, it will end in revolution, bloody revolution. A peaceful, if possible, revolution would, in my opinion, be wiser. 'Come, let us reason together, saith the Lord of Hosts.' *The Star Turns Red* is a warning.
>
> (*Letters*, vol. 1)

The inference is clear: he that hath ears to hear, let him hear. But, in putting across his message, O'Casey does so in his accomplished, light-hearted way; and, tragicomically, the synthesis is successfully achieved.

One of the ancillary themes is false or illusory peace in a conflict-torn world: the same peace which is usually invoked by all mankind at Christmastide, symbolised by the old star – with its images of false Christs and false beliefs – in which the Old Woman and others still place hope. In the play, official representatives of the community – the Purple Priest, Lord Mayor and Joybell (the chattering ministrant of the Christian Front), plus collaborationist elements of trade union leadership (mercilessly flayed in the second act) – are all shown to be false purveyors of 'peace' in a world of spiritual and social decay: cohorts of fascism, derided by O'Casey, making his audience laugh with him (in the manner of Shaw), in this political parable which is both carnival and catharsis.

In Joybell, with his bubbling talk, we see O'Casey flaying false piety and human sanctimoniousness. We listen to him babbling on:

> Nearly here, too, Christmas – only a few hours you might say; just a few more, not more, not many. Grand festival; best of all; dearest, too; jolly times – God rest you merry, gentlemen, you

know, and all that; Immanuel, God with us. Everybody at their best. Holly and ivy; peace and goodwill and plenty; Early Mass, the crib, holy night, and – and – and shepherds watching their flocks – flocks by night – and – and all eyes turned towards the star – your star, my star, his and her star, their star!

Joybell, who suffers reproaches from his fellows with good-hearted, religious equanimity (though one of the workmen in the final act cruelly dubs him 'a praying compound of fear and favour'), is really a mock-representative of a certain section of the Irish Catholic laity, exuding an impenetrable and imperturbable jollity yet blithely unaware and ignorant of most human affairs, and at the same time displaying an unquestioning, almost child-like respect for the doctrines of the Church, as expounded by her ministers ('the Lord's anointed . . . the apple of God's eye', mockingly alluded to in Joyce's *Portrait of the Artist as A Young Man*).

Repressive instincts of a narrow Catholicism, commonly accepted as normal in Dublin – but peculiar only to 'the Pope's Green Island' at the time – are ruthlessly pilloried by O'Casey; when we see Joybell's reaction on being diverted from his usually more pious preoccupations to more natural interests; when, as, in the first act he is suddenly confronted with the desiring glances of Julia, who teases him with her enticing 'Give me a squeeze, a tight one, and make me giddy!' (The same experience and reaction later befall Rankin, the bigoted bricklayer, in the early scenes of *The Bishop' Bonfire*, when Keelin flaunts her winsome sexual charms.) The sudden release of Joybell's suppressed instincts has the momentar effect of near-brutality as the joke backfires and the Old Woman comes out with a typical, grandiloquent, O'Casey-sounding phrase 'This is a quare eye-opener against the innocent look of hol habiliments', capped by Joybell's own protestation, 'It was th streel herself that plucked me into misbehaviour'.

The Purple Priest, who is also introduced in Act One, is a harsh spokesman of the Church, sinisterly portrayed. He exhibits none of the more liberal-minded though ineffective good-will of the Bishop as seen in *Within the Gates*. A sterner, more repressive figure ('dead hearted' he is referred to by Jack) he is ruthless in his broad interpretation of religious aims; in league with reactionary political groups and pressures – in this play, the fascists – to advance th spread of a stultifying faith which has become merely a parody, as emphasised by his droning, religious chant based on rhythms of

church ritual. His language and approach are similar to those of
Shaw's Inquisitor and Archbishop in *Saint Joan*. Allusions to Julia's
scantily dressed attire and Jack's wearing of the Red Star on his coat
in open defiance of the Circle and Flash as flaunted by the Saffron
Shirts – worn, also, in their day by Mosley's followers – reveal
themselves in his Draconian diction:

> I see before me a poor daughter of Eve dressed for a folly that will
> fondle sin with a busy finger; I see before me a son of God wearing
> the badge of the enemy, man's enemy, the Church's enemy,
> God's own enemy. The one must strip off the dress of folly and put
> on a garment meet for penance and prayer; the other must cast
> away a badge that insults the soul of a child of God.

When Jack and Julia refuse to obey, distant drum-beats, offstage,
which earlier had indicated the marching of Saffron Shirts in
readiness to support a rally of the Christian Front organised by the
Church, now give a resounding roll, followed by a terrifying shout of
Hail the Circle and the Flash!' preluding the entrance of the
Leader of the Saffron Shirts, together with Kian and some of their
troopers. The Purple Priest joins in their formal salute, thus
identifying a repressive type of Catholicism with a faceless,
reactionary wing of political power.

Julia is seized and dragged from the room and ordered to be
whipped. The Brown Priest's plea of mercy is unheeded, and the
Old Woman's to Kian ignored, as the leader warns those of the
household: 'Neither drum nor trumpet tells of our second coming:
we come silently, like a thief in the night: we come silently, and we
strike at once!'

The moment of melodrama approaches when Michael, the girl's
father and a rabid supporter of the communists, bursts in upon the
scene and lashes those present with his verbal fury. To the Leader,
after demanding the whereabouts of Julia, he shouts: 'So you're
finding out that in spite of . . . your outstretched paw saluting
cruelty' – a clearly-intended reference to Hitler's bullying tactics in
Europe – 'the workers are getting the guts to fight!' In a frenzy of
fury, Michael, who rushes at the Leader, calling him a 'slug-soul'd
renegade', is shot by Kian, mouthing the cruel slogan of the
movement: 'The Flash strikes those who strike at the rim of the
Circle', reinforced by the Leader's taunt: 'the gaping mouth shall be
shut tight; the violent shall be made meek'. The Old Woman's

shocked reaction is submissively Junoesque: 'Oh, Kian, my son, my poor, sense-forsaken son, what have you done!' The act closes, melodramatically, with the dying Michael's last symbolic, dramatic gesture of defiance, reflected in the words: 'Jack, comrade . . . my arm – raise it, lift it high; lift it up. Lift it up in the face of these murdering bastards – the Clenched Fist!'

The second act changes kaleidoscopically: symmetrical figures are now the illustrious representatives of the General Workers' Union, viewed with a jaundiced eye by the playwright, changing their colours by rotation of socio-religious pressures from those connected with the Christian Front, and constantly scheming among themselves to topple Red Jim from leadership and to abrogate for themselves and their members a more milk-and-water type of socialism in preference to the red-blooded sort envisaged by Red Jim. They represent collaborationist elements of the trade unions: the renegades, as O'Casey sees them, of the Left. All are faithlessly disposed to associate with capitalists, conspiring with the Christian Front to betray the ideals of Jim.

Sheasker's intention is to act the part of Father Christmas at the Lord Mayor's tea-party, sanctimoniously dispensing his favours to the poor, having accepted bribes from hard-line capitalists disloyal to the cause of Labour. Ironically, above them, in the room of the Union building where they meet, is stretched a slogan of true socialists – also employed by Larkin in his day – 'An injury to One i the Concern of All', while, as the act proceeds, they reveal themselves in all their traitorous glory, the hollowness of which the playwright scornfully portrays, from acid comments by those on stage concerning Sheasker's presentation portrait adorning one of the walls of the meeting-room: 'little more like Caesar than a woman's spit'; reinforced by Brannigan's later gibes: 'You golden snouted snails!' 'You tied-up pack of employers' silk and shiny coloured dressing-gowns!', as well as Red Jim's own scathing references to 'a bunch of barking mongrels!' and 'You gang of daws!' (O'Casey, here, adopts Shakespeare's colourful anatomy of swearing.)

In a further twist of irony, there is an interruption in the cabalistic proceedings, when all stiffen in expectation of seeing Red Jim enter, only to be confronted and confounded by one of his henchmen, the brawny, red, rough-spoken, drunken Brannigan, armed in Citizen Army fashion with bayonet, who bursts in upon the meeting expecting to find Red Jim. Unceremoniously flung out by the other for gate-crashing a private meeting, Brannigan's exit becomes a curse-filled departure to the accompaniment of a splendid spit, aimed right in the middle of the eye of an astonished Brallain, invoking memories of tobacco-juice and spits from among crowds that followed Parnell in political demonstrations in County Wicklow, as recollected so incisively round the Christmas dinner-table in Joyce's *Portrait of the Artist*. (Brannigan departs with a self-satisfied, well-flung, Irish-sounding retort: 'You envy-stippled titivated toad'.) Back again, minutes later, demanding maternity-benefit due to his wife, there are more cannonading curses from Brannigan, reminding one, forcibly, of Joyce's disparaging comments, through his characters, on priests who hounded Parnell into his grave: 'Sons of bitches, lowlived dogs!'

In a scene of splendid knockabout, Brannigan, having again been ordered out of the room by the four officials and their bovine secretary, surprises them by whipping out his bayonet and then has them cowering in front of him, while he demands his dues from union funds. At rifle-point, they kneel before a delighted Brannigan and look extremely uncomfortable as a proletarian knighthood is forced upon them from the jeering Brannigan (in a Don Quixote burlesque) to the accompaniment of more rich-sounding expletives in the grand manner. After Brannigan's exultant exit, recriminations mount, forestalled only by the Brown Priest's sudden entry, announcing that Red Jim's arrest is to be sought by the authorities and warning that he must hide. When Caheer pipes up that Red Jim is a danger to everyone, the Brown Priest realises that traitors are within his own camp.

Red Jim's entrance – and introduction – at this stage is the neatest of dramatic ironies as the plot to overthrow him thickens, aided and abetted by his own treacherous supporters. Red Jim invites the Brown Priest to join him in the fight ahead in a moving, eloquent plea, suggestive of a martyr's intuition of his fate and voiced in Shavian-tongued rhetoric, as witnessed in *Saint Joan*: 'To be with us when the star turns red; to help us to carry the fiery cross. Join with us. March with us in the midst of the holy fire'. The Brown Priest, who is not yet fully convinced, declines sadly. 'If I have done wrong may God forgive me!' 'He's forgiven worse!' is Jim's slightly bitter rejoinder.

Red Jim's discovery of apostasy within his own ranks produces venomous and recriminating wrath. The situation has historical parity with that which Larkin himself faced immediately after the

Dublin dispute of 1913. The Transport Union then had a reduced membership and treasury funds were practically nothing. After the Lockout there was no longer a pressing need to preserve a solid phalanx of Labour opinion, and some latent criticism of Larkin, similar to the oblique taunts aimed at Red Jim in this second act, began to make itself heard. Most of it centred round his alleged autocratic manner: 'acting like an arbitrary tribal chieftain', records Emmet Larkin, in his biography of the Irish Labour leader, and his apparent inability to husband money instead of distributing it to every individual case of deserving need. Solidarity inside the Union, as we see repeated in this play, had fallen apart. The stigma was all the more bitter in O'Casey's memory, having himself taken the workers' part and participated in the 1913 dispute, recalling – as he relates in *Drums Under the Windows* – 'the unfolding of the final word from the evolving words of the ages . . . the word En-Masse'.

The dynamism of Dublin's leader – and O'Casey's hero – on which the portraiture of Red Jim is based, is well matched in stirring words from the chapter, 'Prometheus Hibernica' in *Drums*:

> From a window in the building, leaning well forth, he talked to the workers, spoke as only Jim Larkin could speak, not for an assignation with peace, dark obedience, or placid resignation; but trumpet-tongued of resistance to wrong, discontent with leering poverty, and defiance of any power strutting out to stand in the way of their march onward. His was a handsome tense face, the forehead swept by deep black hair, the upper lip of the generous, mobile mouth hardened in fierceness by a thick moustache, the voice, deep, dark, and husky, carrying to the extreme corners of the square, and reaching, Sean thought, to the uttermost ends of the earth.

With vehemence, Larkin castigated his enemies in these words: 'Police, politicians, the Press and the judges on the bench were simply tools of the employing class. No city in the world had a more useless or vicious capitalist class than that of Dublin . . . I am a rebel and the son of a rebel. I recognise no law but the people's law'. Red Jim, an idealised portrait of Larkin, castigates his chicken-hearted supporters in the same forceful way: 'You eel-policy'd pickers and stealers of the workers' courage!'

During Red Jim's altercation with his union delegates, Brannigan is brought in after a drunken rampage between an escort

of armed workers; in the words of Caheer, 'muddying the whole
Labour Movement with his dirty habits!' Red Jim's sarcasm and
scorn is swift and searing: 'He hasn't defiled his dirty habits by
taking fine cigars from Sir Jake Jester . . . The lot of you, joined
together and multiplied a hundredfold, wouldn't make a
Brannigan!' Red Jim's anger at Brannigan's momentary lapse is
keen-edged: 'When you're sober . . . you're the Union's finest
member; when you're drunk, you're a swine!' Then follows a
moving little scene involving temporal-spiritual conversion, classi-
cally achieved, whereby Brannigan renounces his former ways of
weakness:

RED JIM: Give up the drink!
BRANNIGAN (*frightened*): Oh, for God's sake, Jim; I couldn't!
    One of the walls at home is covered with printed
    pledges taken from priests, but I wasn't able to keep one
    of them.
RED JIM: You'll keep this one for me, and sign nothing. I want
    you, Brannigan, I want you. We've enemies every-
    where – even here. (*He indicates the Delegates.*) There's a
    brazen bunch of them! I can't trust you if you drink –
    sober, I'd trust you with my life eternal!
BRANNIGAN (*after a long pause – enthusiastically*): I'll do it, Jim; no
    drink; not once; no more; never again – so help me God!
RED JIM (*gripping Brannigan's hand*): My comrade was dead, and
    is alive again; he was lost, and is found! (*To the escort*)
    Bring forth his side-arms and put them on him.

Then, with a further twist of the O'Casey kaleidoscope, we are
hurled headlong from tragicomedy into farce. As the delegates put
on their top-coats – indicating departure – Red Jim invites them to
pause and reconsider: 'Stay a little longer with us, won't you? We'll
feel rather lonely without you'. Politically and persuasively, they
are being pressed to a vigil, though one, ostensibly, not of their
liking. The delegates, making no reply, move to go, but an escort
blocks the way. Sheasker tells Red Jim to ask his troops to stand
aside and let them out. Red Jim mockingly replies that they are but
'toy soldiers'; with the added rejoinder, to knock them down and
force their way out. Sheasker's wrath evaporates: 'We want no more
of this tomfoolery! I have to act the part of Father Christmas for the

Lord Mayor and I'm late already'. 'The deserving poor'll be disappointed, for you can't go!' counters Jim, who orders Brannigan to detain them, with the consoling retaliation: 'You're safe here. Only, don't do anything to get on Captain Brannigan's nerves!'

After such a tour de force, and with it Jim's quick exit, Brannigan, in sole command, enjoys the remaining splendid moments of the scene's mixture of split-second timing of farce and absurd adulation: to the downhearted delegates, he rejoices: 'We're all comrades, aren't we? Show your joy and delight in the holy star shining in the heavens. What about a carol, boys?' And to Caheer, reaching for the telephone, he snaps: 'That's no use — it's cut!' Brannigan, fulsomely in charge, risibly shouts: 'Up on your feet, you buggers, and do homage to the time that's in it!' The curtain falls on the crestfallen delegates, singing self-consciously the enforced refrains of 'God Rest you Merry, Gentlemen', joined, lustily, by Brannigan and the guards.

In closely-knit synthesis, the third act reverts to the tenement-lodging of the old couple, where, in the room overlooking the church-spire and factory chimneys, the bier containing the body of the dead Michael is lying under the window; reminiscent of the final act, in *The Plough and the Stars*, where the body of Mollser rests in its coffin in the top-floor tenement belonging to Bessie Burgess prior to the funeral. The Old Man and Woman are again arguing; this time as to the outcome of whether the clergy or communists will arrive first to take away the body for burial:

OLD MAN (*jeeringly*): You're a brave one, you are! If the clergy came, you'd be all for him being near the saints; but if the Communists came, you'd want him to have the last honour of a wake among the workers!

OLD WOMAN: Yes; and you'd be posturing in front of the clergy, with your "Yes, your reverence, No, your reverence" till a body would think it was raining reverences, while, in your heart, you'd be pining for bands playing sturdy marches instead of having to listen to the De Profundis!

OLD MAN: I'm not going to start a row in front of the dead.

OLD WOMAN: You always say you're not going to start a row when it's nearly ended.

OLD MAN: I'd soon make up my mind if I got a chance . . .

OLD WOMAN: I thought your mind was made up?

OLD MAN: I have made up my mind; of course I've made up my mind; and once I've made up my mind, I've made it up, haven't I?

OLD WOMAN: The ground trembles when you're making up your mind. It frightened me at first, till I remembered it was only a man's mind moving.

And while the Old Man has slipped out – on the Old Woman's specific instructions to look in at the church opposite and hurry the clergy along – a cross-section of neighbours streaming in from the church enters the house and files round the bier to pay their final respects to the dead man. In a savagely depicted cameo – one of the fiercest pieces of irony in the whole play – O'Casey lets the clipped dialogue speak for itself, almost as if the shadow of Swift were hovering over the proceedings:

YOUNG MAN WITH COUGH: Nearly the same as he was when he was alive; nose a little thinner, maybe; no, not really though, when you look into it. (*He coughs.*) Oh, this cough!

HUNCHBACK: Where's his "Workers of the world, unite!" now? Hid in the dust of his mouth and lost in the still pool of his darken'd eyes . . .

OLD WOMAN: Didn't even give him a chance to say farewell to his friends.

MAN WITH CRUTCH: We all get what's coming to us.

WOMAN WITH BABY (*peering into its face*): Jasus, me baby's withering worse every hour. Born without vital force, the doctor says . . .

MAN WITH CRUTCH: Look at what [the Communists] did in Spain.

WOMAN WITH BABY: The blessed child's slowly dying in my arms!

BLIND MAN: They burned and pillaged the houses of all who couldn't see eye to eye with them.

MAN WITH CRUTCH: Singing a song, they sawed a priest in two, fair in the open air, and the blessed sun shining . . .

YOUNG MAN WITH COUGH: Looka here, if I'd been taken care of I shouldn't be the way I am.

BLIND MAN: It's easy to see how we'd fare if they once got the upper hand here.

HUNCHBACK: We've a world to gain, says they, and nothing to lose but our chains.

WOMAN WITH BABY: A world to gain! Let them throw in the sun,
          moon, and stars as a tilly, and we'll be talking! . . .
HUNCHBACK: A world to gain! Ay, and, at the same time, lose the
          dignity and loveliness that priests say poverty gives
          the poor . . .
YOUNG MAN WITH CRUTCH: Could the Communists say more than
          that – the bowseys!
HUNCHBACK: The Purple Priest patted me on the head, saying
          'You're all the more beautiful in the sight of God
          because of the hump on your back' . . .
YOUNG MAN WITH CRUTCH: 'In God's sight', he says, says he, 'the
          poor and wretched are all clad in gold'.

These are symbolical representations of Dublin's poor: bereft of
everything except their religion; soul-soaked in an arid Catholicism:
they are – for O'Casey – Dublin's spiritual down-and-outs, as he
remembers them; suffering similar degradations himself when
younger but with none of their lethargic, mindless resignation,
savagely depicted in an eulogised world which the red star in its
transformed glory will bring about. Julia,who has pushed her way
through the gaping, prayer-asphyxiated crowd, voices curses on
them, at the same time expounding the playwright's own philosophy through a transcendentalised view of man and the universe:

> You had a rich death, Da . . . Listen. Your last dying sigh is
> swelling into the great chant of 'The Internationale'. You will
> hear it voiced by the workers of the world ere you wither into the
> clay that will shortly hold you tight! And the priests that
> sanctioned your shooting shall fall and shall be dust and shall be
> priests no longer! (*she glances at the crucifix*). Against you, dear one,
> we have no grudge; but those of your ministers who sit like
> gobbling cormorants in the market-place shall fall and shall be
> dust and shall be priests no longer.

Stunned by rage and resentment, the crowd expectantly await the
arrival of the Purple Priest and his ministers for the funeral
entourage but are forestalled, as Jack and some of Red Jim's
followers burst in upon the scene, enquiring of them: 'What do ye
here? This is no place for those whose knees are ever ready to press
the ground'. They murmur they have come to pay their last respects
to a fallen neighbour and to recite a prayer for repose of his soul.

Jack reproaches them with a tenet of new faith – O'Casey's prayer and benediction: 'Then go; go, you dead, and bury your dead: the living sleep here . . . We are the resurrection and the life; whoso worketh and believeth in the people shall never die!' (an echo of Swinburne in *Songs Before Sunrise*: Glory to Man in the highest! for Man is the master of things). The philosophy is Whitman's 'institution of the dear love of comrades' – in an idealised setting; Whitman's *Song of the Axe*, too,

> Where the populace rise at once against the never-ending audacity of elected persons

– Whitman's 'new city of Friends'. (Jack and Julia are Whitman's own pioneers'.) In O'Casey's utopia, in Jack's words,

> brave-breasted women and men, terrac'd with strength, Shall live and die together, co-equal in all things . . .

an echo, too, of Whitman's spiritual creed from the *Song of Exposition*:

> Practical, peaceful life, the people's life, the People themselves Lifted, illumin'd bathed in peace – elate, secure in peace.

Whitman's broad concepts of human love are O'Casey's too: they are voiced by Jack, in open defiance of the crowd and in the face of the Purple Priest, whose peace and benediction betoken an entrance that is now too late to change the turn of events and new order of things. Speaking through Jack, O'Casey foretells:

> The young in each other's arms shall go on listening to the stars thronging the roof of a country lane; their eyes shall see bright joys strolling the streets of the shadowy city; a foggy sky shall be golden, and the hardy pavement shall lift a thick-piled velvet to their passing feet!

This joyous, optimistic, Whitmanesque philosophy of the young-for-the-young is repeated often in subsequent O'Casey plays; it stems from the golden humanitarianism of Blake, as we recollect from *Voice of the Ancient Bard*:

> Youth of delight, come hither,
> And see the opening morn,
> Image of truth new-born.

Countering this note of acclamation is the reactionary philosophy of the Purple Priest, whose diatribe against communism is a ritualistic snarl of protest and condemnation, couched in the inquisitorial style we remember from *Saint Joan*:

> Communism would banish God from your altars: it would change your holy churches into places where bats hang by day and owls hoot by night; it would soil the sacrament of marriage with lust; it would hack in sunder the holy union of the family . . . In the name of God, let us cease to think of Communism! It is the bugle-call of the powers of darkness; it is the fire of hell flaming in its energy!

The Purple Priest's invocation of hate incites the crowd to cry out: 'Burn, maim, kill all that dare to touch it!' (Just as in *Saint Joan*, the sentence passed on the maid by the ecclesiastical court of inquisition incites the impulsive Chaplain of Winchester, John de Stogumber, to a similar virulent outburst with the words, 'Into the fire with the witch'.) And, as with the Inquisitor in Shaw's play ('I am accustomed to the fire: it is soon over'), so brutality does not shock the soul of the Purple Priest (the shot which killed Michael 'was, at least, the hand of authority'; and, in another context, 'God grant the lash may teach the girl the danger of indecent dress and immodest manners'). Like Father Domineer, as we shall see in *Cock-a-Doodle Dandy*, the Purple Priest, following the example of the Jesuits of Clongowes Wood College in Joyce's *Portrait*, approves of driving home the lessons of religion with a big stick. In his narrow suspicion of sex, this prelate is associated particularly with the outlook of the Catholic Church in Ireland during the first half of the twentieth century: the subject for recurrent satire in later plays such as *Cock-a-Doodle Dandy*, *The Bishop's Bonfire* and *Behind the Green Curtains*.

As the body of the dead Michael is about to be reclaimed for Christian burial by the Purple Priest and his acolytes, the Priest is forestalled by Red Jim's sudden forceful entrance and his taunt: ' 'Twere better he had received Christian handling when he was living than to receive it now he is dead'. In the ensuing clash between Jim and the Priest for rites of burial, the Purple Priest brandishes before the crowd the weapon of excommunication; the socialist leader, however, enlists sympathy with shafts of rhetoric:

If the heritage of heaven be the heritage here of shame and rags and the dead puzzle of poverty, then we turn our backs on it,

he storms with outraged passion.

If your God declares that one child shall dwell in the glory of knowledge and another shall die in the poverty of ignorance, then we declare against him . . .

Red Jim, in a moment of triumph – as the curtain falls on this remarkable third act – jubilantly commands Brannigan to 'Take up our comrade and strike up the drums!' The Red Guards lift the bier and lead their followers in the singing of 'Our Comrade's Gone', to the steady drum-roll heard offstage in the street below, while the priests, and those loyal to them, move back in stunned silence to the end of the room.

A return, as Act Four begins, to switch-back comedy and slapstick: in the lounge of the Lord Mayor's residence, two workmen, imbued with a proletarian sense of humour – prototypes of typical creations later dominant in *Purple Dust* and *The Bishop's Bonfire* – are adding the finishing touches to festoons of Christmas decorations. (They approximate to Shakespeare's clowns and always have a touch of earthspun wisdom in their apparent folly.) The Lord Mayor – in Jack's words of Act One, a 'hopabout little bugger' and pawn of clerical authority – trips in and out mincing ineffectual words of encouragement, prompting colourful assertions on the part of the workmen: 'The little under-sized scut', pronounces the first, 'scattering his seeds of kindness, singing a bit of everybody's song', excelled only by the second's observation, 'And all the time he isn't fit to become, even with the help of the saints, a lea in a hidden feather of a mighty angel's wing'. (O'Casey's workmen usually speak in the lyric gold of the Elizabethans.)

As soon as the Mayor's back is turned, they down tools and spray curses on the annual charity-charade of the Christmas festival, ritually expressed at this particular moment in their dialogue and afterwards offset by Joybell's jaunty jabbering: 'Soon we must through darkness go, to inherit bliss unending, or eternity of woe. So keep gay, and keep going!' (Joybell and the Old Man have entered, wearing aprons and chef's caps, and carrying cans of tea.) The Lady Mayoress, over-bedizened and fulsomely exuding feminine charm, chivvies everyone to their duties and pushes the workers back towards their ladders in a flurry of organised ballyhoo, eliciting the dry response from the second workman: 'I can never understand why some workers are ready to fall on their knees the minute a well-dressed cow flits in front of them.'

Then Joybell rushes in again, Hans Christian Andersen style, excitement and elation getting the better of him, with his announcement of 'grand news, great news, good news!': mounted police are on their way to arrest Red Jim. (The downcast workmen are heard mumbling to themselves that their hour of hope when 'the star was about to turn red' is over and workers 'must sing sad and slow, and sleep again'.)

Joybell, the Mayor and Mayoress, together with the Old Man (now dressed as Father Christmas, in the absence of Sheasker detained at Union headquarters by Jim), all show their jubilation at the news of Jim's impending arrest. In the spirit of Christmas celebrations, the Mayor is prevailed upon to sing his specially-composed song. (Most of O'Casey's characters are usually called upon to rhapsodise in song – often embarrassing audiences accustomed only to the obliquities of Pinter or the jocosities of Ayckbourn.) Everyone, with the exception of the workmen, joins in the 'heigh-ho, cheerily' of the mayoral refrain; at the end of which – in an ironical note of total surprise – an 'Assembly' note is blown by bugle-call, offstage, indicating the beginning of insurrection. (Symbolically, the clock has struck!) The workers walk out in significant knowledge that their moment of liberation is at hand. Traditional celebrators, like the Mayor and Joybell, are left wondering and bemused ('What clock were they talking about?'). Even the empty badinage of Joybell and the Old Man is given a symbolically wry twist: to Joybell's 'there must be something up still' is suffixed 'there's nothing up still or down still' (from the Old Man) – an oblique reference to the unfinished hanging of festoons, and ladders astride in the middle of the room, over-topped by the Mayoress's recriminating sigh: 'these workers need a firm hand over them'.

The way for glorious farce is paved as the Old Man offers the Mayor the services of himself and Joybell for the final finishing-off (literally, too!) of the remainder of the hanging-up of decorations

(Joybell's *'deo volente'* gives the game away!) As the Mayor and his wife walk out in illusory hope that finishing touches will soon be completed (unaware of symbolical overtones) the scene is set for moments of the ripest farce, reminiscent of the episode of the telephone skit in the final act of *The Silver Tassie* where the old codgers, Simon and Sylvester, unused to handling the telephone, get themselves hopelessly entangled trying to answer a call at the football club premises. (Joybell and the Old Man are numskulls in the same professional breed.) The ensuing zany conversation hurtles into uproarious farce:

OLD MAN: Slip up, Joybell, as a preliminary, and fix your end first.

JOYBELL: No; you slip up first and see how your end'll hang.

OLD MAN: How my end'll hang? Don't you know well enough how my end'll hang? My end'll hang just the same as your end'll hang!

JOYBELL: My eye is younger than yours, and I'll be able to see if your end is hanging at the right angle.

OLD MAN (*viciously*): Right angle! This is a matter of pluck and hammer and nails, and not a question of aljaybra! There's only one angle to hang it be – the right angle.

JOYBELL: That's just what I'm after saying.

OLD MAN: Just what are you after saying?

JOYBELL: That if you hang it at all, you must hang it at a right angle.

OLD MAN (*shouting*): Good God, man, isn't that just what I'm just after saying!

JOYBELL: No you didn't; you just said that if you wanted to hang it at a right angle you'd have to know aljaybra.

OLD MAN (*shouting*): And what has aljaybra got to do with it?

JOYBELL: Isn't that just what I'm after asking you?

OLD MAN (*shouting*): What are you after asking me, for God's sake?

JOYBELL: I'm after asking you what has aljaybra got to do with it?

OLD MAN (*furiously*): Got to do with what, man?

JOYBELL: Got to do with hanging this strip of decoration at a right angle?

OLD MAN: Amn't I hoarse shouting out that aljaybra has nothing to do with it!

JOYBELL: There you are, you see.

OLD MAN: There I am, I see, what?

JOYBELL: At the end of your argument you have to admit that aljaybra has nothing to do with hanging festoons at a right angle.

OLD MAN (*in anguish*): Oh, isn't an intelligent man nicely tested when he's fronted with a fool!

The level of farce accelerates as the two gaums, unable to carry through their pragmatic task, discourse on the need for displaying 'so many of these coloured vanities at a time like this', with concomitant comments, such as, 'a surging shame of a show-off, I call it', in the midst of farcically-inspired 'chassis'. Mounting their ladders again in a final desperate bid to complete the operation, they clasp their ladders – according to the stage instructions – as if each were embracing a woman! The playwright's directions are riotous: '*The ends of the festoons are wound round their necks so as to leave their arms free to clasp the ladders tightly*', leaving further leeway for more tottering conversation as the slapstick ripens:

OLD MAN: What are we going to do now?

JOYBELL: Pray to God and His blessed saints that we won't fall! . . .

OLD MAN: How the hell can we hug the ladders and fix the festoons at the same time?

JOYBELL: We'll have to think out some way of doing it, that's all.

OLD MAN (*explosively*): Oh, will we? I'm not going to let myself go cantering down through space with nothing definite but the air to stand on!

The farce peters out when the Lord Mayor interrupts the proceedings with a rapid request for a carol and an end to the hammering as festivities are about to commence. Strains of 'Silent night, holy night' are heard from the hall; while, offstage, distant playing of 'The Internationale' cuts across, to sounds of galloping horses and sirens blowing 'shrill and loud . . . from the foundry seen through the window', as the star turns red.

In the climactic melodrama, Joybell's comment, 'We're no sooner out of one trouble than we're pitching into another,' recalls similar moments of bathos in the midst of heightened drama in the climaxes of both *Juno and the Paycock* and *The Plough and the Stars*

Rushing to the telephone for assistance, the Mayor discovers, to his chagrin, the Red Guards have taken over the Exchange. Joybell's and the Old Man's joint-exclamation, 'Where can we go? what shall we do? where can we hide?' is answered by the farcical, mayoral 'Go and hide in hell, you fools, with your great news and grand news and good news!' As Red Guards invade the house and take over the telephone, Red Jim and Brannigan assume command. Protests from the Mayoress are of no avail; and the final hour is one of pitched battle, staged in stylised dumb show.

With support of outside fusiliers, and the conversion of the Brown Priest to their cause, the workers' revolutionary crusade is achieved. Before the final curtain rings down on an electrifying scene, a truce indicates surrender of the fascists and their reactionary allies. Brannigan tells of Jack's death in the fighting. The body is borne in, followed by Julia softly weeping. Kian remains with his dead brother, embracing in the end – by implication – his brother's political faith. In the final rousing chorus and cheering, the climax comes with a triumphant rendering by all, on stage, of 'The Internationale', and Jim's words of adjuration to the mourning Julia: 'Up young woman, and join in the glowing hour your lover died to fashion. He fought for life, for life is all; and death is nothing!' (Human life may be limited, but revolution knows no bounds.)

It is, indeed, an astonishing play, coming from an even more astonishing playwright! It has immense fertility of phrase and driving passion in every line. The Red Jim of this play is no communist spawned of Marxian scholarship and reared in scientific jargon; he is the true, simple hater of injustice and oppression. His eloquence is inspired by the Book of Amos, reflected in the Gospels ('the world as we know it', says St Paul, 'is passing away') and the Mercurial shadow of Walt Whitman: of man's epiphany to man, the victory alone which will overcometh the world: our future faith: faith in humanity itself and faith in the universe as immortalised by the poets. In Red Jim's words, 'thinkers, poets and brave men' have influenced O'Casey's communism; which owes more to traditional sources than to the teaching of latterday theorists and activists. 'Don't read bitterness into one who says a thing that shocks', says O'Casey, in one of his letters. 'Jesus was bitter . . . So was the gentle Blake; so was Shelley. Beware of entering into a sham, lest you become part of the sham yourself'.

In *Inishfallen, Fare Thee Well*, he expands on what he means by communism, and what it means for mankind:

> The Red Star is a bright star . . . It is the evening star, and it is the bright and shining morning star. It is the star shining over the flock in the field, over the mother crooning her little one to rest, over the girl arranging herself for the bridal, over the old couple musing by the fireside, over the youngsters playing in the street, over the artist achieving a new vision in colour, over the poet singing his song . . . over the hammer building the city, over the sickle cutting the corn . . . over the lover and his lass in ecstasy on the yellow sands . . . Red Health of the sick, Red Refuge of the afflicted, shine on us all!

It is Whitman's hope of a larger, deeper life; of a richer experience, no matter how bought. Those who are determined to bow to no idols or false gods, however venerable, but to stand up on their own feet, and confront whatever destiny may bring – these will respect O'Casey and the message that *The Star Turns Red* brings. And, in the endless cycles of progress, all aspirations will have endured, and upon the first-comers will merely lie the duty of helping on the rest.

In its way, and anxiety, to do complete justice to every point of view, this rich and puissant play approaches the thoroughness of *Saint Joan*. In breadth of vision it has much in common with Gorky's novels and plays. Its ending resembles Shaw's later political extravaganza, *On the Rocks* (which O'Casey reviewed in 1934 for *The Listener* and which is included in *Blasts and Benedictions*), though O'Casey's ending is far more jubilant and triumphant, in comparison with Shaw's; instead of the singing on stage of 'The Red Flag', Shaw's extravaganza ends with the comparatively mild and sentimental verses of Edward Carpenter's: 'England, Arise!', together with his weak-hearted Prime Minister (a burlesque on Ramsay MacDonald) exclaiming, 'Suppose England really did arise!'

It must be remembered that *The Star Turns Red* is not a chronicle-play but a parable – an allegory – describing events that have never happened (there never was, for example a struggle between communism and fascism in Dublin resembling the conflict in this play; though the factors and circumstances inherent are present in every European capital to this day). The play offers a vision of the future – when the world will change: in that sense it is both apocalyptic and prophetic.

It is not a tragedy as such, but it has the gravity of the spiritually comic; with moments of farce and melodrama allied to the poetic-symbolic. O'Casey uses a theme from old Christian Morality Plays, the struggle for the possession of an individual soul, in this case the body and soul of the murdered Michael. Revolutionary forces are triumphant.

The play is a masterpiece of theatricality, remarkable in its ability to sustain surprise. The battle-scene of the final act, in stylised dumb show – 'stiff lay figures in various attitudes of death', suggests O'Casey – is bold and effective. Future directors, with an eye to visionary and transcendental effects, must not, however, overlook the drama's other strong points: soul-piercing language and beauty of poetry. (Inadequacies in directorial diction in this field could be disastrous.) In putting across the play's essential message, the director must ensure that the glittering Irishisms are not thrown away. The role of Red Jim calls for an actor of great experience, able to impress his audience with rich verbal magnificence of the lines he has to speak. Larkin was a gifted orator: Red Jim has a golden voice, too.

Red Jim should be tall and strongly built, combining within himself the imagination of an artist and the fire and determination of a leader of a down-trodden class: a persuasive orator, clever at shaping his message, yet with a penetrating sense of humour. He is dressed in a dark-green coat, with a red star on his right breast, faded blue trousers, and wearing a wide-brimmed black slouch hat. He walks, we are told, with a slight seaman's lurch.

Of the two protagonist sons, Jack is a young idealist of twenty-three; slim and sturdy, dressed in light-brown tweeds, a large red star on the right breast of his coat. (He is another version of the Dreamer, and a prototype of Ayamonn Breydon, more fully sketched in *Red Roses for Me*; a throwback, too, from his namesake in the earlier *The Harvest Festival*.) Kian, with Biblical implications of Cain the murderer, is slightly younger; tall and slim, with close-cropped hair and moustache, and dressed in fascist regalia, similar to that worn by the Leader of the Saffron Shirts. Michael is tall and forty-four, his moustache drooping over his lips, James Connolly fashion. Julia is a pretty and vigorous lass of nineteen; she wears a bare-backed, low-cut black pierrette fancy costume. (She and Jack represent not only all the young in Dublin, but the young all the world over.)

The Old Man is short and rosy-faced, with a fine shock of grey hair and matching moustache. The Old Woman is plumpish, of average height, and still has traces of former good looks. Joybell, fat and round-faced, has bushy hair and exudes a false amiability; he is twenty and wears a confraternity robe of rich blue reaching to his heels, with a black cape attached, a girdle of white cord surrounding his waist from which hangs a black cross, and big heavy clumsy boots showing beneath the hem of his robe. The Purple Priest is clad in a violet cassock with cowl, partly covering his face, his cassock breeched with black cord, and he wears a black pectoral cross; he is pale and severe-faced, betokening a harsh, inflexible austerity from within. The Brown Priest wears a brown cassock and cowl, resembling a friar's of the order, most probably, of St Francis of Assisi, the cowl resting on his shoulders, his cassock girded with white cord and he wears a white pectoral cross; he is gentle and kind, but has a look of spiritual bewilderment on his face. The Leader of the Saffron Movement is thirty-two, of medium build and stiff in his bearing; his vivid yellow shirt carries a badge on the right arm of a white circle enclosing a flash on its background (the papal colours suggest links between fascism and the Church); he wears black breeches and top-boots. The Lord Mayor is short, stocky and dark-moustached; he has a faint lisp and is obsequious, wearing his chain of office the whole time, like Binnington in *The Drums of Father Ned*. His wife, forty-five, bustling and self-assured, wears a widely flowing party dress.

Of the Union representatives, Sheasker (whose Gaelic name means 'comfortable'), as Jim's self-appointed heir-apparent, is paunchy and smug-looking, about forty, and is complete with bowler, gloves and watch-chain; Brallain (in Gaelic 'boaster'), as the brains behind the conspiracy – ready to ditch Sheasker when the opportunity arises – is of approximately the same age, only shifty and sly; Caheer ('chairman'), in his mid-thirties, wiry and mean-looking, with a slight hesitancy of speech; Eglish ('petty bureaucrat'), thirty, round-shouldered and more reserved in manner; the Secretary, thin, tall and thirty-five, nervous and evasive. Brannigan is big, brawny and red-faced from his drinking-habits, dressed in corduroy trousers, faded blue jacket and heavy boots. Of the neighbours, most are poorly-dressed and miserable-looking. They are an apotheosis of Dublin's poor; symbols of their macabre existence.

The London *première* on 12 March 1940 at the left-wing amateur Unity Theatre (destroyed by fire in 1975) was directed by

John Allen and ran for over three months – no mean achievement at the beginning of the War. (A revival by Ted Willis at the same theatre was staged, briefly, in July 1946.) Settings for the first production were by Sir Lawrence Gowing, music by Alan Bush and choreography by Louise Soelberg. Notices were cool, save for Agate's accolade, but Robert Lynd conceded: 'Mr O'Casey writes with such imaginative energy and earnestness that the play grips the attention and holds it to the end'. Peter Newmark, as the playwright's specially assigned production adviser, achieved a measure of symbolist interpretation, which the play needs so essentially in performance.

The Irish *première* at the Abbey, as late as February 1978, was bedevilled by bad weather and ran for just a month. The director was Tomas MacAnna, pioneer producer of many of O'Casey's later plays for the Company. (The designer was Bronwen Casson.) Among a huge cast, in what was generally considered a glittering production, Edward Golden played Red Jim, Patrick Laffen played the Purple Priest and Philip O'Flynn played Brannigan. One multi-purpose set with modifications was used throughout. MacAnna described his interpretation as 'a miracle play, Saffron Devil and Red Saviour in final conflict'. Ned Chaillet in *The Times* foretold that 'a major production in London would surprise many critics'.

Abroad, versions have been staged in Sydney, Australia in 1948; in Paris in 1962 at the Théâtre d'Aubervilliers; also in East Berlin in 1968 at the Maxim Gorky Theater, directed by Kurt Veth. A televised performance, to commemorate the centenary of the playwright's birth, was shown on the national network in East Germany. Translations have appeared in French, German, Hungarian, Russian and Chinese.

The Chekhovian influence from *The Cherry Orchard*, as expressed in Trofimov's aspirations, is clear: 'Let's march on irresistibly towards that bright star, shining in the distance!' Chekhov's unfaltering advice is O'Casey's, too.

12 *Purple Dust* (1940): a Pastoral Frolic

Properly staged, *Purple Dust* is one of O'Casey's most riotous comedies: in the words of Nathan, 'a ringing, moving melody orchestrated with a resounding slapstick'. The tone throughout is broad farce, but farce not in the naturalistic sense. There is plenty of irony and symbolism, and fantasy like morning dew; but as the drama unfolds, we are confronted not so much with conventional hilarity as with a strongly suggested atmosphere of an allegory, as apocalyptic in its final vision as in the previous *The Star Turns Red*. (The significance of the subtitle, 'A Wayward Comedy in Three Acts', is a portent.)

Commingling gaiety and levity gives a sense of mystical purpose and foreboding, yet through the outbursts of laughter can be seen some of the playwright's most poetic and idyllic scenes. *Purple Dust* is more lyrical than any of O'Casey's previous plays.

'In a good play', says Synge in his preface to *The Playboy of the Western World*, 'every speech should be as fully flavoured as a nut or apple, and such speeches cannot be written by anyone who works among people who have shut their lips on poetry'. This pastoral romp of O'Casey's is marvellously and felicitously conceived in the poetic and humorous tradition of Synge. Multi-dimensional, as in most of O'Casey's later plays, a concise analysis would defy artistic ingenuity, but Polonius's summing-up in *Hamlet*, of the genre it represents, comes closest to encapsulating in a single phrase the mood of the play: 'tragi-comical-historical-pastoral; scene individable, or poem unlimited'.

In a letter to Nathan discoursing on the nature of the play shortly after its composition immediately before the war (it was ready for production in 1940 – a wayward time, indeed, for any new play to succeed; especially one which gives a hearty guffaw at some of the foibles and follies of the English characters it laughingly portrays) O'Casey wrote:

it is in some ways, an odd play . . . At first it was to be just a skit on the country, but it changed a little into, maybe, a kind of an allegorical form. The idea crept into my head after a visit to a family living in a Tudor House here; suffering all kinds of inconveniences because of its age and history; going about with lanterns and eating in semi-gloom. Terrible torture for the sake of a tumbledown house with a name! I've never gone there since. I was perished with the cold, and damaged with the gloom . . . A lot of the humour is, I think, pretty broad, and a little exaggerated; but we Irish are fond of adding to things.

In the play, O'Casey shows two English financial tycoons, Cyril Poges (a self-made capitalist) and his companion, Basil Stoke (a self-assured but phoney intellectual), accompanied by their two Irish mistresses. Avril and Souhaun – brought over, we are told, with them from England – setting about the hazardous task of trying to refurbish an old Tudor mansion in an effort to revive the pastoral life in the remote Irish countryside at the beginning of the war (as well as escaping from the war – Eire retained its neutrality under De Valera). They are seeking, in the words of John Arden from an article (included in Thomas Kilroy's *Sean O'Casey: A Collection of Critical Essays*, Prentice-Hall, 1975), 'to revive a discredited squirarchal mode of life'. The play shows how, in the midst of their bizarre transplantation – with mock-emphasis on pastoral absurdities – the English characters are foiled and frustrated as events, the weather, to say nothing of the impenetrabilities and unpredictabilities of the Irish themselves (as we know from Somerville and Ross's *The Experiences of an Irish RM*), heap disaster on their ill-fated project, with the river, in the end, rising symbolically around the house. Mixing with relish, fantasy and farce, O'Casey sets out to show that the Irish, with all their fey hypocrisy and charm (though present-day Ireland comes in for its share of mocking criticism), still have a better ideal of a good life than the English plutocrats who dismiss them as an endearing but childish people.

Purple Dust is a full-length cartoon in which caricatured Englishmen are gulled by their witty Irish rivals. Some entertaining chaos follows (in this play the accent is on comical 'chassis') when, in the midst of supposedly hard-bitten Irish realists and equally hard-bitten Irish visionaries (the two are often synonymous), the thick-witted pair, descending at last from their respective high horses, get caught up in the labyrinthine ways of local folly and succumb to all sorts of sorceries and regionalised disasters, in the end getting cozened for their pains by two calculating Irishmen, O'Killigain and O'Dempsey, the one ostensibly a realist, the other an idealist, who carry off their far-from-coy mistresses and leave them bemoaning their fate as the house totters in the flood – prefiguring the collapse of their own outworn civilisation and, indeed, the British Empire. (In Shaw's play, *The Simpleton of the Unexpected Isles*, a similar apocalyptic prediction is suggested – the result of England's decision to withdraw from the Empire. Such radical notions before the advent of World War II must have struck terror and amazement into the hearts of prospective managements in London who used the war and its aftermath as an excuse for avoiding commercial performances of these unusual dramatic fantasias.)

The setting of *Purple Dust* (though not the style and treatment) is not wholly dissimilar to that of Evelyn Waugh's satiric comedy, *A Handful of Dust* (1934); the title derives from T. S. Eliot's *The Waste Land*, wherein Hetton Abbey, an extreme example of a Victorian Gothic country house, in which each bedroom is named after an Arthurian character, becomes a source of dissension and breakdown of marital relations between the inheritor-occupier and his flighty wife, who spends an increasing amount of her time in her London flat and brittle London society of the period, in order to escape from the severities of the country manor and also from her stuffy, pompous husband, who is insensitive to all that is happening because he is too sunk in his dream of English Gothic for which Hetton has become the romanticised symbol. (Unlike O'Casey, Waugh views his hero's delight in what the big house stands for with much sympathy, as in *Brideshead Revisited*, whereas in *Purple Dust* traditions and all that such a way of life represents are finally destroyed.)

'The winds of change come', O'Casey reminds us, in an article relating to the play ('Purple Dust in Their Eyes'), included in *Under a Colored Cap*,

and no one feels them till they become strong enough to sweep things away carrying men and women (however comic and enjoyable), bearing off their old customs, manners, and morals with them. So in the decline and fall of the British Empire (she seems to be in danger now of losing her Commonwealth) many picturesque things, some even lovely, fell with it, and are now but a little heap of purple dust.

It is the endorsement of Elizabethan philosophy expounded by Sir Thomas Browne ('Time antiquates antiquities and hath an art to make dust of all things') or Shakespeare's:

> Golden lads and girls all must
> As chimney-sweepers, come to dust . . .

expanded in the wider context of more embracing beliefs professed by a modern, revolutionary but romantic playwright, such as O'Casey.

Another possible influence on the source and origins of *Purple Dust* may dwell in the explanation given in George Moore's *A Story-Teller's Holiday* – a work O'Casey certainly possessed – which mentions Yeats's strange choice of dwelling-place in a ruined castle in the neighbourhood of Thoor Ballylee in County Galway ('for the sake of spectres', observes Moore acidly, 'himself having become a myth from too long brooding on myths, and myths being, if not spectres, at least of the same kin'). Moore also refers in the same volume to Yeats's idiosyncratic belief in his relationship to the Duke of Ormond: Souhaun, in O'Casey's play, also claims ascendancy to the same ducal family. Again, in his poem *The Tower* – written while he was occupying Ballylee castle – Yeats mentions the incident of a drowned man in Cloone Bog: in *Purple Dust* the setting O'Casey offers is in a remote Irish country village named Clune na Geera.

In the concluding volume of *Hail and Farewell!* (the phantasmagoric style of which is very like the prose-patterning of O'Casey's own autobiographies, especially *Inishfallen, Fare Thee Well*), George Moore mentions, among other topics, the folly of perpetuating elaborate museums, out of which the spirit of life has departed and from which those who frequent them can never awaken imagination, impulse or idea, and 'whether the buying of odds and ends, chairs, fire-irons and decanters, and building at a great cost places in which to store them . . . is not a waste of public money?' The two Englishmen in *Purple Dust* set great store on a Jacobean chair, an Annamese vase and a Cambodian bowl, along with a Quattrocento writing-desk, all of which come to grief in removal and renovation in the course of the knockabout provided by the playwright, who is anxious to show the anachronistic absurdity of excessive preoccupation with the past.

Within the combination of revolutionist and drama-maker, O'Casey is keenly aware of the revolution brought about by the River of Time and the slow-moving or swift-moving Winds of Change; he is also aware that when time and change, in the march of progress, go too slow, life itself takes a hand in the process and shoves dynasties and personalities out of the way, regardless of any sentimental or historical reasons. This is the underlying allegorical theme of his 'wayward' drama: the dust represents the past, principally the dubious past of capitalist England and her outworn ideas of sentimental colonialism, but also, significantly – yet contradictorily – the glorious past of Ireland as represented by her ancient, pre-Christian civilisation.

If we take a closer look at Moore's writings, we discover that some of these ideas are germanely expressed. For instance, in *Vale* (the final book of the *Hail and Farewell!* trilogy) he records, in a fantasised conversation between himself and his younger brother, Colonel Maurice Moore, their differences in outlook on past and present:

'The landlords have had their day, [says Moore] and their day is over. We are a disappearing class, our lands are being confiscated and our houses are decaying or being pulled down to build cottages for the folk. Dialect, idiom, local customs, and character are disappearing, and in a great hurry. I cannot understand how it is that you don't see that Moore Hall represents feudalism. Have a look at it, and tell me, if you can, that it is not an anachronism in the landscape.'

'I think that anybody who would like to live in a comfortable house – '

'But the comfort of yesterday is not the comfort of today. Square rooms and lofty passages conformed to the ideas of our ascendants, and jerry-built villas, all gables, red tiles, and mock beams stand for modern taste and modern comfort; hot water on every landing and electric light . . . Moore Hall is out of date, and it astonishes me that you don't feel it. I wish in a way that I could summon sufficient courage to pull it down and sell it; it would make excellent rubble to build labourers' cottages, and if I could I would cut down every tree and lay the hillside bare. Why not, since I know it will be laid bare a few years after my death?'

The *Hail and Farewell!* trilogy were part of O'Casey's own library and certain passages are prominently and marginally scored by him thus meriting our closer consideration. One such passage is the following, in the continuation of the imaginary conversation between Moore and the Colonel:

'I cannot help being sorry for my poor country [says Moore] that has never been able to show a brave face to the world, not because the Irish are less intelligent than another race, but for some extraordinary curse that seems to have been laid upon this land in the tenth century. Ireland was something then; she had a religion of her own – and she was inventing an art of her own. Up to the tenth century God seemed as if he intended to do something for Ireland, and in the tenth or the eleventh century he changed his mind, and ever since the curse seems to have been deepening. In another fifty years Ireland will have lost all the civilisation of the eighteenth century; a swamp of peasants with a priest here and there, the exaltation of the rosary and whisky her lot. A hundred legislators interested only in protecting monkeries and nunneries from secular inquisition.'

Purple Dust, in its presentation of the real Celtic pre-Christian traditions behind the facade of contemporary Ireland, is an echo of what Moore has been saying, plus the age-long conflict of wits between English and Irish temperaments shown to advantage by juxtapositioning of English characters seeking Hibernicisation in imaginary Clune na Geera; the play also proves to be an entertaining variant on Shaw's *John Bull's Other Island*, though Broadbent is, perhaps, a stronger and subtler delineation than that of Poges, the golden-heeled stockbroker of *Purple Dust*, who is not very good at distinguishing a bull from a cow or any of the other rusticities of his new-found surroundings. Yet O'Casey, in this play, draws on Irish mythology for imagery of heroic liberation and renewal, weaves it into the texture of the play and, in so doing, brings it vigorously to life.

In this entrancing comedy – a humorous poem from beginning to end – he has evolved an imaginative style and technique which he adopts in later fantasies such as *Cock-a-Doodle Dandy*, *The Bishop's Bonfire* and *The Drums of Father Ned*. For the most part dispensing with elaborate symbolic structures and dimensions which served him well in *The Silver Tassie*, and with fine effect in both *Within the Gates* and *The Star Turns Red*, he now, and henceforth (with the exception of *Oak Leaves and Lavender*), relies more intuitively on an original and highly-developed fancy – together with unabashed gusto – as he tilts a Quixotic lance at those inert, soul-destroying forces bequeathed by the established order on what he would endorse with Joyce as our present 'syphilisation'. As he had previously proclaimed, in *The Flying Wasp*, he who would aspire to be an artistic playwright must discover new formulas and new moulds.

In its blend of fantasy, realism and comic involvement, *Purple Dust* is one of the most successful plays in the playwright's later canon. Artistically and wisely directed, to ensure original cohesion of all the disparate but well-known elements involved, it can instil vintage O'Casey and evoke from its audience, as it did on the occasion of its long run in New York, a spectacle of genuine popular acclaim.

Briskly acted, it should romp home amid shouts of laughter. The talk from Irish characters is rich in the kind of sentiments audiences have come to expect from Irish characters (Boucicault's influence) and the play is saturated in bucolic wonder and charm, humour and poetry, which rises throughout to peaks of eloquence. Synge's influence on its gay-hearted lyricism breaks out here and there; and amid scintillating revelry the spirit of Shaw can be seen stalking the background with presentiments of Irish philosophy as expressed in *John Bull's Other Island*: 'An Irishman's heart is nothing but his imagination', and, 'oh, the dreaming! dreaming! torturing, the heart-scalding, never satisfying dreaming' . . .

> An Irishman's imagination never lets him alone, never convinces him, never satisfies him, but it makes him that he can't face reality nor deal with it nor handle it nor conquer it . . .

And, as in Shaw's play lampooning the two countries, all this top-o'-the-morning and broth-of-a-boy and more-power-to-your-elbow business is got up to befool the bedazzled, unsuspecting Englishman. O'Casey's humorists in *Purple Dust* underline the truth of the axiom that when an Irishman is serious an Englishman imagines he is joking and when joking imagines him to be serious. (Seumas Shields's prediction in the first act of *The Shadow of a Gunman*.) Spanning the whole play is an Elizabethan sense of wonder and freshness reminiscent of Shakespeare, so that Troilus's words spring to mind:

> I am giddy, expectation whirls me round.
> The imaginary relish is so sweet
> That it enchants my sense.

Outlining the spirit of the play for American audiences, in 1956, O'Casey stresses:

> There are no politics as such in this play; its foundation, its roof, floor, windows and doors are built out of laughter,

adding:

> The play isn't an attack on England, not even on any particular class in the country . . . It is to some extent, a symbolic play, and unconsciously, a prophetic one too. The auld hoose, beloved by so many for so long, is in a bad way; old things are passing away, and new things are appearing in the sky, on the horizon, and right here in the middle of us. The house is falling, and we hardly know where to start to pick up the bits . . . Within the symbol and the prophecy is woven slapstick and rhythm, a song here, a little dance there, some comic manners of man . . .

In *Under a Colored Cap*, the playwright tells us:

> There are those who clutch at things that are departing, and try to hold them back. So do Stoke and Poges, digging up old bones, and trying to glue them together again. They try to shelter from the winds of change but Time wears away the roof, and Time's river eventually sweeps the purple dust away.

O'Casey's pastoral frolic is dedicated to his daughter, Shivaun, the third of his children, who was born in Devon in 1939. (He was then living with his family in the quiet country town of Totnes, with its ancient and Elizabethan traditions near to Dartington – the progressive school which Shaw had advised for the education of O'Casey's children – before moving, eventually, to Torquay, where he would spend his final years till his death in 1964.) Shivaun, who, in later years became an actress, took part in some of the London productions of her father's plays at the Mermaid Theatre in the late sixties.

Purple Dust is a play rich in dramatic content, where tension is either entirely amusing and satirical or centred in talk that abounds in the abstract-poetical: it is unmistakably comedy of a high order, glorying in its heightened lyricism of star-reaching prose. It is a play which soars and sweeps and dances its way on to the stage in a cavalcade of laughter, transforming theatre into music-hall, pantomime and three-ring circus alike.

Behind the laughter is a bitter joke and beneath the extravaganza undertones of political prophecy, despite the author's earlier protestation to the contrary. Enmeshed in the play is the Shavian doctrine, expressed in *On the Rocks*: 'There is eternal war between those who are in the world for what they can get out of it and those who are in the world to make it a better place for everybody to live in'.

And behind the philosophy expressed in *Purple Dust* is the application of Shaw's 'vision of Judgement' which we come across in *The Simpleton of the Unexpected Isles*, spoken by Pra and Prola, the eugenic priest and priestess of the future: 'New knowledge always contradicts the old, and the new power is the destruction of the fools who misuse it'. (The Dreamer, in the revised edition of *Within the Gates*, also expounds the idea.) In the Unexpected Isles which symbolise the universe, the future lies with those who prefer 'surprise and wonder' to security and soul-destroying rigidity. In the preface to the play, Shaw pronounces: 'In a living society every day is a day of judgement; and its recognition as such is not the end of all things but the beginning of a real civilization' (conceivably, Shakespeare's 'brave new world' too).

Ireland, in *Purple Dust*, is O'Casey's substitute for the Unexpected Isles, where 'everyday must have its miracle' and where those who value life most must 'wrestle with life as it comes' (Shaw's words). The simpletons in O'Casey's play are Stoke and Poges living in their own fool's paradise: they are O'Casey's 'dispensables'. In the apocalyptic vision which this play finally presents, their lives do not justify their existence; so they needs must perish. They – and all the life-denying characters which ultimately have no use, no purpose – must fade out. It is not the end of the world as exponents of orthodox Christianity profess to believe, but the end of a familiar pattern of civilisation based on capitalism, to be replaced, in the eyes of visionaries (including O'Casey), with utopian fervour and good will.

In Shakespeare's vision, it is epitomised by Gonzalo's Republic in *The Tempest*, where all is 'foison' and 'abundance', with

> riches, poverty,
> And use of service, none . . . ;

in Shaw's, the dream of Keegan, in *John Bull's Other Island*, 'where the State is the Church and the Church the people . . . a godhead in which all life is human and all humanity divine'; and for O'Casey, by implication, though not stated specifically as such in *Purple Dust*, an ideology based on his own political faith, whose 'bud-ray shone', he tells us, in *Rose and Crown*, 'when first appeared in life a class that had all, or most, of what was going, became opposed by the class that had little or nothing'; an ideology whose symbol is 'the symbol of a red star. Earlier it was called the sword of light; Prometheus; Lugh of the Long Hand'. In *Purple Dust*, it is signified in O'Killigain's final song, 'Come from the Dyin' ', especially in the phrase:

Where th' lightning of life flashes vivid we go . . .

(set to the tune of 'The Rio Grande' with the playwright's stirring lyrics) and incorporated in O'Casey's own version of a pastoral utopia.

In the play Ireland becomes O'Casey's symbol of a sorcerous, unexpected isle, where 'sounds and sweet airs', 'surprise and wonder', are the order of the day and where no security in the English acceptability of the term exists. Instead of having landed in their quaint repatriation, as they imagined, in a quiet Celtic oasis, Stoke and Poges have unwittingly stepped into an insidious blackguardocracy and are confronted with everything which as English counterparts they hate about the Irish: the workmen appear inefficient and presumptuous, the telephone rarely works and the locals are eaten up with Gaelic lore.

The Englishmen themselves are absurdly comic creations: self-parodies straight out of Evelyn Waugh or P. G. Wodehouse. Their conception of country life is bogus, believing, like so many Ruritanians, that amusements of fishing, shooting and hunting are the country; along with shepherds' crooks and picturesque sur-roundings. They represent the main cartoon-figures in this modern version of a mock-pastoral with its Elizabethan aura of freshness and grandeur. As in *Love's Labour's Lost* and *As You Like it*, we hearken to a festival of words and revel in 'golden cadences of poetry'.

In the characters of O'Killigain and O'Dempsey, we have worldly-wise jesters and wiseacres who are O'Casey's Irish version of Touchstone and Jaques, using their 'folly like a stalking-horse', under pretence of which O'Casey shoots his own vigorous brand of satire and comedy, 'winding up the watch of his wit' (to employ a

Shakespearian metaphor) with true Elizabethan flourish and style. And, as in Shakespeare's comedies, there are monstrous improbabilities, masked by mad fun, laced with symbolism and song, and an abundance of music and dance and wild fantasy, and – in the words of the dust-jacket to the original published version of the play – 'philosophy gushing from the mouth of uninnocent fools'.

In the play itself, a single setting in the room of a Tudor-style mansion in the imaginary village of Clune na Geera in one of the remoter corners of rural Ireland forms the basis of all three acts that comprise this comic wonderland: the time is indicated as 'the present'. The set is 'a wide, deep, gloomy room that was once part of the assembly or living room of an Elizabethan mansion'. The mansion turns out to be a monument of discomfort where every plank conceals a potential pitfall – a structure that might have presented itself, temptingly, in any Chaplin or Buster Keaton film.

O'Casey has lined up fifteen extraordinarily comic characters in this inventive play which tips over into hilarious farce. The main participants are, primarily, Cyril Poges and Basil Stoke, the smug Englishmen: Poges the City man and financial expert (in the words of the Second Workman of the play, 'a smoky bragger who thinks th' world spins round on th' rim of a coin') and Stoke his friend and phoney metaphysician, who has 'passed through Oxford'. With them are a pair of vivacious colleens who are their domiciliary 'wives': Souhaun, the attractive thirty-three year old and concubine of Poges, and Avril, her younger, prettier counterpart, who is Basil's mistress, also Barney their dour manservant and Cloyne their attractive maidservant – instances of Irish servitude rather than civility. Jack O'Killigain is the educated stonemason in charge of renovating the mansion, who, in Synge's colourful expression, 'would face a foxy divil with a pitchpike on the flags of hell'. He is opposed to the Canon's repressive ordinances on free love, and proves himself to be a master womaniser and persuasive in chat. These characters come together with a superb covey of Irish workmen, described in the *dramatis personae* as First, Second and Third Workmen, the second of whom, known as Philib O'Dempsey, is a melancholy dreamer of past poetic fantasies and something of a spellbinding legendiser and harbourer of immemorial hatreds, while the other two are typically country bumpkins, figures of Joxerian fun, passively complying with every wish of their 'paycockian' employers, but never performing anything outright.

Others who peep in and out from the mist of Celtic Twilight –

forming a mysterious backdrop to the whole play – are the Reverend Canon George Creehewel, parish priest of Clune na Geera and local plenipotentiary; a comically-drawn faun figure of a Postmaster; a leprechaun-like yellow-bearded man known as Cornelius, a house electrician with a gift for droll prognostication; and a curious magical creation in the form of a reincarnated river-god in the shape of the Figure of the Flood; plus the stylised head of a cow, which – in the middle of the pantomimic farce – causes its own special brand of horse-play.

The scene opens with the three workmen – two with shovels and one with a pickaxe – at cock-crow on an autumnal morning, discussing the foolish habitat and pipe-dream of their crazy employers; in the words of one of them, 'th' two poor English omadhauns', who, in their mortal misgivings, are wasting their energies in bolstering a tumbledown mansion for the sake of a name and history; in the words of another, 'an' they killin' themselves thryin' to look as if the country loved them all their life'; and, with explicit reference to Avril's flimsy attire, in the words of the third, 'with the young heifer gaddin' round with next to nothin' on, goadin' the decency an' circumspection of the place'.

When foreman Jack O'Killigain enters – 'a handsome, hefty young shripling', we are told by one of the workmen previously, and 'with a big seam in his arm that he got from a bullet fired in Spain' (a reference to the Franco Civil War) – he, too, joins in the derogation of the fool-hardy project to resurrect Ormond Manor in remote Clune na Geera. O'Killigain voices O'Casey's views when he proclaims: 'Give a house a history, weave a legend round it, let some titled tomfool live or die in it – and some fool mind will see loveliness in rottenness and ruin'.

Amid the talk and prognostication, Avril saunters in, dressed becomingly 'in gay scarlet trousers, widening at the ends, and very tight around her hips and bottom' and wearing a 'low-cut black silk bodice, slashed with crimson', and bids them all 'the top o' the morning' and hopes they like the enchanted house they are renovating. O'Killigain's blarney and sarcasm are immediately apparent when he tilts by way of reply: 'Sure, when we're done with it wouldn't it be fit for the shelther an' ayse an' comfort of Nuard of the Silver Hand, were he with us now, or of the great Fergus himself of the bright bronze chariots?' And when, moments later, O'Killigain finds himself alone with the pretty young mistress of the house, he is not slow to press his amorous conquest, extolling her as 'a girl of grace, fit to find herself walkin' beside all the beauty that ever shone before the eyes o' man since Helen herself unbound her thresses to dance her wild an' willin' way through the sthreets o' Throy!' It is this particular sample of flagrant blarney and romantic cozenage which prompts Avril to exclaim: 'But is there an Irishman goin' who hasn't a dint o' wondher in his talkin'?'

Yet Avril herself is also royally touched with entrancing speech, like many a country shebeener out of Synge, when she replies to O'Killigain's invitation to meet him beside the blasted thorn-tree: 'not there: a saint himself would shudder if he had to pass it on a dusky night, with only a sly chit of a moon in the sky to show the way'. With Blakean confidence, O'Killigain reassures her: 'Oh, foolish girl, there never can be evil things where love is living', and so the tryst is established.

Throughout the play, O'Killigain also flirts with Souhaun and Cloyne, lilting his songs of love – Shakespeare fashion – and demonstrating his sexual charm with women. Perhaps his sexual conquest is associated with his prowess as a potential political leader, symbolised in the political annihilation and revolution – brought about by the River of Time – which comes at the end. (Avril is symbolic of spring. There is irony in the fact that her name suggests April showers, and April – in the words of T. S. Eliot in *The Waste Land* – is the cruellest month.)

Soon we witness a verbal display of mock-jousting between the feudal representatives of the manor and their devil-may-care Celtic courtiers. The self-opinionated Poges, a stocky little man with a fussy manner, is quickly foiled in his attempts to win over the independent-minded O'Killigain, when, after a wordy exposition in favour of inhabiting an old house with its 'banners and banneroles', O'Killigain is asked the Wordsworthian question, 'Don't you feel the lovely sensation of – er – er – er – old, unhappy, far-off things, and battles long ago?' Poges fails to elicit any special enthusiasm from the blunt O'Killigain, who replies in true O'Casey fashion: 'I let the dead bury their dead . . . Life as it is, and will be, moves me more'. In front of an astonished Poges, O'Killigain describes Wordsworth as 'A tired-out oul' blatherer; a tumble-down thinker; a man who made a hiding-place of his own life . . . a fool who thought the womb of the world was Wordsworth', and on that derisive note bows out. Poges has obviously underestimated a superior intelligence and after the labourer's exit labels O'Killigain 'a shocking example of bad taste and ignorance'; turning to

Souhaun, he explodes: 'There's one of your fine countrymen for you', and in the irrelevant cross-talk that follows between the swains – the Stoke-Poges duo – and their already disenchanted mistresses, the Irish as a race are judged to be 'quaint and charming' but badly in need of 'control'.

Stoke and Poges – ironically named after the joint place-name of Gray's *Elegy in a Country Churchyard* (O'Casey also had lived for a time in the early thirties in Chalfont St Giles, Buckinghamshire) – are stage Englishmen who elicit the same snobberies and pomposities and chauvinistic ignorance as their Irish equivalents in *Juno and the Paycock*, and rank alongside Boyle and Joxer as memorable 'paycock' creations in the O'Casey charactery. Their lives are a burlesque. As they glide into the play, initially, singing 'Rural scenes are now our joy', they are a parody of all that Gray and English sentiment about the countryside – as entertained by non-rural inhabitants – believe. A rude awakening awaits them, especially at the beginning of the second act, when, instead of experiencing Gray's 'breezy call of incense-breathing morn', the Englishmen find themselves cold and stiff on their mattresses on the floor (the bedrooms being too damp to sleep in); and instead of 'the cock's shrill clarion', they are greeted with deafening early-morning 'jungle noises' from cock and cuckoo (Wordsworth's 'blithe New-comer', the cuckoo, ironically becomes more than just 'a wandering voice' for them!)

In the course of the parody and fun the newly rusticated recruits launch into an absurd discussion, in the first act, on the merits of the primrose: Poges mistakenly ascribing to Shakespeare the lack-lustre of Wordsworth's lines from *Peter Bell*:

> A primrose by a river's brim
> A yellow primrose was to him . . .

thus confirming Souhaun's earlier sardonic judgement on her swain: 'a few little quotations drummed into you at school, is all you know of Wordsworth'. Earlier, when they have been discussing that they ought to invest in hens and cows, Avril remarks that 'a cow might be dangerous', to which the business expert with apt aplomb replies, 'Dangerous? Nonsense; if he was, then we'd simply have to keep him in a cage'.

Some entertaining verbal gymnastics take place following Basil's phoney moralisings on the metaphysics of the primrose (a parody in the style of the late Dr Cyril Joad) which so confound his mentor, the supposedly phlegmatic Poges, that the latter declares it 'a pitiful humiliation to have to listen to a half-educated fool'; interrupted by Souhaun's testy reminder that the conversation is supposed to be merely a friendly little discussion about a common country flower, and topped by Avril's ironic declaration that 'Basil is only trying to share his great knowledge with us'. The diatribe waxes strong with Poges shouting and stampeding: 'he calls that knowledge, does he?' eliciting from Souhaun the dry response that Basil 'passed through Oxford'. Poges's reaction to this is a glorious bit of O'Casey rodomontade: 'I don't care if he crept under it or flew over it; he's not going to punish me with what he picked up there'. Tearfully and wrathfully – shades of The Walrus and the Carpenter in Lewis Carroll's classic phantasmagoria – the deflated Stoke mutters: 'Invincible ignorance, God forgive it', which he follows with a flash of metaphysical inspiration, ' *Quisabit grunniodem expectio porcum* – what can one expect from a pig but a grunt'; and as he leaves the room he shouts back at Poges, peevishly, but more loudly than ever, 'Invincible ignorance!' A parody, we are left in no possible doubt, of Gray's

> where ignorance is bliss,
> 'Tis folly to be wise.

While Poges proceeds to scan his newspaper, the *Financial Universe*, his attention is distracted by (in the wording of the stage-direction) 'a sound of cackling . . . heard outside, and the loud lowing of a cow, and the crowing of cocks'. Barney dashes in to enquire of the bemused Poges whether he wants any 'entherprisin hins', followed by Cloyne asking the same question as to 'startlin cocks' (agents of conspirators are springing up like mushrooms), the First Workman also putting in his spoke for a cow to be offered for sale, 'with a skin on her as shiny an' soft as the down on a first-class angel's wing'. Looking up from his newspaper Poges roars out furiously: 'Hins, cocks, and cows! What the hell do you take me for - a farmer's boy?' (The Irish characters are resolutely determined to show themselves children of this world as well as the children of light!)

The wiles of the workmen begin to manifest themselves when the First Workman, pressing his case for the cow, advises his master to have nothing to do with any of the poultry being offered for sale

'there isn't one o' them that isn't th' essence of a false pretendher!'
The mastermind behind all this tomfoolery and strategy is none
other than O'Killigain, O'Casey's equivalent of Boucicault's
character, Conn the Shaughran; described by Boucicault as 'the life
of any funeral'. The First Workman, with natural guile, tells Poges
he can secure for him 'a sthrain o' pullets' that would give him eggs
'as if you were gettin' them be steam!' Poges phlegmatically
dismisses this ploy and insists that if he wanted poultry he would
summon experts from the Department of Agriculture. The
workman's horrified reaction is reflected in the mock-response
(partly to Poges and partly to Souhaun):

> Oh, listen to that, now! Didja hear that, ma'am? The
> Department of Agriculture, is it? Wisha, God help your inno-
> cence, sir. Sure, it's only a tiny time ago that the same
> Department sent down a special sthrong covey o' cocks to
> improve the sthrain, an' only afther a short probation, didn't they
> give the hins hysterics?

The workman, ignoring Poges's consternation of horror, continues
in the same expansive fashion:

> Ay, an' hadn't the frightened farmers to bring guns to bear on the
> cocks when they found their hins scatthered over hill an' dale,
> lyin' on their backs with their legs in the air, givin' their last gasp,
> an' glad to get outa the world they knew so well! The few mighty
> ones who survived were that stunned that there wasn't an egg in
> th' place for years!

When it becomes clear to even the gullible Poges that this is a recital
of barefaced blarney, he carries on reading his financial newspaper,
bounding up suddenly when his attention is focused on some cement
shares mentioned in the paper and dives for the telephone, which, of
course, isn't working! Souhaun, as bidden, runs to call for one of the
workmen, and the Second Workman, O'Dempsey, saunters into the
room. Not unexpectedly, there is an immediate clash of temperaments between the autocratic Poges and the scornful O'Dempsey,
whom Poges in an explosive outburst calls a fool. The combustion
on the workman's part is slow-burning but deep-seated:

> Comin' over here, thinkin' that all the glory an' grandeur of
> the world, an' all the might of man, was stuffed into a

bulgin' purse, an' stickin' their tongue out at a race that's oldher than themselves by a little like a thousand years, greater in their beginnin' than they are in their prime; with us speakin' with ayse the mighty languages o' the world when they could barely gurgle a few sounds, sayin' the rest in the movement of their fingers.

Poges, with symptomatic English tactlessness, declares brusquely, 'Go to the devil, man, and learn manners!' This produces a further obloquy of disapproval from the disloyal O'Dempsey:

Hammerin' out handsome golden ornaments for flowin' cloak an' tidy tunic we were, while you were busy gatherin' dhried grass, an' dyin' it blue, to hide the consternation of your middle parts; decoratin' eminent books with glowin' colour an' audacious beauty were we, as O'Killigain himself will tell you, when you were still a hundred score o' years away from even hearin' of the alphabet. [*Beside the entrance*] Fool? It's yourself's the fool, I'm sayin', settlin' down in a place that's only fit for the housin' o' dead men! Settlin' here, are you? Wait till God sends the heavy rain, and the floods come!

In the meantime, the current of farce is flowing rapidly as an Irish curse descends not only on the working of the telephone but on the horse Basil has hired for riding, fit as he thinks for hunters to go cantering with ladies of the land, which turns out to be a wild mastodon, flinging its rider, bruised and forlorn, in the middle of a field, while his partner, the bold Avril, canters off instead 'naked and unashamed' with O'Killigain: and to add to the fantasy and hilarity, the locals and workmen embroider the circumstantial unlikelihood of the yarn beyond credibility, to the surprised wonder of one, 'without as much as a gather on her to keep her modesty from catchin' cold'; 'denudin' the disthrict', says another 'of all its self-denyin' decency!' And, crowning the masterstrokes of misfortune, the yellow-bearded electrician has bored a hole in the wrong part of the ceiling, enabling him to thrust his head through at the appropriate time, in the climax of the farce – with exaggeration and fancy so intertwined – bringing the act to a riotous conclusion with the rumbustious rejoinder, 'oh, isn't it like me to be up here outa sight o' th' world, an' great things happenin'!' A rustic variant on the aphorism, 'the best of life is but intoxication' and O'Casey's virtual endorsement of Byron's cynical epigram from *Don Juan*:

There is a tide in the affairs of women,
Which, taken at the flood, leads – God knows where.

The scene and surroundings in Act Two are as before, opening on
a cold, misty morning to loud farmyard noises, offstage, indicating
actualities rather than imagined fancies of the townees' conception
of the countryside, to the chorus, coming vigorously from all
directions, of 'The Farmer's Boy'. The atmosphere is very different
from the elegiac mood suggested by Gray's poem. As the act
proceeds we quickly learn disenchantment of Gray's words as far as
Stoke and Poges are concerned:

> Far from the madding crowd's ignoble strife,
> Their sober wishes never learn'd to stray;
> Along the cool sequester'd vale of life
> They kept the noiseless tenor of their way.

In the air, with all the cackling, crowing and grunting noises that
can be heard, there is anything but the bard's suggested 'solemn
stillness', and the irony of Gray's line:

For them no more the blazing hearth shall burn

is quickly demonstrated by Barney and Cloyne's difficulties in
getting a fire to blaze in the petrified atmosphere of a house of such
primitiveness and gloom. The normally taciturn Barney fulminates
to Cloyne:

Comin' down to this back o' God-speed place for rest an'
quietness! Afther all that science has thried to do for us, goin' back
to lantherns an' candles. Th' only electric light he'll allow is one
over his own desk! Runnin' in the face o' God Almighty's
goodness – that's what it is.

The fanciful *non sequitur* conversation between Barney and
Cloyne, generated by the futile attempt to get the fire going, is
further fanned by Poges's tactless interjection. 'Isn't the fire lighted
yet? Being in the country's no reason why we should be frozen to
death', which sparks off one of those verbal contests between Poges
and Barney that forms part of O'Casey's stock-in-trade, but enacted
with gusto brings its own riotous fun:

POGES (*testily*):You can't light logs with a bit of paper, man. Oh, use your brains, Barney, use your brains.

BARNEY: An' what else have I got to light them with?

POGES: Small sticks, man; put some small sticks under them.

BARNEY: An' will you tell me where I'm goin' to get the small sticks? Isn't the nearest shop a dozen miles away?

POGES: Well, if there's no sticks, sprinkle a little parafin on them.

BARNEY (*sarcastically*): An' where am I goin' to get the parafin? There's no oil wells knockin' about here.

POGES (*severely*): Don't be funny. You 've got to remember you're in the country now.

BARNEY: Isn't it meself that's gettin' to know it well! . . .

POGES: Can't you see that those logs are too big?

BARNEY: I think I do, unless me sight's goin' curious . . .

POGES: There must be an axe knocking about somewhere.

BARNEY: There's nothin' knockin' about here but a bitther breeze whirlin' through the passages that ud make the very legs of a nun numb!

The knockabout continues as Cloyne, who is sent out to find someone to fix the telephone, quickly returns screaming; literally tugging at Poges to save her from, allegedly, a wild 'bull,' whose presence is making itself felt in the entrance hall! Cloyne's (and Barney's) fear is frenetic: to Poges, abandoning all semblance of sang-froid, she frantically shouts: 'Me legs have given undher me. Let me hold on to you, Sir – it's me only hope'. Poges, petrified with panic, calls out to Souhaun and O'Killigain for help; and to Barney he calls out to fetch Stoke to bring down his gun. As soon as Basil appears with the gun and is told about the 'bull', he blimpishly declares, 'Damn it, such carelessness! You must be on guard in the country'. Stoke, on offering his partner the gun, is told,. 'You use it, man; weren't you an A.R.P. man?' and some further ripe exchanges take place on lines similar to the comical dialogue of the popular British television satire, *Dad's Army* by Jimmy Perry and David Croft:

BASIL (*indignantly*): I never did anything more than clay-pigeon shooting! Let whoever let the damned animal in, let the damned animal out! (*He pokes* POGES *with the gun.*) Here, take this, and down him – you're nearer the bull than I am.

POGES (*angrily*): I'm not a toreador, am I? And don't point, don't point the gun at me! D'ye want me to die two deaths at once? What's the advantage of your passing through Oxford if you can't face a bull with a gun in your hand? Be a man, man, and not a mouse.

Basil suggests telephoning the police or the fire-brigade, but is reproved by his friend reminding him that in their present predicament there are no police, fire-brigade or telephone. Then the head of the animal appears round the door, sending Cloyne into a near-faint, and, in the wording of the stage-direction, 'spasmodically tugs the legs of Poges, making him lose his balance so that he topples to the floor, after a frantic effort to save himself', shouting, as he is falling 'My God, he's on top of us! We're done for!' The frightened Basil throws the gun into the room (he is in the passageway) and bolts for his life. In the distance can be heard Barney nervously calling, 'Sing out . . . if you want any assistance!'

The reign of terror comes to an end as the First Workman, who has spotted the cow in the hall, ushers it outside, and enters the room, amazed to see the prostrate Cloyne in a heap on the floor and Poges standing nearby with gun in hand. On learning the truth from the workman, Poges snaps at the terrified Cloyne to get up and take the gun back to Basil, later commenting to the workman: 'Fainting, shouting, screaming, and running about for nothing! No nerves . . . no spirit; no coolness in a crisis'. Buttering Poges, the man replies: 'An' you stood your ground. Looka that now. Prepared for anything'. Flattered, Poges replies calmly: 'The other fellow, Mr Basil, ran for his life . . . British, too, think of that'. Presently, the ladies, bringing in Poges's precious Annamese vase and Cambodian bowl, enquire what all the commotion was about, Souhaun announcing that they had to stop Basil from trying to throw himself out of a window, while Avril gives the news that Barney had got out on top of the roof. Poges, dismissing the cold profanity that he too was afflicted with cowardice, assures them it was nothing, and adds: 'a stray cow in the garden mooed, and Basil lost his head and Cloyne lost her feet'. Avril, however, refutes his assurance by remarking, 'But Barney, when he was rushing past, said that you were out here roaring for help!' In front of them the First Workman, still entertaining sly hopes for an early sale of the cow, craftily counters by reassuring the women, 'Indeed an' he wasn't, for I can testify to that, but standin' here, cool as you like, he was, waitin' for the worst'.

Alone now with the First Workman, after he has ordered the precious relics to be carried upstairs, Poges enquires whether he is the workman who is versed in all the tales and legends of ancient Ireland, but is told he should seek out O'Dempsey, the Second Workman, 'th' powerful man with th' powerful beard'. The First Workman, reminiscing with Poges on the golden age symbolised by the Tudor mansion he is helping to renovate ('Purple nights and golden days, my friend', interjects Poges), reveals himself not so much as a persuasive moonshiner whose talk is poetically touched, but, in the playwright's eyes at least, as a typical working-class toady anxious at all costs to preserve the *status quo* (like Tom Nimmo in *The Harvest Festival*) and belonging, as Swift acutely observed, to

> A servile race in folly nursed,
> Who truckle most when treated worse;

playfully demonstrated when Poges, extolling the Tudor dynasty, wildly exclaims: 'our pride shall be their pride, our elegance their elegance, and the banner of the Tudors shall fly from the battlements again! The King, the King, God bless him!' whereat he is reproved by the workman with the warning: 'I wouldn't say too much about the King, sir; we're a little touchy about kings down here in Clune na Geera'. The workman has his own brand of stylised philosophy, reflected in the words:

> What are we now, what are we all, but a tired thribe thryin' to do nothin' in th' shortest possible time? Worn away we are, I'm sayin', to shreds and shaddas mouldin' machines to do everything for us. Tired, is it? Ay, tired an' thremblin' towards the edge of th' end of a life hardly worth livin'!

And from the First Workman's lips come the first intimations of prophecy: 'It's meself is sayin' ourselves came late, but soon enough to see the finery fade to purple dust, an' the glow o' th' quality turn to murmurin' ashes'.

Poges's tête-à-tête with the workman is abruptly interrupted with screams and squeals, offstage, from Avril and Souhaun, followed by sounds of running feet and breaking of chinaware, as both come tearing into the room clutching remnants of a broken bowl and vase, treasures the pompous Poges values so much. The house has its share of rats as big as badgers, rivalling those of Hamelin's town in Browning's poem. The deflated Poges looks even more crestfallen when the women inform him the relics were only imitation, sold, on the confident authority of O'Killigain, 'in thousands to Singapore and Saigon for suckers to buy them!' Further trouble abounds when Cloyne announces the arrival of a huge garden roller which is dumped, along with garden tools, right in front of the hall door, so close as to impede entry in and out of the hallway. But before Poges tackles the task of its removal, he is enjoined in eager conversation with the mysterious, pensive-looking, strongly-built workman, O'Dempsey.

Poges straightway tackles the dreamy-eyed Second Workman about the share of wonders and treasure-house of history in which the locality is saturated. In poetic vein, the meditative O'Dempsey recounts tales of Finn Mac Coole whose 'spear can be seen with its point in the stars', and with a menacing look at Poges, 'but not with an eye that can see no further than the well-fashioned edge of a golden coin'. Phantasmagorically, too, the workman tells of legends of the 'long-handed Lugh; when the Dagda makes a gong o' the moon, an' th' Sword o' Light shows the way to all who see it', referred to allegorically, as well, throughout O'Casey's auto-biographies, in *Pictures in the Hallway* and *Rose and Crown*.

The character of Philib O'Dempsey may have been influenced, to some extent, by *shanachies* or traditional story-tellers of the West of Ireland, in particular the *shanachie* whom Moore, in *A Story-Teller's Holiday*, introduces from Connaught, Alec Trusselby, the fern-gatherer of Westport: 'an Irish peasant', says Moore, 'but far from typical'. He was not able to forget, he tells us, 'his spare chestnut beard, his moustache and his comely, well-knit figure' together with the fine blackthorn he always carried which he alluded to as 'the Murrigan' (meaning 'great queen' in Irish). In this part of Ireland there were – as Moore noted – plenty of 'gabby tongues'. In similar vein to Synge, Moore declares that 'stories ripe in the mouth are like apples on a sunny shelf . . . trust a good tongue to put a good skin on its stuff'. The traditional story-tellers always looked for inspiration for their yarns by the side of running water shaping their own words into pools and bubbling eddies. In *Purple Dust* it is noteworthy that O'Dempsey waxes even more eloquent as the advent of the presaged flood approaches in the allegorical ending to the third act. And in the final act, as we shall see, the curiously-drawn figure of the

Postmaster wields a finely-carved blackthorn which engages the transfixed attention of Poges.

To a story-teller, what is fabrication? In the Byronic idiom from *Don Juan* – 'truth in masquerade'. O'Dempsey, who – to employ an expression from Synge – has 'as much talk and streeleen . . . as the poets of Dingle Bay', mesmerises the easily gullible Poges with his fine words and images of 'Heber's children' and talk of Shane the Proud and even Parnell 'with his wine-coloured eyes flashin' hathred to England!' (During the spellbinding discourse listened to by the enrapt Poges, O'Killigain has sauntered in unnoticed.) Poges, detaching himself from the spell, enquires: 'And do none other of those you know, good man, see the things you see?' The workman's reply is whimsical as well as prophetic: 'Barrin' a few an' O'Killigain there, they see these things only as a little cloud o' purple dust blown before the wind'.

O'Dempsey, a most winsome colloquist, pitches into Poges (and the modern commercial outlook he represents) with a tyrannical tirade which is characteristically O'Caseyean and caustic:

> Barrin' O'Killigain there an' a few, what is it all now but a bitther noise of cadgin' mercy from heaven, an' a sour handlin' o' life for a cushion'd seat in a corner? There is no shout in it; no sound of a slap of a spear in a body; no song; no sturdy winecup in a sturdy hand; no liftin' of a mighty arm to push back the tumblin' waters from a ship just sthrikin' a storm. Them that fight now fight in a daze o' thradin'; for buyin' an' sellin', for whores an' holiness, for th' image o' God on a golden coin; while th' men o' peace are little men now, writin' dead words with their tiny pens, seekin' a tidy an' tendher way to the end. Respectable lodgers with life they are, behind solid doors with knockers on them, an' curtained glass to keep the stars from starin'!

After the mysterious O'Dempsey has taken up his wheelbarrow and gone out, O'Killigain and Poges enter into another verbal fray:

POGES: What a strange, odd man! I couldn't get half of what he was trying to say. Are there many like him?

O'KILLIGAIN: Millions of them, though few of them have tongues so musical.

POGES: He rather took to me, I think, and looks upon me as a friend.

O'KILLIGAIN (*ironically*): He looks upon you, and all Englishmen, as a rascal, a thief, and a big-pulsed hypocrite.

POGES (*indignantly*): Good God, but that's pure ignorance. Where would the world be without us?

O'KILLIGAIN: The giddy globe would wobble, slow down, stand still, and death would come quick to us all.

POGES (*a little puzzled by this remark*): Eh? Quite. Well, no, not so bad as that, you know, but near it, damned near it.

When Souhaun attempts to remind Poges of the obstacle of the roller, she is rebuked and informed that he is in the middle of 'a serious discussion' with O'Killigain, turning to whom, he remarks, tauntingly:

We, sir, are a liberty-loving people, and have always striven to preserve perfect – perfect, mind you – freedom of thought, not only in our own land, but throughout the whole world . . . every right-minded man the world over knows, or ought to know, that wherever we have gone, progress, civilisation, truth, justice, honour, humanity, righteousness, and peace have followed at our heels. In the Press, in the Parliament, in the pulpit, or on the battlefield, no lie has ever been uttered by us, no false claim made, no right of man infringed, no law of God ignored, no human law, national or international, broken.

Taking the sails out of the pompous windbag, O'Killigain softly interjects: 'Oh, for God's sake, man, don't be pratin' like a pantaloon priest!' Incensed, the furious Poges shouts back: 'I say, sir, that Justice is England's old nurse; Righteousness and Peace sit together in her common-room, and the porter at her gate is Truth!' O'Killigain's rejoinder is derisive: 'An' God Himself is England's butler!' and adding – as the enraged Poges is choking with fury – 'in a generation or so the English Empire will be remembered only as a half-forgotten nursery rhyme!'

Doubtless it was such a passage which unduly upset the normally choleric Agate, who in 1942 in *The Sunday Times* made reference to the play as 'a witless lampoon at the expense of the English, too busy fighting for freedom to answer back'. The timing of the play may well have been unfortunate, yet the essence of the satire remains realistic and convincing, even if devastating as well. Synge's ribald conclusion, in his preface to *The Tinker's Wedding*, is relevant:

I do not think that these country people, who have so much humour themselves, will mind being laughed at without malice, as the people in every country have been laughed at in their own comedies.

Agate, and those of his own persuasion, taking their cue from Poges, who termed O'Killigain's taunts (and, to them, O'Casey's) as 'vile slander', had obviously forgotten the satirical casuistries of Shaw and Wilde – or, in a previous century, Swift and Pope; and perhaps had forgotten completely Byron's wicked little epigram:

> The world is a bundle of hay,
> Mankind are the asses who pull;
> Each tugs it a different way,
> And the greatest of all is John Bull.

In a review of Seumas MacManus's *Donegal Fairy Stories*, in the *Speaker* of June 1902, Synge had written:

> . . . the rollicking note is present in the Irish character – present to an extent some writers of the day do not seem to be aware of – and it demands, if we choose to deal with it, a free rollicking style.

In a letter elsewhere Synge points out:

> The wildness, and if you will, vices of the Irish peasantry are due, like their extraordinary good points of all kinds, to the *richness* of their nature – a thing that is priceless beyond words.

Just as Synge's *The Playboy of the Western World* was singled out for opposition and declared a parody and perversion of Irish peasant life, so Agate and other English critics dubbed *Purple Dust* a libel on English character – unchivalrous both in language and plot. Mocking irony is implicit throughout, just as in the plays of Molière. As Shaw jocularly remarked in defence of Synge: '. . . who is Ireland that she should not be libelled as other countries are by their great comedians?' And England too.

The influence of Dion Boucicault's character, Conn the Shaughraun, can be seen in both Christy Mahon's behaviour in Synge's well-known comedy and jaunty Jack O'Killigain, with his care-free joviality and gaiety, in *Purple Dust*. Histrionic qualitie

which Synge depicted in *The Playboy* – and O'Casey in *Purple Dust* –
are to be found everywhere in Ireland, where dramatic instinct is
strong and where – as Synge was quick to discover – there
is 'a popular imagination that is fiery, and magnificent, and
tender'.

After Poges's stormy exit – following his debacle with the
Irishman – Souhaun teases the handsome O'Killigain – resembling
Synge's Playboy – in the words of Pegeen Mike, 'with a mighty
spirit in him and a gamey heart', and chides him, laughingly, for
provoking Cyril in to such a disagreeable tantrum; whereupon the
unabashed foreman flatters and philanders with the woman who
is supposed to be the consort of Poges. Souhaun responds with a kiss
in the brief romantic interlude which intervenes, quickly followed
by rollicking, rambunctious farce.

The garden roller, looking more like a steam-roller, is pushed into
the passageway by Poges – to the ecstatic consternation of the
workmen and the solicitude of the women, who bemoan his
amateurism in horticultural affairs. In a scene of supramonumental
havoc (Poges resisting all offers of advice and assistance) the roller –
with Poges tugging at it – goes careering down the declivity of the
passageway and crashes through one of the walls, the demented
Poges ending up in a heap of bricks and mortar. The incident causes
Cornelius the 'electrician' to poke his head through the ceiling for a
second time with his comical rejoinder, 'Can't you wait till I'm
down in th' world o' men, and can enjoy these things happenin'!': a
hilarious contrast to the doleful jibe uttered by Poges in his stupefied
state: 'What a rascal that man must be who sold me the roller! In
this country, among a simple people, where the very air is redolent
with fairy lore, that such a dangerous and materialistic mind should
be lurking!'

With scarcely a lull in the farce, the second act ends in riotous
frenzy when O'Killigain alerts everyone that Basil is stalking the
grounds with his gun poised at a dangerous angle. The warning
comes too late as a shot is fired (Poges momentarily believing that
his friend has killed Avril) but from the hole in the ceiling comes the
dire pronouncement that Stoke has killed the poor cow – owned by
none other than Cornelius himself – in mistake for a bull, with the
yellow-bearded eccentric threatening 'the heavy law' on the
English squires by way of compensation, while Poges – sitting on a
mattress on the floor, still writhing in agony, and looking like an
injured Buddha – agonisingly bemoans: 'The curse of the Irish

thorn-tree is on us . . . what an awful country to be living in! A no-man's land; a waste land; a wilderness!'

As dreams of bucolic paradise rapidly fade, the curtain rises on Act Three, with ominous intensity, to sounds of intermittent heavy winds and rain. (The setting is the same as in the previous acts, only later in the day.) Poges – despite his agricultural antics – still asserts himself as the efficient businessman guarding assiduously his financial interests and prepared to reap by telephone (now functioning at last) substantial profits from the War – cashing in, as he terms it, on 'splintered bodies'. (Even from his backwater in Ireland he can still juggle a fortune on the Stock Exchange.) Behind the image of a likeable buffoon lies the more sinister one of shrewd capitalist – exploiting even the efforts of war (an indictable offence which evidently does not trouble his conscience, though, ironically, he would cheerfully 'jail' those like O'Killigain who forecast the end of the British Empire regardless of the eventual truth of the prophecy).

His hypocrisy is also underlined during discussions with Canon Creehewel (a comparatively mild clerical figure compared with Father Domineer of *Cock-a-Doodle Dandy* or Canon Burren of *The Bishop's Bonfire*), who pays a brief visit to the 'paycockian' squires at Tudor Manor to enquire how spiritual interests of the locality can best be served by the acceptable face of capitalism in harmony with feudal life in rural Clune na Geera. Yet earlier on in the play when speaking of the Canon, Poges had mockingly cast aspersions on Ireland's clerical community:

> Oh, these priests, these priests! Thick as weeds in this poor country. Opposed to every decent thought that happens not to have come from them. Sealing with seven seals any book an intelligent human being would wish to read. Ever on guard to keep the people from growing out of infancy. No one should give them the slightest encouragement. Oh, if the misguided people would only go back to the veneration of the old Celtic gods, what a stir we'd have here!

(Echoes of George Moore, in *A Story-Teller's Holiday*, who once declared: 'it would be a wonderful thing surely if the avarice of the clergy turned the Irish into Protestants, the same as it did the English. Be that as it may, what Ireland needs is a new religion, and I pray that she may get one'.)

Although primarily a comic figure, the Canon soon reveals himself as a representative of O'Casey's middle-class hypocrisy – a variant on Shaw's 'middle-class morality', voiced by Doolittle in *Pygmalion* – favouring, to the self-satisfied delight of Poges, 'the slow movement of the past' over 'the reckless and Godless speed of the present'. The Canon flatters Poges's preoccupation with restoring the past, hoping to enlist himself and Stoke in ridding the community of menaces arising from dancehalls, instancing the 'low-cut bodices, defiant short skirts, or shorter trousers, murdherin' modesty with a restless an' reckless hand!' as well as – he bends confidentially towards Poges – the local snake-in-the-grass, O'Killigain! (And, as if to emphasise the Canon's point, the wind and rain can be plainly heard offstage, as a mocking, melodramatic touch.) The Canon's initial remark that 'It is almost a sacred thing to keep an old thing from dying' is intended irony on O'Casey's part, in view of his own commentaries on the play and the conclusion spelt out at the end of *Purple Dust*.

The Canon's hypocrisy is further demonstrated when he turns an apparent blind eye to the excessively bare mistresses of the English squires who have bounced into the room demanding the installation of a bathroom (Poges's taunt that the Tudor period never saw the use of such fripperies is answered by Souhaun's 'In the centre of a hot bath, dear, I can remain in the centre of your civilization') as his gaze is riveted on the cheque which is donated to him by Poges. Ignoring the 'Jacobin' chair, carried into the room by Barney and Cloyne, he departs (in the words of O'Killigain's refrain at the end of the play) 'with a will an' a way, away O!' leaving Poges to comment dryly, 'Ignorance; Irish ignorance!'

In the midst of the removal and hurly-burly, the precious Jacobean chair is jerked, for which Barney is rebuked. He flings back the retort, 'well, if I let a damned chair fall, I didn't knock a wall down!' and while the confusion is going on Avril, fed-up with helping to put 'a foolish old house in order', announces she is going for 'a walk along the bank of the brimming river'. Stoke registers disapproval and rightly suspects O'Killigain; displaying at the same time a petulant fit of temper – in accents far from mild – reminiscent of those English caricature-figures we come across in Carroll's fantasias, but is reproved as usual for his pains. The Stoke-Poges combination, in many respects, is a 'paycockian' variation on the Tweedledum and Tweedledee pair of *Through the Looking-Glass* – the one always shouting 'Contrariwise', the other 'Nohow!'

Souhaun, asking one of the workmen – in this case, O'Dempsey – whether O'Killigain has gone out, is told 'with th' handsome young woman', and is herself flattered by the Second Workman with accents of enchantment rivalling those of Synge's characters – recalling the strange Tramp in *The Shadow of the Glen*, with his 'fine bit of talk', or Christy Mahon in *The Playboy of the Western World*, 'who'd capsize the stars' with his eloquence. It is the same kind 'of a poacher's love' (to use Pegeen's phrase of Christy) that O'Dempsey offers Souhaun – with her handsome, fuller figure, and her shining eyes: 'Soon you'll tire o' nestin' in a dusty nook, with the hills outside an' the roads for walkin'' (Synge: *The Shadow of the Glen*). He captivates her with his winning words: 'You'll hurry away from him, I'm sayin', an' it's a glad heart'll lighten th' journey to a one'll find a place for your little hand in th' white clouds, an' a place for your saucy head in th' blue o' th' sky' (O'Casey: *Purple Dust*).

Romance and idyll quickly give way, once more, with lightning speed, to farce; and in the heightened furore that follows lies one of the play's most hilarious scenes of splendid knockabout: the removal and positioning of 'the oul' codger's bureau', Poges's highly valued piece of period furniture, the gilded quattrocento writing-desk, which not only gets mangled and scratched by the three incompetent workmen but brings down an entire column of the room's archway – prefiguring supernatural events which result from the eventual collapse of the house in the eddying flood-waters in the apocalyptic ending to the play. In the contractual excitement, the desk, as it reaches the entrance, is seen to be a very tight fit, giving rise to a whole concerto of Irish expletives and exasperation

1ST WORKMAN: A little to the ayste, there, a little more to the ayste, can't yous!

2ND WORKMAN: No, west, west; can't yous see it'll jam if yous can it to the ayste? To th' west, I'm tellin' yous! . .

3RD WORKMAN: Where th' hell are yous shovin'? Are yous blind or wha'? No squirmin'll get it in that way (*Recklessly*) Here, throw th' thing up on its hind legs an' let her go! . . .

1ST WORKMAN: See, boys, it's a quattrocento lump o' furniture an' so needs gentle handlin'. (*To* 2ND WORKMAN) You, Philib, there, give it a sudden swing to th' ayste, an' while she's swingin' we'll shoot her ahead.

2ND WORKMAN (*angrily*): How an I goin' to give her a sudden
swing to the ayste when there's no purchase to
get a grip of her? Squattrocento or nottrocento,
I'm not goin' to let it whip a slice outa my hand!

The alarmed Poges looking on in anguish and amazement runs off
to get cushions and pillows to protect the stone-wall from scraping
the sides, while the First Workman mutters to the others, 'J' ever see
such an oul' fustherer in your life? You'd think the thing was on its
way to the kingdom of heaven th' way he's cryin' over it'; capped by
the Third Workman's comment, 'With a look on his ugly oul' gob
like the tune th' oul' cow died of'. A crowbar is suggested to hurry
on the work of 'desthruction', while the rapscallions brace themselves chanting some verses from 'What Shall We do with the Drunken
Sailor' ('*Pull away, an' up she rises*'), in the midst of which the frantic
Poges, on returning, hurtles in – like Captain Ahab in *Moby Dick* –
to the mouth of danger, seizing the edge of the desk and trying to
pull it from the wall, shouting to everyone for help; but before he is
aware of it, the First Workman has leapt on top of the bureau to
come to his rescue, his heavy hobnailed boots scraping the surface,
to his own protestations in self-vindication that 'th' nails are worn so
soft an' smooth they wouldn't mark th' wing of a butterfly'. In the
final predestinating heave, with Poges just having managed to
retrieve his foot in time from under the weight of the turmoil, the
desk shoots forward into the middle of the room – the men looking
triumphant and Poges still rubbing his foot and surveying the extent
of the damage in a state of abject horror. Tempers are not improved,
as Souhaun (followed by Basil) enquire upon entering who caused
all the wreckage. 'Your very clever countrymen', remarks Poges
sarcastically; 'And the high opinion they have of themselves',
interjects Basil mockingly.

After such whelmings, Basil and Poges have a minor *contretemps* of
their own on a point of historical absurdity, only to be interrupted
by the careless O'Dempsey – returning with a barrow-load of bricks
– wheeling past the two disputants through the middle of a newly
laid-out rug on his way to the hall. The irritated Poges instantly
rebukes him, receiving the surly reply, 'What d'ye want me to do?
Take th' barrow o' bricks up in me arms an' fly over it?'

The pace is now set for a grand sparring match between the
English duo on the one hand and the Irish two-man loquacious
wrestling team in a bout of conversational tag on the other

(O'Killigain has duly returned), with Souhaun adding her share of feminine wit. Stoke, who attempts to come to the rescue of his friend, when his *esprit de corps* is challenged, becomes èmbroiled in an embattled encounter with O'Dempsey:

> 2ND WORKMAN (*eyeing* BASIL *with scorn*): Jasus, looka what calls itself a betther man than me!
>
> POGES (*earnestly – to the* 2ND WORKMAN): My man, you're cheeking a cousin of a K.G. whose family goes back to – to – (*turning to* BASIL) – William the Conqueror, isn't it?
>
> BASIL (*stiffening – with proud complacency*): Further back, old boy – Alfred; the last man of the last family fell at the battle of Hastings.
>
> POGES (*impressively*): There, you see.
>
> SOUHAUN (*with a sign of mockery in her voice*): And the ancient gentleman passed through Oxford, too.
>
> O'KILLIGAIN (*from the archway*): The city of dissolute might!
>
> 2ND WORKMAN (*with mock deference*): D'ye tell me that, now? . . . Isn't it an alarmin' thing to hear of the ancientology of a being that I took to be an ordinary man!

and O'Dempsey informs the nonplussed Stoke that his heritage stretches back even further – long 'before an Englishman thought of buildin' a weedy shelther'. After O'Dempsey's exit, O'Killigain is instructed to keep his men and their care-free manners at bay; 'Dignity reigns here', says Poges imperiously.

Portentously, the room darkens and louder thunder is heard in the distance: the workmen decide to knock off as the storm threatens. Souhaun is sorrowful at seeing O'Dempsey leave and previously listening to a musical voice 'makin' gold embroidery out o' dancin' words'. (She has just been offered 'a long sail on the widening waters' by her workman-lover, and Avril, too, is cautioned by O'Killigain to 'come out and join th' living . . . away from where rich ignorance is a blessing, an' foolishness a gift from God'). As fantasy descends upon the scene like a river-mist, Souhaun tells O'Dempsey, invitingly, she would ride away with him if she had a horse; and is told that O'Killigain has provided one. Poges, who senses approaching doom, shouts to the two Irishmen to get out, adding furiously, 'We haven't lived with you long enough to be touched with madness!' O'Killigain promises to call for Avril 'when th' river rises!' As the set darkens, in her frightened dismay, she leaves the room with Basil and soon after Souhaun also disappears leaving Poges to ponder, as the room becomes noticeably darker; and, like the tight-fisted Scrooge of Dickens's tale, he is left to his thoughts and apparitions.

Poges, who has settled down at his injured writing-desk busying himself with papers from a drawer, is suddenly confronted with a little leprechaun of a man, dressed in a rain-soaked mackintosh, with a blackthorn stick in his hand, who peeps round the room at him and then trots around dancing a polka: it is the curious village Postmaster, who carries his own special pixie brand of whimsicality and humour. Even though he is pure fantasy he is not unlike James Stephens, the poet and author of *The Crock of Gold*, to whom O'Casey later dedicated *Cock-a-Doodle Dandy*, but in manner and deportment he most resembles his counterpart, the porter of a general store in that same play, and also the strangely comical railway porter in the later play, *The Bishop's Bonfire*. He is a fey figure straight out of the Irish mythological past. Like all such romancers and legendary tale-bearers he carries a fine blackthorn, or shillelagh, which Poges greatly admires and wishes to examine but is not allowed to touch because the cudgel has been closely and mysteriously associated with the downfall of Parnell.

Darkness and gloom are visibly descending as thunderclaps and the sound of a galloping horse are heard in the distance. Poges is reluctant to detain the Postmaster procrastinating at his side, but the little man has come, ostensibly, about the late-night telephone calls which Poges has been in the habit of making thus causing, with the existence of an old-fashioned manually operated telephone switchboard in the area, the official's lack of sleep, and the fantastical postmaster hovers around for a pledge on Poges's part to cease using the telephone late at night, but in reply for his pains is given only a curt, autocratic refusal and told in firm tones to take himself and his shillelagh away from the house.

As the scene darkens and the wind and rain beat with velocity, even the one electric light (which has engaged the energies of the weird Cornelius throughout the whole play) is seen to flicker in the darkening gloom. As the Postmaster turns to go, he and Poges are confronted with an even stranger apparition, 'dressed from head to foot in gleaming oilskins', with a black hood giving a glimpse of a blue mask, 'all illumined by the rays of flickering lightning, so that

The Figure seems to look like the spirit of the turbulent waters of the rising river'. The antediluvian sprite is as unrealistic as Nuard, Lugh and Fergus – and all the other legendary and mythological names mentioned in the course of the drama from Ireland's ancient past. By the back entrances come Basil, Barney and Cloyne, each holding a lighted lantern and looking very frightened. They too stare at the Figure, whose words of prophecy are Biblical in foretelling the end of the present manner of civilisation as we know it: 'Those who have lifted their eyes unto the hills are firm of foot, for in the hills is safety; but a trembling perch in the highest place on the highest house shall be the portion of those who dwell in the valleys below!'

As the frightened assembly is arguing about what to do, the Postmaster thwacks his blackthorn on the quattrocento desk with a loud crack and issues instructions for scrambling on the roof or improvising a raft in face of the rising waters. In the midst of the terror Avril appears wearing a green mackintosh and with case in hand ready to depart. All ask where Souhaun is and Avril tells them in a soft-spoken voice: 'Gone with the wind; gone with the waters; gone with the one man who alone saw something in her!' And in the recriminations which follow, O'Killigain is heard outside loudly shouting for Avril to brave the storm and follow him. Then he appears inside, his trench-coat and hair soaking (most of the playwright's heroes and virile young men are dressed in trench-attire, suggestive not of gunmen but gallants; wayward young gaffers who are jubilant in their unwavering self-determination). To Poges, as he carries off the betrothed Avril, he flings the final retort: 'You have had your day, like every dog. Your Tudors have had their day, and they are gone; and th' little heap o' purple dust they left behind them will vanish away in th' flood of the river'.

The play ends, dramatically, as O'Killigain snatches his girl from the hands of the outwitted English (as in the fairy tales of old Ireland) and rides her off through storm and flood, as the sound of oars can be heard splashing the waters, to O'Killigain's singing of 'Come from the Dyin' ' – set with the playwright's own words to the familiar refrains of 'The Rio Grande' – as in the injunction of the final stage direction: '. . . the green waters tumble into the room through the entrance from the hall'. In the passageway, the distraught Poges finally cries out, in a mocking parody on the playwright's part on Browning's celebrated lines: 'Would to God I were in England, now that winter's here!'

Since the play is designed almost wholly in terms of fantasy, it is not an easy drama to produce: the mixture of styles – rhapsodic farce and low comedy – with its infusion of poetry and song make it a daring and challenging play both to stage and act in. Yet O'Casey's play – along with the irrepressible *Cock-a-Doodle Dandy* and the much later *The Drums of Father Ned* – is a happy comic diversion which makes it a prime candidate for staging among his later works, and it needs to be played with tremendous verve. It has the usual marvellous flood of glittering words we associate with O'Casey. Whilst the play has been successfully produced in America and elsewhere abroad, the few English productions, on the whole, have been disappointing failures. Surely, O'Casey's rumbustious comedy and frolicsome satire is not impossible to produce? An intelligent and imaginative producer should be able to present the word-play and horse-play in successful combinations, bearing in mind the drama is grand, irreverent fun, even for Anglophiles. Farce is combined with symbolism and poetry as it becomes richly and maddeningly apparent that the type of English mind portrayed in this play will never understand the Irish – epitomised so well in the magic of Whitman's lines, from 'To a Certain Civilian', which O'Casey was fond of quoting:

> . . . go lull yourself with what you can understand, and with piano-tunes,
> For I lull nobody, and you will never understand me.

Although it may be an awesome task to impart O'Casey's devastating Irish irony across the footlights – especially in translation or styles suitable to foreign audiences – temptations to overplay laughs and stage tricks at the expense of lyricism and fantasy must be resisted and an overall balance preserved. O'Casey's power, his flashing stream of metaphor, wit, passion and excitement in this entrancing comedy and masterly satire will shine through if handled with sensitivity and care. Even a bad production will not altogether stifle O'Casey's voice; but a play of this extraordinary felicity deserves nothing less than golden performances, and, so far, in England, we have not seen a satisfactory professional production.

The play has had a history of unpopularity among certain theatrical managements in this country, though entirely without justification. Agate's original outburst, in April 1942, at the height of the war, was shrill and silly, but may have left its prejudicial mark:

the London *première* at the Mermaid Theatre for the Sean O'Casey Festival in 1962 did little in the way of grand homage to O'Casey's reputation. Predictably, hardened patriots might still take offence at the 'pro-Irish' flavour of the play and the portrayal of English characters as such ignorant and stupid buffoons, though forgetting that nation-wide popular burlesques, such as *Dad's Army* – lampooning the antics of the war-time Home Guard – contain characters as equally crass and riotously funny. (Stoke and Poges are forerunners of Wilson and Mainwaring.) The satire on the stiff-upper-lip attitude and political reference to the collapse of the British Empire will offend few English audiences these days; no more than an Irish audience at the end of the century would take exception to the portrayal of a couple of Irish girls returning to their native land as the 'kept women' of two prosperous Englishmen. Critics from the past may have been shocked by the 'scandalizing of Ireland's holy name' (to quote what the Postmaster in the play says about Parnell), with memories of Synge's aspersions on the face of Irish womanhood in the 1907 *Playboy* riots; though such dusty recollections must by now be almost extinct. More perceptive Anglophiles might, with some reason, have expected better butts for the wit of the vivacious Irishmen; more solid obstructions, along the lines of Shaw's Broadbent in *John Bull's Other Island*.

The play demands excellent all-round acting, even among fey characters in the final dream-like atmosphere of the last act. Whilst Irish accents are not essential, O'Casey's lines must not be thrown away or spoken up-stage; and rich cadences of Irish speech, as reflected in the dialogue – especially among the workmen and on the tongues of O'Killigain and the women – must be impressively and distinctly conveyed to an enraptured audience, mesmerised by the sheer cascade of words as well as by the cavalcade of humour and burlesque.

The role of Jack O'Killigain is important: he is O'Casey's hero, one of his great romantics, and one who in a way is a young and gayer Shaughraun, ready with song and dance and great with hyperbole of chat, and one whom O'Casey admires because he can work with his hands as well as mouthing honeyed words. He is a tall, fair young fellow of twenty-five; dogged-looking, handsome and clean-shaven. Although, we are told, he has had a pretty rough life, he is very self-confident; and extensive reading has increased his confidence. He is dressed in blue dungarees and wears a deep yellow muffler (similar to that worn by the Dreamer in *Within the Gates*).

There is much of the playwright himself in the portrait.

Poges – the caricatured capitalist – is sixty-five, stoutish and with a protruding belly. He is self-opinionated and fussy. His partner, Basil Stoke, is lean, cadavorous, and thirty; hatchet-faced, with a gloomy, mock-philosophical air. Avril is vivacious, pretty, and twenty; Souhaun comely and thirty-three. Both are dressed in fashionably-styled English costumes. Cloyne is a stoutly-built country collecn of twenty-five; Barney is a middle-aged domestic with a disgruntled face and manner. O'Dempsey – the Second Workman – is a powerful man of fifty, with gleaming eyes and a dreamy look, and a wide, strong beard, faintly touched with grey. The First Workman is tall, lean, with a 'foxy' face; the Third, stouter than the rest. They are dressed in soiled clothes and wear high rubber boots. The Canon is portly, with hair balding at the front and bushy hair greying at the back and sides. He is dressed in outdoor clerical garb and a black, rain-sodden cloak when he makes his entrance in the third act. The Postmaster is a dapper little man with a stout face and a huge fiery-red beard like a leprechaun. Legendary-looking, too, is the eccentric electrician, Cornelius, the yellow-bearded man. The Figure, dressed from head to foot in shiny black oilskins, is a river-sprite illumined by rays of flickering lightning. He is a fantasy creation.

Although only one setting is required throughout, the set should be readily dismantlable to allow for the yellow-bearded workman to stick his head down through a hole in the ceiling. Besides a few minor difficulties with crumbling sets and props, an imaginatively-minded director will have to interpret in a visionary way the playwright's final stage direction in the climax of the extravaganza regarding the tumbling waters surging into the set.

The play had its world *première* on 16 December 1943 at the People's Theatre, Newcastle-upon-Tyne: a plumed occasion for its director, Peter Trower. Its first professional English showing immediately after the war at Liverpool Playhouse by the Northern Company of the Old Vic, directed by Eric Capon, featured Kieron O'Hanrahan (better known by his film-name, Kieron Moore) in the lead. Sam Wanamaker's 1953 Glasgow Royal Theatre production, despite an excellent cast which included Miles Malleson, Walter Hudd, Liam Redmond and Siobhan McKenna, never reached London. The Mermaid's 1962 production (directed by Peter Duguid for Bernard Miles) disappointed many (the fantasy was underscored), even though a promising cast featured Ronald Fraser,

Peter Bowles, Ronald Hines, Annette Crosbie and June Tobin. A major production in London is long overdue.

Singularly, in America, the stage-scene was the reverse. The New York venture at Cherry Lane, opening on 27 December 1956, and directed by Philip Burton (the designer was Lester Polakov), was enormously successful and ran for fourteen months – the longest time for any O'Casey production. In Ireland, the play was first performed professionally in 1973, at Belfast's Lyric Theatre, paving the way for its Abbey production in 1975 (both directed by Tomas MacAnna).

Among foreign productions, the Berliner Ensemble's in East Germany in 1966, directed by Hans-Georg Simmgen, was outstanding. (It enjoyed a run of more than 270 performances.) Much of its success was due to Andreas Reinhardt's décor. By contrast, the Paris version in the same year by the Theatre National Populaire was less successful. The West German production in 1978 at Wiesbaden, directed by Hermann Kleinseelbeck, scored a notable triumph. Translations include those in French, German, Italian, Hungarian, Czech, Russian, Chinese, Japanese and Persian.

13 *Red Roses for Me* (1942): a Phantasmagoria of Dublin

Red Roses for Me, written during the early part of World War II, is generally regarded as the most autobiographical of all O'Casey's plays.

Dr Ronald Ayling – one of O'Casey's bibliographers – states that the play 'clearly owes a great deal to the Playwright's experience in writing *Pictures in the Hallway* during the same period. Several episodes in the drama – notably the transformation scene in Act 3 – closely parallel episodes in the second autobiographical volume'.

The main plot of a young worker – Ayamonn Breydon – killed in a strike and the profound influence of his mother and friend, the local Protestant Rector, is derived from an earlier play; *The Harvest Festival* (1918–19), published in America for the first time in 1979, and in Britain in 1980, to mark the centenary of the playwright's birth.

Earlier intimations were conveyed by O'Casey in a letter to Nathan, dated 18 April 1942: 'The play is built in a wholly new way on a theme sent many years ago to the Abbey Theatre by the name of *The Harvest Festival*. Of course, there was little or nothing then to the play; though I think this one isn't bad'. Stylistically and synthetically, the two plays are wide apart. *The Harvest Festival* can now be seen as an example of early apprentice-work – naturalistic in design – whereas *Red Roses for Me* (the title derives from a song O'Casey wrote, called 'She Carries a Rich Bunch of Red Roses for Me', which he includes in the chapter, 'Touched by the Theatre', in *Pictures in the Hallway*) belongs in the later canon which weds fantasy to story, comedy and song to pathos and heroics.

As the dust-jacket of the 1942 English edition – written by O'Casey himself – suggests:

The play is woven out of many moods, forming a lively pattern. The characters are clearly and vividly painted in rich, dancing dialogue. The play shows how many things, thoughts and activities cross and recross the minds of the Dublin people; and shows – though some are blind to it – how all from the Protestant Rector down to the street flower-seller are correlated in a strange, sometimes sad, and always vigorous relationship. The Dublin of myth and misery, of darkness and light, of the shrinking sigh and the aggressive shout stands in the play with her Civic Crown balanced rakishly on her head.

Against a vivid background, differently projected – here in a stylised, phantasmagoric way – showing the Dublin of the tenements; the Dublin graphically portrayed in *Inishfallen, Fare Thee Well*, the plot is a simple and moving one: that of a young, dedicated, self-educated Protestant railway worker – reared in poverty – with strong social and personal convictions and wide-ranging loyalties to class and colleagues, who involves himself in an industrial and political dispute on behalf of his fellow-workers and dies for their cause. It is a simple, meaningful drama: in Brooks Atkinson's words, 'original in style, pungent in humour, beautiful in its language and resolute in spirit'. In form, it is prismatically conceived, and has the rare quality of splendour.

Of O'Casey's Dublin phantasmagoria, the Yeatsian scholar, Dr A. G. Stock, has testified in Ayling's 'Modern Judgements' volume on O'Casey: 'Of all his later plays this one seems to me to be the strongest affirmation of faith, and in a way the most generous. In Ayamonn Breydon [O'Casey] has shaped a positive heroic image, ideal but not incredible because it grows convincingly out of a real environment'. With its interpolated songs and dances and texture of golden words, it mirrors O'Casey's own struggle in terms of romantic tragedy. O'Casey has written a compassionate allegory of the plight and fulfilment of those who refuse to be bound by poverty or side-stepped by convention.

Dr Stock reminds us that there are a number of heroic women in O'Casey's earlier plays who outface and outclass the qualities of their men-folk. But, in *Red Roses for Me*, Ayamonn Breydon

is conceived somewhat in the spirit of epic, at once mythical and authentic: an ideal image, but shaped by real experience of workers' life. He is not the creature of a doctrine . . . He is pictured as a whole man, whose capacity to use the riches of the world to the full gives him a natural right to possess them. In sheer excess of life he takes death in his stride, and the continuance of the world is his immortality.

Predictably, he is an idealised self-portrait, revealing at the same time strengths and weaknesses of the distanced personality of the younger playwright, and an indication in some ways of his inward integrity and intrepidity.

The exuberance of other living characters, Mrs Breydon, Ayamonn's mother, in particular, recalling stoical qualities of O'Casey's own mother (again, vividly recounted in *Inishfallen, Fare Thee Well*), sweeps through the finely spun canvas and golden labyrinth of the play. All are rugged individualists, caught in the crossfire of each other's emotions, reflecting the uncertain environment of Dublin in 1911–13.

The beginnings of class struggle among poorer sectors are manifest, leading to industrial turmoil which culminated in the intensive and bitter Lockout of 1913, in which the playwright himself was agonisingly involved. ('By bettering your own conditions', author James Stephens, who also had experienced intense poverty, had told Dublin workers in *The Insurrection in Dublin*, 'you are going to better the conditions of everyone . . . You are as truly the liberators of the world today as were those twelve other workingmen who long ago threw up their jobs to follow the penniless Son of the Carpenter and your battle will not be a bit easier than theirs was'.)

Although the background of *Red Roses for Me* was widely assumed to be those terrible events of 1913 – in which thousands of workers in transport and ancillary spheres were implicated (many killed and injured in street rioting with mounted police in a number of disturbances and baton charges; others made redundant and unemployed for opting to join a trade union of their choice, and eventually starved into submission by the ruthless determination of the employers themselves) – O'Casey corrects such a misapprehension in a programme-note specially written for a later performance of the play at the University of California in May 1964:

Though the play is dedicated to the gallant men and women who took part in the long and bitter fight for freedom to join the Union of their choice, under the leadership of the great Jim Larkin, the play doesn't deal with that Lockout, but with a strike of Railwaymen of the British Isles long before Jim Larkin was known to any Irish worker . . .

Thus the 1911 Rail Strike in Dublin and in the rest of the British Isles (when the playwright still worked for GNRI) is the real representative background, though subsequent events soon escalated into a cauldron of industrial ferment which left its permanent scars in Dublin immediately before the outbreak of World War I.

According to one eye-witness, a retired London secretary of the National Union of Railwaymen:

> The 1911 railway strike was something of an uprising. It was a terrifically hot year and a series of spasmodic strikes broke out, starting in Liverpool and spreading throughout the country. I believe it started there with a demand for a shilling rise, but for many of us there were no specific demands. We took advantage of the opportunity to do something about our rotten conditions – fourpence an hour for a 10 hour day, 60 hour week, no annual holidays, getting time off only when things were slack. And railway workers were considered privileged because, though the pay was rotten, it was 'regular'.
>
> (R. A. Leeson (ed.), *Strike: A Live History 1887–1971*)

A former branch official of the Transport and General Workers' Union at Liverpool docks has also testified:

> In Liverpool in the 1911 strike the big point made was for recognition of the Dockworkers Union and against the Cunard Co. which had transferred all its work to Hull, where it was half a penny cheaper per man ton. The whole lot were out, dockers, carters, seamen, railwaymen; it was known as the general strike of Liverpool. Churchill said it was not a strike but a Civil War.
>
> (Leeson, as above)

Fighting between mounted police, Scots Greys – mounted with lances and flags – and strikers broke out and went on, we gather, 'all Sunday night and the best part of Monday. Wherever people gathered they attacked them . . . Bloody Sunday; that's what they called it'. And what happened in Liverpool, O'Casey foresaw, could happen in Dublin.

Two years later, there were worse scenes of general bloodshed and disorder in Dublin itself during the notorious Lockout of 1913. The play is a telescoping of these two events in history.

But *Red Roses for Me* is really not so much a play in the historical idiom as a poetic allegory. With this play, O'Casey returns to the Dublin of his dreams, which he views through a kaleidoscope, and writes his allegory in terms of its politics: the conflict between Catholic and Protestant; the battles of Irish Labour and the resurgence of a better life to follow, portrayed in the 'bridge of vision' scene in the notable third act – infused by the richness of O'Casey's language, glowing with colour and the lyrical splendour of song and dance. 'Behind all', says J. C. Trewin in *Three More Plays*, 'is O'Casey's great heart and compassionate mind. And overall is the knowledge that Shakespeare and the Elizabethans have been tapping at the window-pane, that Sean O'Casey has stood with them upon the bridge of vision'.

Although the play is dedicated in spirit to those who struggled for a better life in the 1913 dispute (Larkin's goal was a 'Co-operative Commonwealth for Ireland'; O'Casey's a similar ideal for the whole of mankind), the play, being a reflective cameo of the playwright's own struggle for self-determination and realisation, is dedicated, in fact, to one of his great friends in Dublin who helped achieve this: 'To Dr. J. D. Cummins in memory of the grand chats around his surgery fire'.

Joseph Cummins, who had been a surgeon at Dublin's Royal Victoria Eye and Ear Hospital where O'Casey was treated in the early twenties for the renewal of the chronic ulcerated cornea condition of his eyes, had taken a personal interest in the rising playwright (following the jubilant acclaim of *Juno and the Paycock*) and had made friends with the dramatist, we are told in *Inishfallen, Fare Thee Well*. In Cummins's home in Merrion Square they chatted in the evenings on literature and art, including, as O'Casey joyfully recollects, 'the tempestuous writings of James Joyce'. (*Ulysses*, only just published, was still the great literary talking-point.)

The significance, in the play, of rose symbolism (which derives from both title and theme) is its expressiveness in legend and history: the symbol of valour and of love. 'Let the timid tiptoe through the way where the paler blossoms grow', says Ayamonn, during an altercation, in the first act, with the girl he loves, the sweet-faced but faint-hearted Sheila Moorneen: 'my feet' (he says) 'shall be where the redder roses grow, though they bear long thorns, sharp and piercing, thick among them!' Throughout the age of chivalry, the rose had become an emblem of honour and reward for valour – recollected, at the beginning, when Ayamonn and his mother are rehearsing a scene from Shakespeare's *King Henry VI, Part 3* for a fund-raising rally of transport workers in the event of a strike. The Red Rose was the emblem of the House of Lancaster and many rose myths sprang into being during the Wars of the Roses.

The rose is also a magical symbol, especially in affairs of the heart (Browning's 'Still more labyrinthine buds the rose', and Burns's 'My Luve is like a red, red rose'). But the flower of love and life is also the flower of death. In poetry, the rose is often a symbol of perfect beauty, swift to fade. 'Gather ye Rose-buds while ye may', says Herrick, and 'Go, lovely Rose!' is Waller's plaintive chant. Such poetic regret is assuaged by stouter aspirations from the Irish poet, Thomas Moore, in his poem, 'Farewell! But Whenever You Welcome the Hour', the concluding verses of which O'Casey quotes on the title-page of the first English and American editions of *Red Roses for Me*:

> You may break, you may shatter the vase, if you will,
> But the scent of the roses will hang round it still.

To the Druids, especially, the rose became a symbol of its own immortality, signified in the mystical lines of Yeats – in 'To the Rose upon the Rood of Time' 'Red Rose, proud Rose, sad Rose of all my days!'

Sheila, at the close of the play, places a bunch of red roses on Ayamonn's coffin. But truer significance is realised in the final song, sung by Brennan – and peculiarly associated with Ayamonn's memory – the lyrics of which are those of the playwright:

> A sober black shawl hides her body entirely,
> Touch'd be th' sun an' salt spray of th' sea;
> But down in th' darkness a slim hand so lovely,
> Carries a rich bunch of red roses for me!

Through life's dark poverty and ignorance, the younger O'Casey –

personified in the character of Ayamonn – finds gleams of richer colours which he continues to clasp throughout his courageously fought and nobly achieved artistic life as an international playwright.

In France, the Red Rose is also a symbol of socialism.

Whereas the principal theme of *The Star Turns Red* is the perpetual struggle between the forces of fascism and communism, the main subject of *Red Roses for Me* is shown in the international struggle between Labour and Capital, which, in Ireland's history, reached crisis-point in the notorious Dublin Lockout of 1913–14. The event remained a watershed in O'Casey's own life and provides some of the inspiration and much of the raw material behind the present play. And what is shown in the struggle is not Yeats's 'utter change' and 'terrible beauty' being born (the subject of scorn in *The Plough and the Stars*) but a subtle change and tentative beauty – the beginnings of a new social era and contract. (Ayamonn's martyrdom at Easter is significant.) There is nothing didactic about *Red Roses for Me* – O'Casey's lyrically inspired tragicomic ode – which is described, in unaffected terms, by the playwright as 'A Play in Four Acts'.

The setting in the first two acts is the interior of the living-room of a dilapidated ground-floor tenement-lodging in Dublin – home of the Breydons; while that of the third is a panorama of a Dublin street, beside a bridge overlooking one of the quays of the River Liffey; and in the fourth act, part of the grounds surrounding the little Protestant church of St Burnupus in the northern suburbs, in the East Wall district of the city. The time is described as 'A little while ago'. More specifically, from detailed scenic stage directions, the first act opens on an early mid-spring evening to the accompaniment of torrential rain; the second, at about ten o'clock of the same night, save that the rain has ceased, revealing 'a fine moon sailing through the sky'. The third act – a little later in time – is loosely inferred as dusk merging into a glorious sunset, forming the allegorisation of the play, whilst the time-span in the final act is 'a warm, sunny evening, the Vigil of Easter'.

As the curtain rises on the first act, Ayamonn and his mother are alone in their drab living-room, the whitewashed walls of which 'are dwindling into a rusty yellowish tinge'. Both are rehearsing a rousing scene from Shakespeare, giving a moment of inspiration –

the gilded costumes they are wearing over their normally dull-looking clothes adding a gleam of colour to their everyday precarious existence: a foreshadowing of the transfiguring moments to be glimpsed in the irradiating third act.

Not the social background so much as Ayamonn and his mother constitute the driving force in the play. Ayamonn, doomed Protestant idealist who sees the shape of a new world in the shilling-a-week for which the railwaymen are striking, is in love with a Catholic, Sheila Moorneen. She is the daughter of a Royal Irish Constabulary Sergeant, a girl, whom Mrs Breydon, in the opening scene, describes as 'a fine coloured silken shawl among a crowd of cotton ones', though as the first two acts unfold, a girl, we see, blinded, increasingly, by querulousness and a narrow understanding of all that Ayamonn's poetry and painting and union activities signify – 'the light of the burning bush', to him; 'a wide branching flame' (in his words). She complains that his life is widening into too many paths instead of treading safely and securely through a single passageway, making it possible, as she would wish, for their two lives to come close together.

Mrs Breydon is the zealous, hard-working personification of O'Casey's own widowed mother, displaying the same courage and humanity as Juno herself, or the tireless devotion to begrudging neighbours – in another context – of Bessie Burgess; and the same equal determination to ensure life blossoms in the drabbest of surroundings. Her floral emblems, like those of Mrs Casside in O'Casey's autobiographies, are the musk, geranium and fuchsia, flowering bravely in biscuit-tins standing on a roughly made bench beneath the window of the dimly-lit lounge, enlivened by a brilliant fire burning within a large, old-fashioned grate.

In addition to Catholic neighbours resident in the upper rooms of the same tenement – Eeada, Dympna and Finnoola, who are flower-sellers by the quayside of the Liffey – together with others described as First, Second and Third Man, respectively, among regular visitors who frequent and befriend the Breydons is a beguiling old Protestant vagabond, the melodion-playing Brennan o' the Moor, a parsimonious old landlord but generous with his time and devotion to Ayamonn and his mother, an outlaw and songster ('bold and yet undaunted') like his name-sake in the Irish ballad surrounded as he is by the conventions of his Catholic neighbours. In Brennan, Eileen O'Casey tells us, 'Sean remembered a Totnes character he used to see at the market, and who doubted whether a

bank was really safe enough for his money. Says Brennan to Sheila
in the play, 'with cunning confidence, tell me what you think of the
Bank of Ireland? . . . Safe as if St. Pether himself had the key of
where the bonds are stationed, eh?'

Among those who enjoy the special confidence of Ayamonn are
two diversely comic friends: Roory O'Balacaun, a fervent
Nationalist who cannot see ordinary people in his limited dream of
an Irish Ireland, and the atheist Mullcanny – 'mocker of sacred
things' – who brazenly tells the astonished Brennan, 'Haven't you
heard, old man, that God is dead?' (To which the shocked
septuagenarian counters, 'Well, keep your grand discovery to
yourself'.)

A sympathetic onlooker, overall, is the Reverend E. Clinton,
Rector of the church of St Burnupus, where Mrs Breydon worships,
who still staunchly defends the present activities of her son, who was
once active in his church, even though – in his quest for wider
knowledge – he is drifting away from conventionalised thought and
orthodox religion. The Rector and his mother do not oppose the
newer idealism of Ayamonn, even though they do not share his
views. Says Dr Stock, in her fine analysis of the play: 'because they
are his equals in magnanimity, neither makes any assault on his
integrity'.

In contrast to the Reverend Clinton, who is a composite portrait
based on both Reverend Edward Martin Griffin, one-time rector of
St Barnabas' church, Dublin (to whom *Pictures in the Hallway* is
dedicated, ' . . . a man of many-branched kindness, whose sensitive
hand was the first to give the clasp of friendship to the author'); as
well as his predecessor, the Reverend Harry Fletcher (both, overtly,
too 'Romish' for the Select Vestry of St Barnabas) there are two
bigoted vestrymen in the play named Foster and Dowzard, who are
presented as proof that Catholics are not alone in their representation of a spectacle of narrowmindedness and hypocrisy. The saintly
Rector's Churchwarden also happens to be the brash, angry
Inspector Tom Finglas of the Mounted Police, who violently
disapproves of Ayamonn's political support for the strike (and
contempt for law-and-order) and who pointedly gives his support to
the virulently Protestant demands of the Machiavellian duo (Foster
and Dowzard) who claim that flowers around the altar, as such, and
a daffodil cross, especially, are unbecoming in a Protestant church.
(Subsequently, the vestrymen register their disapproval by trampling on a floral cross, a gift to the church which Ayamonn has

provided.) And, when told by the bigoted pair that Ireland is on the verge of a 'hoppy Romish auto-dey-fey', the Rector jovially replies: 'Well, let the Loyola boys and King Bully fight it out between them' (a spectacle – outside the play – since witnessed often and tragically enough in Ulster), adding, by way of corollary after the bloody battle between strikers and Finglas's police has resulted in Ayamonn's death – whose interment is fiercely opposed by the Rector's biased henchmen – 'It is a small thing that you weary me, but you weary my God also'. Resolutely, he tells them: 'Stand aside, and go your way of smoky ignorance, leaving me to welcome him whose turbulence has sunken into a deep sleep, and who cometh now as the waters of Shiloah that go softly, and sing sadly of peace'.

Clinton bears most of the hallmarks of the Reverend Griffin in *Drums Under the Windows*, who 'couldn't suffer fools gladly . . . endearing him all the more to Sean, who himself had a hasty temper and hated fools fiercely'. The Rector's annoyance is seen in his contact with his foolish verger, Sexton Samuel (who, if he bears no special resemblance to Mary Webb's character of the same name in *Precious Bane*, has a comparable Irish parity in that his tongue is full of circumlocutions), and exasperation shows itself in his relations with Foster, Dowzard and the Inspector. Whereas the sexton in *The Harvest Festival* is intentionally verbose, his counter-part in *Red Roses for Me* is more that of a typically Dublin verbarian, showering sparks on ignitable conversational farce:

SAMUEL: It's not for me to remark on anything that manoeuvres out in front o' me, or to slip in a sly word on things done, said, or thought on, be th' pastors, masthers, or higher individuals of th' congregation; but, sometimes, sir, there comes a time when a true man should, must speak out.

RECTOR (*with a sigh*): And the time has come to say something now – what is it, Sam?

SAMUEL (*in a part whisper*): This mornin', sir, and th' dear spring sun shinin' through th' yellow robes of Pether an' th' purple robes o' Paul, an' me arrangin' th' books in the pews, who comes stealin' in, but lo and behold you, Fosther an' Dowzard to have a squint round. Seein' they're Select Vesthrymen, I couldn't ask them why they were nosin' about in th' silence of th' church on an ordinary week-day mornin'.

RECTOR (*patiently*): Yes; but a long time ago, you said something about daffodils.

SAMUEL: I'm comin' at a gallop to them, sir.

RECTOR: Good; well, let's here about the daffodils.

SAMUEL: Aha, says I, when I seen th' two prowlers with their heads close together, whisperin', aha, says I, there's somethin' on th' carpet.

RECTOR: Is what you have to tell me something to do with Dowzard and Foster, or the daffodils?

SAMUEL: Wait till you hear; sometimes Fosther an' Dowzard'll be to th' fore, an' sometimes th' daffodils. What can these two oul' codgers be up to, says I, sidlin' up to where they were, hummin' a hymn.

RECTOR: Humming a hymn? I'm glad to hear it; for I'd be surprised to hear either of them humming a hymn.

SAMUEL: Me it was, sir, who was hummin' th' hymn; for in a church, I like me thoughts to do with th' work I'm doin', if you know what I mean.

RECTOR (*impatiently*): It'll be nightfall before you get to the daffodils, man.

(Act Four)

Timid species and taciturn figures are unusual in the O'Casey repertoire, though Sammy, the shy singer who accompanies Brennan in the first act in a brief, self-effacing performance, shares common ground in this respect, with Mr Gallogher in *The Shadow of a Gunman*. The shy Sammy of *Red Roses for Me* (not to be confused with the loquacious Sexton of the same name) is described by his fellow-minstrel – the vagabond Brennan – as 'extravagant in shyness, an' sinks away into confusion at the stare of an eye', though after he has rendered his song, the audition is greeted with Brennan's fanciful 'A second Count McCormack in th' makin'! An' whenever he sung Mother Mo Chree, wasn't there a fewroory in Heaven with the rush that was made to lean over an' hear him singing' it!'

Of the twenty-one characters who figure in the play, more than half are but lightly-sketched in this tapestry of poetic fantasy, yet footlights are focused on the principal ones that linger in the memory: Ayamonn, whose Red Badge of Courage brings him to an untimely death; Mrs Breydon, forebearing in her suffering; the Rector, whose wisest counsels prevail; Sheila, whose love is weak;

Brennan, whose bigoted heart outshines his less charitable kinsmen; Roory, mistaken ideologist; and Mullcanny the sceptic, above religious and political dissensions tearing Ireland apart, yet remote from the gleam in the people's heart.

Two of Ayamonn's fellow-workers – described as First and Second Railwaymen respectively – figure among the remaining subsidiary characters, though only briefly at the end of the second act, soon after the Rector himself has called upon Ayamonn – in the presence of Sheila – to inform him of the worsening industrial situation; the men beseeching Ayamonn to lead them in the face of intransigence from their determined employers. Amid horror-stricken pleas from Sheila to the Rector to persuade Ayamonn not to become embroiled, the minister replies in unwavering rectitude: 'Who am I to say God's against it? You are too young by a thousand years to know the mind of God. If they be his brothers, he does well among them'. By endowing a filial blessing on them in the name of Christianity, O'Casey shows that Protestant clerics of the calibre of the Reverend Clinton, who counter the entrenched ignorance within their own flocks in the Church of Ireland, and progressive Catholic priests, offering greater enlightenment to their parishioners (his later play, *The Drums of Father Ned*, is dedicated to the valour of such high-minded champions of spiritual liberty), are worthy torch-bearers in the fight for truer happiness and a more just society.

The street lamplighter who passes by the grounds of the church, where crowds are gathered, in the final act, to mourn the passing of Ayamonn, completes the range of supplemental characters who drift in and out of the scenario; his salty repartee betraying his Shakespearian origins. He is a minor tragicomedian in the true O'Casey mould.

The strength of O'Casey's play, applauds Eric Bentley, lies in familiar O'Casey virtues: 'rich dialogue, strong situation, deeply-felt characters, stark contrasts of mood and texture'. Some critics have compared the play unfavourably with *Juno and the Paycock*, but to do so is to misunderstand the genre it represents. *Red Roses for Me* is not a chronicle play but a lyrical, visionary drama that has all the sweeping force of an allegory and, perhaps, too, the formula for conversion into a musical, if deftly interpreted and translated successfully. Although both plays are tragicomedies and cameos of Dublin, the choreography and scenes of symbolism are more richly developed in the later play.

The epiphany effect of the third act has the redemptive quality of those transfiguration episodes we encounter in the works of Joyce: both in *The Portrait of the Artist as a Young Man* and in *Ulysses*. (In Joyce, too, surrealistic techniques are more keenly developed in his later work.) Both Ayamonn Breydon and Stephen Dedalus – in consummation of a fuller life – experience transcendental epiphanies, as their souls fly 'sunward above ordinary and everyday existence' – a revelation, as Joyce proclaims, 'of the artist forging anew in his workshop out of the sluggish matter of the earth a new soaring impalpable imperishable being'. In O'Casey's play, the audience, too, feels this transmutation. It is, indeed, a theatrical catharsis. Few plays are endowed with such heightened imagination and emotional magnetism – stirring excitements that spring from the ordinary highway of everyday life. Yet, beneath the transformation and phantasmagoria O'Casey tells us, as Yeats would have recognised, lies 'the point of the spear whose handle is our daily life'.

Ayamonn's plight lies at the heart of the drama: he is the centre of the entire web. Significantly, he is O'Casey's most fully-rounded male hero, because, like Stephen Dedalus, he is an autobiographical creation. In most of the playwright's other dramas the heroic function is invested, majestically, in the women: the men are either absurd idealists or buffoons. But Ayamonn is different: he is the idealised heroic image. We see embryo portraits of him in Jack in *The Star Turns Red*; and, to some extent, the other Jack (Rocliffe) in the early play, *The Harvest Festival*; Davoren in *The Shadow of a Gunman*; as well as the Dreamer, though less defined, in *Within the Gates*; and O'Killigain, more extrovertly and humorously drawn, in *Purple Dust*.

In the first half of the play in both the first and second acts, Ayamonn is almost continuously at the centre of the stage: all the characters are drawn towards him and reveal their flamboyance because of him. To these divergent types – Brennan, Mullcanny, Roory, Sheila – in their agonised sparring, and of course, to his own mother, and in his relations with the Rector, he is both savant and sympathetic friend. Diversified opinions he welcomes with rare tolerance (like Davoren, he takes interruptions in his stride), echoing his creator's philosophy when he says: 'I'll stand by any honest man seekin' th' truth, though his way isn't my way' (Act Two).

'Sketchin', readin', makin' songs, an' learnin' Shakespeare' – as his mother remarks – apart from his union activities and addressing meetings (in a seemingly overcrowded life); his life needs them all.

'The Sword of Light' – symbol of Irish Independence and the goal to which militant Fenians like Roory aspire – must merge, for Ayamonn, into a brighter flame, the lamp of Truth, stemming from knowledge as well as disbelief, the prerogative of Mullcanny and other agnostics, whom the creed-coveting crowd despises and whom Ayamonn resolutely defends; offset by bigotry (symbolised by Brennan in his flashes of vehement Protestantism and Sheila in her narrow Catholicism). Ayamonn's sword of enlightenment surpasses all these: it reflects the empirical beliefs of his creator, echoing the philosophy which James Stephens expounds, in *The Crock of Gold* and elsewhere, that when one constantly lives in the dark (a reference both to blindness – a condition which Joyce and O'Casey came close to – and the dimly-lit atmosphere of the slums; the experience of both Stephens and O'Casey), the only light surrounding such darkness is the flame of Truth, as the early auto-biographical works, *I Knock at the Door* and *Pictures in the Hallway*, testify.

Ayamonn, therefore, is able to shrugg off such taunts as Roory's 'What's in this Ruskin of yours but another oul' cod with a gift of the gab?' because his light of freedom is more strongly poised: to rid humanity, like Ruskin (and later Shaw) of poverty and ignorance. Ayamonn's sword is the sword of Excelsior (resembling, perhaps, Arthur's legendary Excalibur, or even Caladbolg – of Irish legend – the sword capable of consuming everything).

Ayamonn's ideal of freedom differs from Roory's. He, in fact, expresses O'Casey's own truer ideal, in the course of the second act:

> Roory, Roory, is that th' sort o' freedom you'd bring to Ireland with a crowd of green branches an' th' joy of shouting? If we give no room to men of our time to question many things, all things, ay, life itself, then freedom's but a paper flower, a star of tinsel, a dead lass with gay ribbons at her breast an' a gold comb in her hair. Let us bring freedom here, not with sounding brass an' tinkling cymbal, but with silver trumpets blowing, with a song all men can sing, with a palm branch in our hand, rather than with a whip at our belt, and a headsman's axe on our shoulders.

A clear rebuke to the Nationalists in their narrower vision. There is a good deal of the playwright's former Nationalist friend – Ayamonn O'Farrel, the tram conductor – traceable in Roory's portrait (he is focused in the chapter, 'The Sword of Light', in *Pictures in the Hallway*).

Most Nationalists – with the possible exception of James Connolly – were not particularly interested in Ireland's social questions or the problems of Labour, and that is why O'Casey had become disillusioned with them. Ayamonn's sympathies, in the play, match those of O'Casey. 'My sympathies', the dramatist was to explain, in an issue of the *Irish Statesman* of 7 February 1925, 'were always with the rags and tatters that sheltered the tenement-living Temples of the Holy Ghost'.

Ayamonn's philosophy – and that of O'Casey – is embodied in the wisdom we find expressed in George Eliot's *Middlemarch*:

> Let the high Muse chant loves Olympian:
> We are but mortals, and must sing of man.

And when Ayamonn remonstrates with Sheila for always choosing the conventional, easy path – 'safely ensconced in a clear space in a thicket of thorns' – his thought, again, reflects the bolder, more independently-minded outlook of George Eliot:

> I would not creep along the coast, but steer
> Out in mid-sea, by guidance of the stars.

If Sheila Moorneen is one of the least promising of O'Casey's young heroines (she has her origin in 'Nora Creena', O'Casey's first-love, portrayed in *Inishfallen, Fare Thee Well*, where we learn that 'Nora wasn't for him: she would forever shelter in the lee of a credulous respectability'), Ayamonn's widowed mother, by contrast, shows a quickening, tempered resilience, akin to the courage of Juno, based adroitly on the indefatigable hardihood of O'Casey's own mother, who is eulogised at length throughout the auto-biographies. Mrs Breydon's maternally realistic attitudes in Act One are in deliberate contrast to Ayamonn's initial innocence or Sheila's unheroic conventionalism, and reveal themselves in her own words: 'I did an' dared a lot for you, Ayamonn, my son, in my time, when jeerin' death hurried your father off to Heaven'. She knows – like some of George Eliot's worldly-wise heroines – that our deeds are but fetters we forge ourselves and that it is the world itself which brings manacles that restrict. Instinct and experience tell her that heroes do not exist: men are either saints or knaves, pilgrims or hypocrites.

Wise in her daily work – to fruits of diligence, untowered by passionate ideals – she wears an heroic heart, shaped by the earth rather than the sky. Downward rooted, she has an upward eye, readily acknowledged by Ayamonn:

> When it was dark, you always carried the sun in your hand for me; when you suffered me to starve rather than thrive towards death in an Institution, you gave me life to play with as a richer child is given a coloured ball.

Elements of tragedy which stem from the course of ordinary human lives have touched Mrs Breydon's large heart: she is widowed – as was O'Casey's mother before him, when he was six – and bringing up a family in the grim poverty of Dublin's dilapidated houses has meant years of struggle and hardship as well as heroism – though such suffering has not, as yet, entered her soul, in the same way as it has entered her son's. Unheroic circumstances have not as yet affected his nature: his highest personality, in the first act, has not been subjected to its fullest development. (His stature is to progress with the play; his charisma of greatness is seen at the end.)

Mrs Breydon's steadfast qualities are recognised by all of her unfortunate neighbours. 'A shabby sisther of ceaseless help she is', says Eeada, echoing Dympna's 'his poor oul' mother's feet has worn out a pathway to most of our tumbling doorways, seekin' out ways o' comfort for us she sadly needs herself'. And, in a vision of unnourished hope, Finnoola – the youngest – proclaims: 'For all her tired look an' wrinkled face, a pure white candle she is' (Act Three). Exasperated at one stage by his mother's extreme unselfishness, Ayamonn alludes to her, in a scathing aside, as 'an imitation sisther of charity' (Act One).

Although opposed to Ayamonn's diverse activities, just as Sheila is, she clearly emerges as the nobler woman because, in the second act, she demonstrates her bravery by rescuing the atheistic Mullcanny (of whom she disapproves) from stoning by a gang of bigoted marauders (a similar state befalls Loreleen in *Cock-a-Doodle Dandy*), who pursue their victim to the front parlour of the Breydon household, where Brennan and Roory have been wrangling in the O'Casey grand manner, and, indeed, continue to do so whilst crouching on the floor to avoid reprisals which come crashing through the windows. (Tragicomedy gathers momentum as Brennan, who begins the argument by claiming St Patrick for a Protestant – in the words of the playwright, 'mixes mirth with madness' – with Mullcanny, from his position on the floor, fueling the discussion by championing the claims of the evolutionists, stressing that monkeys, like man, have a taste for beer – and everything suddenly blossoms into bizarre, conversational 'chassis'.)

Without realising it, Mrs Breydon has identified herself with Ayamonn's broad concept of complete tolerance. She is now poised for her own part in the co-tragedy, in the final act, in understanding the spirit of Ayamonn's self-sacrifice, which she faces with Junoesque forbearance.

As she pauses in front of a rowan-tree, in the churchyard, in the final act – in the presence of the Rector – after the bier bearing the body of her dead son has passed into the church, she utters a natural eulogium – a cry of mournful praise – reflected in her words:

> There's th' three he loved, bare, or dhrenched with blossom. Like himself, for fine things grew thick in his nature, an' lather came the berries, th' red berries, like th' blood that flowed today out of his white body.

Pain, in her glorified life of tragedy, becomes an understanding compassion; and what lesser mortals and onlookers would count as despair, for her assumes the saintly suggestion of unrealised hope.

Ardent souls – Ayamonn's included – are always ready to commit themselves to fulfilment of their own visions. As Ayamonn, who has undergone a finer heroism in Act Two, remarks to Brennan: 'To know the truth, to seek the truth, is good, though it lead to th' danger of eternal death'. The leader in Ayamonn, in the second act, outshines the dreamer. He denounces Sheila's suggestion of betrayal of his fellow-workers with a vehemence which indicates his social conscience is above personal considerations: 'Go to hell, girl, I have a soul to save as well as you'. And, to one of the railwaymen, he proffers the arm of leadership, in the imminence of strike action, saying: 'Tell the Committee, Bill, I'll be there; and that they honour me when they set me in front of my brothers'. (Earlier, he had exclaimed, in moment of self-prophecy: 'When a true man dies, he is buried in th' birth of a thousand worlds'.)

Visionary power, says Wordsworth, in *The Prelude*, is embodied not only in the viewless winds, but in the mystery of words; and, we may add, in the play's context of heightened possibilities, reflected in the momentary suspension of action and denouement. Thus, the expressionistic fantasy of the third act serves not only to maintain suspense – an interval in the action (Ayamonn has been at the centre of the footlights for most of the first two acts) – but also as a medium for the playwright's visionary purpose. The technique so arresting in *The Silver Tassie* is equally impressive in this scene in its total and prismatic effect.

Dublin, the city itself, now becomes the focal point of the scene and manifests itself in its many moods through O'Casey's kaleidoscope. On stage, a bridge across the Liffey occupies the centre, with its panoramic view of the city's tall gaunt houses and streets peopled with divers citizens, a distant church steeple and silhouettes of quayside landmarks presenting a far-off view. At the foot of the nearside parapet linger tired slum-folk, among whom, with their expressionless faces, are flower-sellers, Ayamonn's poorest neighbours, who have appeared briefly in the previous acts. Here, in this scene, they are even less cheerful as Finnoola, in the greyness of their surroundings, gives vent to their heart-felt cry:

> A gold-speckled candle, white as snow, was Dublin once; yellowish now, leanin' sideways, an' guttherin' down to a last shaky glimmer in th' wind o' life.

(Richness blossoming forth, indeed, from such secondary characters, though we experience it, too, in a tranquil way, in the night-fable of *Finnegans Wake*: 'While the dapplegray dawn drags nearing nigh for to wake all droners that drowse in Dublin'.)

Snatches of passing conversation can be heard at intervals from those who cross the bridge. Firstly, we see the Rector conversing with Inspector Finglas, showing, for the most part, how out of touch both are with the continuing march of common humanity, as affecting those huddled beside the quays; the 'flotsam and jetsam', as the Inspector derisively calls them (including Ayamonn along with them), though the Rector rebukes him with something of the former indignation of his ancestor, Dean Swift, for his lack of charity: 'Ayamonn Breydon has within him the Kingdom of Heaven. And so, indeed, may these sad things we turn away from'. (The unreality of their unawareness has already banished reality from the scene and prompted fantasy-musings from the flower-sellers speaking among themselves – the young Finnoola, in the shabbiness of her attire, conjuring visions of splendour when 'their shabbiness was threaded with th' colours from the garments of Finn Mac Cool of th' golden hair, Goll Mac Morna of th' big blows, Caoilte of th' flyin' feet, an' Oscar of th' invincible spear'.)

Secondly, we observe Brennan, lingering with his melodeon and begging for coppers, with what one of the quaysiders castigatingly calls his 'sootherin' songs o' gaudy idleness!' (even though, in this instance, the song he sings is one specially written by O'Casey – beguiling in its sweet-sounding 'I stroll'd with a fine maid', and its enchanting refrains of 'An' I tuck'd up my sleeves for to fasten her shoe').

And, thirdly, we watch Roory, entering the scene anew with Ayamonn, at the conclusion of Brennan's song (which the stage onlookers have declared heathen in tone), prompting a character-istic sally from the feckless Fenian, in the direction of Brennan: 'Isn't it a wondher, now, you wouldn't sing an Irish song, free o' blemish, instead o' one thickly speckled with th' lure of foreign enthertainment?'

As despondent men and women chant their weary litany of despair ('It's a black an' bitther city'), Ayamonn rouses them with the call: 'We hold a city in our hands!' (He urges them to cast off their lethargy, as Ireland itself is stretching and arising, as it were, from sleep.) To accustomed eyes, *Dubh-Linn* may signify 'Dark Pool', but the Seventh City of Christendom, reaffirms Ayamonn, is 'what our hands have made her'. Echoing O'Casey, himself, he reminds the city-folk: 'We pray too much and work too little. Meanness, spite, and common patherns are woven thick through all her glory; but her glory's there for open eyes to see'.

A divergence in attitudes between Ayamonn and Roory – the one a zealous reformer, alive to progressive thought and all that socialism can bring; the other a narrow sectarian idealist, enshrined in Nationalist fervour – flares up in a short confrontation in the following exchange:

ROORY (*impatiently*): We waste our time here – come on!
AYAMONN: Be still, man; it was dark when th' spirit of God first
     moved on th' face of th' waters.
ROORY: There's nothin' movin' here but misery. Gunpeal an'
     slogan cry are th' only things to startle them. We're
     useless here. I'm off, if you're not.

AYAMONN: Wait a moment, Roory. No-one knows what a word
may bring forth. Th' leaves an' blossoms have fallen, but
th' three isn't dead.

ROORY (*hotly*): An' d'ye think talkin' to these tatthered second-
hand ghosts'll bring back Heaven's grace an' Heaven's
beauty to Kaithleen ni Houlihan?

AYAMONN: Roory, Roory, your Kaithleen ni Houlihan has th'
bent back of an oul' woman as well as th' walk of a queen.
We love th' ideal Kaithleen ni Houlihan, not because she
is false, but because she is beautiful; we hate th' real
Kaithleen ni Houlihan, not because she is true, but
because she is ugly.

Ayamonn's reiteration of the playwright's own views on his native
society run counter to traditionally held patriotic ideals; and so the
irritated Roory goes off, disgruntled, in the opposite direction.

The scene has now darkened and buildings and people have
become shadows and silhouettes. Ayamonn's role henceforth is to
transform the minds and outlook of his lethargic slum-dwellers and
to fill the hearts of these down-and-outs of society with an enlivening
mystique of fantasy. (Poetry and poetically-conceived drama justify
such an approach.) His poetic speeches contain the core of his
militancy: 'Our sthrike is yours. A step ahead for us today; another
one for you tomorrow. We who have known, and know, the
emptiness of life shall know its fullness'. To Eeada, he beckons, 'The
apple grows for you to eat'; to Dympna, he exhorts, 'The violet
grows for you to wear', and to Finnoola, 'Young maiden, another
world is in your womb'. (Ayamonn, in the words of Keats, is no
bardic, 'pale-mouth'd prophet dreaming'.)

Suddenly, the scene has transformed itself, in the manner of an
aureole, as sunset over the river garnishes stage and surroundings,
irradiating characterisation and speech. 'Don't flinch in th' first
flare of a fight', Ayamonn soliloquises; and gazing meditatively
down the river, he rouses his fellow-citizens in an ecstasy of spiritual
revelation: 'Take heart of grace from your city's hidden splendour . . .' As houses and streets have taken on a new appearance –
in the wording of the stage direction, 'decked in mauve and
burnished bronze' – the flower-sellers appear dressed in brighter
array, in traditional costumes, their faces ecstatic in the vision which
has transfigured them and their city, Finnoola exclaiming: 'She's
glowin' like a song sung be Osheen himself, with th' golden melody

of his own harp helpin'!' (It is a pantomimic, almost Cinderella-like effect.)

The majesty of the city is revealed, as Dublin becomes the central character of the scene to which Ayamonn pays homage:

> There's th' great dome o' th' Four Courts lookin' like a golden rose in a great bronze bowl! An' th' river flowin' below it, a purple flood, marbled with ripples o' scarlet; watch th' seagulls glidin' over it – like restless white pearls astir on a royal breast. Our city's in th' grip o' God!

(The aurora of scene has the same magnetic effect as the river, Anna Livia Plurabelle, in Joyce's *Finnegans Wake*.)

Ayamonn chants a hymn of praise to the city which has reared and moulded him:

> Fair city, I tell thee that children's white laughter,
> An' all th' red joy of grave youth goin' gay,
> Shall make of thy streets a wild harp ever sounding,
> Touch'd by th' swift fingers of young ones at play!

to which the rest join in, in chorus:

> We swear to release thee from hunger an' hardship,
> From things that are ugly an' common an' mean;
> Thy people together shall build a brave city,
> Th' fairest an' finest that ever was seen!

Ayamonn's 'fair city' is Dublin, but O'Casey's, like Shakespeare's, is 'the great globe itself'.

In the scene's transcendentalism, Ayamonn is not only protagonist, but singer and dancer too. To the sound of a distant flute, Finnoola, in the urge of jubilation, dances to the tune that wafts across the bridge, and, as the pace quickens, she is joined in rhythm by Ayamonn; the rest of the onlookers clapping approvingly to the tap of the dancers' feet, each shouting praises of their nation ('Sons an' daughters of princes are we all, an' one with th' race of Melesius!'), until the two dancers become tired and part. (The old are regenerated by the spirit of youth represented by Ayamonn and Finnoola.) As Eileen O'Casey remarks, in a programme-note included in *The Sting and the Twinkle: Conversations with Sean O'Casey* (Macmillan, 1974):

> Finnoola, especially, is poignant in her beauty with her dreams, which Sean's imagination has conjured up, bringing great beauty, gaiety and joy to Ayamonn's life for just a short while, with all ugliness gone. Because life has not yet marred her grace, charm, and beauty, this makes it overwhelming, as one knows what life and poverty can do to the Finnoolas of this world.

When the dance-sequence comes to an end, Ayamonn, in an earnest parting, tells the wild-hearted Finnoola: 'May you marry well, an' rear up children fair as Emer was, an' fine as Oscar's son', and bids her good-bye. (The dance episode derives from an autobiographical incident described in *Pictures in the Hallway*, although actual details resemble more the playwright's encounter with Mild Millie of *Drums Under the Windows*, the model for at least two of his other stage characters: Nannie, in *Nannie's Night Out*, and the Young Whore of *Within the Gates*.)

Ayamonn's dance with Finnoola ends abruptly when he hears his fellow-strikers marching in unison in the distance. His leave-taking is as sudden as the resurgent note indicating the eve of insurrection in *The Star Turns Red*. (Ayamonn's joining the strikers and dying in defence of their struggle with the police are events which happen offstage, forming the spear-head to the final act.) Bewilderingly drab reality descends once more at the close of this memorable third act, as Ayamonn's dream will have lingered in the hearts of the slum-folk, and the distant sounds of trampling feet remind spectators – on and offstage – that dreams and actualities go together and that dreams have to be fought for.

In the last act, Ayamonn's appearance is brief, but it provides a moment for his affirmation of faith and cause for which he is willing to die. To the Inspector, in his harsh disavowal of the strikers' claim, he insists: 'A shilling's little to you, and less to many; to us it is our Shechinah, showing us God's light is near; showing us the way in which our feet must go . . . the first step taken in the march of a thousand miles'. But the remonstrating words of the Inspector are no deterrent: 'Remember . . . when swords are drawn and horses charge, the kindly law, so fat with hesitation, swoons away, and sees not, hears not, cares not what may happen'.

Ayamonn's death is an implied necessity – an inevitability – in the forward thrust betokening a brighter humanity. The Rector is told of his death later by the injured Finnoola (herself a victim offstage in the cavalry charge) who just manages to crawl to the churchyard to impart the news: 'He whispered it in me ear as his life fled through a bullet-hole in his chest'. And, gasping for breath herself, she hesitatingly but with due emphasis manages to convey Ayamonn's last message: 'He said this day's but a day's work done, an' it'll be begun again tomorrow . . .' (Tomorrow, or the next day – as O'Casey allegorically affirms in *The Star Turns Red* – as all our yesterdays, in the foretelling words of Macbeth, will have led the way to dusty death and be replaced – is O'Casey's hope – by an immortalised and reinvigorated life here on earth.)

Thus, we realise, the embodiment of Ayamonn is the ecstasy of a true life: the essence of self-sacrifice. He is a masculine version of Shaw's Saint Joan or Shakespeare's Imogen: their sensibility shaped by suffering. Ayamonn is a true protector and fighter for an ennobled existence. What survives him is of greater importance: a new life, a new beginning. His immortality lies in the present; his memorial enshrined in the future.

The Reverend Clinton is deeply affected by Ayamonn's death, and remains a truer Christian because of it: 'Oh Lord, open Thou mine eyes that I may see Thee, even as in a glass, darkly, in all this mischief and all this woe!'

Resembling the Brown Priest in his conversion in *The Star Turns Red*, he sees secular glory in such upheaval and sacrifice and noble self-immolation. And he echoes O'Casey's own philosophy when he asserts:

> From the clash of life new life is born . . . All things in life, the evil and the good, the orderly and disorderly, are mixed with the life of the Church Militant here on earth. We know our brother, not for what may have been an error in him, but for the truth for ever before his face. We dare not grudge him God's forgiveness and rest eternal because he held no banner above a man-made custom.

He stands by Ayamonn with the whole of his faith and sees his death as a victory which, in the familiar words of the evangelist, not only 'overcometh the world' but which – translated in terms of O'Casey's unique vision – means being 'alive and laughing in the midst of God's gay welcome' (the Rector's consoling words to

Ayamonn's grief-stricken mother). Thus, the Rector's God, in the end, like his creator's, is firmly on the side of life. O'Casey's God, like Joyce's, may be but 'a shout in the street, a joy manifest; but the shout is never a manifesto or creed.

In *Red Roses for Me* – as in so many of O'Casey's other plays – it is invariably and inviolably the shout of a social need: the shout of a people for bread, or the shout of a multitude for a richer, fuller life – the riches, kingdoms of this world supplanting poverty, degradation and guileless self-exploitation.

The underlying message of the play lies in the implied assumption that failure in the eyes of the world may well turn out to be an eventual success, rather than apparent success for all to see which may result in failure. We can never be certain, as O'Casey remarks at the end of *Rose and Crown*, that 'failure isn't success in a shroud'. Dr Stock is so right in her final analysis: 'Ayamonn died for love of this world's joy, and the red roses that symbolise it are a truer close to the play'.

In the final stages, and with a significant change of sympathy and understanding, Sheila is heard to remark: 'Maybe he saw the shilling in th' shape of a new world' – realising, irreducibly, Ayamonn's loss, and thus confirming her previous innermost fears, when, at the end of the second act, after trying her utmost without avail to dissuade Ayamonn from aligning himself with the conflict, her choking cries are submerged in the tenement-women's hymn to their Patroness, Our Lady Queen of Sorrows:

> Oh, Queen of Eblana's poor children,
> Bear swiftly our woe away,
> An' give us a chance to live lightly
> An hour of our life's dark day!

At the close of the play it is neither hymn nor anthem that is sung as the lights are left burning (at his mother's request) in the church where his body lies, but the words of his own haunting song, 'Red Roses for Me', sung, fondly, by Brennan as 'a finisher-off to a last farewell'.

All O'Casey's plays are, to greater or lesser extent, extravaganzas and extravasations of fancy escaping from the mainstream of fact. In *Red Roses for Me*, effusion is achieved in remarkable and total synthesis, and with a surer touch than in some of his other later works. Throughout the play, the playwright's feet are firmly in the grime and serio-comic atmosphere of the Dublin slum; but the love of life and colour keeps breaking out; as reflected in Ayamonn's painting, poetry and song-writing, and his veneration of Shakespeare, Shelley and Ruskin – his chosen writers – or, in his mother's case, the flowers that continually bloom on the window-sill in old biscuit-tins. As O'Casey once told a London interviewer, 'For you can't sever yourself from humanity, for there's nothing else that counts. Didn't Synge say, "Although his head may be in the stars his roots must be in the earth"?' This is the quintessence of O'Casey's own art and dramatic technhque: his path is always from the plough to the stars – heaven's glories resplendent in earthly achievements.

In the transcendental third act, which begins in stark drabness, changing into an aureole of splendour with the sun's rays over the Liffey and finally back to the original overcast scene in the wake of sundown, reality and vision are merged in an effusion of wonder and actuality. The sunset which irradiates the dull houses by the quayside and ordinary specks of humanity who dwell there – and who are without hope – is transcendentalised by O'Casey and serves as a dream-epiphany with which to inspire his audience. The concept is that which inspires *Within the Gates*, but with *Red Roses for Me* – in this phantasmagoria of Dublin – the synthesis is more finely achieved and burnished with a richer gold, as an imaginative and sympathetic director will quickly discover.

Some of the roles in this expressionistic fantasy are fully-rounded: Ayamonn, Mrs Breydon and the Rector are kindlingly flesh-and-blood; others, such as the flower-sellers and tenement-folk, mere ciphers (though, in Finnoola's case, transition from one to the other is part of the transubstantiating effect of the third act); while others, such as Roory and Mullcanny, are typed midway between the two, with their inner essences rooted in humanity. Ayamonn, alone, cares enough for the dregs of his people to want to share his vision with them, and his concept of life and vitality transfigure them before their own eyes. As in *The Star Turns Red*, we are in the realms of fantasy, but what has passed from him to them is real, for at the end the city-dwellers support his cause, as the strike has succeeded in its first beginnings. Empirical designs of both plays are identical, though the more lyrical *Red Roses for Me* – an ode to the sanctity and beauty of life – will always remain more popular with audiences and producers, though to directors the same problems remain.

In *Red Roses for Me*, O'Casey has succeeded in staging a play on a poetic level in which eloquence and everyday speech, characters, visions and symbols, meet. Tragicomedy – against a background, as one critical voice has termed, of 'delightfully entertaining sectarian wrangling' – is, to a degree, present, but no longer fills the stage. The play is virtually a nameless 'tragedy': a tone-poem, showing hideous pathos of baulked lives; the stage martyrdom of the main hero rouses the playwright to an uplifting awareness and eloquence encompassed only by a flame of faith and pinnacled by persuasive hope. The 'Chassis', for the most part, gives way to visions resulting in achievements no less vivid than those from the more naturalistic drama of the 'paycock' and his cronies. The afflatus results from an altogether different genre, but equally impressive. The aggrandisement of human nature, implied in word and action, can only be realised by a commensurate and consummate production. The magic of iridescent drama alone – presided over by a sensitive director – will serve to transform such munificence into one of O'Casey's most passionate and urgent plays, the least preoccupied with incident or diversion.

The raging swirl of images and words needs lyrical Irish actors and a production of haunting, almost epic proportions. In *Red Roses for Me*, transitions from reality to supra-reality and back to everyday humdrum existence are made with great skill. In a worthy production it is essential to convey such an impression. The first two acts are semi-naturalistic for the most part, and comic in conception (the production, as in *Juno and the Paycock*, should catch the claustrophobic realism of the crowded slum), though the chorus of slum-dwellers moving in and out of the tenement should be imaginatively portrayed, preparing audiences for the visionary leap of the second half of the play, which is truly a compassionate allegory. It is the phantasmagoric third act – with its scene near a bridge over the Liffey – which makes most demands on a production, showing the dullness of lives without dreams, transfigured by Ayamonn's dazzling dream of a just and golden future, with its apocalyptic overtones. (In the pantomimic effect, the Celtic gods are reinvoked to achieve miraculous, if fleeting, transformations). In this act, especially, the onus is on both director and designer. Settings should reflect the change before our eyes; and the infusion of poetry which the playwright provides must be injected into a keenly sensitive direction and illustrious production.

Lack of incident should not befool any director into imagining the play to be oversimplistic: well-springs of tragedy lie deceptively, significantly, beneath. Although in the final act there are initial scenes of tragicomic laughter, the mood is unnaturalistic: news of Ayamonn's death must lend an expressionistic slant if it is to have its fullest impact.

Lighting and music are important. In the final scene, Mrs Breydon's soliloquisation to the Rector of her son's virtues, which she illustrates by reference to the rowan-tree in the churchyard, should not be spoilt, for example, by clumsy timing, allowing chapel lights to get switched off – as has happened on occasions – half way through the soliloquy. Designer, director, and electrician, must be alert as the climax descends. As the flower-sellers and tenement-dwellers envision a splendid Dublin bathed in gold and bronze, the action swings into a gay and jubilant dance, making demands on choreographer and producer alike. But, most of all, the play is drama of verbal splendour in the breath-taking O'Casey idiom. No actor can afford to muff his lines or jar the beauty of iridescent speech. The whole play wears a golden robe of words. But, despite the lustre of its style, the acting must have its feet rooted firmly in the ground. Central parts call for brave and moving interpretation, and even minor characters emerge in gusty performances that give the play its human scope.

Ayamonn Breydon – a magnificently drawn cameo of a young hero who carries the world on his shoulders – is a youth with stars in his eyes and fire and steel in his soul. He is tall and well-built and aged about twenty-two or so. As a railway worker who spends most of his money acquiring books and tries to learn all about the truth of the universe in one fell swoop, he is a recognisable portrait of the playwright himself. He is clad in working attire, wears heavy hob-nailed boots and black corduroy trousers, except in the first scene when he dons Shakespearian costume for the rehearsal sequence. His Shakespearian imagination provides his fellow-characters in the rest of the play with an inspiring and unified view of themselves, reflecting their deepest needs and longings.

Mrs Breydon, patient mother who gets on with everything and who grits her teeth against a harsh background of poverty and is never too worn to sit up with a sick neighbour, is a replica of the playwright's own widowed mother. Mrs Breydon is approaching fifty, and, although she bears the marks of hard struggle on her face, a glint of cheerfulness always breaks through.

Sheila, as Ayamonn's sweetheart, at twenty-three has a fine grace and figure. She has an open sympathetic face but marred – in the playwright's own words – by 'a cloud of timidity'. (She is frightened by Ayamonn's poverty and wild ideas of religious toleration and classlessness.) Dressed in a tailor-made costume of brown tweed and matching accessories, she represents – says the playwright's widow – 'any young girl incapable of standing by her love and unable to fight against her own upbringing'.

The Rector, the Reverend Clinton, a handsome man of forty, has a grave scholarly face and a warm, endearing twinkle. He wears a brown, pointed beard, faintly turning to grey, and is dressed in clerical black. His gentle compassion mirrors the wider, fiercer tolerance of Ayamonn.

Brennan – the old strolling vagabond – is unswervingly Protestant though spluttery of speech; he is friendly and impish by turns. A long, white flowing beard gives him a resemblance to St Jerome. He is dressed in shabby-genteel fashion and wears a soiled mackintosh. A faded bowler crowns his bald head. His face is broadly wrinkled, but his eyes are bright and peering. He should be played subtly, with combined humour and melancholy. He is a tragicomic character.

Roory O'Balacaun – the violent patriotic Catholic with a tangy sense of humour which thrives in argumentation – is middle-aged and dressed in rough homespuns, cap and trench-coat. His character is not fully drawn in the sense that Ayamonn's is; he lacks the personal magnetism displayed in Ayamonn.

Equally fanatical is supercilious, atheistic Mullcanny – a comic blasphemer – whom the playwright describes as 'young, lusty, and restless'. He is attired in ill-fitting tweeds – his tweed-cap set rakishly on his head. He pours conversational oil on the heads of troubled disputants – the Protestant Brennan locked in perpetual combat with the Catholic Roory – reflecting narrow sectarian divisions that have plagued Irish history through centuries. Mullcanny is a cartoon-character.

The faces on Ayamonn's Catholic neighbours are stiff and mask-like; 'holding tight an expression of dumb resignation' in the playwright's words, like those portrayed in *The Star Turns Red*. The flower-sellers – Eeada, Dympna and Finnoola – are symbolical of hard-pressed working-class women of the tenements: the expression of Eeada is an old woman's; Dympna's that of middle-age, and Finnoola's a young girl-of-the-people. Faces of the men-folk and other neighbours are expressionless. Seams of poverty have destroyed their lives and expunged hope. The young singer who arrives with Brennan in the first act to give a rendering of Ayamonn's song also has a mask-like expression which shyness fails to alleviate. He is a taciturn figure in the Gallogher mould. The railwaymen who acquaint Ayamonn of the intended strike are stony-faced, too, in their resignation. Their peaked caps banded in red are pulled well over their heads.

Inspector Finglas, the Rector's churchwarden, is clad in a blue, silver-braided uniform, big blue helmet and highly-polished top-boots, and carries an impressive silver sword. His cavalrymen are not only servants of the King's peace but harbingers of the hard-hearted ruthless law of the employing class. This is made clear to Brennan in the fourth act: 'keep clear of unruly crowds – my men don't wait to ask the way you worship when they raise their arms to strike'.

Bigotry and dissension which divide Ireland nationally also divide her parochially, as illustrated by Foster and Dowzard who are members of the Rector's vestry and who are Orange to the core. Foster is small and scraggy, 'with aggression for ever lurking in his cranky face'; he has a squeaky voice which rises to a scream when angry. (So, also, has Rankin, the Catholic workman in *The Bishop's Bonfire*, when roused, drawing attention to his bigotry.) Dowzard is fat, red-faced and beefy and bulldozes his way into a perpetual state of self-invented discontent. Both are dressed as railway foremen and wear silver-braided peaked caps. As extreme Protestants from Belfast, who have come to work in Dublin, they view with disfavour the Rector's 'Romish' activities. They denounce the minister as Ichabod and shout for Breydon's head. They refer to the strikers as 'th' Pope's bullies' in the ranting manner of some of today's Northern Irish political leaders.

Samuel, the foolish verger, is sixty and prey to tantrums of the bigoted vestrymen. His woebegone manner is reminiscent of sexton Waugh's in *The Harvest Festival* and he is equally circumlocutory, though in a more comical and less conscious fashion.

The theme-song – from which the title of the play derives – is based on a semi-traditional air known as 'Eamonn a' Cnuic' ('Ned o' the Hill'): O'Casey adapted it to suit the words he had specially written, as he did with so many others in his various plays. Balladry often influences his choice of characters' names: Ayamonn and Brennan in this play; Robin Adair and Marion in *Cock-a-Doodle Dandy*; the mysterious Ned – the priest who never appears but whose spirit is omnipresent – in *The Drums of Father Ned.*

Since the first published versions of *Red Roses for Me* in 1942 and 1944, some slight revision has been made by the playwright, following the London post-war production in 1946, during which the author attended a performance of his play. These changes embraced mainly cuts in the final act to give it tighter synthesis: erasion, for instance, of two minor 'Humpty Dumpty' characters, both victims of police-cavalry-charge in the strikers' demonstration rally offstage; one with a brass tuba battered down over his head – comical-looking in his state of surprised confusion; the other stuck fast into a batoned drum surrounding his body in egg-shell style, looking even more comic-pathetic; both evincing sympathy from the Rector but only scorn from the hypocritical Foster and Dowzard. The dramatist, on reflection, must have decided to curtail the comedy incident in order to lend more heightened and persuasive effects prior to the sombre news of Ayamonn's death, through the lips of Finnoola. The scene is absent from all subsequent editions of the play, including the one which appears in *Collected Plays,* vol. 3.

For the later New York presentation, O'Casey made a few further changes and revisions, incorporating additional scenes and characters in the second half of the play. (These can be seen in *Six Great Modern Plays*, New York: Dell Publishing Company.) Yet subsequently, in the collection *Three More Plays* (1965), the second paperback anthology of the main plays to appear appealing to a wider readership, O'Casey omits any such additional material, the text being virtually the same as the one which is included in *Collected Plays,* vol. 3 with the addition, solely, of a short simple scene in Act Three, involving three workmen speaking excitedly on the bridge and speculating among themselves as to whether the military will be called out if the dispute intensifies. Current productions, for the most part, seem to favour the version published in *Collected Plays.*

The world *première*, with unauthorised cuts, at Dublin's Olympia Theatre in 1943, occurred during wartime, directed by Shelah Richards, with designs by Ralph Cusack. Another version, drawing hostile religious comments in the press, was staged by Ria Mooney (Noel Purcell excelling as Brennan) at Dublin's Gaiety Theatre in 1946. The first English presentation was pioneered in 1943 at Newcastle-upon-Tyne's People's Theatre, and Ria Mooney also directed in Sir Bronson Albery's first London production in 1946 (staged, successively, at Swiss Cottage's Embassy, Hammersmith's

Lyric and the West End's New and Wyndham's Theatres). English reaction, on the whole, was adulatory and, in some quarters, even rhapsodical. Kieron O'Hanrahan (Kieron Moore) played the lead, with a cast which included Maureen Pook, Eddie Byrne and Tristan Rawson. In 1954, Joan Littlewood's version in London's East End (the designer was John Bury) passed unobtrusively. The Mermaid's 1962 production (directed by Julius Gellner for Bernard Miles), despite fine performances from Donal Donnelly and Leonard Rossiter, lacked the soaring beauty in the symbolic third act. Tomas MacAnna's 1967 staging at the Abbey, with Jim Norton in the lead, excited its audiences but enraged its critics. Belfast, at the height of the Ulster troubles in 1972, witnessed a more moving interpretation at the Lyric, directed by Mary McCracken. The Abbey's second production in 1980, for the centenary celebrations, achieved a persuasive realism in Hugh Hunt's interpretation in a cast which included Stephen Brennan, May Cluskey and Ray McAnnally. By comparison with the BBC/RTE televised adaptation the same year (featuring John Kavanagh, Pauline Delany, Niall Buggy and Colin Blakely), it was less finely construed.

The New York *première* at Broadway's Booth in 1955–6, directed by John O'Shaughnessy with sets by Howard Bay and featuring Edward G. Marshall and Eileen Crowe, was received ambivalently and ran for a month. Among foreign productions, Jean Vilar's at Paris's Théâtre National Populaire in 1961 captured popular attention, as did Leo Mittler's in 1957, at West Berlin's Schlosspark-Theater, though critical dislike of its alleged 'operatic' impact led to an unnatural social-realist interpretation in Ernst Kahler's East Berlin version of 1963. The West's Schiller revival in 1977, by Wolfgang Heinz, was too strongly lyrical with insufficient stress on comedy. Translations have included French, German, Italian, Spanish, Danish, Bulgarian, Estonian, Persian, Polish, Russian and Roumanian.

14 *Oak Leaves and Lavender* (1946): an Oleograph of World War II

O'Casey's play about England during World War II, *Oak Leaves and Lavender*, is a commemorative tribute to the Battle of Britain telescoped in an oleo of fantasy and realism depicting heroism in the postlude of international fratricidal conflict and near-national strangulation: 'its dialogue ablaze like the leaves of a beechwood in autumn', comments Trewin in *Dramatists of Today*, and 'in terms of . . . impressions of Britain in her hour of danger, quivering on the edge of death', notes Wilson Knight, 'is beautifully apprehended'; the synthesis of past, present and future moulded into a chronological dream-drama, as ethereal as Shaw's *Heartbreak House* or Chekhov's *The Cherry Orchard*. Plot is minimal; mood impressionistic and the theme of an heroic life-death struggle culminates in a visionary optimism. Colloquial expression and folk-poetry blend with songs and choruses; and, although humanity's 'still, sad music' is present throughout, the final message is Blakean:

> He who bends to himself a Joy
> Doth the winged life destroy;
> But he who kisses the Joy as it flies
> Lives in Eternity's sunrise.

In tone, the play is more symbolic than either *Purple Dust* or *Red Roses for Me*, and to stage is as fully comprehensive and demanding as *The Star Turns Red*, or even *Within the Gates*.

Peremptory opinions have declared, on the evidence of one, totally inadequate, immediate post-war production, that *Oak Leaves and Lavender* is the dramatist's most obvious failure for the stage. In the vicissitudes of stage history, O'Casey's least remembered play has become his most underrated to the extent that present enthusiasts recall notions of it only through the medium of the printed text. Critics of the play, with only an arm-chair view to conjure, compare it unfavourably with the rest of O'Casey's plays. Certainly, within the conspectus of paper dimensions, it gives the impression of being less vibrant than some of his other dramas, so there remains the question of whether this particular play will revivify in a cosmic production it patently merits.

J. B. Priestley, when reviewing the play on publication, had serious reservations. Blatantly, he blamed style and method. 'What we have here is not drama in the ordinary sense but a kind of verbal opera', overloaded, he implied, with too much symbolism. Despite compensations of the 'gorgeous rhetoric' achieved, genuine dramatic action, he declared, had been lost. O'Casey's predicament – according to Priestley – was how to dramatise the essentially undramatic nature of the average inarticulate Englishman, investing him with powers of heightened speech which he does not notably possess. ('English conversationalists', quipped Oscar Wilde, 'have a miraculous power of turning wine into water'.)

Yet, in *The Art of the Dramatist* (1957; reprinted 1973), Mr Priestley the playwright – as opposed to Mr Priestley the critic – stresses:

> Everybody and everything on the stage have this double character; they are seen in the strange light and shadow of belief and disbelief; they belong to a heightened reality that we know to be unreal. It is this experience, unlike any other, that I call dramatic experience, and that the Theatre exists to provide for us.

Exactly. So, is Mr Priestley being unusually double-visioned? Echoing, unconsciously, Shaw and O'Casey in their theatrical pronouncements, he goes on to assert:

> And I suspect that it is this strange link with these moments of mystical insight that has given the Theatre, no matter how tawdry and trivial it may appear to be, a central place in most civilised societies, and has brought the drama close to religion.

Precisely; and yet, when reviewing *Oak Leaves and Lavender*, Mr Priestley the critic – abandoning the logic of his 'Doctor Jekyll' dramatic theory and donning instead the mask of 'Mister Hyde' – proceeded to bare his critical fangs, as follows:

He [O'Casey] has enlarged his method, heightened his manner, done more and more telescoping and symbolising, and piled on the rhetoric, to make up for the loss of all that Dublin flung into his lap, to show us what a Communist Celt of genius can do even with English life and character. Much of the drama has gone, and we are left with opera without the orchestra.

Tintinnabulatory clap-trap! In *The Green Crow*, Mr Priestley is referred to by O'Casey as 'A minor moper acting the part of a prophet in the wilderness', and the sting is not altogether undeserved. When urged to go back to the method of *Juno and the Paycock*, O'Casey was reluctant to tread again what he himself has described as 'the wasteland of self-derivative art'. As he further explains: 'dramatists cannot go on imitating themselves, and, when they get tired of that, imitating others. They must change, must experiment, must develop their power, or try to, if the drama is to live'.

One of the ways in which truth in the theatre – as in life – is achieved is through 'super-naturalism'. The great playwright is he who has a deep love of and a mystical feeling towards his art. Like Eugene O'Neill, the 'theater of creative imagination' for O'Casey represents the perfect 'theatrical' theatre of his dreams. The old 'naturalism' no longer applies; O'Casey had accepted O'Neill's philosophy (which the American playwright had expressed in a playbill-article of 1924) that 'we have endured too much from the banality of surfaces', and the dramatic soul must somehow transcend what O'Neill terms 'the ignoble inarticulateness of flesh'. The proper solution – as both playwrights foresaw – lies within the spiritualistic, or seraphic, sphere: what, in essence, Wilson Knight describes as 'the impact of the numinous' on the drama. This is realised to a large extent in *Oak Leaves and Lavender*, which, although denigrated by many critics, for Wilson Knight – at least – remains 'a work of exact and impersonal integration'. He also proclaims: 'A new dimension is felt, with the impingement of spirit-beings on man's transitory life. Humanity touches the unseen'.

The Biblical maxim: 'In the midst of life we are in death' was recognised by O'Casey as being especially appropriate during the crisis-years of World War II. Never before had the fear of death become such a universal factor even on the civilian front, with its aspects of civil defence, its images of land girls and women's auxiliary service forces, farmers and others in the Home Guard, its daily news bulletins announcing either victories or, more often crushing defeats: life and death were locked in armed combat and in ceaseless strife.

In *Oak Leaves and Lavender*, Death's presence regulates the tempo of tragicomic events in the midst of an ever-present realisation that Britain is at war. The play is described by the author, in a letter in 1946 to the Macmillan Company, New York, as 'an O'Casey tribute . . . to the big fight here [in England] against Nazi domination'. Later, in another letter, the playwright declares: 'Oak Leaves would hardly be welcomed in Germany, for the mood of the play towards Germany is the mood of all of us to her in 1941, during the big bombing of our cities and towns'.

The action of the play passes in a West Country manor house 'during the Battle of Britain'. Purple represents the colour of death. In a masque-like Prelude, spirits from an eighteenth-century world dance in the shadows to the tune and rhythm of a minuet and converge on events of the present. These ghostly dancers also parade at the end of the play, though there is no indication of a postlude as such: the tempo of past and present has by then converged on the future, and eventuality and circumstance have joined hands with each other, showing a telescoping of the time-sequence – rather like the Time plays of Mr Priestley's own creation. The undertones of war (forming the main synthesis of the play) are sandwiched between the two shadow-masques in a fantasia of stage surrealism, reminding us of the supernaturalness of Shelley's words from 'Adonais':

> Earth's shadows fly:
> Life, like a dome of many-coloured glass,
> Stains the white radiance of Eternity.

A variation, too, of the strange theme we encounter in Blake: 'Eternity is in love with the productions of time'.

Throughout the play, death is close. History, the past and death are inextricably intertwined: it is an extension of the *Purple Dust* theme: the influence of the dead on their posterity, symbolised by the scent of lavender which drifts through the rooms, superimposing itself on the common purpose of the English people during the war, when the familiar symbol from the past – Hearts of Oak – was invoked in a battle for survival.

A single setting informs all three acts and the Prelude which comprise the play: 'The great room of a Manorial House of a long past century', its stylised panelling lending itself to adaptation, in the final act, to factory workshop conditions in the pressing plethora of war-time emergency conditions. The ghostly apparitions that haunt the house point the moral: the House is England, redolent of past glories, as well as corruptions, on the verge of national collapse, in O'Casey's version of *Heartbreak House* of the war – in the spirit of Hector Hushabye's words in Shaw's play, 'We do not live in this house: we haunt it'. The idea of a symbolic house occurs in *Purple Dust*, when the house which is finally submerged represents feudal powers of capitalism. Such abuses – implies O'Casey – the war must eventually sweep away in the common cause of survival and freedom.

In his autobiographical *Sunset and Evening Star*, the dramatist applauds the national spirit of communistic activity and brotherhood of man:

> Men and women were measuring out life now, not with coffee spoons, but with rifle, tommy-gun, sling, splint, and badge. A bitter change, but not all evil. Common life had to go on, but with a very different rhythm. Things were changed, changed utterly . . . All political diversions ran from the stage as the curtain rose upon war.

(More than one political commentator has avowed that Britain came close to being a socialist society in the war years.) O'Casey's scene is at once familiar and high-fantastical: it is Britain, working-class and aristocracy alike, united in common bond, poised on the brink of survival, following the fall of France, bracing herself against the threat of German invasion. The spotlight focuses on the home front in a corner of the South-West during the relentless bombing of cities and towns such as Plymouth – Duxton in the play – in the wake of the Battle of Britain showing the supreme testing-time of civilian endurance and bravery.

The play is dedicated to one of many who were called upon to exercise the highest gallantry in the service of international freedom: 'To little Johnny Grayburn, who, in his sailor suit, played football with me on a Chalfont lawn and afterwards gallantly fell in the battle of Arnhem'. Johnny Grayburn had been a playmate of the dramatist's son, Breon, and is mentioned in *Inishfallen, Fare Thee*

Well as Lieutenant John Grayburn 'who died holding a Rhine bridge at Arnhem', clad 'in the muddy-yellow of England's battledress', fighting for the world's freedom and 'swallowed up in the greed of eternity' (a reference to Blake's aphorism). Meanwhile, in Britain, on the civilian front – O'Casey tells us in the autobiographical story – 'busy people were getting ready for their own burial', as the Nazis were plunging the whole European amphitheatre into holocaust and ruin.

The play is sub-titled, 'A Warld on Wallpaper' – that is world-war on wallpaper (by telescoping two worlds into one) – a punning reference to Yeats's letter rejecting *The Silver Tassie*, O'Casey's earlier play about the World War I, emphasising that in a good play 'The whole history of the world must be reduced to wallpaper in front of which the characters must pose and speak'.

In *Oak Leaves and Lavender*, characters pose and speak in dialectical as well as dialectal idiom and in colourful metaphor: Devonian and Cornish accents jostle – not always in sweet harmony – with those of Feelim O'Morrigun, the Irish butler in the household from Knocknawhishogue, who is the central character and one of the most entertaining figures in the drama, as is William the waiter, whom he resembles, with his 'quiet voice with a gentle melody in it', a leading favourite among Shaw's creations in *You Never Can Tell*. Both charaters exist to please and serve: never at a loss, always ready at the right moment, never in the way; unextravagant eccentrics who have to deal with rather dotty dependants but who manage withal to preserve their equanimity. An American critic – with whom O'Casey corresponded – Dr Horace Reynolds, has observed of Feelim that in war he has some of the authoritativeness shipwreck gave to the Admirable Crichton. But Feelim O'Morrigun is no English butler: he is, says Dr Reynolds, 'the Irish blood-brother to the immortal Fluther Good' (*New York Times Book Review*, 11 May 1947).

Some commentators have suggested, superficially, that the Dame of the play, Dame Hatherleigh, who is of aristocratic background and who later in the play loses her airman son, is based on Lady Gregory. But Dame Hatherleigh (only her upbringing and circumstances suggest a comparison) is obsessively strange and does not match up to the illustrious qualities of Lady Gregory – as outlined in the Chapter, 'Blessed Bridget o' Coole', in *Inishfallen, Fare Thee Well*.

An extensive cast comprises O'Casey's portrayal of a cross-section of an English community, moulded to heroic measure, during war. Even allowing for doubling of minor parts, the resources of a large company will be called upon to do justice to the dramatist's intentions. Dame Hatherleigh's West Country Manor acts as a focal point for local Civil Defence operations and is peopled with all sorts: the Dame herself, with Feelim, her butler and major-domo, who has also been given the role of Head Warden of the district; their sons, both pilots in the Royal Air Force and actively engaged in the battle of the skies (in history, known as the Battle of Britain). Drishogue, Feelim's son, has formed a romantic attachment with Monica, the daughter of a local farmer, Abraham Penrhyn (with a severe puritanical outlook and surly disposition, who, when adversity occurs, hastens to the bottle) and Edgar, Dame Hatherleigh's son, has similar designs on local land-girl, Jennie Frome – one of O'Casey's golden, voluptuous lasses with a Rabelaisian enjoyment of life. Other land-girls of lesser stature include Joy and Felicity; counterbalanced by farm workers, Mark and Michael, defence volunteers in the local territorial Home Guard, whose amateur attempts at soldiering inspire both ridicule and trepidation in Feelim. (A similar-styled burlesque on the Home Guard, or Local Defence Volunteers, as they were officially named, under the title of *Dad's Army* by Perry and Croft, won popular appeal and laughter later on English television screens.)

In addition to minor parts, such as Third Home Guardsman, there are: a pair of constables known as Sillery and Dillery, blundering and conceited, West Country versions of Shaksepeare's Dogberry and the Watch; Mrs Watchit, the Dame's Housekeeper, eccentric almost as the Dame herself; visitors to the Manor, including a Russian refugee, Mrs Deeda Tutting, harbinger of political hatred and doom, who has her counterpart in Mrs Creeda Stern in *Sunset and Evening Star*; a Mr Constant, local resident eager to get his wife to America, away from the dangers of the bombing; a man leading a deputation demanding air raid shelters; a farm-hand called Pobjoy, a pilloried figure of scorn, who is a conscientious objector; plus other land-girls, ATS and WRNS, representatives of Women's Auxiliary Services; farm workers and factory operatives, including Old Woman of Seventy and Foreman of Factory (who appear in Act Three); a Seller of Lavender, chanting her wares at the beginning and end of the play; as well as ghostly apparitions who appear in the Prelude of the Shadows and return at the postorbital conclusion, comprising First, Second and Third Lady

Dancers and their Gentlemen partners; and, finally Young Son of Time, instrument of Change and humanity's flame-thrower, 'symbolical of youth's earnest and warm vigour'. Such is the gallimaufry of characters in this time-fantasy of the war.

In the prologue, ghosts of eighteenth-century aristocratic worthies – represented by various sets of dancers – dance their minuets in flickering shadows of the dimly-lit atmosphere shrouding the great interior of the rococo mansion. (The light playing on them – says the stage instruction – 'seems to come from the ghosts of many candles'.) In this expressionistic scene – similar to the Bridge of Vision transfiguration scene in the third act of *Red Roses for Me* (where stage lighting is exploited to its fullest to illustrate the significance of the dialogue) – light from burning London, emblazoned against a background of the Blackout, reflects the glare of incendiary bombs dropping all around the capital and impinges on the shadow-masque of dancers. As the distant sky becomes red – turning to mauve – the ghostly dancers sense danger as the flames of war leap higher threatening the heart of London. 'Look', says one of them, 'The buildings topple like the town of Troy . . .' And, says another, 'There, in the midst of the red foliage, the dome of St. Paul's stands out like a black and withering lotus blossom!' Leaning against the clock, Young Son of Time intervenes with the remark that England is bereft and 'orphan'd' of her greatest men. 'She is alone at last, and she is lost.' Her political leaders have betrayed her, and Churchill has not yet proved himself the bulwark of war-time leadership which history has since acknowledged. Swords have rusted, observe the spirits (mindful of the warning in *Othello*) and sophisticated weapons replaced them: time has brought about a change. 'Burning torches now are in the hands of others', remarks one of the shadows, quizzically.

This masque – like those in Elizabethan drama and, notably, Shakespeare's *The Tempest* – has an allegorical force: it is conjoined with the one at the end of the play – foretelling victory and revolutionary change. The shadows return at the conclusion of the play, as one cries out: 'The lavender will bloom again, and oak leaves laugh at the wind in the storm'. The lavender song sung at the end of the Prelude (' . . . buy my bonnie lavender') acts as a bridge between two worlds: the world of the past and the world of futurity; or, the world of *status quo* and the world of change.

In the giant leap between the two – symbolised by the present – (mild stage lights now reveal the interior of the room), the beginning of Act One finds Britain entrammelled in feverish war-time preparations. The war's first rude, dramatic effect upon the public was the imposition of the Blackout on 3 September 1939. From then onwards, for the duration, every home and building as well as every vehicle and moving object were compelled to function with reduced lighting as air-raid precautionary measures took effect. Compliance with lighting restrictions, and the importance of affording protection against the blast from bombs, presented major security problems because of the conflicting demands of the necessity to maintain a normal semblance of public life. This is demonstrated tellingly and amusingly throughout the first act during the 'phoney' war period when nothing at all happened on the civilian front; yet stringent preparations, of course, went on.

Protection against blast was provided by sandbags and bricking-up of windows in the case of larger and more vulnerable buildings. Other protective devices included anti-splinter netting affixed to windows and doors and the provision of steel shelters for use in gardens and homes. The exercise of civil defence was in the hands of specially selected wardens, such as Feelim in the play, whose responsibility it was to assist local fire brigades in provincial towns to deal with conflagrations resulting from enemy bombings. Improvised medical-aid posts were quickly established everywhere and also anti-aircraft control stations in defence of Britain's skies. Policemen on patrol were vigorously enforcing the hated blackout conditions.

At the commencement of Act One, Monica is helping Feelim to darken the windows with appropriate blackout coverings, the scent of lavender – foretelling death – floating in through the windows. Death has become more than an old wives' tale; everyone – the autobiography tells us – 'was learning anew and in a fresh way that God was Love'. The sinister Blackout was accompanied by an equally faceless operation whereby 'all road sign-posts were swiftly taken down, all names of places blotted out from railway stations, so that all England quick became a land without a name . . . Henceforth, the world would form its life to the beat of Hitler's heart'.

While men were fighting on European battle-fronts, women were recruited, because of shortages in man-power, in various capacities in engineering and agricultural grades and in territorial auxiliary fighting services. Home Guard units were established in towns, cities and villages. Equipment was sparse and hybrid at first: in the country – as we see later in the first act – pikes and other implements preceded arms and rifles, as all kinds of amateur weapons were pressed into service.

In the absence of Colonel Hatherleigh – fighting at the front – Feelim's duties, in his own words, included the managerial and tactful supervision of 'a house haunted by night, an' a bedlam by day with workers on th' new aerodrome, Home Guard units, air-raid wardens, first-aid post, Land Girl hostel, an' rest camp for th' bombed-out evacuees' with himself 'in th' centre an' on th' fringe to keep harmony an' ordher!' He bemoans his fate that his chief war-time preoccupation is not only to keep an eye on Hatherleigh's eccentric wife but all the rest of the women engaged on war work in the Big House who are predisposed to talk him 'into a wild dilerium!' When Dillery the policeman reprimands him for con-travening regulations by showing too much light, Feelim remarks: 'Fuss an' fury. God must ha' had a rare laugh when He made a serious Englishman'. Later, when the tramp of marching recruits on Home Guard manoeuvres can be heard outside the windows, he makes the comment: 'It's pathetic. They think they're marchin' through Georgia'. And, of the antics of these West Country versions of *Dad's Army*, Feelim remonstrates: 'Old men manoeuverin' themselves into an early grave'. While Feelim is securing the manorial blackout fixtures from a ladder, a crash of breaking glass from the spearhead of a careless pike indicates that the local Home Guard are on 'playground' duty again!

The phoney war was thus highly conjectural as well as comical in its conjuration. The Dame's housekeeper, Mrs Watchit – a rural oddity in herself – brews tea without the infusion, in her forgetful-ness, offering Feelim the solemn discourtesy at the supposed moment of refreshment that ''Usband says as 'ow 'ee thinks as it would buck you up like' (Feelim's reaction to this volte-face is a scolding adjuration to Mrs Watchit to 'keep your mind from whirlin' when you're makin' tea; an' when you make it, make it with tea, and don't thry to make it with a miracle!'). Another of the housekeeper's foibles is to cut off the gas from the mains in the kitchen when she goes out shopping, taking the key in her pocket 'to 'usband fuel'. Home Guardsman Sergeant Mark is yet another of the innocent eccentrics inhabiting the household. In the drive for energy conservation initiated by Feelim he offers the Ruritanian advice: 'Best way conserve fuel, I says, is keep aturnin' down gas-tap, don't light fires, keep poker locked up, mark time with hot water, riddle-me-ree th' ashes, an' don't light no light that 'tisn't necessary'. To which Feelim retorts: 'And never get outa bed!'

O'Casey's first act has a number of farcical episodes in which people just muddle through the war. In the second act their courage has already been tested as, unceasingly, throughout night and day, the endurance of heavy bombing attacks has become a regular hazard, as sleepless, harried men and women toil cheerfully about their normal daily tasks. The scene's interior, although basically the same as in the first act, appears changed, with blackout coverings remaining up and electric lights on all the time, against a background of constant air-raid alerts, with their attendant daily havoc and disruption.

Threats of invasion have loomed menacingly and refugees have already poured into the South-West from London and the Eastern counties. Reflecting on dangers from a possible German invasion, Jennie is asked by her land-girl colleague, Joy, after a particularly long, wearisome 'alert' lasting six hours, how she would react: 'Live on if I can; die in my lover's arms, or die fighting them, if I can't'. The significance of the reply is only realised towards the end of the third act when the two airforce pilots, Edgar and Drishogue, are killed when their combat air plane crashes over the local aerodrome and Jennie dies trying to rescue her lover from the burning wreckage.

In the hundreds of fields and scattered acres all over the country, thousands of women took up farming in the national 'Dig for Victory' campaign and millions of tons of vegetables were produced for vital consumption in canteens and homes. Choruses and songs of tribute to the role of these women and land-girls are given voice, led by Jennie and Joy, praising their tireless efforts.

> toiling on farm and in wold,
> Digging hard, digging deep, in the morning!

And, in precious moments of relaxation, Jennie counsels Joy not to be afraid 'when your hair gets tangled in the stem and leaf of the myrtle': in the stark reality of war 'The stormy night of your harum-scarum god is over'. The righteousness and earnestness of war are now crucial issues: in the second act, the comedy has a keener edge, whereas, in the first, farce is in the ascendancy, to match the anti-climatic mood of the early non-eventful stages of the war.

Now, war's deeper dimensions predominate: dangers to individual predicaments; hazardous lives of pilots, especially, as expressionistic stage-effects in sound and colour warn menacingly of war's inexorable outrage. Tongues of flame and fire light up the sky and windows of the set to the sound of rushing music, at the conclusion of the act, of Wagner's 'Ride of the Valkyries', with flashing of swaztikas on radio panels as German warplanes are heard rumblingly offstage. The Manor shivers and windows shake. (Gone are bangs and the naturalistic sounds which accompanied the earlier dramas such as *The Shadow of a Gunman* or *The Plough and the Stars*. O'Casey's aim, in *Oak Leaves and Lavender*, is to portray the spirit and essence of the war.) Onstage, the crowd – led by Mark of the Home Guard – chants encouragement to the British flyers: to the 'Young, lusty lads in Air Force blue', honoured in the choric refrain of 'Sons of England!' O'Casey's attitude to the conduct of World War II reflects in large measure Shaw's during World War I: that war would be won ultimately in the sky rather than in the trenches; therefore, aerial bombardment was the key to victory. 'All wars', Shaw maintained, 'are decided by breaking through a military barrier and getting a bayonet or bomb against the brains and stomach of the nation as represented by the civilians of the capital' (quoted in Weintraub, *Bernard Shaw, 1914–1918: Journey to Heartbreak*, 1973).

In the play, Monica remains apprehensive over Drishogue's plight: as her air-pilot lover his life has become, ironically, a die-dream. Drishogue possesses something of his father's tenacity and reassures her, giving her strength and succour with the words:

> And you must be as the Irish lass of twice a hundred years ago, who sold her rock and sold her reel and sold her only spinning-wheel, to buy her love a sword of steel to fix him fitly in the fight for the rights of man.

Drishogue, whose views resemble some of those of Red Jim and the Dreamer, is not in the war, he tells Monica, solely for England's sake: internationally, he supports it as an internecine struggle against fascism; an extension of the Civil War which strangled freedom in Spain. His attitude (and O'Casey's) is the wider view that patriotism is a lively sense of collective responsibility. 'Nationalism', he would agree with Richard Aldington, 'is a silly cock crowing on its own dunghill'.

In addition to the scare of lavender scent penetrating the house –

with its forebodings of death – Feelim becomes a victim, too, of household hallucinations: he imagines he feels flounces against his step from the swish of ghostly dancers who haunt the mansion. Woven into the texture of the play is the philosophy of Thomas Campbell from 'Lochiel's Warning': 'Coming events cast their shadows before'. (References to the Scottish poet surface throughout O'Casey's work.) In the midst of ever-present fantasy, Feelim exclaims: 'Oh, isn't it enough to have to contend with corporal enemies, without havin' to deal with spiritual ones too!'

Among many 'corporeal' hazards Feelim has to put up with are the prying antics of Constables Sillery and Dillery – a pair of solemn asses – ever on the watch for unobscured lights in contravention of blackout regulations; well-to-do citizens, such as Constant, whom Feelim sees as 'surgin'' round Dame Hatherleigh tryin' through her, to touch American bankers, ambassadors, an' consuls, in an effort to get their children an' relatives quick to the States'; deputations, too, from civilians for more shelters, and Home Guardsmen clamouring for more up-to-date rifles and effective amunition; as well as denunciations from hostile tongues seeking to disparage the efforts of those directing the local war-effort; in Shakespeare's indicative words, from *As You Like It*:

> Jealous in honour, sudden and quick in quarrel,
> Seeking the bubble reputation
> Even in the cannon's mouth.

And, in 'the slings and arrows of outrageous fortune' which torment Feelim in a different fashion, Feelim – following Hamlet's example – is forced 'to take arms against a sea of troubles'. When he breaks the news to his fellows of America's Lend-Lease agreement and an ensured supply of further arms and tanks for Britain while she stands alone against Hitler he breaks into impassioned song – 'To arms', intoning:

> March on, march on, serfdom is past,
> Set free th' world at last!

The tragic significance of the second act is finalised with last-minute instructions from their squadron to Drishogue and Edgar to return to their aerodrome for flight bombardment, which, for the assembling crowd in seeing them off – as well as for theatre audiences themselves – produces moments of agonised hope and trepidation akin to the mixed emotions accompanying the final scene of the first act of *The Silver Tassie* when the boat leaves for the Continent to take Harry Heegan and the rest of the troops to the trenches.

Drishogue – an enthusiastic young communist (with similar ideals to Jack and the Dreamer) – realises he is risking his life every time he plunge into battle in the tormented skies. (During the Battle of Britain a pilot's life was not expected to exceed eight weeks.) He is a sensuous, vitalistic young hero – 'a sweet sky pilot', to adopt a phrase from Shaw, in a different context – who bids his lover, in this scene, a death-fraught 'farewell', flushed with the O'Casey philosophy of 'a lover's kiss is an eternal thought!' Monica's parting words have their own simplistic poignancy: 'Goodbye! A beggarly word braving it out to parting lovers like sorrow in a coloured coat'.

The parting between Edgar and vivacious Jennie is, perhaps, more tragic because it mirrors an unreflecting heartbreak induced by the unimaginable horrors of modern warfare. Jennie's attitude is O'Casey's. Earlier in the play her words echoed the beliefs of the dramatist: 'Though life's uncertain, we ought to edge its darkness with a song!' In retrospect, the parting at the close of Act Two is strewn with sweet sorrow, the numinously implied words constituting an unrealised epitaph for both: in Jennie's words, 'When I see you again, let the breast of your Air Force blue glitter with stars like the sky of a winter's night!' Soon, the glittering stars will serve as a perpetual *de profundis* in memory of both. Eternity's grasp is not simply within the reach of a selective few – whether brave lovers or undaunted heroes. This is the sombre message the play imparts in the life-drama of world catastrophe. Pursuit of freedom – when humanity is at its darkest ebb – knows no bounds, even to uncharted realms of death. 'Brave death', says Shakespeare's Hotspur in *King Henry IV, Part 1*, 'when princes die with us'.

The immolation of Drishogue, Edgar and Jennie, harbingers as well as potential inheritors of the freedom which victory will bring – gay, youthful and intrepid in their love of life and vitality, wantonly sacrificed in the brutality and waste of war – is a cumulative tragedy hard to accept even in the face of international war, especially one in which, in Drishogue's words, 'righteousness and war have kissed each other: Christ, Mahomet, Confucius, and Buddha are one'.

The purpose of the war, while firmly endorsed in the peroration of Drishogue in the first act –

Go forth to fight, perchance to die, for the great human soul of England. Go forth to fight and to destroy, not the enemies of this or that belief, but the enemies of mankind . . .

– does not necessarily imply acceptance of the evils of war in general. Shaw's death-bed wish, as O'Casey informs us in *Sunset and Evening Star* (Eileen, the playwright's wife, was at his bedside shortly before he died), was that youth might not be wasted in another war. In this play, it is the indomitable hope of O'Casey, too.

The elegiac utterances of most of the characters in the play bewail the extent and enormity of the loss of life through war. In many respects, *Oak Leaves and Lavender* is O'Casey's saddest and most sombre play. But a beautiful sadness prevails, fortified by victory and hope and inviolability of earth's endeavour. Of life there is no ending; so optimism is triumphant. 'Even the winter has her many beauties', says the aged playwright in the closing paragraphs of his final autobiographical volume,

even for the old who shiver, . . . the cold mists of morning, the fretted framework of the trees against the sky, the diamantling frost biting a harsh beauty into the earth's soft bosom; the stillness of the earth herself under it all, waiting for the spring. Ah, yes; to the old, spring and its budding bring a welcome as well as to the young. Sweet spring, full of sweet days and roses.

The same stoical belief in survival and progress which occasions the autobiographical writings pervades the plays as well, even this war-torn play; even the utterances of Dame Hatherleigh herself – immersed as she increasingly becomes in dolours of suffering and grief – reflected in the cycles of nature whose changes affirm the indestructible texture of beauty:

Is the crimson cherry brown? The apple-blossom black? The sky for ever grey? No, no! The cherry is as red as ever; the apple-blossom rosy; and the sky is often blue; sweet lavender rears tops of gentle purple; many a sturdy oak shall strut from a dying acorn; and a maiden's lips still quiver for a kiss.

(Act Three)

The finality of war is effectively demonstrated by the sudden transformation, in Act Three, of stage settings and design: the interior of the Manor has now been converted into a local munitions factory. Increasing war production has become an urgency since Hitler – at this stage in the war – had invaded Russia; and German bombers which, previously, had been busily attacking London and provincial cities, were suddenly switched to the Eastern Front. Spare-time factories now sprung up all over Britain to assist in greater manufacture of aircraft components, shells and the construction of tanks. In the bustle of emergency, the role of every individual citizen was vital: it was a war of nerves as well of attrition: civilians were put to the final test – and ingenuity pushed to its utmost limits – in a unique phase of unparalleled civilian courage and co-operation; and, though phosphorous bombs, V-weapon rockets and other deadly projectiles fell upon the population in the final, strenuous efforts with greater concussion than ever before, national morale remained dauntless in the face of these new threats and dangers.

Throughout – as events in this act suggest – public attitudes towards conscientious objectors become severe in their disapprobation. Pobjoy – the conscientious objector introduced in this act – bears the brunt of dissension from farm workers who refuse to work with him. Feelim tries to persuade Pobjoy of the futility of his 'anti-violence' outlook: 'Birth is noisy, and death isn't quite a quiet thing'. But Pobjoy replies sourly that he has a conscience. 'Let them who take the sword perish by it', he counters; to which, Feelim replies, 'Thousands of children who never took the sword perished by it; perished by it because we took it into our hands a little late'. Mrs Watchit voices the opinions of the crowd when she remarks: 'Waste o' time talkin' teh 'ee. Smack in th' jaw is grace o' God teh folks like 'im, 'usband says'.

When Feelim attempts to lecture Pobjoy on the illustrious heritage of England and the brave risks servicemen are making to enable rations to be imported to English citizens, the indifferent Pobjoy flings back the taunt of Irish neutrality: 'Those brave men are blown to bits while your Irish eyes are smiling. Get your own rats to go into the fight, and then you'll have a surer right to lecture us'.

The taunt is also taken up by an Old Woman from the rest-centre who remarks that Feelim is too comfortable over here 'makin' a nice livin' outa th' soft-hearted English'. She is also supported by one of the land-girls, Felicity; and a one-sided discussion develops, similar to the episode in Joyce's *Ulysses*, where the Citizen – full of nationalistic prejudice and chauvinism – boasts and rants and

abuses Bloom in a mood of single-minded arrogance which is also
characteristic of some of O'Casey's 'paycockian' typed characters.
Like the passage in *Ulysses*, the scene is one of burlesque inter-
polation and gathers absurdity as it proceeds. It also cuts deeply into
contemporary pretentiousness and hypocrisy.

The Old Woman, a septuagenarian old virago herself – the
equivalent of Joyce's Citizen – is vitriolic at the expense of the
Irish, though exempts Ulster's role in the war effort:

> OLD WOMAN: As for me, no-one's prouder than me of the North-
> eastern Irish, who are men, an' not rattlesnakes or
> scum, for they belong to a different race altogether.
> FEELIM: (*sarcastically*): Didja not know that before, me girl? We
> Irish are only human: The North-eastern boyos are
> specially adapted for divine purposes.
> OLD WOMAN (*furiously*): North-east Ireland will remain where it is,
> in spite of your venom, ignorance, an' audacious
> intolerance. That's why your tribe never gets any-
> where. After all, th' whole world knows we English
> are th' supreme examples of unity an' orderliness! I
> hope to see all foreigners sent back to where yous
> came from; an', regardin' yourself, I wish you a
> bomb-strewn passage over your Irish sea!

In the midst of the disputation, Farmer Penrhyn rushes in abusing
Feelim and his men – those practised in stirrup-pump duty (though
most of those in the Auxiliary Fire Service had never fought a fire in
their lives) – for failing to extinguish the blaze caused by an
incendiary bomb setting fire to Penrhyn's farm. 'All is ashes an' all is
dust. Us's a broken man', he moans. Cursing Providence as he
leaves, Feelim calls after him, 'I'll not let you insult God! Say what
you like about Feelim O'Morrigun; but you must show ordinary
respect to God Almighty!' Feelim's conciliatory words to the
bigoted Presbyterian farmer, no less than to the one-sided disputants who are goading him into defending what they see as a
nation of cowards, are in the same spirit of tolerance and broad-
mindedness as Joyce's Leopold Bloom, who confronts bigotry with
the observation that 'Some people . . . can see the mote in others'
eyes but they can't see the beam in their own'.

Although Feelim, like his counterpart in *You Never Can Tell* – the admirable waiter, William – is an accomplished and amiable appeaser, he does show some remarkable, forthright, Flutherian qualities which suggest he is in the genuine O'Casey mould. The foreman of the factory is also Irish, and in a brush between the two over abrogation of duties, Feelim, in a quick-tempered exchange, deprecates his colleague's 'devalerian authoritarianism', and despite his own loyalties to the Catholic faith of his upbringing, Feelim launches a fierce attack on the new Irish theocracy under De Valera that has the familiar O'Casey ring to it: 'Turnin' th' poor people into shock brigades of confraternities an' holy sight-seein' sodalities, so that they're numb with kneelin' , an' hoarse with th' dint of recitin' litany an' prayer!' Some of Fluther's blarneying tactics are also demonstrated when Feelim is faced with a revolt from the farm workers on his hands because of the presence of Pobjoy in their midst. The land-girls are by no means displeased with such a disquisition coming from the lips of Feelim as the following:

> If I told yous what I think yous are, it's not diggin' th' land yous would be, but sportin' about in the whitest o' linen an' gayest of silks, with young an' handsome gallants festooned with ordhers, an' swords danglin' from their hips, cravin' a dance in a lighted hall, or a long kiss outside, under a tree, an' the twilight fallin'!

The distorted views about the Southern Irish – voiced by the land-girls and local inhabitants – are vigorously denied by Feelim, who resents imputations of cowardice, when Irish soldiers have linked arms with European armies both in the present and the past, demonstrating the truer conviction of T. E. Lawrence 'that Irishmen persuade only the rest of the world'. To a brave man, therefore, every soil is his qwn country.

With deepening combat, 'the meteor flag of England' – to quote Campbell in 'Ye Mariners of England' – was being blown about unrecognisably in the stormy tempests separating Southern England from German-occupied Northern Europe. Britannia's bulwark no longer towered 'along the steep' (Campbell's words) and her march beyond the mountain-waves and 'ocean-warriers' was insufficient to deter the Hun. Her commanders were discovering the truth of Shaw's previous assertions that the war would ultimately be won in the sky and not on the battlefields or on the seas. This, too, is the implicit lesson of *Heartbreak House* – and the experience that gives it its ending. In broader terms, the time sequence in *Oak Leaves and Lavender* is manipulated to include, significantly, the Battle of Britain – in its widest sense – by telescoping the major phases of the war. With the help of the Russian torch and American trumpet and 'thunders from her native oak' (Campbell again), Britain was able to quell the floods and avert the stormy winds from blowing on her shore. On the Continent, instead, the battle raged loud and long and 'the fiery fight' was fierce; and for many, it was a case (as in 'Hohenlinden') of

> on, ye brave,
> Who rush to glory, or the grave!

The factory-house of the play is buffeted by the stormy winds of war, the crowd chanting 'The house is trembling and the windows shake!' (Subsequently, O'Casey told Nathan in a letter that 'there is ne' er a bang' in the whole play: he had outgrown 'these bangs', though conceded they were present often enough in his early dramas.) A voice announces, expressionistically, in stentorian tones over the radio, that a desperate struggle is being waged till fascism is destroyed; and singing voices are heard proclaiming the 'Heart of Oak' intentions of national endeavour and collaborative effort.

In the heart of the struggle comes news of the deaths of Drishogue, Edgar and Jennie. The crowd with heads bent murmur reverentially: 'They died for us all. God be good to them!' Brokenly, but defiantly, Feelim vows to take up the fight where Drishogue laid it down, proving to the onlookers not only that Irish valour still exists, but proclaiming, eloquently, the torch of resistance and freedom, with the words: 'Hearts of steel, well tempered with hate, is what we are . . . Hearts of oak don't last; so hearts of steel we are!' In war, says O'Casey in *Sunset and Evening Star*, there is neither song nor sermon, only lamentation and desolation; the world sinking into a world of ruins, the accompanying pain, says Shaw in *Heartbreak House*, being one that goes mercifully beyond the powers of feeling. 'When your heart is broken', says Shaw – through the voice of his Ellie Dunn – 'your boats are burned: nothing matters any more. It is the end of happiness and the beginning of peace'.

Resettlement, the ending of O'Casey's play implies, is expressed by the Tennysonian philosophy underscoring *The Lotos-Eaters*, and, in itself, may be a confusion worse than death:

Trouble on trouble, pain on pain,
Long labour unto aged breath,
Sore task to hearts worn out by many wars
And eyes grown dim with gazing on the pilot-stars.

The final act ends with Monica's explaining to Feelim that she was secretly married to Drishogue and now carries his child. Feelim exclaims: 'Oh! Which is worse – th' burden of th' dead who are with us now; or that of the living still to come!' The moral is that whatever the losses, life must go on, the war must be won. A slow lament – 'Oh, Bend Low the Head' – is sung, in conclusion, to accompaniment on trumpets and drums offstage, honouring the coffin bearing the body of Drishogue, draped with a Union Jack and half covered by a silken strip of green, followed by Dame Hatherleigh, dressed in a sable cloak, her head covered by a silver cap similar to that worn by the Young Son of Time in the Prelude to the play. The mourners include farm workers, factory operatives, and representatives of the women's auxiliary services. Preceded by Feelim and Monica, the crowd follows the coffin out; the two Home Guardsmen bringing up the rear.

As Dame Hatherleigh stares impassively out of the window at what was once the garden-path, the cortège passes by: the music becomes fainter in the distance and the young Foreman of the factory – after a reverential silence and ignoring the staring, grief-stricken presence of the Dame – blows his whistle sharply and the room suddenly becomes alive once more with the movement of machinery and the hustle of factory activity: the belts travel, the wheels turn and the drop-hammer rises and falls.

The transition is complete: we must all suffer change; our household hearths, says Tennyson, grow cold, and we return as household ghosts – as our sons and posterity inherit us. The lavender blossom in O'Casey's play has replaced the lotos in Tennyson's poem: both have the same symbolical function: death-in-life; 'dark death, or dreamful ease'.

In the fusion of time, the stage darkens and the room rapidly becomes dark; and Dame Hatherleigh, in a sad, almost toneless voice, remarks: 'We must all go soon. Our end makes but a beginning for others'. The future, the playwright signifies, is in the hands of the young. Thus, the play, besides being a 'supernoctural' fable (to apply Joyce's pun), a dream-phantasmagoria in the style of *Finnegans Wake*, is an allegory of youth. 'Only the rottenness and ruin must die', says Dame Hatherleigh. 'Great things we did and said; things graceful, and things that had a charm, live on to dance before the eyes of men admiring'; a variation of the lotos-philosophy expressed by Tennyson and the *Morte D'Arthur* theme of 'The old order changeth, yielding place to new'.

The Dame's last words have the wistful significance of death: 'The scent of lavender's in every breath I draw, and the dancers are very close'. In the darkening shadows revealing the dancers of the Prelude, Dame Hatherleigh intermingles with them, slowly sinking down — in the words of the stage-instruction — 'to lean her body against the clock' (the position occupied by Time's Son in the beginning). To the dancers she exclaims: 'Wait for me . . . for I am one of you, and will join you when I find my son'.

'The lavender shall bloom again!' says one of the shades, and the chorus repeats the cry as the dancers, to the accompaniment of a slow minuet, as in the prologue, mingle with the shadows, while the Lavender Seller, as before, is heard chanting her wares, signifying that customs, traditions — even street-cries — fade into the whirlpool of existence and cycles of fast-vanishing history and ever-changing life.

History is cyclic, suggests O'Casey, echoing Joyce, who in turn was influenced by Vico; just as Priestley, in his concept of time and space, was influenced by Dunne, whose *An Experiment with Time* (1927) offered a theory ascribed to telepathy or clairvoyance.

Oak Leaves and Lavender — to adapt a phrase from the Frenchman, Louis Gillet, Joyce's friend and admirer, as applied to *Finnegans Wake* — is 'a sort of ontological reverie'; a phantasmagoria without beginning or end: a death-view of man's life, as *Ulysses*, in Joyce's case, is a daytime spectacle and *Finnegans Wake* a nocturnal fantasy. (The latter, we know from O'Casey's letters, made a great impression upon him. '*Finnegans Wake* is me darlin'! The dream of Finnegan's the world's nightmare', he told a correspondent in 1940, 'and the clap of thunder is in our ears [Earwicker's ears] once more. We are waiting here for it to break in flames over our heads. "Sheshell ebb music wayriver she flows" is Joyce's own parody, & a lovely parody it is, too.') O'Casey, like Joyce, uses the techniques of dream, since, as Richard Ellmann has observed in his commentaries in *Selected Letters of James Joyce* (1975), 'in dreams all ages become one' and 'conventional barriers disappear' (including those of class). Consecutiveness and matter-of-fact happenings are therefore irrelevant to a dream-sequence.

An endless fantasy and spectacle like the *Wake*, *Oak Leaves and Lavender* can be viewed either as a foreshadowing or – in Joyce's own words – 'a fadograph of a yestern scene', or, basically, as a resurrection dream in which the answer to the mystery of death and the notion of eternity is given by time itself, symbolised in the play by the character, Son of Time; akin to the River Anna Livia Plurabelle, endlessly flowing, as in Joyce's epic: the image of sentient experience that ticks by from day to day, lost in the shroud of history and yet, miraculously, living on in future epochs.

The magic of O'Casey's play – like the *Wake* of Joyce, on whose warp and woof it is based – depends, essentially, on a fantasy interpretation. The play is cast in an ethereal mould throughout. The dancers who appear at the beginning and end suggest a ballet interpretation with proportionate emphasis on dance, music and words. The Prelude and – by implication – postlude of the play provide a *danse macabre* with dialogue indicating cataclysmic events to follow, in a *saecula saeculorum* sequence. Emphasis is on choreography and choric songs. A sensitive director must share an endearing enthusiasm for this particular blend of stylised drama: one who has preferably had previous experience with Chekhov and Strindberg at least, and, perhaps, may have had the good fortune to have come into contact with the stage adaptation of *Finnegans Wake* in the dramatisation by Mary Manning (*The Voice of Shem*) and who will, therefore, not have to experience the birthpangs of this particular genre.

Versatile actors, clever and imaginative lighting, and ingenious sound effects are essential to a satisfactory production of *Oak Leaves and Lavender*. The words – a glowing example of O'Casey's eloquence – must be clearly heard, as in all his productions. The Blackout scenes, dream sequences and adroit use of colour where indicated in the text must be skilfully reproduced. Lyrical intelligence is needed in the handling of this play.

The role of Feelim is important: the melody of his speech and his sure timing make his part memorable. The remainder of the characters – with the exception of Jennie – are archetypal or symbolic.

The Celtic derivation of the name Phelim or Felim is 'the ever good'. The surname, O'Morrigun, is also derived from the Irish; it signifies 'god of destruction'. The name Felim in ancient Irish history is synonymous with Felim O'Connor, who headed one of the bloodiest battles ever fought between English and Irish in 1315, when ten thousand Irish – according to the poet Campbell – including most of the O'Connor family, whose chieftains were considered the flower 'of Erin's royal tree of glory', perished in one day. The historical significance of the name, therefore, is associated with 'arms bearing' – a role O'Casey's Feelim assumes. Tara – in the annals of pre-Christian Ireland – was invested with a political importance lost today: it was the convention-centre of a triennial assembly, or parliament, of Druids and other learned men. The psaltery of Tara became the grand national register of Ireland, though there is, of course, no mention in it of Dame Hatherleigh's faddist preoccupation with the lost tribes of Israel being associated with Celtic forebears. Such theories have their comparison in an utterance of Shaw's, at the beginning of World War II: 'If he [Hitler] conquers these islands he will certainly add my country-men, the Irish, to the list [of killings and racial exterminations], as several authorities have maintained that the Irish are the lost tribes of Israel' (quoted in Shaw, *Platform and Pulpit*, ed. Dan H. Lawrence, Rupert Hart-Davis, 1962).

Feelim is described as a man of forty-five, 'wiry, slender, and as cunning as a fox (except when he is in a temper), which he somewhat resembles with his thin protruding nose and reddish hair, now tinged, though very slightly, with grey'. He is dressed like a butler except that he wears the army-trousers of a Home Guard. Dame Hatherleigh is about the same age, 'well figured, though tending, ever so slightly, towards plumpness'. She is austerely dressed in a tailor-made suit of dark green, relieved by a scarf of deep orange. Drishogue (Celtic: *driseog*, a thorn – perhaps, because of his left-wing views and ideals; a thorn, maybe, in Feelim's softer flesh) is a tall lad of twenty with a thin, tense face; Edgar, almost as tall and of the same age, has a plumper, more placid, though less imaginative face. Both are dressed in Royal Air Force blue uniform. Monica is a young lass, 'sweet and twenty' but a little pensive-looking; Jennie, a voluptuous lass of twenty-four, honey-blonde and possessing a Rabelaisian confidence. Joy, her colleague, who is slimmer, is less ebullient. Both farm-girls wear the land-girl uniform of brown breeches, with vivid green jerseys when wearing walking-out costume, or brown smocks, peasant-wise, and high rubber boots when working. Home Guardsman Mark, is tall, well-knit and twenty-seven; Michael is 'short, stout, bull-necked' and gasps a

little, we are told, after every sentence. Mrs Watchit is fifty with
white hair – elaborately permed – and 'moves with a slow, stiff trot'.
Deeda Tutting is a gaunt, plain-faced, querulous woman of forty
or so; her manner positive and dogmatic. Abraham Penrhyn,
Monica's father, a Cornish farmer – with a strong accent – is fifty or
more, with bushy grizzled hair and a long grizzled beard; narrow-
minded and bigoted. Constable Dillery is lanky and melancholy-
looking, with a drooping grey moustache; Sillery is fat with a
rubicund face. Both wear ridiculously protruding peaked caps and
carry large torches. Mr Constant is tall and thin. Pobjoy is a slim
thirty-year-old – 'intelligent in a curious aloof way'. The factory
Foreman is dressed in brown overalls and speaks with an Irish
accent. The Old Woman of Seventy is quarrelsome and spokesman
of a one-eyed arrogance. Young Son of Time is a handsome lad of
twenty or so, clad in a close-fitting suit of emerald green, and around
his shoulders he has a deep sable cloak, indicative of the threat of
inevitable old age; he wears a conical hat of gleaming silver. His
voice – when he speaks – is 'clear and bell-like' resembling Ariel's
(the Air-sprite of *The Tempest*), and there is a note of authority and
finality in what he says. He is O'Casey's Time-Spirit and dramatic
embodiment of the unity and ubiquity of time, and symbol of youth.

The ethereal quality was totally absent from the only professional
English production the play received in London, at Hammersmith's
Lyric Theatre on 13 May 1947. The director-designer was Ronald
Kerr. Feelim was played by Fred Johnson, Dame Hatherleigh by
Mary Hinton, Drishogue by Edward Golden (who also played Red
Jim in the Abbey's production of *The Star Turns Red* in 1978), Edgar
by Alec Ross, Monica by Sheila Sim, Jennie by Joyce Marwood,
Joy by June Whitfield, Pobjoy by John Whiting and Penrhyn by
Oliver Burt. The play attracted plenty of attention and argument
but only had a short run. It was, recalls Trewin, 'one of the most
thoroughly botched productions' of that decade. Even the playwright sadly records in *Sunset and Evening Star*:

> . . . critics often tolerant of things done badly, declared it to be a
> butchery of a play . . . The play, admittedly, was a difficult one,
> probably a clumsy one, possibly, even, a bad one; but the
> shocking production failed in every possible way, to show
> whether it was one, or all, of these; failed to give the slightest
> guidance to an experimental playwright.

Although the playwright, afterwards, tended to hold the play in disesteem, a critical accolade, when the play was published, was bestowed in the pages of *The Times Literary Supplement*:

It is not easy to judge the effect on the stage of a play which must depend upon imaginative production and upon acting with plenty of bite and guile; but in the reading it would seem to have great poetic and dramatic power, and to be the first play in which Mr O'Casey has succeeded in smoothly blending comic characterization with poetic grandeur of event.

We should take heart from this prediction of assurance, and attempt a worthier production of *Oak Leaves and Lavender*; one whose qualities are attuned to finer possibilities in the theatre-fare of the future. A Swedish production at the Helsingborgs stadsteater preceded the London one, and translations exist in French and Spanish.

15 *Cock-a-Doodle Dandy* (1949): a Mock-Allegorical Fantasy

In O'Casey's next play, Ireland is once more the setting; for, like Joyce, he confesses, 'it is only through an Irish scene that my imagination can weave a way'. The result is a superb comedy with tragic overtones – a mixture, as always, of the grave and gay; a challenging mixture of down-to-earth reality though couched in unrealistic terms and encased in its own special forms of magic and laced with erotic fancy and comic raillery. O'Casey's original extravaganza is the out-pouring of a humorous imagination and balletic whim taking its cue from no one tangible source, save, possibly, Shakespeare himself.

In *Cock-a-Doodle Dandy*, there are moments of unmistakable echoes of *The Tempest* and *A Midsummer Night's Dream*. O'Casey's Irish comic fantasy – with allegorical implications – is even more richly inspired than *Purple Dust* in its extravagant exploitation of farce and satire. The younger Granville-Barker, in *Plays and Players* (October 1959), described it as 'a rollicking fantasy that burns with compassion and crackles with wit'. The play is seen by Dr David Krause, editor of the playwright's letters, as a 'mock-battle between allegorical forces of good and evil'.

In the theatre, as Brooks Atkinson has stressed: '*Cock-a-Doodle Dandy* has to be played like a dance – all lightness and improvisation, bursting with spontaneity'. No doubt, these very qualities moved Joan Littlewood to comment, in a letter to the playwright in 1949: 'I have not felt so delighted with a play for many years'. Her enthusiasm was also shared by Nathan, who wrote of the play's exuberancy (quoted on the dust-jacket of the first-edition):

The theme is the rightful joy of life and the proper dismissal from all consideration of those who would fetter it. Employing a gay

297

mixture of symbolism and wild humour . . . O'Casey filters through his natural cynicism as lively and amusing a slice of fantastic drama as one can imagine.

The philosophy behind the play is that expressed in O'Neill's tempestuous *The Great God Brown*, which O'Neill sums up as: 'the creative pagan acceptance of life, fighting eternal war with the masochistic, life-denying spirit of Christianity . . .' (quoted in Sheaffer, *O'Neill: Son and Artist*, 1974).

In an explanatory article, reprinted in *Blasts and Benedictions*, O'Casey suggests:

The play is symbolical in more ways than one. The action manifests itself in Ireland, the mouths that speak are Irish mouths; but the spirit is to be found in action everywhere.

O'Casey is rigorously opposed to cant and hypocrisy; is against world-wide repression, as the same article makes clear:

Joyce said that 'God may be a cry in the street', and O'Casey says now that He may be a laugh or a song in the street, too. Political fellas in the U.S.A., in the U.S.S.R., in England, and especially in Ireland – everywhere in fact – political fellas run out and shout down any new effort made to give a more modern slant or a newer sign to any kind of artistic thought or imagination; menacing any unfamiliar thing appearing in picture, song, poem, or play. They are fools, but they are menacing fools, and should be fought everywhere they shake a fist, be they priest, peasant, prime minister, or proletarian.

The enchanted Cock in the play, we are told, represents 'the joyful, active spirit of life': an apocalyptic figure (Bird of Dawn and Herald of the Morn), like the prognostic birds of Gaelic folk-lore, embodying the playwright's own distinctive, comic symbol of life-force. O'Casey's image of a life-sized, jubilant dancing bird is derived, he tells us, from resplendent words voiced in a favourite play of Yeats – *The Dreaming of the Bones* – wherein the First Musician sings:

> Red bird of March, begin to crow!
> Up with the neck and clap the wing,
> Red cock, and crow!

Blake's advocacy, in *The Marriage of Heaven and Hell*, of an increase in sensual enjoyment as a means of releasing men from their self-limitation, also remains a prescriptive influence.

Because O'Casey's play represents, in Joyce's phrase from *Finnegans Wake*, 'a funtasy on fantasy', a fantasy-burlesque, amock with episodes of profane joy and wild, rollicking Celtic humour, purists have tended to dismiss it as yet another insignificant Irish satire with limited audience appeal. In the midst of such churlish ululation is a failure to distinguish any allegorical significance behind the lampoon.

It was not unnatural immediately after the world-wide upheaval of World War II (Yeats's prophetic words from *Last Poems* of 'irrational streams of blood staining earth' and 'tragedy wrought to its uttermost' having been realised) that O'Casey's thoughts should have dwelt on his own native Ireland – the unsceptered isle – which, because of its neutral stance, had steadfastly avoided the rigours of the enveloping international nightmare.

It had not escaped the ironic attention of O'Casey that De Valera's Ireland was preening itself on having become one of the foremost spiritual nations in the Western world; a rigid, prayer-blown theocracy, enacting 'a censorship of brittle badinage and dainty disdain', we are told in *Inishfallen, Fare Thee Well*, where priests and rulers were intent on dragging the people into heaven by the scruff of their necks, and where – in the words of Joyce – 'Christ and Caesar are hand and glove!'

This is illustrated tellingly in *Cock-a-Doodle Dandy*. Dickens, in a letter of 1846, had declared: 'I have a sad misgiving that the religion of Ireland lies as deep at the root of all its sorrows, even as English misgovernment and Tory villainy'. Engels, the social revolutionary, had written as early as 1869:

Ireland still remains the *sacra insula*, whose aspirations must on no account be mixed up with the profane class struggles of the rest of the sinful world. Partially, this is certainly honest madness on the part of the people, but it is equally certain that it is partially also a calculated policy of the leaders in order to maintain their domination over the peasant.

(The situation was still largely true in 1949, when the play was published in London. Significantly, a separate edition was never published in America.)

During the war, O'Casey was able to observe, from the English side of St George's Channel, that the Emerald Isle had become selfishly immersed in her own problems; or, as he claimed, 'busy saving her soul'. In *Sunset and Evening Star*, he scathingly observes:

> All Ireland's temporal activities had been placed under saintly protection – Textiles under St. Clotherius, Buildings under Saints Bricin and Cementino, Brewing and Distilling under St. Scinful, Agriculture under St. Spudadoremus, Metal Work under Ironicomus, Pottery under St. Teepotolo, Fishing under St. Codoleus, Book-making under St. Banaway, the whole of them presided over by the Prayerman, St. Preservius, a most holy man of great spiritual preprotensity, who was a young man in the reign of Brian Boru, and who passed to his rest through a purelytic seizure the day he tried to read the first few lines of Joyce's damnable *Ulysses*.

The social change undergone by Ireland after the Civil War is the subject of perpetual scorn not only in later volumes of the playwright's autobiography but in all his post-war plays following *Oak Leaves and Lavender*. The emergent bourgeois class in Eire (after battles for independence) had forsaken the original concepts of social progress, and was obsessed with the intricacies of power and privilege and respectability – absent while the struggles had lasted – one manifestation of which was the donning of a tall-hat on all occasions of public ceremonial. 'It won't be long', reflected O'Casey, 'till the gold harp's taken out of the green flag, and a bright, black tall-hat put in its place. The terrible beauty of a tall-hat is born to Ireland'. In *Cock-a-Doodle Dandy*, with its satirical emphasis, the symbol of a tall-hat becomes mock-representation of national as well as civic pretentiousness; an apparition of foolish fancy and false national pride.

In this Swiftian, symbolical comedy of love and hate, O'Casey presents an Irish village, called Nyadnanave – which means in Gaelic, 'Nest of Saints', but the name also contains the ironic pun, Nest of Knaves. Earthy, entrenched Irish reactionaries – mostly the men, old in years and older still in spirit – have a hard time coping with what they believe to be the demon-antics of the creatures of joyous fantasy who are in league with the women representing, as O'Casey sees them, youth and life. The Cock, O'Casey's symbolic character, dances in and out of the action in a brave attempt, though ultimately unsuccessful, to save those of the play's characters – the women, especially – from the repression, bigotry and intolerance that stem from authority and denial of individual liberties. A pantomimic farce ensues, as richly comic havoc wrought by the Cock produces supernatural events – alluded to by one of the characters as 'demonological disturbances' – to the fear and holy terror of the establishment. The play bubbles with impish and inordinate humour, and fantasticalities include collapsible chairs, a quaking house, a whisky bottle whose contents will not spill, and a blast of wind that pulls the pants off a civic guard. It is a whirlwind of riotous, intoxicating fun.

In the midst of the frenzy and petrification, O'Casey drops his poison. The play weaves a warning of hate into the comicalities, spelling death and destruction if the evils of repression are not fought all around us. At the end, O'Casey – in the manner of Prospero – breaks the spell of fantasy in order to remind us that the symbol of the Cock-a-Doodle Dandy is, after all, only a poetic myth, a state of mind. The Cock is defeated and the young people all emigrate. The revels are over and the 'significality' of O'Casey's parable is now clear: the gay bird can ridicule forces of repression and mock them with its miracles, but it cannot destroy them. O'Casey employes the Cock in almost the same way as Shakespeare employs Ariel.

O'Casey's most amusing play is also his bitterest. It is a searing indictment of modern Ireland, which may account for the reason why there was no professional performance in Ireland until 1975. Of all his later plays – written in fantastic style – it is, as Brooks Atkinson reminds us, the best constructed and one which especially deserves a scintillating production. It is another of O'Casey's unjustly neglected plays. The dialogue, as in all his dramas, is wonderfully vivacious: the golden symmetry of dancing words resplendent throughout, just as in *Red Roses for Me*. In *Blasts and Benedictions*, O'Casey makes the claim: 'It is my favourite play; I think it is my best play – a personal opinion; the minds of others, linked with time, must decide whether I'm wrong or right'.

The play is dedicated 'To James Stephens, the Jesting Poet with a Radiant Star in's Coxcomb'. Both playwright and dedicatee were wedded to the concept of the fantasy in their writings, based in turn on Blake's vision of 'an Endeavour to Restore what the Ancients called the Golden Age' and what Stephens meant when he wrote that 'poems, too, are to me prophesies, and there will be a gay old world sometime'. O'Casey touches on this aspect in his article pertaining to the play:

> To me what is called naturalism, or even realism, isn't enough. They usually show life at its meanest and commonest, as if life never had time for a dance, a laugh, or a song. I always thought that life had a lot of time for these things, for each was a part of life itself; and so I broke away from realism into the chant of the second act of *The Silver Tassie*. But one scene in a play as a chant or a work of musical action and dialogue was not enough, so I set about trying to do this in an entire play, and brought forth *Cock-a-Doodle Dandy*.

Twenty characters participate in this stage-kaleidoscope of fantasy. Although illusory, they are founded on flesh-and-blood reality: all are recognisable vignettes. Prominent are Michael Marthraun and his companion, Sailor Mahan, a former sea-faring crony – another of O'Casey's celebrated duos – the corner-stone of rich, rumbustious comedy, in the traditions of music-hall and musical comedy. Both are cartoon-capitalists from the countryside, waxing spiritually prosperous in De Valera's Isle of Caprice. Bog-owner Marthraun was a one-time small farmer; now a thriving businessman, local councillor and confraternityman. His spiritual jackal, Mahan, is also a thriving local magnate and gombeen man and devout son of the church for reasons mutually beneficial to both. The mustard-seed of the their success is turf, and turf allied to theology makes their world spin. Mahan has many of the tendencies advertised in 'Captain' Boyle's spurious career on the high seas. The inspiration behind his personality – the playwright tells us, in *The Green Crow* – stems from 'what I saw, not in London, no, not even in Dublin, but in New York'.

As the play is in the tradition of Pastoral Tragicomedy (one of Polonius's categories) it is unsurprising that there are several heroines – Loreleen, Lorna, and Marion – because of various love plots. Loreleen is the bewitching young heroine – Marthraun's daughter by his first wife – and herself the living embodiment of the Cock's magical influence and instrument of some of the super-normal events; her sway induces superstitious fears in the hearts of Marthraun and the rest of the male community. There is Lorna, gay young second wife of Marthraun, whose loveliness and youth become sources of dismay and disturbances not only to her timorous older husband but to those encased in the fear-laden atmosphere and 'moody misery of th' brown bog'. The romantic lead, however, is invested in Marion, the maid – helper in Lorna's house – timid at first, but when influenced by the gaiety and transforming marvels of the Cock and love of the Messenger, Robin Adair (balladry becomes a source of name-inspiration in O'Casey's later Ruritanian comedies), shakes off indigenous fears and indiscernible suspicions. She is one of O'Casey's attractive Irish soubrettes.

The Messenger, who is one of O'Casey's golden lads – with the emblem of intrepidity across his shoulders – is in love with Marion. He is a freedom-fighter in the same mould as the Dreamer from *Within the Gates*, only Robin is a surer-styled, gayer creation. With him is the Cock, who appears from time to time pirouetting on stage – a wordless wonder and gorgeously plumaged – the author's champion of primordial virtues and the inspired magician of the play. (His role is similar to Ariel's or Puck's – he is O'Casey's own version of Robin Goodfellow.) He is also the satiric mocker of local hypocrisies rampant in rural Ireland.

The instruments of repression to which the Cock is opposed are represented by the stern, puritanical Father Domineer, the parish priest of Nyadnanave who is a symbol of clerical dominance; Shanaar (the name signifies 'old man' in Gaelic), a crawthumping bigot; with able assistance from a peasant-lad, One-Eyed Larry – a sinister younger version of Shanaar – who acts as sacristan to the priest in the eventual exercise of exorcism of the Cock.

Other agents in the work of 'desthruction' and repression are two peat-workers – described as First and Second Roughfellows – peasants working on Marthraun's bog who at first are swayed by proletarian shouts for improved conditions but who later succumb to dominant middle-class pressures. (They, too, become slaves of repression and fear; willing acolytes in Father Domineer's fear-ridden, clerically dominated society.) Other subsidiary agencies include a Sergeant of the local Civic Guard – a Dogberry of ineffectuality – whose influence, like the 'polis' in *Juno and the Paycock*, in the immortal words of Maisie Madigan, 'is Null an' Void!'; a town crier, or Bellman, dressed in the role of fireman; together with a Porter of a nearby general store, from a neighbouring town, a zany rural oddity in himself (who bears a likeness to the eccentric Postmaster in *Purple Dust*).

Remaining secondary figures are Jack, Mahan's rebellious foreman lorry-driver; Julia, Lorna's sister – a paralytic on a visit to Lourdes; her father, speechless and stony-faced, who accompanies her, hopeful of a 'cure'; a Mayor and Mace-Bearer, attendant on the public proclamations. Finally, a select assemblage of villagers constituting 'A crowd' in the veneration ceremony accompanying the departure of Julia for Lourdes. (Altogether, 'miracles' and wonders play a prominent part in this fanciful tragicomedy.)

The three 'scenes' (as O'Casey prefers to call them) take place in the garden in front of Michael Marthraun's house in the airy local habitation of Nyadnanave. The ethereal quality recalls *The Cherry Orchard* and the final act of *Heartbreak House*. All three plays have outdoor settings.

Cock-a-Doodle Dandy owes no allegiance to time (in the basically unchanging rural climate of Ireland). In the first 'scene', it is a brilliant summer's morning, symbolised by giant sunflowers against the garden wall; in the second, a less sunny midday; and in the third, dusk – the sunflowers, by then, having become 'solemn black' in appearance. Near the wall is an Irish Tricolour fluttering from its flag-pole. (There is a flagstaff, we recall, in the garden of Shaw's *Heartbreak House*, too.) The directions tell us that Marthraun's house is 'black in colour, the sash and frame of the window in it is a brilliant red'. The allegorical meaning behind the words in Chekhov's *The Cherry Orchard*, spoken by the student Trofimov at the end of the second act, the celebrated 'The whole of Russia is our orchard', applies equally to O'Casey's fantasia: the whole of Ireland is symbolised by the house and setting in Nyadnanave.

In the first 'scene' of O'Casey's play, sunshine has bathed the garden in 'a deep pool of heat' and the grass has already turned a deep yellow. At the opening curtain – before anyone appears – the Cock enters and weaves his spell by dancing jubilantly around the garden. In the distance – beyond the wall – can be seen a purple bog with a sky stretching over it canopied in silver-grey. The Cock, who, in appearance, is a life-sized bird of deep-black plumage with a big crimson crest over his head, is a Yeatsian-inspired creation in yet another sense. 'His face', we are told, 'has the look of a cynical jester', putting us in mind of that notable early poem of Yeats, 'The Cap and Bells':

> The jester walked in the garden:
> The garden had fallen still;

> He bade his soul rise upward
> And stand on her window-sill.

As the play unfolds its spell and interlaces its magical influence, the role of rooster is identified with that of jesting playwright: waving his cap and bells on stage and at audience alike, singing his notes of enchantment both inside the house and out; and like the jester in Yeats's poem, 'Had grown sweet-tongued by dreaming'.

As soon as the cynical Cock disappears, Michael and his Sailor 'butty' make their entrance into the garden from the porch, each carrying a kitchen chair, and enter into discussion seated as far away as possible from the house. The appearance of two old soul-mates locked in conversational combat – 'oul' butties' as they are termed – has become a familiar hallmark in several O'Casey plays, from *Juno and the Paycock* onwards; and these typical O'Casey argufiers are in disagreement about 'lyin' hallucinations' and 'sinisther signs appearin' everywhere'. The Sailor is sceptical, but the landowner is convinced that Loreleen, since her return from London, has cast a spell on the house and that the three women – Loreleen, Lorna and Marion – are, bewitchingly, the cause of all the disturbances and 'evil evocations floatin' through every room'.

Mahan, a man of the world who has not by any means renounced his pleasures, enquires 'what kinda evocation an' significality is there?' Marthraun replies that he is petrified at the mysterious wind which follows his daughter through the house, allegedly turning the 'frenzied faces' of holy pictures to the wall; 'an' another time', he tells his incredulous companion, 'I seen th' image of our own St. Pathrick makin' a skelp at her with his crozier; fallin' flat on his face, stunned, when he missed!' (The humour is Rabelaisian, outrageous and reminiscent of Joyce in *Ulysses* and *Finnegans Wake*.)

And, when Mahan insists that 'there's nothin' evil in a pretty face, or in a pair of lurin' legs', Marthraun counters – echoing O'Casey's view of Catholicism – 'Oh, man, your religion should tell you th' biggest fight th' holy saints ever had was with temptations from good-lookin' women'.

Aside from preliminary considerations of personal animosities, poisoned by clerical influence and fear, we are given a quick glimpse into an even greater malaise which bites into the soul of modern Ireland: the swamping emphasis placed on greed and monetarism which is also satirised, scathingly, in the author's later one-act play, *Time to Go* (and, again, in *The Bishop's Bonfire* and *The Drums of*

Father Ned). Louis MacNeice, in *Eclogue from Iceland*, says of the Irish: 'Their greed is sugared with pretence of public spirit'.

The two flint-hearted capitalists, in *Cock-a-Doodle Dandy*, readily turn aside from their primeval preoccupations to count, not their blessings, but the state of their coffers; and a hard-headed business wrangle ensues. The Sailor reminds his fellow 'butty' that he owes his prosperity to the turf-boom and that this has brought its share of honours: that of local Councillor, Justice of the Peace, as well as public recognition as 'th' fair-haired boy of the clergy'.

While the two are arguing hammer and tongs over who should meet the extra amount involved because of the lorry-men's demands, Loreleen passes by on her way to the garden-gate and ejaculates, in mocking tones: 'Lay not up for yourselves treasures upon earth, where moth and rust doth corrupt, and where thieves break through and steal!' The conniving pair pretend not to have heard, but the sudden entrance of the two workmen from the bog (the two 'Roughfellows'), brushing past Loreleen, with ultimations for increased pay and better conditions, produces a taunt from Marthraun to one of the workmen: 'That's a social question to be solved by th' Rerum Novarum'. The second workman's answer is cynically derisive: 'Fifty years old; not worth much when it was born an' not worth a damn now'. And, Marthraun is told: 'Give a guaranteed week or the men come off the bog!'

The Roughfellows, who have admired Loreleen's alluring beauty ('Deirdre come to life again', says one, in silken compliment), are astounded at seeing her transfigured before them, in the shape and form of the Cock, and a crowing sound heard in the distance. (The play, which is fancy-inspired, has much to do with 'miracles' in the sense of transformation of attitudes.) The Cock is the embodiment of pure fantasy, a subjective spirit: he has no equivalent in the world of women and men; even Loreleen – who changes into him at times – is not his complete incarnation: he is the fulfilment and fulguration of joy and the antithesis of intimidation and denunciation. In political terms, he represents a focusing-point of unifying, transforming social power, though he is not in any way God-inspired. (O'Casey would seem to have endorsed the philosophy expressed by Yeats, at the conclusion to his play, *Calvary*: 'God has not appeared to the birds'.)

Whilst the two old humbugs quarrel among themselves as to the amounts each will have to pay to finance the workers' claim (strikes play a prominent part in O'Casey's dramas), Marthraun testily declares: 'It's this materialism's doin' it – edgin' into revolt against Christian conduct. If they'd only judge o' things in th' proper Christian way, as we do, there'd be no disputes'. But, in the midst of their dissensions over wage negotiations, the Sailor is not yet ready to 'hoist th' pennant of agreement': Christian ethics – O'Casey suggests – are tied to the cassock-strings of capitalist values. (Yeats had also implied as much, in his short play, *The Land of Heart's Desire*, where God's heaven is in alliance with the world of human society.)

As angels and devils clash in mid-air, and passionate, proud hearts below are enthroned in an aura of their own preoccupation with mammon, O'Casey (with an experienced playwright's consummate skill and timing) introduces, at this stage in the comedy, his arch-buffoon, a crawthumping old yokel by the name of Shanaar who has the confidence of Marthraun though not yet the conviction of Mahan, and around whom, along with the forces of repression, the butt of his satire is directed. He is O'Casey's version of the cult of the holy fool.

With a propensity for spouting dog Latin (referred to by the Sailor as 'bog-Latin') and self-proclaimed pseudo-assurance in the exorcism of evil spirits, Shanaar is satirically presented; his venerably-regarded, worldly-wise antics and superstitious beliefs bringing their own share of rich havoc, along with offsetting disruptions from the Cock and illustrating the rumbustiousness of O'Casey's rural extravaganza:

SHANAAR (*shoving his face closer to* MAHAN's): Ah, me friend, for years an' years I've thravelled over hollow lands an' hilly lands, an' I know. Big powers of evil, with their little powers, an' them with their littler ones, an' them with their littlest ones, are everywhere. You might meet a bee that wasn't a bee; a bird that wasn't a bird; or a beautiful woman who wasn't a woman at all.

MICHAEL (*excitedly*): I'm tellin' him that, I'm tellin' him that all along!

MAHAN (*a little doubtfully – to* SHANAAR): An' how's a poor body to know them?

SHANAAR (*looking round cautiously, then speaking in a tense whisper*): A sure sign, if only you can get an all-round glimpse of them. (*He looks round him again*): Daemones posteriora non habent – they have no behinds!

MICHAEL (*frightened a lot*): My God, what an awe-inspiring, expiring experience!

To the incredulous Mahan, Shanaar relates the tale of a cuckoo (to the superstitious, always a bird of misfortune) whose call enticed a holy monk to commit adultery and murder; who, when discovered, was hanged; and whilst sobbing on the scaffold, the mocking laughter of a girl and the calling of a cuckoo could be heard. (In moments of hilarious melodrama, these same sounds are re-echoed in the wings, instilling shock and surprise into the sober ears listening on stage. Their stern whimsicalities become targets for rip-roaring farce.) Heads huddled, the three continue their farcical deliberations:

SHANAAR (*in a tense whisper*): Say nothing; take no notice. Sit down. Thry to continue as if yous hadn't heard!
MAHAN (*after a pause*): Ay, a cuckoo, maybe; but that's a foreign bird: no set harbour or home. No genuine decent Irish bird would do a thing like that on a man.
MICHAEL: Looka here, Sailor Mahan, when th' powers of evil get goin', I wouldn't put anything past an ordinary hen!

Shanaar then relates another tall story, at the end of which the sound of a corncrake echoes offstage, and all are counselled to 'take no vocal notice' and parley the object of ill-omen with a tirade of Latin, which – in Shanaar's words – always sends it into 'a helluva disordher'.

No sooner has this strange remedy been promulgated than Marthraun's house becomes the centre of commotion, as loud, commingled cackling, crowing and crashing of crockery interrupt the collocution in the garden; and a cup, followed by a saucer, flies from a window past the heads of the three crimping wiseacres. Marion rushes out with the announcement that a wild fowl inside is creating domestic havoc, unceremoniously having overturned the altar-light, clawed holy pictures and pecked at the Councillor's tall-hat! When they hear this, the three chauvinists outside are overcome with fear and ready to duck behind the garden wall, particularly the expert on sorcery. Their reactions are predictably unheroic:

MICHAEL (*pleadingly* – *to* MAHAN): You've been free with whales an' dolphins an' octopususas, Sailor Mahan – you run in, like a good man, an' enthrone yourself on top of th' thing!

MAN (*indignant*): Is it me? I'm not goin' to squandher meself conthrollin' live land-fowl!

MICHAEL (*to* SHANAAR – *half-commandingly*): In case it's what we're afraid of, you pop in, Shanaar, an' liquidate whatever it is with your Latin.

SHANAAR (*backing towards the wall*): No good in th' house: it's effective only in th' open air.

In the midst of the comical frenzy, Marthraun instructs Marion to fetch Father Domineer. On her way out she encounters the Messenger, Robin Adair (he is named after the light-of-love from the traditional song, 'Eileen Aroon', and has the same sterling qualities as his more familiar namesake-hero, Robin Hood) and, although he is come with an urgent missive for the bog-owner, he tarries awhile talking to Marion at the gate, only to be shouted at by the arrogant Marthraun with frenetic pleas to release her and telling Marion to redouble her efforts to get hold of the parish priest: a mission, of course, which Robin ridicules, and reinforces, by handing the cowering bog-owner a telegram on behalf of the turf-workers, which the possessively preoccupied Councillor promptly pockets, in his fear, without even opening or reading.

Seeing the three men watching the house so affrightedly, the bold gallant enters the house, despite all the ructions from within, to prove to the Cock-shyers 'there's no harm in him beyond gaiety an' fine feelin''. To the astonishment of the onlookers, Robin later emerges from the house – after commotion and loud crowing within, followed by puffs of smoke issuing from the window – triumphantly leading a docile Cock (suitably beribboned), instilling trepidation on the faces of the demented householder and his sailor crony, who have meanwhile rushed to join the inauspicious soothsayer (cowering behind the garden wall) whose Latin exorcisms have not ruffled a single feather of the indomitable bird. The Cock's joy-pervading influence, Robin suggests – responding to sympathetic glances from the women as opposed to menacing looks from the men – will soon be felt when it leads them 'through a wistful an' wondherful dance'. O'Casey's lively message of joy is imparted jointly by Messenger and Cock, as Robin declares beckoningly, to the Cock, in Yeatsian tones: 'Go on, comrade, lift up th' head an' clap th' wings, black cock, an' crow!'

The implication is that instead of praying for 'miracles', we should join in 'the dance of life', summed up in the lines of Toller's poem: 'In dance is dreamed the holy song of the world', the cornerstone of O'Casey's own philosophy, expressed in all the plays and enunciated, especially, in *Within the Gates* onwards (hinted at, too, in the final act of *The Silver Tassie*): such participation, O'Casey infers, would in itself constitute a 'miracle' of human achievement – as Yeats reiterates, too, in his play, *The Cat and The Moon*.

The Cock is O'Casey's colourful equivalent of the Lord of the Dance, though he is not a symbol of divinity: he represents intrinsic *joie de vivre*; the elixir of life; unfettered gaiety as opposed to all unnatural repression. (Joyce, in the drowsy dream-language of *Finnegans Wake*, draws a similar parallel: 'The kissing wold's full of killing fellows kneeling voyantly to the cope of heaven'.) O'Casey's bird emblematises the epitome of joy-in-life; the spirit of courage and adventurousness, whose magic is potent to transform menaces resulting from the forces of anti-life – the kill-joy atmosphere initiated by repressive regimes and administrations everywhere. Its miracle of transformation succeeds in winning the hearts of the women characters in the play, but its transubstantialising effects are lost on the men – with the sole exception of Robin Adair. The transformation is complete, when – in a farcical interlude – Messenger and Cock march offstage together doing a goose-step, to the consternation and comicality of all present. The buoyant jubilation of the women is at once reflected. As for the astonished-looking men, a gleeful Marion pokes fun at their stunned, gloomy, stupefied faces: 'Me faltherin' tongue can't impart th' fun I felt at seein' yous all thinkin' th' anchor was bein' weighed for th' next world!'

The conversation takes on an objurgatory twist as soon as Marion has returned indoors and as the colloguing hypocrites – joined by the inauspicious prayer-blower – have returned to their seats in the garden. Marthraun comments reprovingly on the change in Marion: 'Th' ignorant, mockin', saucy face of her afther us bein' in danger of transportation to where we couldn't know ourselves with agony an' consternation!' Shanaar warns:

Watch that one, Mr Marthraun. Women is more flexible towards th' ungodly than us men, an' well th' old saints knew it. I'd recommend you to compel her, for a start, to lift her bodice higher up, an' pull her skirt lower down; for th' circumnambulatory nature of a woman's form often has a detonatin' effect on a man's idle thoughts.

The soothsaying old idiot attributes sources of evil and disruption to the 'scourge of materialism sweepin' th' world . . . An' women's wily exhilarations are abettin' it'. These nostrums go down well with Marthraun, but the Sailor listens in silence.

The old prognosticator, however, is encouraged by his one-man 'Amen chorus' – 'An' th' coruscatin' conduct in th' dance-halls is completin' th' ruin' – which draws the solemn response from Marthraun: 'Wise words from a wiser man! Afther a night in one of them, there isn't an ounce of energy left in a worker!' And the pious old fraud whispers a final warning: 'Don't forget that six thousand six hundhred an' sixty-six evil spirits can find ready lodgin's undher th' skin of a single man!'

The sceptical Mahan is unconvinced by all this crawthumping pi jaw. As soon as Shanaar has made his departure, the Sailor tells Michael: 'That Latin-lustrous oul' cod of a prayer-blower is a positive danger goin' about th' counthry!' His companion does not agree: 'A little asthray . . . but no cod'. Mahan complains:

Aw, th' oul' fool, pipin' a gale into every breeze that blows! I don't believe there was ever anything engenderogically evil in that cock as a cock, or denounceable either! Lardin' a man's mind with his killakee Latin! An' looka th' way he slights th' women. I seen him lookin' at Lorna an' Marion as if they'd horns on their heads! . . . They wouldn't tempt man if they didn't damn well know he wanted to be tempted!

As the capricious humour develops, the Cock's magic proceeds to play merry havoc with the men's susceptibilities and fears, ensuring that real horns have sprouted from the decorative heads of the women, as well as putting a spell on the whisky they are drinking and whipping up a tempestuous wind later on: phenomena, apparent only, in the words of Lorna, to the 'two oul' life-ighteners' and the rest of their chaw-bacon confraternity.

In the cockpit of caprice, the 'scene' ends with a sharp twist of ony as Lorna's sister, Julia, who is dying of an incurable disease, is arried into the garden on a stretcher, accompanied by her father, together with the Mayor and Mace-Bearer, plus a crowd of well-wishers. She is on her way to Lourdes, in the hope of finding a miracle that will save her life. Father Domineer enters to lead a prayer so that public aspirations will be granted and 'Julia will bring us back a miracle, a glorious miracle'. As the name Julia signifies 'divine', the significance of the remainder of the play revolves around a contest between the miraculous wonders of the Cock and 'miracles' at the hands of Father Domineer.

In the second act or 'scene' – as O'Casey specifies – we see the whole village alerted by Father Domineer to fight the influence of the Cock. Much of the play is now couched in bitter, sardonic terms, as the playwright castigates those forces and personalities whom he sees as destroying the moral fibre of present-day Ireland. As in Rimsky-Korsakov's *The Golden Cockerel* – the libretto of which is based on a tale by Pushkin – *Cock-a-Doodle Dandy* ridicules authority in the guise of Church and State; the characters in both works belonging to realms of fantasy. (Like Pushkin's tale, the only logic of plot is the logic of a fairy-tale.) Elements of similarity exist between Pushkin's tale and O'Casey's fanciful play: in each, wizardry and the magical powers of the cockerels are striking auguries. Loreleen, too, is akin to Pushkin's beautiful princess, whose beauty, in the words of the Russian writer, 'is so great that by day it frightens away the sun and by night illuminates the earth'.

The ethereal, outdoor setting of the first 'scene' merges into the equally hallucinatory atmosphere of the second, where the revels continue but with greater emphasis. The Cock-a-Doodle Dandy, though rarely on stage, is omnipresent and weaves his spell continuously, with merry devilment, like Shakespeare's Robin Goodfellow or Puck. In O'Casey's play, embodiment of the Cock is invested in Robin Adair, the Messenger, as well as Loreleen (from the Gaelic, *Laor*, meaning 'plenty'); the same exuberant qualities, as the drama develops, manifest themselves in those who come under the Cock's influence, namely Lorna and Marion. The men are too much under the spirit of clerical domination and 'Nyadnanavery' to be counted worthy of consideration among the Cock's disciples and devotees.

At the beginning of the second 'scene', when the stage is deserted (the whole village having turned out, in 'an edifyin' spectacle', to witness the departure of Julia for Lourdes, in a buoyancy of hope and a cavalcade of prayer), Mahan and Marthraun stroll into the garden, marvelling to each other on the train of events which have led the district astir and the significance of miracles to the tiny township thriving in the turf-age. Their conversation waxes excitedly – in the manner of Boyle and Joxer – with jests and jeers thrown about in a well-flavoured dialogue of indignation and derision:

MICHAEL (*indignantly*): Looka, if you were only versed in th' endurin' promulgacity of th' gospels, you'd know th' man above's concerned as much about Nyadnanave as he is about a place where a swarm of cardinals saunther secure, decoratin' th' air with all their purple an' gold!

MAHAN (*as indignantly*): Are you goin' to tell me that th' skipper aloft an' his hierarchilogical crew are concerned about th' Mayor, the Messenger, Marion, me, an' you as much as they are about them who've been promoted to th' quarter-deck o' th' world's fame? Are you goin' to pit our palthry penances an' haltin' hummin' o' hymns against th' piercin' pipin' of th' rosary be Bing Bang Crosby an' other great film stars, who side-stepped from published greatness for a holy minute or two to send a blessed blast over th' wireless, callin' all Catholics to perpetuatin' prayer!

MICHAEL (*sitting down on a chair*): Sailor Mahan, I ask you to thry to get your thoughts ship-shaped in your mind.

In argument with the Messenger – who has joined them in the garden – the discussion plunges into the high seas of farce:

MAHAN (*to* MICHAEL): Looka, Mick, if you only listened to Bing Crosby, th' mighty film star, croonin' his Irish lullaby, (*he chants*) 'Tooral ooral ooral, tooral ooral ay', you'd have th' visuality to see th' amazin' response he'd have from millions of admirers, if he crooned a hymn!

MESSENGER: I was never sthruck be Bing Crosby's croonin'.

MICHAEL (*wrathfully – to* MESSENGER): You were never sthruck! An' who th' hell are you to be consulted? Please don't stand there interferin' with the earnest colloquy of betther men. (*To* MAHAN): Looka, Sailor Mahan, any priest'll tell you that in th' eyes of heaven all men are equal an' must be held in respect an' reverence.

MAHAN (*mockingly*): Ay, they'll say that to me an' you, but will they say it to Bing Crosby, or any other famous film star?

MESSENGER: Will they hell! Honour be th' clergy's regulated by how much a man can give!

MICHAEL (*furiously – to the* MESSENGER): Get to hell outa here! With that kinda talk, we won't be able soon to sit steady on our chairs. Oh!

(*The chair he is sitting on collapses, and he comes down to the ground on his arse.*)

MAHAN (*astonished*): Holy saints, what's happened?

MICHAEL (*in a fierce whisper – to* MAHAN): Take no notice of it, fool. Go on talkin'!

MAHAN (*a little confused*): I'll say you're right, Mick; th' way things are goin' we won't be able much longer to sit serene on our chairs. Oh!

(*The chair collapses under* MAHAN, *and he, too, comes down to the ground.*)

MICHAEL (*in a fierce whisper*): Don't notice it; go on's if nothin' happened!

MESSENGER (*amused*): Well, yous have settled down now, anyhow! Will I get yous chairs sturdy enough to uphold th' wisdom of your talkin?

Mad pranks and merry jests continue, when the two old butties resort to a drink, as relief from their troubles, but find that the 'bewitched' whisky foils them in the attempt. The Sailor is not amused: 'You'd think good whiskey would be exempt from injury even be th' lowest of th' low'. In the war of attrition which follows, freedom rears her beautiful brow but repression fights a subjugable skirmish, when the full forces of a witch-hunt sanctioned by Church and State are brought into play. The Civic Guards as well as local presbyter want an end to the hilarities and disturbances, which they regard as 'deranging thrickeries of evil'.

As fantasticalities develop, a curious Porter from a nearby store staggers in and heaps further fun on the comicalities, carrying the battered remnants of a tall-hat to be delivered to one who is addressed as self-styled Councillor and 'a Jay Pee'. The character, who bears some resemblance to the leprechaun-figure of the Postmaster in *Purple Dust*, is something of a Ruritanian absurdity, though his roots are firmly enough in Irish country soil. He clashes with the autocratic Marthraun, but, indigenously, does a quick equivocating conversational turn-round when he discovers that Michael is the man to whom the hat should have been delivered:

MICHAEL (*with importance*): I'm a Councillor and a Jay Pee.
PORTER (*with some scorn*): D'ye tell me that now? (*He bends over the wall to come closer to* MICHAEL): Listen, me good man, me journey's been too long an' too dangerous for me to glorify any cod-actin'! It would be a quare place if you were a councillor. You'll have to grow a few more grey hairs before you can take a rise outa me!
MICHAEL (*indignantly*): Tell us what you've got there, fella', an', if it's not for us, be off about your business!
PORTER (*angrily*): Fella yourself! An' mend your manners, please! It's hardly th' like of you would be standin' in need of a silky, shinin' tall-hat.
MICHAEL: If it's a tall-hat, it's for me! I'm Mr Councillor Marthraun, Jay Pee – ordhered to be sent express by th' firm of Buckley's.
PORTER (*with a quick conciliatory change*): That's th' firm. I guessed you was th' man at once, at once. That man's a leadher in th' locality, I said, as soon as I clapped me eye on you. A fine, clever, upstandin' individual, I says to meself.

When the comically-styled Porter is instructed to hand over the hat, he prevaricates, explaining that 'th' hat's been slightly damaged in thransit' and then goes on to stupefy his astounded hearers that whilst delivering it, 'someone shot a bullet through it, east be west!' When Marthraun dismisses the idea as nonsense ('who'd be shootin' bullets round here?'), he is informed that the Civic Guards were out trying to shoot down an evil spirit 'flyin' th' air in th' shape of a bird' (the Cock being the instigator of such absurdities).

In the antic confusion, more shots are heard, and the petrified Porter offers Marthraun the mangled hat and flees. As the two gaums view, forlornly, the damaged head-piece, a buffoon of a Police Sergeant – from the local Civic Guard – enters with rifle poised ready to shoot the ostracised fowl and quell the 'demonological disturbances'. The Sergeant turns out to be a prevaricating Dogberry, and a bit of a prognosticator, too, into the bargain. When Marthraun and Mahan ask him what it is he has been pursuing and shooting, he parleys with circumlocutions which

give rise to a rich episode of farcical banter, which practitioned
audiences will instantly recognise:

MAHAN (*despairingly*): Thry to tell us, Sergeant, what you said
      you said you seen.
SERGEANT: I'm comin' to it; since what I seen was seen by no man
      never before, it's not easy for a man to describe with
      evidential accuracy th' consequential thoughts fluttherin'
      through me amazed mind at what was, an' what couldn't
      be, demonstrated there, or there, or anywhere else, where
      mortals congregate in ones or twos or crowds astoundin'.
MICHAEL (*imploringly*): Looka, Sergeant, we're languishin' for
      th' information that may keep us from spendin' th' rest of
      our lives in constant consternation.
SERGEANT: As I was tellin' you, there was th' crimson crest of th'
      Cock, enhancin' th' head lifted up to give a crow, an' when
      I riz th' gun to me shoulder, an' let bang, th' whole place
      went dead dark; a flash of red lightning near blinded me;
      an' when it got light again, a second afther, there was the
      demonised Cock changin' himself into a silken glossified
      tall-hat!

As Michael and the overawed Mahan discuss the 'significality' of all
this – and view with apprehension the battered hat lying in the
garden – the Sergeant is asked whether it bears any resemblance to
the object he shot at, and they are told: 'It's th' dead spit of what I
seen him changin' into durin' th' flash of lightning!' He tries to
describe how he fired, when the garden is suddenly plunged into
darkness for a few moments, followed by fierce lightning; the hat has
disappeared, and where it stood now prances the Cock. During
lightning flashes, the lusty crow of the Cock is heard. When the light
suddenly returns, Cock and tall-hat have vanished – reminiscent of
the disappearance of the cockerel in Pushkin's tale. Stage direction,
at this point, is riotous: '*Michael and Mahan are seen to be lying on the
ground and the Sergeant is on his knees, as if in prayer*'. The Sergeant's
reaction is one not usually associated with constabulary duty: 'Holy
St. Custodius, pathron of th' police, protect me!' And Sailor and
farm-owner mutter that they are done for!

   When, afterwards, the three sit down to talk over the strange
happenings, resolving to consider taking seriously the clergy's
warnings – curtailing 'th' gallivantin' of th' women afther th' men'

and heeding those who extol the dangerous influences of books
('Th' biggest curse of all!') – they are interrupted by the hurried
appearance on scene of the Bellman – dressed as a fireman –
heralding a warning of the Cock's arrival 'in th' shape of a woman!'
His advice is oddly Ruritanian: 'Into your houses, shut to th'
windows, bar th' doors!' Ignoring the Bellman's counsel, they
remain sitting on the ground, with Sailor Mahan singing a sea-
shanty to bolster their dejected spirits.

Whilst they are hoisting musical sail, Loreleen enters – bathed in a
golden glow – greeting them with a note of irony in her voice: 'Ye do
well to bring a spray of light, now and again, into a dark
place . . . The song is heard, th' wine is seen, only th' women
wanting'. Running over to the porchway, she shouts into the house
to entice Lorna as well as Marion to come out and join in the
'enthertainment'.

This is the signal for a fancy-dress ball – with mystical
enchantments – reminding us of *The Tempest* with its 'majestic
vision' of harmonious spirits as part of Prospero's 'insubstantial
pageant', where Shakespeare's nymphs of the wandering brooks –
called Naiads – are invoked in a pleasure-bestowed principle: in
much the same way, the Cock-a-Doodle Dandy and its allies, in
O'Casey's mock-carnival and pageant, prepare their onlookers –
the Nyadnanaves – for an orientation and reinvigoration of outlook;
and, just as the theme of Shakespeare's masque in the fourth act of
The Tempest is an allegory of marriage-bliss, so the fancy-dress ball
in *Cock-a-Doodle Dandy* – initiated by Loreleen (but in reality the
work of the Cock) – is an allegory of unfettered joy and harmony-in-
life: both playwrights urging men – in Shakespeare's words – to 'be
merry' and 'make holiday'.

The fun-fair in the garden begins as bewitching comedy: the
magic of the Cock can be seen in the wiles of the women, whose
enchantments gradually win over for a time the men, whose
unchanging mental rigidities are revealed when Marion exchanges
the Sergeant's gun for a newly-delivered top-hat (in contrast to the
earlier 'mangled monstrosity') which she brings out to Marthraun,
who immediately shies away from it thinking it bewitched. The
three men stare at it, as if expecting fresh 'horrification' to happen
and 'thrained tenacity of evil things'.

Ignoring the woe-begetters and toasting themselves from the
contents of Michael's whisky, the women offer a toast to 'Th' Cock-
a-Doodle Dandy!' Thereafter, a sense of delighted animation steals

over the faces of the woebegone worriers, who now join in the toast, as Robin Adair appears, in the background, playing softly on his accordion. In the enchanted atmosphere, an encomiastic change comes over the conversation of the men: they cease to haggle over money; Michael, in an excess of charity, offers Mahan double his original request 'without a whimper, without a grudge!' and Mahan reciprocates, 'We're as good as bein' brothers!'

Although Biblical phraseology is invoked when Sailor Mahan ejaculates, 'Looka th' lilies of th' field, an' ask yourself what th' hell's money!' it is in effect – though in an allegorical way – a vivid endorsement of the Shavian view of world politics and our sham democracy, whereby Shaw, in one of his last prefaces (*Farfetched Fables*, 1948), reveals his disgust with

> our politicians and partisans [who] keep shouting their abhorrence of Communism as if their Parties were cannibal tribes fighting and eating one another instead of civilized men driven by sheer pressure of facts into sane co-operation.

The toast, the transformation of attitudes and the Messenger's accompanying music prompt the couples to participate in a lively dance – akin to the whirling spectacle beside the river in the 'bridge of vision' scene in *Red Roses for Me*. Both dance and dialogue are indicative of new feelings of brotherly love and humanitarian awareness; but, suddenly, in the pantomimic effect, vivid ornaments on the women's headgear are seen to sprout horns (as yet unnoticed by the men); in the wording of the stage direction, 'the cock-like crest in Loreleen's hat rising higher as she begins to move in the dance'. At the peak of excitement, a loud clap of thunder, followed by a long, lusty crow from the Cock, preludes the ominous appearance of Father Domineer, and, in an instant, the revels are ended; the carnival is over.

In a declamatory outburst, the priest reminds his hearers that 'pagan poison is floodin' th' world, an' that Ireland is dhrinkin' in generous doses through films, plays, an' books! . . . Th' empire of Satan's pushin' out its foundations everywhere', and promptly orders them to cease their 'devil's dance', spraying a Latin curse on their gaiety, '*ubique ululanti cockalorum ochone, ululo!*' The phraseology of the priest's peroration has an echo of those nineteenth-century hymnists, such as Father Frederick Faber, who in hymnody have declared that:

Deep night hath come down on this rough-spoken world,
And the banners of darkness are boldly unfurled,

encapsulated, as well, in the words of the hymn, 'Star of the Sea',
sung at the close of the first scene as an accompaniment to the sick-
procession bound for Lourdes:

Mother of Christ, Star of the Sea,
Pray for the wanderer, pray for me.

Father Domineer is one with Fabians of hymnology who view
mankind as 'sojourners in this vale of tears' and, therefore, to be
saved 'from peril and from woe'; and the recurring words of the
refrain, *'Pray for the wanderer'*, have, for O'Casey and, indeed, for all
Irish exiles a note of implicit irony, reflected in those self-confessed
words in *Inishfallen, Fare Thee Well* wherein he admits he is 'a
voluntary and settled exile from every creed, from every party, and
from every literary clique'. Such alienation also applies to such life-
embued figures as Loreleen, in the play, whose failures to re-adapt,
after several years abroad, to circumstances and rusticities of Irish
city as well as provincial life, have earned them the fierce and
perpetual scorn of those in the motherland.

Thrown on life's surge, O'Casey insists, we are captains of our
own fate, as Shaw's Major Barbara, previously, had reiterated (re-
echoing Nietzsche's philosophy that in order to live joyously man
must live dangerously). The voyage of life advocated by O'Casey is
Whitman's, expressed in *O Captain! My Captain*:

The ship has weather'd every rack, the prize we sought is won,
The port is near, the bells I hear, the people all exulting . . .

The playwright's rebuke to stern, unyielding predictabilities, as
practised by the forthright, puritanical Father Domineer – is
summed up in a colloquial passage in *Sunset and Evening Star*:

Say what you like and pray how you may, there'll always be a gay
song deadening the sound of a *de profundis*. It would be a big,
bright blessing in disguise if even a few of our bishops had some of
the imagination of Yeats, a tittle of the wit and deeper sense of
Shaw, and a little of the royal ribaldry of Joyce to test our
thinking.

After Domineer's hysterical outburst, O'Casey's satire turns savage in its Swiftian irony, and the mood of the play – like the concluding scenes in *Purple Dust* – darkens into one of bitter allegory ridiculing the Dark Rosaleen. Joyce, in his poem 'Gas from a Burner', had already instilled a note of mockery in his comment:

> O Ireland my first and only love
> Where Christ and Caesar are hand and glove!

In the remaining scenes of *Cock-a-Doodle Dandy*, O'Casey develops a saturnine picture of post-independence Ireland, which he sees as a theocracy ruled by Armagh in the north and Dublin in the south in a coalition of unenlightened coadjutorship whose ancient faith, the Messenger declares, is founded on fear and whose modern axiom is: 'fear is your only fun', replete with *mea culpas* and *mea, maxima culpas*!

In front of the priest, the two 'fostherers of fear', as Marion, previously, has dubbed them, Marthraun and Mahan (Father Domineer's right-handed Confraternity and Sodality men) publicly recant for their part in the dance, though Loreleen remains obstinately defiant and unrepentant. Sailor Mahan is instructed to dismiss from his service one of his best lorry-drivers, Jack, because, allegedly, according to the priest, he is reputed to be living with a woman 'in sin'. Mahan upholds the man as an upright person as well as a fine worker, and says his employment is in the national interest. Father Domineer counters that *he* is 'the custodian of higher interests'. The wheedling Marthraun assures the dominating priest that, as a faithful son of the Church, Sailor Mahan will obey.

As Mahan mutters his refusal, the lorry-driver himself appears on stage to have a word with his employer. Shying away from the priest (who showers abuse on him for his personal conduct), the lorry-driver has come with an ultimatum for Mahan, informing him that the workers are about to leave the bog, as no reply has come in response to their telegram delivered earlier – in the first scene – by Robin and since forgotten about by the two employers in their state of 'spiritual' psychosis.

Ignoring imputations of the turf-dispute, and more solicitous over any potential flouting of his own spiritual authority, Father Domineer turns viciously on the lorry-driver, uttering a curse that God should strike him dead. In an ironic turn of divination, it is not God but the priest who fulfils his own curse: in a burst of fury he lunges forward at the unrepentant driver and hits him, unwittingly, a fatal blow on the side of the head.

Such a moment of grim melodrama surprises the spectators by its suddenness, and is scarcely mitigated by tenseness of dialogue which brings the second scene to a sombre close, with ironic exchanges between priest and Messenger. 'I murmured', says the voice of clerical authority, in supposedly mock-humble tones, 'an act of contrition into th' poor man's ear', to which the Messenger – quietly playing his accordion – in a softly satirical voice, replies: 'It would have been far fitther, Father, if you'd murmured one into your own'.

A true happening O'Casey assures us. No matter; audience and playwright have conspired to dwell in an imaginary world with – some will allege – expressionist 'distortions' (though, justifiably, within a playwright's licence). For playwrights, according to Shaw – along with poets, mathematicians and philosophers – are functionaries without whom civilisation in its fullest sense would not be possible. And, whether from the earth around him a playwright draws, in Shakespearian parlance, 'rotten humidity', or sings of

> The heartache and the thousand natural woes
> That flesh is heir to . . .

– his quest is still the quintessential quandary, whether in the form of 'aspics' tongues' or 'adversity's sweet milk', or life's sick dreams. By Shelley's definition, in *Defence of Poetry*, 'Language, colour, form, and religious and civil habits of action, are all the instruments of poetry', with which O'Casey – within the conspectus of drama – would concur. 'All weakness that impairs', says Matthew Arnold, 'all griefs that bow', find similar expression in imperishable verse and genuine dramatic feeling. Indeed, often, the very light the poet walks in, darkens sun, moon and stars.

In the grim final moments of the macabre ending to the second 'scene' of *Cock-a-Doodle Dandy*, O'Casey would seem to have approved the significance of Swinburne's translucent thought from 'A Marching Song' in *Songs before Sunrise*:

> From the edge of harsh derision,
> From discord and defeat,
> From doubt and lame division,
> We pluck the fruit and eat;
> And the mouth finds it bitter, and the spirit sweet.

In the third 'scene' – with its equally dark overtones – we witness the acceleration of the ridiculous witch-hunt, wherewith the forces of authority, in league with the superstitious inhabitants of Nyadnanave, pursue the hated Cock (and his female accomplices) as though banishing a cacodemon. (Black cocks, in legendary times past, were viewed with suspicion as agents of the Devil.) Hysterical influences are aground everywhere; and under the *imprimatur* of bell, book and candle, Father Domineer is determined to expunge the rebellious influences of the Cock, and succeeds, even at the expense of driving people from the land. (Ireland's emigration-rate was rapidly soaring in immediate post-war years.) The play's final message is that individuals may be 'exorcised' or ostracised and driven out, but the spirit of freedom never. In the worldwide fight for human rights, we are all prisoners of conscience.

Says Lorna, at the beginning of the scene: 'How can they destroy a thing they say themselves is not of this world?' And, of the proposed exorcism, Sailor Mahan comments: 'Waste of time, too. It'll take a betther man than Father Domineer to dhrive evil things outa Eire'.

The priest brings with him an inane assistant in the form of One-eyed Larry – Cyclopean in moral matters, too – to help him carry out the futile exorcism operation. The half-idiotic Larry is satirised by the playwright as another bigoted crawthumper – a younger version of Shanaar – in whom are seen the foundations of holy madness. In the Joycean concept of 'A priestridden Godforsaken race!' O'Casey demonstrates that the laity, too, are sometimes equally strange and simple in their ways and willing instruments of repression. (Joybell – the confraternity acolyte we encounter in *The Star Turns Red* – is another religious simpleton in the same vein.)

In the mock-contest which follows, all action centres round the house, which, in this saga of comic absurdity, becomes an emblem of bitter 'heartbreak' proportions. The house shakes as flashes of lightning and thunder-claps rend the air, punctuated by sounds of breaking crockery and cackling of barnyard fowl. In the words of Shanaar, the house is being 'purified an' surefied' of supposedly evil influences. And, as if to illustrate the soothsayer's false accusation that 'women's wily exhilarations' are one of the root-causes of the country's moral degradation and ruin, Loreleen rushes in, in disarray, having been pelted by some local bigots for alleged lascivious conduct and for strutting an air of mettlesome defiance and independence – reminiscent of Jannice in *Within the Gates*.

Whether she is to be reviled or punished, she affirms, 'I'll still be gay an' good-lookin' '.

Becalmed by Lorna, she throws a challenge: 'Let them draw me as I am not, an' sketch in a devil where a maiden stands!'

Whilst the follies of exorcism shake the house to its foundations (the spiritual significance of which is not lost on the audience viewing the house as representing Ireland), Sailor Mahan (reduced to the role of sceptical onlooker, while his fellow-magnate, Michael, has joined in the expunging operations with Father Domineer and One-eyed Larry) offers help and financial assistance to get Loreleen away from the scene of venomous unrest and vindication. A covert meeting-place is arranged, when, suddenly, the dotty sacristan, rushing out of the house, battle-scared, declares:

They're terrible powerful spirits. Knocked th' bell outa me hand, blew out th' candle, an' tore th' book to threads! Thousands of them there are, led be th' bigger ones – Kissalass, Velvetthighs, Reedabuck, Dancesolong, an' Sameagain.

(Ben Jonson's humours invested with Joycean irony in O'Casey's version of Blake's Marriage of Heaven and Hell!)

The whole play is a Pandora's Box of puns, irreverences and mocking Hibernicisms: full of blasphemous orisons, in truest Ossianic tradition. O'Casey belongs in the Irish heritage of parody. Like so many of his countrymen, before and after him, he is – to employ a phrase from *Finnegans Wake* – a 'bawd of parodies'. We recall similar irreverences from pens of other Irish writers, notably Joyce, Shaw, Yeats, Stephens, Moore and Brendan Behan; and, we remember, too, the barbituric utterances of Synge in *The Playboy of the Western World*.

Meanwhile, as the game of high cockalorum goes on in the house, the trembling continues until the flagpole totters, followed by blue and red lightning flashes from the window and a loud peal of thunder which rends the garden: then all becomes silent. In the garden, the spectators shiver with fear, except Loreleen, who remains cynical and quietly imperturbable throughout. Like Imogen in *Cymbeline*, she fears no more the 'all-dreaded thunder-stone' or 'censure rash', neither can 'exorciser' or 'witchcraft' harm her: bondage, as well as death-in-life, she has renounced; as Emily Brontë had done in 'No Coward Soul is Mine' and in equally stoical beliefs reflected in another of her poems, 'The Old Stoic':

Through life and death, a chainless soul
With courage to endure!

'Now, like Father Faber's 'tempest-tossed Church', all eyes are on the suddenly bestilled house, as Father Domineer and Michael emerge from within, battered and bruised, their clothing torn and the priest's face smeared with smoke. Blissful, as well as boastful, the priest gives an assurance that 'evil things have been banished from the dwelling. Most of the myrmidons of Anticlerus, Secularius, an' Odeonius, have been destroyed. The Civic Guard and the soldiers of Feehanna Fawl will see to the few who escaped'. And then, with delicious irony on the playwright's part, the priest says: 'We can think quietly again of our Irish Sweep'. The women are then counselled to return to their 'proper place' in the house and to straighten it out 'and take pride in doing it' – in what the priest imperiously and old-fashionedly proclaims as 'th' only place for th' woman . . . Th' queen of th' household as th' husband is th' king'. (The double irony is implicit, as O'Casey, obviously, has endorsed the Shavian viewpoint, expressed in *Man and Superman*: 'Home is the girl's prison and the woman's workhouse.')

However, unrest returns, as the towsled Marthraun remembers there are still some dangerous books hidden in the house. At which, the irrational Domineer behaves like a demon possessed – though the episode sparks off some spicy comedy for which O'Casey is richly renowned:

FATHER DOMINEER (*startled*): Books? What kinda books? Where are they?

MICHAEL: She has some o' them in th' house this minute.

FATHER DOMINEER (*roaring*): Bring them out, bring them out! How often have I to warn you against books! Hell's bells tolling people away from th' thruth! Bring them out, *in annem fiat ecclesiam nonsensio*, before th' demoneens we've banished flood back into th' house again!

(MICHAEL *and* ONE-EYED LARRY *jostle together into the porch and into the house to do* FATHER DOMINEER'S *bidding*.)

LORELEEN (*taking her leg down from the chair, and striding over to* FATHER DOMINEER): You fool, d'ye know what you're thryin' to do? You're thryin' to keep God from talkin'!

FATHER DOMINEER: You're speakin' blasphemy, woman!

MAHAN: What do people want with books? I don't remember readin' a book in me life.

(MICHAEL *comes back carrying a book, followed by* ONE-EYED LARRY *carrying another.* FATHER DOMINEER *takes the book from* MICHAEL, *and glances at the title-page.*)

FATHER DOMINEER (*explosively*): A book about Voltaire! (*to Loreleen*) This book has been banned, woman.

LORELEEN (*innocently*): Has it now? If so, I must read it over again.

FATHER DOMINEER (*to* ONE-EYED LARRY): What's th' name of that one?

ONE-EYED LARRY (*Squinting at the title*): Ullisississies, or something.

FATHER DOMINEER: Worse than th' other one. (*He hands his to* ONE-EYED LARRY) Bring th' two o' them down to th' Presbytery, an' we'll desthroy them.

A scuffle breaks out as Loreleen snatches the books from the sacristan. In the Battle of the Books, One-eyed Larry tries to prevent her, but a sharp push from their owner sends the wild-eyed sacristan toppling over. At great speed, Loreleen darts out of the gateway and disappears. The men endeavour to give chase, on the priest's instructions, but remain helpless, their feet as if stuck to the ground. Seconds later, the Cock suddenly springs over the wall and pirouettes in and out of the garden: a signal for further magical disturbances. The stage blackens and there are thunder-claps as well as rifle-shots: with the return of daylight, the men remain prostrate and stunned. Father Domineer is nowhere to be seen, having been carried off by the Cock, in a sudden, surprised coup.

Hilarity, for a while, becomes a riotous spectacle of burlesque as the two hypocrites, Mahan and Marthraun, moan that they have been shot. In the centrifugal chaos, the women are beyond hallucinations and past caring (Mary Boyle and Juno in transposed circumstances). In a fanfaronade of fancy, the victims produce cigar-sized bullets from their breast-pockets and declare themselves – in the face of feminine incredulity and disbelief – blood-brothers in perpetuity. Irony is immediately apparent when the argumentative sparring resumes, as the mock-brothers remember their financial differences. 'D'ye want me to ruin meself to

glorify you?' is a taunt flung by one of the opposing blood-brothers
to offset the gracious corollary of the other: 'I'd see you in hell first!'
(The mammon of iniquity sends the two totemists into an orgy of
disagreement as the tarnished lasses – Lorna and Marion – look on
as reluctant witnesses, in clouds of despair, viewing with growing
apprehension and impatience the role of their countrymen in the
rat-race of cupidity and preoccupied gain in the face of ecclesiastical
connivance.)

A banshee-wind – whipped up by the frenzied Cock – fails to
affect the women but has the men clutching their trousers, like
clowns in a pantomimic farce. Chasing gull and moon, it sweeps
One-eyed Larry into their midst, spinning glorious fabrications
about Father Domineer's 'miraculous' escape from the clutches of
the Cock and safe delivery to his presbytery on the back of a
supposedly 'white duck'. As the frolicsome wind continues, the
Bellman is lifted across the stage, too, adding another version to the
telling of the strange wonder: the bird which carried the priest to
safety was, he affirms, a 'speckled duck'. Tongues of confusion break
loose and a minor 'miracle' quickly turns the whole countryside into
a babel of confusion or – in Shakespeare's telling phrase – 'a kind of
excellent dumb discourse'. In the middle of the argumentation, the
Sergeant, who is also blown on stage, but trouserless, declares the
bird was a 'barnacle goose'. (Like Synge's *Playboy*, O'Casey's play
roguishly exploits what Lady Gregory once devastatingly termed
'our incorrigible Irish talent for myth-making'.)

Mocking the ridiculous spectacle of unconstabulary authority,
Marion exclaims: 'It's lookin' like th' blue bonnets are over th'
bordher!' but the joke is lost on the local raconteurs wrangling
amongst themselves in confusion. The wind intensifies, piping gales
of bewilderment everywhere, to the amusement of the women,
watching the men gripping their waist-bands, joined by Robin, in
his usual nonchalance, playing a gentle melody on his accordion
and unaffected by the general disorder. The Messenger is scornful:
he feels only a breeze carrying with it the scent of pinewoods. In the
greyer air of Nyadnanave, he sees that young trees and saplings are
not flourishing, and no drums are throbbing in these woods or
trumpets sounding!

The fierce wind eventually blows the fiercer machinations of
Father Domineer into the spotlight. (After his arrival on stage, the
wind ceases, leaving 'a sombre silence' behind it.) He rallies his
troops in a mock-fight against moral turpitude. In punning

reference to the Irish folk-song, 'I Know Where I'm Going' – and other lyrics – he and his crusaders declare:

FATHER DOMINEER: We know where we're goin', an' we know who's goin' with us.

MICHAEL: The minsthrel boy with th' dear harp of his country, an' Brian O'Lynn.

BELLMAN: Danny Boy an' th' man who sthruck O'Hara.

ONE-EYED LARRY: Not forgettin' Mick McGilligan's daughter, Maryann!

Father Domineer's shock-troops soon hunt down their intended victim: Loreleen is dragged – bruised and dishevelled – bleeding and disgraced, before them, in the presence of the priest, having first been manhandled by the two Roughfellows, at the bidding of Father Domineer, and then spat upon by a mob of vigilantes, in a fit of sectarian righteousness, when it was learnt she was in the company of a married man; that of Sailor Mahan. The irony of Joyce's invective is recalled:

'Twas Irish humour, wet and dry,
Flung quicklime into Parnell's eye . . .

In a similar fit of 'righteous reprobation' the priest condemns Loreleen's conduct and upbraids her as a 'shuttlecock of sin!' He condemns her to be driven out of the country – a banished child of Eve, unfit to live in Eire's Eden. (Earlier in the play, he had suggested American deportation!) Self-vindicated, the foolish presbyter remains – in the aphoristic words of Blake – 'A fool tangled in a religious snare'. And Blakean sentiment is behind Loreleen's taunt, in telling the priest: 'When you condemn a fair face, you sneer at God's good handiwork. You are laying your curse . . . not upon a sin, but on a joy'.

Condemned to exile, she is joined first by Lorna, then by Marion and finally by Robin – all anxious, in the words of Lorna, to be 'free from th' Priest an' his rabble'. As exiles, they go fortified in the belief that they leave behind them only vilification and harassment and an awareness – as O'Casey has proclaimed elsewhere – that 'The loneliness of an exile among strangers is nothing like the loneliness of a man exiled among his own people'. Joyce also admitted:

It is to be safe from the rabid and soul-destroying political atmosphere in Ireland that I live here [in Paris], for in such an atmosphere it is very difficult to create good work, while in the atmosphere which 'Father Murphy' creates it is impossible.

At the end of the play, the misguided voice of Father Domineer informs the unhappy Marthraun: 'Be of good cheer, Michael; th' demon is conquered – you can live peaceful an' happy in your own home now' (alone, and palely loitering, of course!). And the old hypocrite, Shanaar, also declaims: 'An' fortunate you are, for a woman's always a menace to a Man's soul. Woman is th' passionate path to hell!'

The Messenger, who has been playing softly on his accordion and lilting 'Oh, woman gracious' – a gentle exordium to Eire's golden youth – pledges his love for Marion, who accepts, but in the greater freedom of exile (' . . . not here; for a whisper of love in this place bites away some of th' soul!). Love, strength and tempest – these they will share; but not within the boundaries of their native land (as the playwright, from his own experience, had known so well).

In the darkening mood of inclemency and despair, which descends on the final scene, the dolorous return of Julia from her visit to Lourdes, uncured, and unattended now, save for the ceaseless and careworn devotion of her father – public venerations now having vanished – proclaims the anguish of the incurably sick. As O'Casey himself was to comment, poignantly, years later in *Under a Colored Cap*, on the occasion of the death of his own beloved son, Niall, at the unexpectedly early age of twenty, from leukaemia:

There are no miracles these days: Meshach, Shadrach, and Abednego have ceased to live . . . Science alone can, like Hercules, stand between death and the dying young. It is Science alone which can mend God's image, when the image is hurt; and when Science fails in its mending, then God's image falls away into dust.

The consoling words from the Messenger to Julia – who hears of the flight of the young – are ones of bravery and courage in the face of adversity: 'Evermore be brave' (Emily Brontë's 'courage to endure'). His cruellest shaft is directed at Marthraun: 'Die. There is little else left . . . for the likes of you to do'. And, as the disconsolate turf-owner buries his head in his arms, Robin follows the example of the women *émigrées* – singing softly his ballad of love and hope – setting out 'To a place where life resembles life more than it does here'; along the path of exile; and away from the rural attitude in Ireland, which prompts Pegeen, in *The Playboy of the Western World*, to satirise with stinging condemnation: 'it's sooner on a bullock's liver you'd put a poor girl thinking than on the lily or the rose?'. The desertion from Michael is similar, too, to Dan Burke's, in the ending of Synge's other play, *The Shadow of the Glen*, wherein his wife goes off with the musical-voiced Tramp, while the other farm-hand, Michael Dara, condoles with Burke, wishing him future 'happiness', without the consolations of female companionship, which, curiously, is how both Father Domineer and Shanaar wish that God will reward Michael Marthraun, in the loveless future, in *Cock-a-Doodle Dandy*.

In *Sunset and Evening Star*, O'Casey concedes: 'There are brave men and women in Ireland still; and will be, will be, always, for ever'. But his message to forward-looking youth, in such stultifying circumstances, is to fly the country – along with the wild geese and exiles of yesteryear; to stand still would be to sink in the bog. This is the tocsin of the play; the feeling behind most of the later tragicomedies. Confronted by persecution and repression in De Valera's Ireland – reflected in the tens of thousands of young Irish emigrating annually from their country in the post-war years – the dramatist felt that his own particular exile had been justified as well as rewarded; feeling 'livelier in a livelier land'. The worst type of exile – O'Casey concludes – is exile of a countryman among his own people: an exile from civilisation and from every decent, cultural and acceptable way of life.

Cock-a-Doodle Dandy, like many of the author's previous dramas, is based on a vision of comical 'chassis' and conflict. Thus, the taming of the Cock becomes the sportive preoccupation throughout, giving rise to a lively comedy which dances along surefootedly among a merry circus of magical props and pitfalls with counter-opportunities for tongue-rattling Irish wit, extravagant fun and colour, song and dance, and risorial slapstick.

Less imaginative producers may be deterred by its diverse fantastical elements and potpourri of styles: for example, the close alternation of farce and melodrama, and the skilful admixture of gaiety and gravity tightly suffused. Sensitive directors will not find the play (in Nathan's words in another context) 'a rooster too difficult of winging', but will revel in the lilt and surge of a boisterous comedy, renowned for its boiling wit and vitality. But even to a gifted practitioner, this satirical, fantastical work will remain an untamed masterpiece in an hitherto inexperienced genre.

Among stage difficulties are certain trick technical effects, such as disappearances, collapsing chairs, banshee-winds, a quaking house and other instances of hurly-burly and fantasticality. Design and costumes must reflect a fantasy approach. The set – horeshoe in design – consisting of a front garden outside a symbolical Irish cottage, should be colourful as well as unrealistic. The dramatist's own detailed stage-instructions should be closely followed. Cadences of Irish speech are essential. In all, the resources of a protean company and the resourcefulness of a skilled director are vital.

The director's task should be to find a style of presentation whose contemporary relevance is clear. (Time remains unspecified in this timeless morality-comedy.) Conflicts in the play are intrinsically, perennially, contemporary: between young and old; between sexually repressed and those who wish to be free; between established authority and those who rebel against it; between workers and employers, women and men.

This fantasy-burlesque, with its charming nursery-rhyme, fairytale-like quality, needs to be played with spontaneity and wild exuberance. The successful director will discover how to transform the text into a soaring spectacle of lively improvisation on freedom of spirit and buoyancy of purpose; how to enact the robust, antic humour, coruscating into an unusual synthesis. In this play, of all O'Casey's dramas, the dramatist has succeeded in achieving a brilliant fusion of those elements which constitute the special magic of theatre. The play's fanciful nature does not depend on dramatic gimmickry or directorial whim. The play weaves its own spell, due to O'Casey's extraordinary technique, and it is this which sustains interest and suspense throughout. When the play is brought to shining life, we have a surging, irreverent mixture of music, dance, magic, drama and farce, seldom experienced, even within the confines of modern extravaganzas. The language is a coruscation in itself: a challenge to all but the finest of actors. *Cock-a-Doodle Dandy* is funny on many different levels at once; it is a play, too, with sad overtones. Its ending is both Arcadian and Elysian, though tragicomic; its three rambunctious 'scenes' circus and ballet in one.

Although O'Casey's extravaganza is trenchant and derisive – a satire on contemporary Ireland – its director, in triumphant interpretation, should always aim for a lyrical course, bearing in mind the cautionary advice offered by Brooks Atkinson, on the occasion of the New York production, in 1958:

> *Cock-a-Doodle Dandy* is more like *Peer Gynt* or a ballet with spoken dialogue . . . Unless a company can play it in balanced tones and rhythms it comes close to being 'a helluva disordher', as one of the characters remarks.

Echoes of *Within the Gates* sound throughout the play. The Messenger recalls the Dreamer; and *Cock-a-Doodle Dandy* has both the outdoor setting and ballet-like beauty of the former play.

The Cock of the title is the symbol of life and joy, as well as of revelation and courage. The cock is a world symbol, familiar to Shakespeare; and a symbol for France. Although the Cock, in the play, has no lines to speak, he is magnificently plumed and wattled: a monstrous feathered Puck, prancing about, flapping his wings and crowing loudly. He should be played with impudent elegance. (Most of the play should be performed as broad caricature. In fact, one of the most exhilarating performances should stem from the house itself, trembling, in a display of torment, that is both Bacchanalian and Biblical in its upheaval.) The unloosening of the Cock, as the playwright's archetypal symbol of youth and passion, weaves a warning of discomfiture to all 'crawthumpers' and moralists everywhere and prefigures even sterner forebodings in *The Bishop's Bonfire*. As the harum-scarum events wreak their havoc, the Cock becomes the playwright's vital agent. At the end of the mock-carnival ceremonies and pageant, the hypocrites are punished, as the fearless walk out in the direction of their own Utopia – as in the ending, too, of *Purple Dust* – leaving behind only a decaying garden and dying village, symptomatic of Ireland itself.

The admirable rooster is brilliantly and strikingly costumed. In the description of stage-directions:

> He is of deep black plumage, fitted to his agile and slender body like a glove on a lady's hand; yellow feet and ankles, bright-green flaps like wings, and a stiff cloak falling like a tail behind him. A big crimson crest flowers over his head, and crimson flaps hang from his jaws.

Although the Cock's magic is responsible for the general feeling of irreverent fun, it is typical of O'Casey's category-defying analysis that the dramatist never once brings the curtain down on such moments of boisterous comedy. At the end of the first scene, we witness a paralytic young girl setting out for Lourdes; while the second curtain closes with the death of a young lorry-driver felled by an adventitious blow from a heavy-handed priest; and the play closes with a haunting cameo of infinite misery – the loneliness of a bereft man whose narrow-mindedness has only served to drive away from house and home the affections of his young wife and daughter in search of a more humane and sympathetic society. The skein of phantasmagoria matches Blake's: in the aphorisms of the poet:

Excess of joy weeps; Joys impregnate. Sorrows bring forth.

As in all O'Casey's plays, we have a Dickensian profusion of marvellously absurd characters who inspire audience-appeal with their exuberant, larger-than-life turmoil. In *Cock-a-Doodle Dandy*, the twin pillars are Michael Marthraun and Sailor Mahan, whom Atkinson sees as imparting 'tight-jawed fanaticism of hot-tempered hypocrites who are intoxicated with the sound of words they do not understand and advertise their ignorance with literary bravado'. They are counterparts not only of Boyle and Joxer but demonstrate, as well, some of the absurdities of Mutt and Jeff (Sailor Mahan is American-inspired).

Marthraun is in his sixties, 'clean-shaven, lean, and grim-looking'. Dressed in a dark tweed suit, with leggings to match, he wears a gold chain across his waistcoat, complete with winged collar and bow-tie. Mahan is fifty; stouter and more serene, with a short, pointed beard, tinged with grey, underlining a ruddier, more rugged complexion. He is attired in light-grey flannels with double-breasted coat of royal blue and white scarf over a light-blue shirt.

Of the women, Loreleen is an attractive eighteen-year-old, dressed in darkish green with dark-red emblems – the colours of the Cock – on her bodice and skirt. Her hat is also emblematic of a cock's crimson crest. Lorna is between twenty-five and thirty-five, much younger than her husband and still very good-looking; she is dressed in contemporary Irish costume. Marion is twenty or so, short-skirted, and has, like Loreleen, a saucy air of insouciance. She wears a 'scarf-bandeau' around her head, dark-green uniform, flashed with brighter green on the sleeves and neck.

Robin is twenty, cheerful and light-hearted, and dressed in a silver-grey coat buttoned over his breast – a scarlet emblem on the right side. He wears a bright green beret. He is a harmonious tunesmith, singing his own songs and accompanying himself on his accordion. He also has a sly sense of humour. According to one commentator, Dr W. A. Armstrong, he 'resembles the legendary love-god, Angus; his music and songs symbolize a poetic principle'. (Loreleen is aptly compared by the playwright to Deirdre, returning to her native land only to find grief and disillusion.)

Shanaar is old and wrinkled, with long white hair and a grimy beard. His peasant costume is threadbare; his corduroy trousers patched, and his thick boots worn-looking. On a sack-cloth waistcoat he wears a brass cross. His strange appearance is offset by a wide-brimmed, black crumpled hat. (He is a kind of local spiritual witch-doctor: stalwart of the Church and revelling in pseudo-theological mumbo-jumbo and amateur supernaturalism.) The Sergeant is dressed in the Irish police-officer uniform of the Civic Guards and carries a rifle; his age is between forty and sixty, and he is in a perpetual state of frenzy and fear. The Porter is middle-aged with a grizzled beard. He is wry and obdurate – the wide-peaked cap he wears accentuating this fact. One-eyed Larry is twentyish; alternately sinister and stupid-looking. He is dressed awkwardly in a black cassock or soutane with red braiding. With his phoney religious fervour, he is a potential Shanaar. (His yarn about the loss of an eye due to a destructive bout with an evil spirit from a bottle is as persuasive to the ears of the local community as to the strange soothsayer's.)

Father Domineer is tall, heavily built and forty; breezy in manner and severe in his pronouncements and judgements. He is dressed in outdoor clerical garb and a wide-brimmed black hat. The two Roughfellows are sturdy and robust and dressed in peasant costume with contrasting-styled shirts and scarves. Mahan's foreman lorry-driver, Jack, is thirty, with an air of self-determined independence; he is dressed in leather jacket, khaki trousers and oily-looking peaked cap. The Bellman – dressed as a fireman – wears brass helmet, red shirt and blue trousers. Julia, supported by a high pillow and stretcher, has the forlorn marks of the gravely ill. Her father, sturdy and fifty, is poorly attired and carries an impenetrable, stony-faced resignation. The Mayor and Mace-bearer are robed cere-monially: the Mayor being stout, his acolyte tall.

The world *première* was staged at the People's Theatre,

Newcastle-upon-Tyne on 10 December 1949 (the third O'Casey *première* there), directed by Peter Trower. Its first London professional showing was at the Royal Court Theatre in 1959 (a re-run of the successful Edinburgh Festival production), directed by George Devine (the designer was Sean Kenny). A zestful cast included J. G. Devlin and Wilfrid Lawson in the leads, with Joan O'Hara, Etain O'Dell, Norman Rodway, Patrick Magee and Eamon Keane. (An Arcadian version adapted itself to the Minack open-air theatre, Porthcurno, Cornwall in 1965.)

In America, the play has made greater strides. Its first staging was in Dallas, Texas, by Margo Jones in 1950, with a version at Yale University in 1955. The New York *première*, by Lucille Lortel and Paul Shyre (previewed in Toronto), was directed by Philip Burton in 1958 (the designer was Lester Polakov). The run was disappointingly short. The 1968 revival at Stanford University provoked fresh interest, resulting in the classic 1969 Broadway production by Jack O'Brien and Donald Moffat, considered by many to be its iconoclastic best.

The play's publication in 1949 led to bitter reaction in Ireland, where, until 1975, it was almost totally taboo. Tomas MacAnna's first professional showing at Belfast's Lyric paved the way for a Dublin *première* at the Abbey in 1977, which he again directed in settings by Brian Collins. Edward Golden, Bernadette Shortt and Maire Ni Ghrainne were among the leads. Despite well-attended performances, the critics voiced their expected animadversions.

Among foreign productions, the Berliner Ensemble's in 1971 was noteworthy, as was Hansjorg Utzerath's West Berlin version of 1969. In France, the 1971 version at Nice was successful, as was Guy Retore's Paris production in 1975. Its English neglect is unjustified. There are translations in French, German, Italian, Spanish, Dutch, Polish, Roumanian, Slovak and Japanese.

16 *Time to Go* (1951): a Satiric Fantasy-Sketch

In theme and manner, *Time to Go* resembles *Cock-a-Doodle Dandy*. It is what one of its characters would term an 'effervesacatin' substratum of Irish post-Revolutionary society; similarly treated, in fact, to the conceptual world of *Within the Gates*, only in miniature. The lighter side of Irish life is accentuated, but with an excoriating wit.

The fact-seeing, illusion-proof characteristic of the modern Irishman, epigramatically exposed by Shaw in *John Bull's Other Island*, is reaffirmed, with intoxicating vigour, by O'Casey, in this semi-mystical but enchanting little play, which, in essence, is a kind of inversion of the Irishman's now suspected contempt for rationality.

The playlet, together with two other one-act pieces – *Bedtime Story* and *Hall of Healing* – was first published in 1951. (They are included in *Collected Plays*, vols. 3 and 4, and later published separately in *Five One-Act Plays*, in 1958.) These shorter interludes range from allegory and fantasy to naturalism and realism, impregnated with farce and burlesque, along the author's now familiar tragicomic lines. *Time to Go* is both allegory and comic farce in one, and, if it is to be successful, needs to be staged whimsically.

O'Casey describes his little play as 'A Morality Comedy in One Act'. It is a microcosmic, sardonic view of mid-twentieth-century rural Ireland – 'Priest-puffin island!' as one of the characters quips, with more than an inkling of foreknowledge or folk-lore. From beginning to end, the play is pure satiric fantasy, reminiscent of the dramatist's earlier political one-act fantasy-skit, *Kathleen Listens In*.

In *Time to Go*, O'Casey portrays a country where alliance between Church and prominent business leaders has impaired, if not denied, true Christianity. Huckstering peasants, as well as the gombeen greed of shop-keepers and publicans, contribute as much to the decline and fall of post-independence Ireland as the priests themselves, despite the fact that Ireland, as one character opines, is a positive 'bird-sanctuary' for the clergy. The final impression, as Liam O'Flaherty in *A Tourist's Guide to Ireland* also confirms, is one of 'a beautiful sad-faced country that is being rapidly covered by a black rash'.

The basic contradiction, in this miniature phantasmagoria, lies between spurious and authentic Christianity, providing roystering fun and tragic polemics. The scene, in the author's own words, 'is the butt-end of an Irish town'; time, the ever-unchanging present.

In a wide-ranging cast of thirteen characters, some realistically portrayed, others mere stereotypes, the main roles are represented by Michael Flagonson, a typical publican; his 'effervesacatin', prodding wife, and his business ally, Bull Farrell, owner of a general store, who, between them, demonstrate that God and Caesar are indissolubly linked throughout the length and breadth of rural Ireland. And, through varied business activities at a country fair – involving impecuniousness as well as greed from several types of farmer (Barney O'Hay, Cousins and Conroy) in comparison with the different traditional attitudes of two especially contrived mythical figures personified by Widda Machree (whose cardinal sin has been she has asked too much from the sale of a cow, and now repents of it) and Kelly from the Isle of Mananaun (who, in turn, has given too little for it, but regrets the fact) – O'Casey offers two contrasting kinds of commitment: one of simple generosity that is genuinely Christian in its original sense; and the other of modern hypocritical significance that unites business and worship in a bond of pious fraud (as aided and abetted by Sergeant Killdooey of the Civic Guards and his two lumpen-cohorts).

The moral of the play, set above numerous sub-themes, is the need for absolute, dedicated unselfishness.

Music, songs, colour and dance all interlace, enchantingly, in a miniature web, glowing with irridescent speech.

A transmogrified theme – one of encomiastic change (similar to that employed in epiphany-episodes featured in *Red Roses for Me* and *Cock-a-Doodle Dandy*) – is used, seraphically, in the finish, to point the moral, in the form of an uplifting 'halleelucination' (to quote another of the endearing neologisms!). O'Casey's 'butt-end' village, whether it be the fictional equivalent of Buttevant, or, simply, Nyadnanave (or any of the O'Casey-styled locations), is condemned to a vision of death, when its potential saviours and golden youth decide that 'it's time to go'.

The mammon of iniquity is left to go its own vicarious way, confusing its own jingle of profits with the gentler sound of the Angelus or Mass bell. 'I wondher what would Brian Boru think of it, if he was alive today!' exclaims the generous-hearted, forward-looking Young Woman of the play; 'Or the Fenians before him', echoes her male companion, 'who set honour an' truth before comfort or safety'. Hotheaded the Celtic heroes may have been, but were never coldhearted.

'I don't really loathe the Roman Catholic Church', the playwright confessed, with saintly infidelity, in a letter to Desmond MacCarthy, in 1949. 'I loathe those who are turning her liturgy into vulgar nonsense and her temples into dens of thieves'. *Time to Go* is an eloquent testimony of such staunch scepticism, consistently preached throughout O'Casey's later colourful dramas, in the spirit and practice of Emerson's Beautiful Necessity, which excludes nothing of earthly significance and ensures that everything in the cosmic universe is done bravely and done well.

Along with *Bedtime Story*, the play was first produced, professionally, in America, by a group of Off-Broadway actors on 7 May 1952, at the Jugoslav-American Hall, New York, directed by Albert Kipton (décor by May Callas). It was revived in 1960 at the Theatre de Lys, sponsored by Lucille Lortel.

In London, it was first staged at the Unity Theatre in 1953, where it was featured in the billing, 'Three in a Row' (along with *The End of the Beginning* and *Hall of Healing*). The director was Ivor Pinkus. In a letter to the producer, O'Casey warned that *Time to Go* was the most difficult of his one-act plays to stage, because, as he euphemistically warned: 'It is when fancy and imagination strikes into a play that the English Theatre staggers about'. Although fantasy and sharp comedy were to the fore in this interpretation, the symbolic note was missing.

Although this kaleidoscopic little play remains surprisingly neglected, even abroad, a brave amateur presentation in 1971 attracted attention in County Cork, when members of the Fermoy Youth Club produced it with vigour, in a lilting programme which included folk-music, hornpipe and song, in a rare feast of song and words. Translations exist in French and Russian.

17 *Bedtime Story* (1951): a Sophisticated Farce

Although this farcical one-act caprice is subtitled, 'An Anatole Burlesque' – in the gayer manner of Schnitzler's man-about-town sketches (collectively known as *Anatol*) – O'Casey, in a programme-note to his own-styled 'unconsidered trifle', chooses to emphasise the light-heartedness of his sophisticated satire by underscoring his belief that: 'Here is a little play in which there are neither good nor bad judged seriously, with a laugh at the beginning and another at the end'.

This pert little effervescent piece was included by Brooks Atkinson in his selection of nine favourite plays among his 1968 collection, *The Sean O'Casey Reader: Plays, Autobiographies, Opinions*, published by Macmillan. (It is the only one-acter represented in the collection.) Although, says Atkinson, 'the hearty laugh of theatrical enjoyment' is present in all the author's one-act soufflés (as it is, of course, to an even greater degree in the full-length plays), alone amongst them – in Atkinson's judgement – the playlet merits special admiration and remembrance for its unflagging exuberance and 'sustained mockery'. On stage, it is a sheer romp.

Teasingly, it tells of a young Catholic bachelor, overtly pious and ultra-respectable, who, on impulse, invites a 'gay lass' (who is more than a high-spirited soubrette) into his lodgings in Dublin one night, but his efforts to keep her quiet after their nocturnal idyll leads him into all sorts of unforeseen troubles (not only with his fellow-lodger and land-lady, but with a doctor, nurse and police-man, in the finish). The hilarious episode is a salty little satire against those morally self-righteous young men (they abound still in Dublin and elsewhere in Ireland) who yearn for sexual intercourse, but who are, because of predominantly Catholic influences and upbringing, obsessed by a futile sense of sin. (Joybell is another representative of this breed.) The behaviour of John Jo Mulligan, the timorous twenty-four-year-old bachelor, contrasts, markedly, with fun-loving, vivacious Angela Nightingale, who, after their long day's night of promiscuity, with its clouds of remorse, on Mulligan's part, afterwards, revenges, thwarts and swindles him not only of outward self-respect but of belongings and cash which so effect his subsequent behaviour that his apparent disorders lead Daniel Halibut (his fellow man-about-town lodger) and Miss Mossie (his prim land-lady) to suspect he may be mentally deranged; whence, in an uproarious *volte-face* at the end, they summon outside help and try to have him committed. On realising the situation that has overwhelmed him, Mulligan finally sinks, forlornly, into his chair in a dead faint. (Miss Nightingale, in common with her sister-representatives, Nannie and Jannice in O'Casey's previous dramas, delights in upsetting the withers of false respectability, with whorish unconcern and unaffected self-enjoyment.)

The cascade of fun generated by this explosive little vignette is O'Casey's unquenchable variant on the all-too-familiar stage concept of bed-room farce. In the playwright's own words: 'It shows what odd things may happen when a pietist ceases to pray for a moment; how bewildered and lost he becomes because of a first lingerieing [sic] glance at lace on a petticoat'.

O'Casey's description of the pagan Angela's attributes are also recorded for us in his programme-note (included in *Blasts and Benedictions*):

The child of this world, Angela Nightingale, is far cleverer, wittier, and more alive, than the child of light, John Jo Mulligan. She is more honest, too, as wickedness is as often a virtue, for piety is often stained with pride, while wickedness is in too much of a hurry to bother with anxiety about pretence; eager to keep, not himself, but his little name unspotted from the world. Angela's cleverness, her honesty, her gift of seeing through another, and her humour, are lost, ill-used, or not used, a condition happening to many another woman, too.

The sketch, in effect, is a variety-turn for two players: the whore and the hypocrite. The land-lady and Halibut are merely ancillary, and the policeman, doctor and nurse enter just before curtain-fall and have no speaking parts.

In Britain, though never performed professionally, the playlet has attracted a measure of philistine reaction, failing to take account of its outrageous, extravagant fun. In 1954, in the British Drama League's annual competitive festival, it was banned outright by an adjudicator from Essex. As O'Casey commented, ruefully, in *Under a Colored Cap*:

> So this little play has never been performed in England, as far as I know, except by the students for the students of the R.A.D.A., for fear it might weaken the moral fibres of the elderly, bringing the land to a decline and fall into the depravity of whoredom, though this, at least, would be better and brighter than the decline and fall into the drab and malicious menace of puritanism.

Unsurprisingly – underneath the heroics of hilarity where the absurdities of puritanism are the play's chief comic target – reaction has also been cool in Ireland, where intolerance is often mistaken for moral fervour. In 1969, at the annual Irish Universities Drama Association Festival, Micheal Mac Liammoir, in his role as adjudicator, poured scorn on the choice of the play as an entry from the students of University College, Dublin. *Bedtime Story*, he declared, was 'a dreadful example of senile or teenage meandering'. The play certainly lampoons the average Irishman's dilatory, I'm-done-for amatory technique in a brilliant, devastating exposure of national failing, in mercilessly amusing fashion; and physical love and its subconscious aspects are expressed with wit and skilful psychological insight, just as in Schnitzler's *Anatol* and *La Ronde*. (O'Casey's short story, 'I wanna Woman', included in the collection, *Windfalls*, is in a similar sardonic vein.) Mac Liammoir's outburst did not deter Bangor's Drama Club from entering – and winning – with the play in the All-Ireland One-Act Drama Festival in 1971, precipitating the Abbey's 1972 *première* at the Peacock with John Lynch's direction.

Abroad, away from taunts of puritanism, the scene is the homeland story in reverse. Its American début in 1952 in New York by Joseph Papirofsky (Joe Papp), paved the way for its 1959 Broadway showing by the Cronyns, who played it as straight comedy. In Paris there have been several versions, from the early successful Montparnasse showing of 1960. It was also performed in Nevers in 1972, along with *A Pound on Demand*. The Burlesque also scored a hit in East Berlin in 1959, and there was a revival at the Schiller-Theater Wekstatt in 1967. Translations have appeared in French, German, Spanish, Polish, Hungarian, Estonian, Persian and Russian.

18 *Hall of Healing* (1951): a Therapeutic Diversion

Hall of Healing is the most tragicomic of O'Casey's one-act diversions, even though the dramatist labels it 'A Sincerious Farce in One Scene'. It is based on memories of reprehensible medical conditions operating at the turn of the century, and afterwards, among dispensaries of the poor and the notorious Red ticket system in Ireland – a method of communication between patient and doctor, and one of many evils condemned by Larkin, Connolly and others alike – that exacerbated such conditions. Some of these memories, too, affecting the playwright's early childhood, are recounted in his first autobiographical book (especially, in the Chapter, 'The Hill of Healing'), *I Knock at the Door*.

In a letter to the *Irish Times* of 28 December 1951, O'Casey wrote: 'Little did I think, when I wrote *Hall of Healing* that the conditions of fifty years ago in the dispensaries of the poor would be the same today'. And, with additional emphasis, he affirms: 'These dens, called dispensaries, exist still! . . . I have been in many dispensaries, where the ragged, the cold, and the sick poor gathered, hustled in and hustled out again, as if they had no claim on life, and it was an impudent thing for them to be seeking the comfort of health'.

In characteristic grotesquerie, the little play depicts, in a light-hearted, tragicomic way, treatment of the poor in a Dublin medical dispensary during a typical winter's day. The grubby yet fascinating world is portrayed in a semi-stylised, memorable way.

The theme of the play is the universal, mistaken, unnecessarily forebearing quality of resignation – as irrational in its origins as its implications – affecting not merely dispensary patients, as portrayed in the guise of the Old and Young Woman, Green, Black and Red Muffler (and, even more tragically, Grey Shawl, Red Muffler's wife): visionary characters sketched with vivid veracity, but affecting, too, in heartless fashion, doctor and apothecary, as well as

341

soulless attendants looking after such chambers of horrors. As one patient in O'Casey's surgery bitterly remarks, all the people in the dispensary are in a dance of death. Most are unaware of it and blandly continue their blind existence.

The dance motif is evident by emphasis on movement. Each patient hops to his place in the queue, and the attendant, the Caretaker of the Dispensary, Aloysius (nicknamed 'Alleluia'), dances a wild jig whenever he hears music from an adjoining church. In O'Casey's grotesque farce, he is one of the jesters – forever browbeating and 'expostulating' with the patients. Others are Jentree, the alcoholic, whose nerves are ruined from excessive drinking, and the Old Woman, who shows childish delight in other people's ailments. When told by the doctor to swallow half a gallon of water a day to nullify the effects of alcohol, the Old Woman points out to 'Alleluia' (with which Jentree wholeheartedly agrees): 'If th' poor man has to negify th' wine with wather, and then has to negify the wather with wine, sure th' poor man'll burst himself thryin' to find a solution for his ailment'.

The characters' stoical resignation has genuinely unforeseen tragicomic results. We see its comic attributes in the child-like satisfaction which the same characters derive from getting one particular coloured medicine rather than another, as instanced in the Old Woman's facile observation to Black Muffler (inordinately pleased with the change of colour in his niggling physic): 'Be th' look of it, son, that should do you a power o' good. This fella thinks more o' bottles than the th' other fella did – I'll say that of him!' We see its comic absurdities in the rule that each new patient must supply three different bottles (one for each colour of medicine the doctor might prescribe), though when Green Muffler is fobbed off with pills, instead, he soliloquises to the patients in the waiting-room that this form of malpractice is 'cruel'! (His portrait is an echo of the Ballad Singer in *Nannie's Night Out*.)

The comic-macabre element is accentuated when the Old Woman is shown to prefer to wait outside in the cold until the dispensary opens rather than cross swords with 'Alleluia', and in the finicky fussiness displayed by the attendant himself to placate the uneasy quirkiness of the doctor, torn between futile resignation, hopelessness, and the subconscious need to alleviate the plight of his never-diminishing panel of poor. 'He'll take a long time between patients today', quizzes the Old Woman, 'always does when he's bad from booze'. The sombre mood of the play, as affecting the malign world of the poor, is reminiscent of the playwright's earlier one-act (though sketched in a different technique), *Nannie's Night Out*.

In *Hall of Healing*, the mindless resignation among the patients which forms the basis of this comic grotesquerie is challenged, single-heartedly, by Red Muffler, who, alone, refuses to accept, without success, despite hopeless odds, its permeating, soul-destroying effects. He, most of all, is in direst need of immediate, therapeutic consideration; and, whilst he is forced to sit and wait his turn, in the face of trumpery regulations, his wife – a forlorn figure in a thin faded skirt and broken boots – enters the surgery, before it closes, at the finish of the play, and breaks the chilling news to him of their baby daughter's death (from croup); and so it is futile waiting any longer. (The poster on the surgery-wall drawing attention to vigilance over diphtheria and other deadly ailments is doubly ironic.)

The experience of Red Muffler and his wife was the tragic experience of O'Casey's parents in the harsh poverty-surrounding environment of Dublin in the latter half of the nineteenth century. Red Muffler's broken response is reflected in his bitter outburst: 'Death has sometimes a kindlier touch than many a human hand'. And his final aggrieved message to doctor and patients is couched in the threat: 'Yous are afraid to fight these things. That's what's th' matther – we're all afraid to fight!' (the slogan-cry that motivates, but breaks, Jack Rocliffe in *The Harvest Festival*, or Ayamonn Breydon in *Red Roses for Me*).

In the Biblical maxim, 'the destruction of the poor is their poverty'. That is why, in this relentless detestation of poverty and other social ills, O'Casey, like Shaw, in Browning's words, 'was ever a fighter'. He himself possessed titanic force to rise above his early privations; and, being composed of steel as well as flame, was strong enough to have overcome the odds and triumphed. Red Muffler is thus a stereotype of fighting resolve and the personification of battling mankind in a socially deprived world. Black Muffler and Green Muffler, on the other hand, are symbols of faceless, irresolute humanity, akin to Eliot's 'hollow men' and 'stuffed men' ('Shape without form, shade without colour'), inhabiting 'death's other kingdom'; and similar, too, to O'Casey's own down-and-outs, portrayed so hauntingly and graphically in the sharper labyrinth of *Within the Gates*.

'Alleluia' and Jentree are humanity's clowns, whose motley rests in laughter. The Old Woman has a salty tongue, like so many of her kind in various plays from *Within the Gates* onwards. The doctor and apothecary are, in Lady Macbeth's illuminating phrase, 'night's black agents' that 'scarf up the tender eye of pitiful day'. The rest of the charactery belongs to the inner, painted veil of humanity, comic-pathetic in the grey pathos of outward nemesis. An inextricable mixture of comedy and tragedy is present in this poignant little diversification – taking its place, with justification, alongside the author's renowned tragicomedies.

The play is tragicomedy in its fullest sense, and both elements should be emphasised strongly in the acting. Tragedy lies in the setting and situation and is brought to a head by the final incident of the play. Comedy rests in the characterisation and dialogue, especially the extravagantly colourful turns of speech. Although the setting is Dublin, the play, like so many others of the author's, has a universal significance. O'Casey's targets are not merely the vagaries of doctors in the conditions in which they are forced to practise – plus poverty in general – but hypocrisy of all kinds. However, although O'Casey sympathises with the poor, he also blames them roundly for being spineless and defeatist, but this does not imply, as some critics have insisted, that he shows 'contempt for the poor'.

Joe Papp's New York *première* in 1952 was in conjunction with *Bedtime Story* and *Time to Go*, with settings by May Callas. In Britain, there were performances at London's Unity Theatre in 1953, in a three-part billing (featuring *Time to Go* and *The End of the Beginning*), directed by David Dawson (with designs by Kate Amaral and Robert Dyson). In Dublin, Tomas MacAnna directed for the Abbey in 1966 (the designer was Brian Collins). There was also a revival at the Peacock in 1971 by Peadar Lamb.

Abroad, Jean-Pierre Vincent staged a successful French showing at Strasbourg in 1978, and it was featured in an O'Casey triple bill by Adolf Dresen in Berlin in 1965. Robert Keller's East German 1968 version at Cottbus was duly acclaimed. Translations are known to exist in French, German, Russian and Turkish.

19 *The Bishop's Bonfire* (1955): a Celtic Lament

'A Sad Play within the Tune of a Polka' is the wistful sub-title of O'Casey's next full-length play – known, generally, by its more familiar title of *The Bishop's Bonfire*. Again, the terrain is rural Ireland, where rhetoric is the fire-water of the natives and rank Jesuitry the specific balsam bestowed on a long-suffering population adjusting – though with the occasional glint of a drollish mind – to De Valera's sinister yet subtle, spiritual blackguardocracy. 'It's an outspoken play', O'Casey told a correspondent in 1955 – shortly before the world *première* in Dublin – 'with a good deal of humour and some sad moments'. In the introductory parts, the play is mostly bubbling talk, in O'Casey's fluent style, though an *allegro con brio* in the finish darkens the plot, bringing the drama to an unexpected and extraordinary conclusion – couched in firm melodrama in truest Boucicaultian manner.

Although less ebullient than the gay and more imaginative *Cock-a-Doodle Dandy*, it caused a storm of controversy when it was first produced in Dublin (Dubliners had not seen a major production of a new O'Casey play within its capital for close on thirty years), even though it played to crowded houses in its five-week run. Amid smiles and laughter from audiences, the reaction from critics and establishment was scarcely mollified by the sweet inclinations, in a programme-note, from the seventy-five-year-old playwright:

> Here's what's called a play by what is called a playwright. O'Casey's the name, and here he is trying once more to dance a polka on the stage. See him dance the polka. He hopes you'll like it, and he hopes you'll laugh. We writers are inclined to be a cocky crowd, thinking so often that what we say should be, not written down on paper, but graven deep down in marble so that newcomers to life won't miss the great news; when, in reality, most of what is written by us are but plumes of smoke getting into

the eyes to make them water, and into the nose to make us sneeze . . .

Well, here's another plume of smoke which I hope may have a little flame in it to light up life for a moment or two; to make us think again of some of the problems Ireland has to face in the midst of the sound from the singer's song and the politician's shout.

The Bishop's Bonfire is not a play about the banshee-world of giants, fairies, monsters or phoukas – though survivors from that leprechaun's kingdom are to be found in this mid-twentieth-century burlesque. The play, O'Casey was later to pronounce, 'is . . . about the ferocious chastity of the Irish, a lament for the condition of Ireland, which is an apathetic country now, losing all her energy, enthusiasm and resolution'.

Six years later, in 1961, in a programme-note written specially for the London production at the Mermaid Theatre, his lament had become a lacerating condemnation of contemporary Ireland's theocratic and puritanical stranglehold on life, reflected in the following premonitory paragraphs:

The play shows an aspect of Irish life – the terrible fear of the sight of a lover and his lass among the rye or half-hidden in the bracken, in a dance at the cross-roads, or walking together down a country road or lane; a land where Chastity has become one of the worst vices; the marriage rate the lowest in the world and the birth rate, too; with the younger and more vital ones streaming out of the country – last year 60,000 left Ireland probably for ever, hurrying to Australia, America, Canada, and, mostly, to England.

Says a speaker over the Irish Broadcasting: 'The place of least enjoyment is the place of least engagements towards marriage. If gaiety and enjoyment are hidden from the young, the young will go where they are to be found'. Of course, they will. And these things are shown in my play.

But in Ireland we have an almost all-powerful clergy, and the Roman Catholic Bishops are ipso facto the Government of the country. The play shows this in the show of piety and profits, venomous puritanism, and the ignorance of all around, laced into timidity against tradition and clerical authority – 'An ignorant priesthood teaching an ignorant peasantry', as an angry Irish

University Professor recently declared, though a Catholic himself.

In the play, the saucy Keelin, the sad but open-minded, and sensible Father Boheroe, with the gay spirit and gay songs of the Codger, try to bring some life, some courage to the town of Ballyoonagh. It is an effort to be symbolic of the thought and conduct and outlook, when all's forgotten save the preparations to give a right royal welcome to a Bishop arriving for a visit to his native town.

The subsequent theme and happenings and prevailing mood are summarised in the words of the dust-jacket of the English edition of the play, published later in 1955:

> O'Casey's latest three-act play brings us down again to rural Ireland at a time when all are busy providing a colourful welcome to a Bishop about to pay a visit to the little town he was born in. There are gorgeous goings-on to entertain him in the house and home of Councillor Reiligan, the big man who owns all the body and half the soul of the little town of Ballyoonagh.
>
> Through all the busy hilarity there runs a steady undercurrent of revolt against what the President of Dublin's University College called 'The strange fog of unreality which seems at the moment to have penetrated every corner of Ireland's national consciousness'.
>
> Love, marriage, and the flight of the young from the land are touched on in O'Casey's sad and gay way amid the hurry, zeal, rancours and rivalries of the Ballyoonagh folk; and within the dusk shine a young priest's conscious, and an old peasant's unconscious, efforts to lift up the people's hearts, and bring down some of the light from the stars to the way of the plough.
>
> As in the author's other plays, his characters manifest themselves, and strive, laugh, and argue among heady gusts of talk.

In the little rustic oligarchy of Ballyoonagh – O'Casey's comic wonderland – those who hold sway are the local Councillor, personified by Reiligan, and the parish priest, represented by Canon (later Monsignor) Burren, both portrayed, alternately, as braggarts and poltroons, comic-pathetic figures, who try to influence their fellow countrymen into a turgid, spiritual obedience, shaping them unnervingly in preparation for the life of the next world – the *Tir-nan-og* of eternity. Such stern predictabilities, as the play comically reveals, are no match against the eruptiveness of native veterans and Vesuvians – the irrepressible yokels and born buffoons – represented in the persons of the Codger, the Prodical and Daniel Clooncoohy, as well as histrionic rebels such as Manus Moanroe, the disillusioned spokesman of aspiring youth, supported by their clerical sympathiser, the endearing Father Boheroe (an idealised, if less inflexible, portrait) whose civilised revolt, between them, fails, in the end, to dislodge the hymns of puritanical gloom or devouring dogmas offered providentially in black bile. Throughout such a chillingly pervasive atmosphere, the leaps of youth and aspirations of freedom-fighters are dashed.

'In the midst of our deepest emotions', says George Moore, in *Celibate Lives*, 'we are acting a comedy with ourselves'. So it is in the spectacle O'Casey creates in *The Bishop's Bonfire*. Behind the laughter are bitter salt tears shown in those who fight against repression but who fail to win through. 'God gave us our human nature', stresses O'Casey (reiterating Moore), and, again, in the words of Moore, 'Body and mind . . . are not two things, but one'. In the wholeness of his nature, argues O'Casey, man must live integrally.

Just as Moore, in *The Untilled Field*, chooses to depict the inhibitions and frustrations of rural Ireland, so O'Casey, in *The Bishop's Bonfire*, similarly portrays contemporary Catholic Ireland, emphasising its pious mediocrity, its middle-class respectability and superstitious religiosity. The same faults that are the subject of scathing satire in *Cock-a-Doodle Dandy* are again flayed in coldly perceptive irony with a vividness of presentation in an accompanying prose-style whose rhythm and texture are as unquenchable as ever.

Throughout the drama, the titular Bishop is the subject of much ridicule, even though he never actually appears. The pompous and pietistic are satirised. Scorn is heaped on those – personified by Foorawn – who, in their religious servitude, place chastity before charity; on those, such as the Councillor and Canon, who lack charity and are therefore shown, in the Pauline phrase, as sounding brass and tinkling cymbals, as well as on those who rely, for their well-being, on the intercession of saints – stultifying individual and national initiative. 'When we have problems', says Father Boheroe, 'ourselves are the saints to solve them. Our weakness – and our strength'. 'Man has to finish what God begins', says the Codger, in an explicit piece of Shavian doctrine handed down from the time of *Major Barbara* – a favourite theme with the ageing playwright and the subject of epiphany in his panorama-of-life drama, *Within the Gates*. ('I feel now as if there was nothing I could not do, because I want nothing', says Shaw's Ellie Dunn in *Heartbreak House*. 'That's the only real strength', replies Captain Shotover, with confident conclusiveness. 'That's genius'.)

Although in basic attitudes *The Bishop's Bonfire* infuses plenty of bite and comedy, it must be remembered that in the newly created ecumenical atmosphere among Christians everywhere in the wake of Pope John's Vatican Council in the early sixties, the play is now less topical in some of its aspects of social and ecclesiastical criticism. Pope John's intuition of a Catholic humanism as an indispensable beginning for the basis of a revivalism throughout the universe – free from dusty and narrow conventions – has changed Catholic thinking and even made inroads in Catholic Ireland. Its chief stumbling-block – as O'Casey suggests in the play – lies in the cultural weakness the Church, in a predominantly Catholic country, has to offer. In the fifties, as O'Casey stresses, it was rigorously opposed to any sort of humanist standpoint at all, enacting, in self-defence, a rigidly evil system of censorship, which became the laughing-stock of the free world. A humanist culture, favoured in many countries where mixed societies prevailed, was frowned upon in Ireland where a narrowly theological viewpoint predominated.

But the play's basic assumption is still incontrovertibly true: namely, the great barrier to Irish development in the twentieth century was not so much British Imperialism as Irish puritanism. It was this aspect of the play which caused such a rumpus among higher echelons of Dublin's society when it was first staged in 1955.

Like Yeats – in his final phase – O'Casey sees himself as 'a passion-driven exultant man [who] sings out' and who possesses 'an old man's frenzy' and 'an old man's eagle mind'. Yeats's fears and aspirations accord with those of the ageing playwright:

> Whatever flames upon the night
> Man's own resinous heart has fed.

Despite their assumed anger – their alleged arrogance – both writers identify themselves closely with their own 'indomitable Irishry'. In both there beats a truly 'fanatic heart'. With O'Casey, a love-hate relationship with his native land emerges, enshrined in the demonstrative word of the autobiographies as 'Spireland': an echo of Joyce's satiric sobriquet in *Finnegans Wake* – 'Shamrogueshire'. Behind O'Casey's allegorisation lies the fervent hope that such mid-twentieth-century stigmas and aspersions in Ireland will eventually disappear; and, indeed, towards the end of the twentieth century, there seem some slightly encouragingly hopeful signs.

In the golden glow of *The Bishop's Bonfire*, there is – in Nathan's panegyrics (foreword to *Five Great Modern Irish Plays*) – 'a passionate undertone, a brave resolve, and a hint of spiritual music'. Behind the profligate beauty and lyric spirituality – so reminiscent of Blake – is a tale of august heartache, overriding the surface of which, to re-echo Nathan, is 'a compassion for humanity drenched in the tears of a great pity's understanding'. The language therein matches Shelley's 'Orphic song' in *Prometheus Unbound*; in Milton's words, from *Reason of Church Government*, the elderly playwright is seen as 'A poet soaring in the high region of his fancies with his garland and singing robes about him'.

O'Casey's 'understanding' is closely allied to Shelley's in his *Address to the Irish People* (1812):

Oh, Irishmen! I am interested in your cause; and it is not because you are Irishmen or Roman Catholics that I feel with you and feel for you; but because you are men and sufferers.

The liberty which Shelley and O'Casey both champion is the liberty, above all liberties, advocated long ago by Milton (as expressed in *Areopagitica*): 'the liberty to know, to utter, and argue freely according to conscience' (so eloquently expressed, too, in *Red Roses for Me*).

The philosophy behind the play is also strikingly Shelleyan; it sums up the mood and misfortunes of O'Casey's tragicomedy:

Can there be worse slavery [asks Shelley] than the depending for the safety of your soul on the will of another man? Is one man more favoured than another by God? . . . God values a poor man as much as a priest, and has given him a soul as much to himself. The worship that a kind Being must love is that of a simple affectionate heart, that shows its piety in good works, and not in ceremonies, or confessions, or burials, or processions, or wonders.

Take care then that you are not led away. Doubt everything that leads you not to charity, and think of the word "heretic" as a word which some selfish knave invented for the ruin and misery of the world, to answer his own paltry and narrow ambition.

Yet, Ireland, as O'Casey has affirmed in *Blasts and Benedictions*, 'is a kaleidoscope of amazing contrasts'. Boasting the oldest civilisation in Europe, she is still, as a newly independent nation, very young at heart. Believing everything, even, says O'Casey, 'the legend of Eden's garden', she is at heart inquisitorial; always searching, always asking questions. Her popular imagination, as Synge had discovered, is 'fiery' and 'tender'. Paradoxically, as O'Casey has also noted: 'She believes that all authority comes from God, bowing low in consecrated submission', yet, agonistically, 'lifts her right hand to strike at an authority she dislikes, or thinks unjust'.

Strands of hope are woven into the tragicomic fabric of the play, but diminish as the play heads darkly to its conclusion. In the unnatural atmosphere created jointly by priest and politician, faith, in its truest sense, has been stultified and charity banished completely (it being recognised that charitable love emanates from the human heart and understanding).

In Ireland, an ancient and almost universal conviction sees conflict between bodily, sensuous experience and the pursuit of religious ideals. To seek liberation, therefore, in solely traditional religious values – in the way Church and State decree – means to renounce, as far as possible, bodily pleasures and affections, and to mortify – or deaden – impulses that remain. This widespread belief in punitive asceticism, with a fundamental distrust of human emotions and laws of the flesh, is relentlessly practised in Ireland as a country predominantly Catholic, in conjunction with a joint political-ecclesiastical shaping of a modern theocratic state.

Ignoring genuine spontaneity and transcendent rhythms which the body aspires to, such traditional asceticism produces – as the play reveals – unhealthy distortions and harmful attitudes, which O'Casey, in *The Bishop's Bonfire*, expressly condemns. Celibacy, too, because of negative attitudes towards the human body – and in particular sexuality – is roundly condemned as an impairment of the human spirit; a misuse of man's higher potentialities. Denigration of sexual love; the absence of any humanistic, cultural ideals (resulting in national psychological immaturity) are some of the features heavily censured by the play, together with total condemnation of a vicious censorship narrowly operating in the fields of books and television.

How different, O'Casey implies, from the passionless tones of the Irish catechism and ecclesiastical pastorals is the rich sensuousness of certain passages in the Bible (underplayed in Catholic teaching), such as the *Song of Solomon*:

> As the lily among thorns, so is my love among the daughters . . .
> Stay me with flagons, comfort me with apples; for I languish with love.

No wonder *The Bishop's Bonfire* – with strong denunciations of clerical rule and the mishandling of human lives within the Republic of Ireland – angered both Press and establishment. The fiercely pietistic newspaper, the *Standard*, openly disassociated itself from O'Casey's drama of dissent, regarding the play as sheer Quixotism, as well as morally offensive to the broad stream of Irish Catholics. More enlightened students, however, from University College, Dublin, in public debate, overwhelmingly deplored the attitude of the *Standard* towards the play. Blasphemy was very much in the minds of beholders.

O'Casey's strictures – over a longer period – had also been voiced from within the walls of Ireland's leading Catholic seminary, Maynooth, by an independently minded churchman, Dr Walter McDonald, a professor of theology on the staff of the college for forty years. This big-hearted priest, whom O'Casey held in the highest regard (*Inishfallen, Fare Thee Well* is dedicated to him; likewise, in part, his last full-length play, *The Drums of Father Ned*), had laboured incessantly to endeavour to bring about changes in moral and cultural climates to meet the challenges of modern humanism.

In his *Reminiscences of a Maynooth Professor* (1925) – frequently quoted throughout the playwright's later volumes of autobiography – McDonald states (in his censure of Ireland's theocratic dictatorship):

> We are behind the times in many ways; mainly because our thoughts, from being clad in old-fashioned garments, have become themselves old-fashioned.

McDonald died in 1920 (his reminiscences were published post-humously), alienated and disturbed by the realisation that resistance to all semblance of reform was largely due to the adamantine efforts of intolerant, insensitive clerics and their cruel, short-sighted elders – the Bishops of the Church – whom McDonald, in the end, realised would do anything to withstand any winds of change. McDonald, like O'Casey and Joyce, recognised the national malaise: episcophobia! (Milton, in his day, viewed bishops as 'a sad and doleful succession of illiterate and blind guides'.)

The Bishop's Bonfire, besides being a Quixotic comedy with a jaundiced eye, of contemporary Ireland, is a light-hearted palliative, seeking to bring about a more liberated spirit of universal harmony to those lands – Ireland in particular – where oppressors and imposters tie in a living tether not only the collective endeavours of their peoples but the very vital contributions of their own princes of thought. The play has an exhortative appeal, emblazoned by the splendour of its language, matched only by the silver-sounding rhetoric of Shelley himself. O'Casey's aspirations are at heart Shelley's:

> May every sun that shines on your green island see the annihilation of an abuse, and the birth of an embryon of melioration! Your own hearts – may they become the shrines of purity and freedom, and never may smoke to the Mammon of unrighteousness ascend from the unpolluted altar of their devotion!

As an exordial indication of the promptings of human conscience, *The Bishop's Bonfire* remains more than just another exercise in social corrective; in the context of Shaw's exhilarating words on theatre, it is seen as 'an armoury against despair and dullness, and a temple of the Ascent of Man'.

Adopting Shavian principles, O'Casey camouflages his ideals within the play's comic superstructure, with its opulent reminders of superb music-hall technique and its gallimaufry of characters, who, derivatively, owe their existence as much to the gorged delights of pantomime as to the groundswell of natural material to be found in the soil of the Irish countryside. O'Casey's rogues and vagabonds are more rumbustious than ever: grotesques, in the same mould as Dickens's larger-than-life whimsical creations. They exist – as Eric

Bentley once observed – in 'a dream world of sublime infantility'. O'Casey gives us – in the persons of the Codger and the Prodical – a creative ensemble of clowns straight from the world of mad nonsense, which admirers of Lewis Caroll – as well as audiences from the times of Shakespeare and Burbage to those of Grimaldi, Chaplin, and Laurel and Hardy – have always enjoyed. In the play itself, where comedy and farce have become so interfused, we have one of the characters – the young priest, Father Boheroe – making a reference, at one stage, to 'the punch and judy show of Ballyoonagh' (Act Two).

In the fictitious wonderland of this bogland town, feverish preparations are in full swing for the intended visit of the Right Reverend William Mullarkey, the much-talked-of dignitary who never appears, but whose formal absence sets the stage for prime disasters among the Councillor's work-force, painted in thickest slapstick in the manner of *Purple Dust*. In the first act – and in much of the second – O'Casey gives us a liberal supply of muddleheaded 'chassis', ending with the elderly Codger spilling a whole bag of cement on the new carpet in Reiligan's lounge – the room specially set aside for the duration of the Bishop's stay. The happenings – and hindrances – all take place within the Councillor's home, except in the first act, where the scene is outside the drawing-room window, leading to the garden, and where improvements are being undertaken, including the building of a garden-wall; the time being around Angelus on an autumn evening, and in the remaining acts later during the same evening.

Reiligan is one of the two prominent worthies of the local establishment who dominate the proceedings to such an extent, we are told, that he owns the local dance-hall, public house and shirt-factory, as well as a slice of land showing impotent signs of agricultural decay. From the author's stage-instructions, we learn that he is 'the biggest money-man in the district, a loyal pillar of the clergy, and has great power and influence in the affairs of the state – the local member of the Dail could never climb into a seat without the backing of Councillor Reiligan'. When we reflect that the Celtic derivation of his name originates from 'reilig', a cemetery, we would probably expect him to own the local hearse and maybe add 'funeral director' to his many local functions as well. We discover, early in the play, he has just been appointed a papal Count, which occasions the Codger's ribald jest: 'Ballyoonagh lifts herself up a step nearer to heaven!' The Count's prerogative is to lavish expensive as well as extensive preparations within his own habitat for the Bishop's intended arrival.

The other worthy in the local hierarchy is the Very Reverend Timothy Canon Burren – parish priest of Ballyoonagh – a comic-pathetic figure exercising within his special orbit full plenary powers; his name in Gaelic signifies 'pride'. In the Canon's archetypal world, Ballyoonagh is viewed as a central place of penance and prayer: cultural enlightenment would only serve to distract it from its main spiritual course. The Canon believes, as a matter of principle, in hay-forking his parishioners into realising their opportunity of a hiring-fair in the next world: heaven not only lies about us, in the Canon's eyes; heaven *is* Ballyoonagh. He is at spiritual odds with his young curate, the more enlightened Father Boheroe (whose name in Gaelic means 'Red Road'), described by the dramatist as a 'man of the world as well as man of God', with strong suggestions of the Brown Priest in his make-up, and displaying those sterling qualities which Dr McDonald, and others like him, adopted during O'Casey's earlier lifetime.

The Canon and Reiligan between them succeed in squeezing the spiritual strength from the community. They are Gog and Magog of the little town: representatives of God and Mammon exercising their own unholy alliance. The Count's eager ambitions are abetted by the Canon's, but obstructed, comically, by his wilier, downtrodden domestic workers, who in their glorious incompetency footle their way through the scenario in a riotous misinterpretation of their subservience. One is Dick Carranaun – otherwise known as 'The Prodical' (Ireland is renowned for its rural nicknames), a lanky Protestant mason with a pugnacious air, whose one failing is to lay his hands on a drink (his reformist intentions give an added twist to his wry sense of humour). The other is his cadaverous colleague, Richard Rankin – a fiercely Catholic zealot – who is both dangerously misogynic and puritanical (Keelin in a flaunting display of femininity arouses his opprobrium); the playwright, in his textual description, stresses 'He chooses to pray than to whistle when at work' – his fantaticism being mirrored in a piping, falsetto voice. Both bricklayers are engaged in building a garden-wall and are assisted by a nonchalant factotum rejoicing in the name of Daniel Clooncoohy (his surname, in fact, suggests 'a cuckoo in the meadow') who is a young 'come-day, go-day' type of workman, who walks about in an idyllic dream, believing himself to be in love with Keelin – Reiligan's younger daughter – but on concerted pressure from his employer and the Canon, is obliged to give up notions of marrying her, and, being too weak-willed to counteract authority, abandons Keelin to the anguish of lost love.

An elderly odd-job man, Michael Sleehaun – known, affectionately, as the Codger – is also employed in Reiligan's house and on his land – 'Meadows', the forthright workman declares, 'that haven't felt the rousin' rift of a plough for fifty years'. He is a jaunty, defiant, crisp-tongued octogenarian and commentator shrewd in age – symbol, perhaps, of O'Casey himself, in his riper, mellower years – who adds to the fun and fantasticalities with his capricious songs and vagabondish wit. In the eyes of the Canon he is seen as an idle scamp, but to most onlookers – including audiences in sympathy with the playright's vision – he is characterised as a lovable vagabond. His half-astringent asides complement the subtler pronouncements of Father Boheroe, whose main concern is sanctioning the epicurean path of progress for young lovers and revolutionaries alike.

Of the Councillor's daughters, the younger, prettier Keelin, alone, is saddled with fatigues and the responsibilities of household routine; as relief from which she delights in flaunting her sexual attractiveness to those around her – like Avril in *Purple Dust*, or Julia in *The Star Turns Red*. She is desperately in love with her father's workman, Daniel Clooncoohy and wishes to elope with him but later agonisingly realises that ineradicable forces – those of her father and the Canon – are firmly against the association. Her defiance is crushed in stultifying circumstances that prevail in such a theocentric atmosphere. (Clooncoohy turns out to be a moral coward who surrenders to the dictates of his employer and the Canon; Father Boheroe gives advice and encouragement but can do nothing in the existing lacuna of a repressive situation).

Her elder sister, Foorawn (the Gaelic 'fuar' suggests an unnatural frigidity), has stifled her love for her former lover, Manus Moanroe, who has turned out to be an ex-seminarian or 'spoiled priest'. She has taken a perpetual vow of celibacy, with the strong and bitter disapproval of her ex-lover – now her father's foreman – though with the absolute blessings of both her father and the Canon. A nun, therefore, in everything but name, she has within her house her own prie-dieu, or praying-desk, and her own special saint – St Casabianca – to intercede with, in prayer. She prays while her younger sister 'slaves' in the kitchen. (The Biblical Martha-Mary situation, as applied to modern, domestic, rural Ireland, is given a wry twist.) Professor Bernard Benstock, in his shrewd analysis of O'Casey's characterisation as a whole, has aptly commented that 'Foorawn's doom is as preordained as was Jannice's, her cold heart as fatal as the young whore's ailing heart'.

The 'wounded' hero in the drama is portrayed by Manus Moanroe, a renounced Catholic and steward to Reiligan, who is paid a mere pittance for his workmanship. He carries bitterness around with him like an oversize chip on his shoulder and in the same downcast spirit of despondency as Harry Heegan in *The Silver Tassie*. His bitterness stems both from the lost love of Foorawn – entrenched in her life-long vow – and an awareness of the 'dead' world around him. Despair finally ovecomes him and he becomes a nursling of grief, broken in spirit, like the maimed hero of *The Silver Tassie*. Although of sturdier material than Daniel Clooncoohy – who succumbs readily to outside pressures – he lacks the lesser man's gaiety of outlook which is more in accord with the playwright's approved affirmation of life, voiced by Daniel, in the second act:

What's it matter whether a man's born under turrets or under a thatch? It's the man with the gay heart that rides the waters an' the winds; who shakes life be the hand when life looks fair, an' shakes her be the shoulder when she shows a frown.

Clooncoohy's words are bigger than his resolve, blighted by a native hue of irresolution which is reluctant to upset the *status quo* (a younger version of Tom Nimmo in *The Harvest Festival*).

Two remaining characters of lesser importance, among the dozen cornucopian ones appearing in the play, make their impact in the second act (for the sake of additional comic relief). The Councillor's son – Lieutenant Michael Reiligan – in the dark-green uniform of the Irish Army, rushes in during the preparations, looking for his 'oul' fella'. The elder Reiligan, he makes clear, is as tight-fisted in his allowance to his son as he is in rewarding Manus for his practical stewardship; but the son, as officer in charge of a Guard of Honour to meet the Bishop, means to keep up his standing with his fellow-officers by adopting the same life-style as practised by his socially ambitious father. He finds a ready sympathiser in the person of Daniel, whose artless admiration for the younger Reiligan's 'stattus' fails to bamboozle his wiser and wilier colleague, the Codger.

The other short-lived character of comical persuasion is the zanily-sketched Railway Porter – whom the Codger refers to as

Hughie Higgins – whose idiosyncratic Irishness is in the same vein as his namesake, the Porter (of a general store), in *Cock-a-Doŏdle Dandy*. He arrives outside Reiligan's house – on his way from the station – out of breath and in a perturbed state. He is supposed to have brought with him the statue of the Bishop's special saint – St Tremolo, – the saint-with-a-horn – but he arrives empty-handed since he alleges the statue kept on blasting his horn at him, reminding him of his own past misdeeds and transgressions: 'knew I was a toss-up for heaven or hell; head or a harp. So he kept blowin'; oh, me poor ears – a piercin' blast!' (Consequently, he left the statue at the 'Polis' Station, though Rankin fetches it later.) Although his stage appearance is brief, his strange utterances are as astute, in their way, as those of the golden-voiced dustman of *Pygmalion*, Doolittle, when talking to Professor Henry Higgins. In his rare, captive moments – and with his capricious manner – he proves himself a fine soliloquiser:

> Them they call saints is right enough on a pedestal, half-hidden in a church frustrated with its own dimness; but out in the light, they're dazzlin', an' there's danger in the dimension of their shinin'. Dimpled dangers the lot of them. (*With conviction*) No, no; I'd rather look for heaven in a cracked lookin'-glass at home.

He enquires of Reiligan whether the statue of this new saint, whom the Porter quaintly refers to as 'this bookaneeno boyo', is going to remain a permanent fixture in Ballyoonagh; he would, he says, like to be forewarned. (Earlier on, the Codger had quipped: 'The one thing increasin' in Ireland, the population of stone an' wooden saints'.)

Whimsically, the curious Porter utters a large chunk of O'Casey philosophy, when he pronounces:

> They're queer, these holy men an' holy women. Never have a minute's peace if you let them get you thinkin'. Give one of them ones a chance to get a grip on you, an' he'll have you worryin' God for help to do what you should be damn well able to do yourself without botherin' God at all.

His strange talk prompts Reiligan to declare: 'It's drink. He's not himself. He's coloured his mind with drink, and it's separatin' into pictures like ones in a stained-glass winda. It's drink'. Ignoring the imputation, the Porter carries on with his individualistic pro-nouncements, waving his arms about in an excited manner: 'What are we doin' but weavin' a way through life, content with an odd prayer to propel us towards where none of us wants to go! How'r we to know if we're comin' up upstream, or goin' down downstream?' (The philosophy is reminiscent of the workmen in *Purple Dust*.)

O'Casey, who had worked as labourer in Dublin, for the Great Northern Railway, Ireland, at the beginning of the century – among the many manual jobs he held before turning professional playwright – amusingly told a correspondent, in 1955: 'I'm sure you never heard a Railway Porter talk as the one did in *The Bonfire* – though I know one, a Louis Blad of Dublin, who could talk, and knew Shakespeare and Shelley quite well; and who was an eloquent blatherer when he had drink taken'.

The theme of exile runs all the way through the play, just as it does, though less covertly, in *Cook-a-Doodle Dandy*. The Codger, at the beginning of the first act, confides in the young curate, Father Boheroe: 'I'm the sole Sleehawn left standin' here in Ballyoonagh. Wife dead (rest her soul), two daughters an' three sons away, away in America, leavin' me the one lone, mohican Sleehawn left standin' in Ballyoonagh. Fly away, Peter, fly away, Paul; fly away, Susan, fly away all – a fly-away country, this of ours, Father; this country of ours'. This is exemplified by the dedication and quotation – in Irish – on the title-page.

The play is dedicated to the playwright's mother and to his daughter, Shivaun: 'To Susan Gone and Susan Here'. The Gaelic quotation:

> *Cad dbeanfamaoid feasta gan adbmad,*
> *Ata deire na g-coillte ar lar*

is explained by the dramatist in a letter of 24 March 1955 to Thomas Mark, of Macmillan and Company (O'Casey's publishers) as follows:

> The Irish motto is the first two lines of a famous and rather lovely, Irish lament; one for the loss of chieftains fled away from Ireland to France and Spain; the beginning of the flight of the "Wild Geese". The best English I can think of is –
> "What shall we do for timber
> Now that the last tree in the forest is down?"

Published in both Britain and America in 1955, only a few months after the Dublin *première* (in Britain with the seal of a Book Society recommendation), the play made a fresh impact, scarcely before the smoke of controversy had blown away from the Irish capital itself (summed up, colourfully, in the playwright's own article, 'Bonfire Under a Black Sun', included in *The Green Crow*).

O'Casey's drama-bonfire, in the first two acts, is mostly – to echo the phrase of one of the masons, in the beginning – 'a tangle of talk'. The two bricklayers squabble amongst themselves like a couple of 'paycockian' pantaloons, the Prodical reiterating, furiously:

> Me soul's me own particular compendium. Me soul's me own spiritual property, complete an' entire, verbatim in all its concernment.

> (Act One)

Malapropisms, misunderstandings and pusillanimous prognostications abound. When the two bricklayers are joined by Clooncoohy and the Codger, the sparring becomes a convivial bout of conversational wrestling. Factotums of 'factuality' and *'primae facie'* examples of 'a perspective contingency' are wantonly flung about in a cascade of verbal nonsense and orgiastic splendour. It is a pantomime-world where the characters roar their opinions in gargantuan self-abuse:

> DANIEL: Don't be actin' the eejut, Codger!
> CODGER (*angrily*): Who's actin' the eejut?
> DANIEL (*as angrily*): You are, the way you're talkin'!
> CODGER (*close up to him*): Eejut yourself!
> DANIEL (*placing a hand to* CODGER'S *chest, and shoving him backwards*): Aw, go away!
> CODGER (*rushing back, putting a hand to* DANIEL'S *chest, and shoving him backwards*): You go away!
> DANIEL (*swiftly returning, and giving the Codger a fiercer shove backwards*): You go away!
> PRODICAL (*remonstrating*): Gentlemen, easy! Can't yous see yous are turnin' your own opinions into *ipso factos*?

> (Act Two)

Talk itself becomes such a prepossessive potency – and inactivity a contagious notion of hilarity and farce – that work, in its familiar, realistic sense is banished from the setting. And, from such scenes of prestidigitation, 'chassis' rules supreme.

Man – through the glorious ineptitude of O'Casey's characters – is a contextual illustration of lampoonry, confirming Pope's satirical judgement: the glory, jest and riddle of the world! The furious Reiligan, along with promptings from the pompous, umbrella-stick proddings of the Canon, chivies his dream-sullied workmen into fits of bemused awareness of extrinsic reality, instilling a mutative world of fear and forced achievement, where, in the cynical words of Manus Moanroe,

> We have to keep building our temples higher and higher till the shouting of heavenly pride encases and hides the growling-grumble of men.

Whenever he sees bricks left lying around his garden, which is in a glorious state of unfinished chaos, or pots of paint abandoned on his mahogany table in the lounge, and cement on his carpet, the demented Councillor is driven to shouting: 'Good God, is this the way you're helpin' the work to welcome the Bishop?' His anger explodes into a comical adjuration which exposes itself, finally, in the absurdity:

> From this out, there's to be no talkin'; and if anyone does talk, everybody is to listen to nobody.

While the workers dream and fly their tenebrous course, God's rural representatives of 'Grandmother Church' (to quote Joyce's all-embracing term from his poem 'The Holy Office') make friends with 'Mammon's countless servitors' (the Joycean metaphor is apt), and such union tightens its control over 'Stepmother Erin' that most of her 'daughtersons', Joyce reminds us, find they need the religious balm and spiritual unguent of prayer and indulgences. Prayer-safe in their own little spiritual countrysides, few Irelanders outside what O'Casey, in *Inishfallen, Fare Thee Well*, terms 'a prelatian-led crowd of ding-dong dedero devotees' would dare to speak out against pronouncements of their bishops for fear of excommunication. In extremes of heterodoxy, those who challenge clerical authority – is the implication of the play – are driven to swift exile, where, in the Joycean phrase, they can flash their antlers 'unafraid, unfellowed . . . . and alone' and remain as 'indifferent as the herring-bone'.

The play's masculine hero – spiritually maimed and psychologically alienated – is Manus Moanroe, who, like Drishogue O'Morrigun in *Oak Leaves and Lavender*, we are told, had left his country to fight in the Royal Air Force during the Second World War; a petulant soul who spurns the soul-sour atmosphere of clerical domination. He, too, like most eventual exiles, becomes self-doomed, friendless and alone. He is particularly bitter towards the Canon and Church for robbing him of the woman he loves:

> Oh, Foorawn, Foorawn, time shall toss wrinkles on to your sweet face, shall wither your breasts, shall bring your knees to a bending; but no bonny breeze of life shall ever blow your skirt aside.
>
> (Act One)

By the end of the play, his hatred is entrenched and manifests itself in self-expressed objurgation:

> When I think of the Bishop who's coming, and look at the Monsignor who's here, I'm glad I escaped from the honour and glory of the priesthood!
>
> (Act Three)

In the intellectuality of his bitter negation there is something arid and cynical about his isolation from the generosity of his fellows; he fails to win either their sympathy or respect. Yet he is a true disciple of Joyce; a true exile-in-the-making, as exemplified in Joyce's poem, 'The Holy Office':

> And though they spurn me from their door
> My soul shall spurn them evermore.

In a bleak encounter, towards the end of the first act, Manus is reminded by Foorawn that she is 'now under the pure white moon of Heaven . . . I am no longer a lure to your seeking eyes'. He counters that he is still 'a man with the same soul, the same mind, the same defiance of shabby life, and the same outlasting and consuming love' for her, as ever. The humane Father Boheroe endeavours to give him moral comfort, but is unable to console him, any more than the crippled, wheel-chaired priest, in Graham Greene's play, *The Living Room* (1953), is able to console the distraught Rose, bent on her suicidal path of despair. In a moving passage in O'Casey's play, we witness similar anguish and heartbreak:

> FATHER BOHEROE (*from near the window – softly*): Be a man, Manus. She is too deep now in the vainglory of her chastity to come to you.
>
> MANUS (*impatiently*): Oh, you! You who stifle and tangle people within a laocoon of rosary beads!
>
> FATHER BOHEROE: I wish, not to tangle them with rosary beads, Manus, but to join them with life . . . Come, let yourself fall in love with life, and be another man.
>
> MANUS (*sarcastically*): At peace with all things.
>
> FATHER BOHEROE: At war with most things.
>
> MANUS: You are a kind, good man, Father. [*He pauses.*] Would you do me a great favour?
>
> FATHER BOHEROE (*eagerly*): Of course I would. You've but to tell me what it is, Manus.
>
> MANUS (*tonelessly*): Just leave me alone.

O'Casey's priest is more mettlesome than Greene's, who says: 'My senses don't feel it' – about his faith – 'they feel nothing but revolt, uncertainty, despair – but I know it at the back of my mind'. Father Boheroe, on the other hand, is a priest in a similar individual mould, but has greater inner strength and simplicity and mirrors his creator's distinctive philosophy: 'All places are sacred . . . the church we pray in, the homes sheltering us, the shops where we get the things we need to go on living, the halls we dance in; yea, the very place we walk on is holy ground . . . Too much formal prayer sometimes makes a soul conceited; and merriment may be a way of worship!' To Keelin, he counsels: 'a man in a woman's arms may indeed be close to God'.

The Codger and Father Boheroe between them are spokesmen of O'Casey's fervent, simplistic belief. Says the Codger: 'Man has to set his face to face things, eh, Father? God's more than a mere melodeon-player. Yis, man has more to do than just sing for his supper'. Father Boheroe re-echoes this when he exclaims: 'God is unhappy when we don't do what we can with what He gives us'.

The elderly Codger, besides being a vortex of fun and gaiety, is a fount of soulspun wisdom. He echoes his creator's convictions when he tells his colleagues – including the Protestant bricklayer, the Prodical – who seems to be rejoicing at the Bishop's coming:

> What are the things that God gives to one man to the things God gives to all? What's the gold on a bishop's mitre to the gold on the gorse? The sheen of his satin shoon to the feel of a petal on the wildest rose? What's a bishop's purple to the purple in the silky plume of the speary thistle?

And, when the Prodical counters that the Bishop's visit will bring a few golden days to the locality, the wise octogenarian retorts: 'Ay, golden days of penance an' prayer . . . but not for me. Me golden days is over'. And he chants gaily, as well as a little gloomily, a lilt of Irish expectancy, stifled in the bud-ray of counter-revolution and repression:

> Ah, them were th' golden days with an arm round a waist,
> When everything shone so shy an' gay;
> When a man had heart to toss the girls as well as time to toss th' hay –
> Oh, them were th' days when life had something fine to say!

Its conceptual origins stem from Blake, as we recall from several of the poems in *Songs of Experience*. For instance, the poignant conceits expressed in 'The Sick Rose', whose crimson petals have been destroyed by the invisible worm; or the wilting radiance of the poet's 'Sunflower', after the sun has ceased to shine (an influential factor in the setting of *Cock-a-Doodle Dandy*); or, again, in *Gnomic Verses*, wherein Blake declares:

> Abstinence sows sand all over
> The ruddy limbs and flaming hair,
> But Desire gratified
> Plants fruits of life and beauty there.

The mood of the play reflects Blake's contraries – expressed in the words of the Codger as 'merrily mournful': the 'humorous sadness' we also find in Shakespeare (referred to in *As You Like It*). The ending of the final act is almost identical with that of the first: a sad, sonorous sigh, in song, as the two lovable clowns – the Codger and

Prodical – together softly intone, 'My Bonnie Lies Over the Ocean' – with its inborn echoes of exile and never-to-be-forgotten memories of previous happinesses which can neither be expunged nor recaptured on homeland soil again. An inextricable dream-curse come true, with years of exodus ahead; in Aytoun's grief-stricken words from 'The Island of the Scots':

> The deep, unutterable woe
> Which none save exiles feel

though Tennyson (whom O'Casey admires) experiences it, too, 'from the depth of some divine despair',

> In looking on the happy Autumn-fields,
> And thinking of the days that are no more.

Slapstick and farce, within the musty precincts of Councillor Reiligan's lounge – despite new appearances and renovations – form a comic interlude throughout most of the second act. There is an hilarious episode in which Reiligan's officer-son – home on leave – outlines his crazy, hypothetical scheme to resist what he considers to be an imminent danger – a Russian invasion of Ireland. By having jeeps and jeep-drivers with walky-talkies posted all over the country, he is convinced that Irish military strength can repel threats of any potential invader. (A notable irony, since arguments over the total destruction of the world by the use of atomic weapons waxed furious in Britain in the mid-fifties, leading to the Campaign for Nuclear Disarmament in the sixties and revived, again in the eighties.) Lieutenant Reiligan's crack-brained scheme of jeeps dashing about Irish roadways generates a glorious bout of histrionics, involving Daniel, the Codger and Prodical, all confounding and confuting each other, in a series of typically 'unconfutable arguments', in O'Casey's broadest farcical manner: the whole episode being pure codology and word-play from start to finish.

Blarney and poetry are suffused: the workmen's tongues are royally touched, and the Codger's songs add merriment to the scene.

In striking contrast is the behaviour of Foorawn, who being in love with religion and obeying unquestionably the narrower edicts of the Canon, is intent not only in suppressing her own sensual feelings but those of all around her, as penitential preparation for the Bishop's visit – with all its attendant civic welcoming ceremonies and its bannered bonfire celebrations to destroy all dangerous and heretical literature. Foorawn's narrow religiosity is drawn in exact contradistinction to Shaw's Saint Joan, whose religious sense, although simplistic, is broader, embracing both body and spirit and believing in the holiness of the imagination and inviolability of the senses. Joan's cry of recrimination when sentence has been passed on her by her misguided, ecclesiastical judges – to spend the remainder of her days in perpetual imprisonment – brings forth avowals of the sacredness of the natural world as well as the eternal: 'to shut me from the light of the sky and the sight of the fields and flowers . . . and keep from me everything that brings me back to the love of God when your wickedness and foolishness tempt me to hate Him' has its parallels, as well, in *The Bishop's Bonfire*.

The Codger – and later Father Boheroe – uphold such strong Shavian ideals and re-echo the fervent, sentient feelings of Joan. Foorawn, in the narrow prison of her puritanism, tells the Codger that Ballyoonagh will have a new spiritual lease of life with the Bishop's visitation and the Codger must amend his personal habits: renounce smoking and drinking and 'senseless singin'', as well. At which, the Codger humbly retorts: 'I don't know how I'm goin' to give up the singin'; I've been singin' all me life. After all, Miss, the birds sing, the angels sing, an' I don't see why the poor oul' Codger shouldn't sing too' (Peer Gynt's belief, as well, that 'Singing is the art of being *us*'). Foorawan's reply is coldly dismissive: 'You're neither bird nor angel, Codger, but only a poor old man on his way to th' tomb . . . we're all steppin' our way to th' tomb'. But Codger's counter-reply is equally derisive: '. . . goose-steppin' it, right enough, Miss'.

Later, when Father Boheroe has an angry exchange with Canon Burren, he exclaims: 'God help us, Monsignor, for by fear, we have almost lost our love for our neighbour; even our worship is beginning to have the look of the fool's cap and the sound of the jester's bells' (Act Two). And, in the third act, the young priest, when offering advice to Foorawn in the difficulties of her subsumed state, offers a firm naturalistic stand, based on Shavian belief:

Ah, Foorawn, it is easy to turn one's back on things, but it is better and braver to face them. I shall never turn my back on a beautiful world, nor on the beautiful flesh of humanity, asparkle with vigour, intelligence, and health; and as for the devil, what we often declare to be the devil is but truth who has at last mustered the courage to speak it.

Courage is the mainsail of Father Boheroe's actions. In his vital, full-blooded grasp of human relations he offers a consoling strength, but is vitiated because of the superior power of the Canon and the more influential hold of the Church hierarchy throughout the land. The Canon's attitude is dominant and brooks no interference. He reprimands Father Boheroe with a withering remonstrance:

> You're clever, Father – and sincere, I hope – but your cleverness seems only to make persons more unhappy than they were. I'm afraid I cannot commend the way you try to lead my poor people towards illusions. Can't you understand that their dim eyes are able only for a little light? Damn it, man, can't you see Clooncoohy can never be other than he is? You're very popular with our people, but remember that the love they may have for you doesn't come near the fear they have for Reiligan [*he pauses*] or the reverence they must show for their Parish Priest.

As his own limitations are brought home to him, Father Boheroe recognises that his hands will always be tied. Keelin breaks down in front of him at the end of Act Two and bemoans her forsaken plight, after telling him that Daniel lacked the moral courage to continue with their relationship in the face of such unrelenting opposition. Like Dr McDonald before him, Father Boheroe recognises that the Cold Wind of Repression (shown in the symbolical ending to the second act) will forever outweigh any individualistic attempts at forward-looking change.

Twenty-five years after the play was written and first performed, Irish novelist, Brian Moore – living in self-imposed exile in California – could declare, in the course of a *Radio Times* article prior to a BBC televised interview:

> I left Ireland in 1942 because I felt that nothing would ever change. Now I come back [each year] precisely because nothing has changed.

So, the Ireland of 1980 – which happens, also, to have been the centenary of O'Casey's birth – remains, basically, the same as the Ireland of sixty years ago, in 1920 – the year of McDonald's death.

Irish Catholicism, as Sean O'Faolain was keen to point out in *The Times Literary Supplement* (he reiterated the charge, characteristically, in his eightieth year – also in 1980), is a wholly indigenous brand of Christianity, in no way resembling its counterpart abroad or even in Europe. (The puritanical streak alone should be sufficient proof, he alleges.) Distinctive hallmarks of Irish Catholicism, he maintains, are an accompanying 'egregiousness' and 'patriotic memories that reinforce it'. According to Dr O'Faolain, the Irish love of sport, good company, good cheer, boundless talk and a sense of humour are only one side of the same coin: 'an escape from the grimly mysterious, the mystical, the ominous, the sad'. *The Bishop's Bonfire* certainly reflects such a dichotomy in the Irish nature: the jovial, hunting, drinking and singing Irish on the one hand, and the praying and breast-beating Irish on the other.

The Christian who decries humanism is wrong is the play's conclusion. Religion and humanism are not antithetical: they are complementary. 'Society', says Shaw, in *Everybody's Political What's What?*, 'cannot be held together without religion'. But by religion, he means, what he terms, 'anthropomorphic Deism':

> Man must not look to God to do his work for him. He must regard himself as the fallible servant of a fallible God, acting for God and thinking for God, because God, being unable to effect His purposes without hands or brains, has made us evolve our hands and brains to act and think for Him: in short, we are not in the hands of God, but God is in our hands.

This is the whole philosophy implicit in *The Bishop's Bonfire*, too.

Father Boheroe and the Codger are persuasive exponents of Shaw's humanitarian creed. Indeed, the sanctity-of-life principle is taken even further by O'Casey, who has his young priest proclaim, when answering the narrower charge levelled against him by Foorawn that he has offered no religious encouragement to the Protestant Prodical knocking at the threshold of Faith in the Catholic Church:

> He serves God as a mason better than I do in my priesthood, or you in your chastity.

By helping to build hospitals, homes and churches, the Prodical (says O'Casey's priest) has demonstrated in more pragmatic way his essentially humanitarian needs: a practical combination, as far as O'Casey is concerned, of true Communistic principles and Marxist ideals based on Christian tenets:

> Every man who puts his best effort into his life and work, be he a doctor or a bricklayer [O'Casey once remarked, in an interview], is a Communist whether he knows it or not, for he's helping to improve the common good, making the world a better place for himself and his family and his country, and all the countries of the world.

In *The Bishop's Bonfire*, the playwright stresses that love – in the broadest meaning of the word – is the real touchstone and panacea essential to humanity; only within its broad bounds shall we find basic freedoms and universal happiness.

While, in the final act, the empty celebrations of the Bishop's Bonfire exert their meaningless hold, the play's chief characters are absent from its profitless celebrations. Father Boheroe's path lies, he remarks, in an opposite direction, 'where, though there be no cedars, at least, I shall walk under the stars'. The Codger and Prodical go off drinking, 'trying to get a glimpse' (in the priest's earlier words) 'of heaven through the wrong window'; thereby catching a glimpse of their own preferred paradise in a *moment musical* of their own.

The hovering clouds of black comedy catch up with Manus and Foorawn, who enact between them a macabre scene sketched in bleakest melodrama, whereby Moanroe – as her former lover – exacts his toll of fullest revenge on the Church he despises and its ally, his employer, by robbing Reiligan's bureau, over which, in the lounge, the votive light is burning before the statue of St Casabianca (Foorawn's favoured saint) and (hollowest of ironies) takes the gun left on top by Lieutenant Reiligan during his homecoming. Stealing the money set aside for ecclesiastical pontifications, he notices the abandoned gun, which he slyly slips into his pocket, commenting sourly: 'Saint Casabianca, you're a bad boy: over the money and beside the gun. The lack of a gun and the loss of the money will make you a little more like a saint'.

He is caught in the act by Foorawn, who abuses him, calling him a 'gaspin' throw-away from the Church eternal!' In retaliation, by way of self-vindication, he voices a stream of fraudulent practices carried out in the name of piety and religion that would do justice to

Joyce. A furious altercation ensues, with Foorawn's hurling the charge of 'sacrilege' in his face, and Manus flinging back the wounding retort: 'you mournful, empty shell of womanhood!' Tempers increase, and, as she lifts the telephone, threatening him not only with police intervention but total ruin throughout district and countryside, in his fury he shoots her. Dropping the telephone, she staggers to a chair by the table. Momentarily stunned, she utters a wild, ambivalent cry of anguish: as different in its wild, melodramatic despair as the more naturalistic reaction of Bessie Burgess (when shot in error by one of the British snipers, in the ending of *The Plough and the Stars*). In melodramatic outburst, Foorawn cries out: 'You ruffian! Oh, Manus, darling, I think I'm dying'.

Spotting pen and paper lying on the table, she calls hastily to Manus to hand her the gun. Staring at her in dazed fashion and slumping forward over the table, he challenges: 'Go on, shoot me, before the strength of hate leaks away from your weakening white arm'. Then, scribbling a suicide-note to exonerate Manus, she reaffirms her deeply-felt lost love, and dies. In stifled anguish (we are reminded of Donal Davoren), he sobs: 'Oh, my poor Foorawn! My sombre musk rose; my withered musk rose now!'

Switching out the light, revealing the red glare in the darkness of the sky of the Bishop's Bonfire (to the sounds of distant cheering and shouting), he hides behind the curtained window leading to the garden where the Codger and Prodical are lingering, lilting, in semi-drunken fashion, their merrily-mournful ditties, as they chorus between them softly and significantly, 'My Bonny's Gone Over the Ocean' in the final curtain-fall of a scene of extraordinary, melancholic melodrama, in the finely balanced, tragicomic, moving O'Casey-style.

'The whole play's symbolical', retorted O'Casey, when challenged to defend the killing of Foorawn:

> The critics say that I spoil the last act with melodrama. But the shooting's symbolical. If that hadn't been done, if it had ended with Keelin's man going away, that would have meant death just the same, a life of frustration and despair . . . I don't see why there shouldn't be a little bit of melodrama. It's a play, you see, the theatre's make-believe.

The blending of farce and tragedy – as well as comedy and poetry – call for directorial dexterity. In *The Bishop's Bonfire*, as in most of the later plays, a phantasy interpretation is necessary, though the play is less fantastical – more a blend of realism with fantasy – than its uproarious predecessor, *Cock-a-Doodle Dandy*, offering acting opportunities which can be eagerly grasped by an enterprising company. Instead of a strong story line shaping the action, changes in characterisation tend to shape the drama, as in the case of *The Silver Tassie*.

Frank Dunlop, who directed the first London performance in 1961, has described, in *Plays and Players*, some of the problems facing a director:

> The sort of construction adopted here puts a great deal of strain on the actors, who must shape the drama as well as just play the parts. An actor, too, will find that O'Casey often brings him on to achieve a different atmosphere. He does not use a change of situation to bring about a change in pace and atmosphere, but instead brings a different character to achieve this.

Reiligan, for instance, being a sort of shouting character, is frequently utilised to generate excitement in the comedy.

The Bishop's Bonfire is not an easy play to produce: unexpected both in theme and manner. O'Casey's drama is full of mood and challenge: diaphanous, yet passionate with conviction. One enthusiastic commentator, apparently versed in quick-change scene-transformation, has noted that in the first act alone there as many as 'fifteen or sixteen short scenes verging into each other'; but the structure is not nearly as complicated as this comment would have us believe. At the other end of the scale, in extremes of criticism and commentary, lies the assertion that the action of the play consists simply of a revolver-shot in the third act! In the realm of fancy, diaphanousness is the play's singular charm. The poetry and psychological insight into moral anguish of several of the characters, giving rise to high tensions in crisis-moments, requires uncompromising simplicity and conviction in the acting. The characters of Keelin and Foorawn, together with Manus and Father Boheroe, find themselves in a terrible dilemma: a dilemma the playwright exploits to its utmost limits. Cast and director, although concerning themselves, naturally, with the harrowing consequences of Catholic belief which O'Casey poses, should concentrate foremost on the inner understandings of the characters themselves as individuals within the framework of the play; and then absorb the style and mood in which it is written.

Broad foundations have much in common with popular types of entertainment, such as *commedia dell' arte*, music-hall and melodrama (Boucicault's influence, here). Repression and pietism are successfully ridiculed within the creation of O'Casey's world of mad merriment, in the same zany tradition as *Juno and the Paycock*, *The Plough and the Stars* and *Purple Dust*, giving rise to an inspired gallery of glorious clowns (Shakespeare's influence, recognisably). Subsidiary characters are important, too; as in Shakespeare's dramas. (There is more than a striking resemblance to the Porter in *Macbeth* – with his eloquent muttering and cursing – in O'Casey's character of the same name.)

Father Boheroe, the sympathetic priest – full of human understanding – requires an actor of subtle strength and integrity. The priest is a man of worldly wisdom, in his thirties, of medium height and build: his face, the playwright indicates, is ruggedly cheerful and thoughtful; his eyes bright and searching and capable of a roguish twinkle when encountering acts of human foolishness. His clerical garb is worn; he is hatless and has dark and bushy hair. (Undoubtedly, he is a younger version of Shaw's Peter Keegan.)

The Codger is tall and wiry for his eighty-four years. In the playwright's description, he 'carries his age about him in a jaunty and defiant way'. He has thick white hair, moustache and beard, and his dark eyes are alert and sparkling. He wears a gay, cotton checked shirt and old black trousers, belted without a waistcoat.

Manus Moanroe, 'warped by a sad and sullen look', is a tall figure in his thirties, well-built but slovenly looking, his old air-force trousers frayed and his cotton shirt soiled. He is a restless, disenchanted rebel, though his pragmatic talents endear him to Reiligan if not to the Canon.

Foorawn, tall and austere-looking, though handsome withal, is twenty-seven, dressed in a black tailor-made suit, which, to quote O'Casey, 'is meant to be solemn and sober, but which plainly hints at the slim, trim figure beneath it'. Her sister, Keelin, is a pretty, auburn-haired, vivacious lass of twenty-five, dressed in a short, dark-green skirt, nylon stockings and white blouse, partly covered by an apron.

Daniel Clooncoohy is twenty-five and good-looking. His face, we learn, is 'open and innocent, though sometimes shadowed with a furtive look; neither sure of himself nor sure of his future'. He wears grey flannels. Of his other fellow-workers, the Prodical is long and lanky and humorously pugnacious-looking. (We are not told his age.) He evidently squanders much of his time in drinking, and, in spite of resolute attempts to give it up, never entirely succeeds. Rankin, his fellow-mason, who is forty, is also thin and cadaverous, his face 'obsessed with a sense of ever-present sin, and his nostrils frequently sniff the fogs of hell' (the playwright's fanciful description, in his stage-directions, is a pointer to his character). Rankin is bald; the Prodical has thick, bushy iron-grey hair; both wear faded bowlers and thick heavy boots, stained with mortar.

Councillor Reiligan is short, stocky and has a sturdy paunch. He is between fifty and sixty. His striped trousers and frocked coat give him a baggy appearance and he pompously carries in his hand a silk tall-hat – recurrent symbol of satire. Canon Burren is also short and plump; he trots when he walks. The Lieutenant is a young officer decked out in full marching order with a dark-green uniform. The whimsical Railway Porter is middle-aged, dressed in corduroys and wears a peaked cap. He has whiskers under his chin, a wide mouth, and spectacles protruding from weak eyes. His eyes twitch open and shut many times in conversation, instilling added curiosity into a curiously-phrased manner of speaking.

The play's world *première* in Dublin on 28 February 1955, at the Gaiety Theatre, was produced by Cyril Cusack and directed by Tyrone Guthrie. It played to overwhelming houses in its five-week stormy run. Irish critics, for the most part, denounced the play and many Catholic clerics joined in the condemnation, and there was a raging controversy in the Dublin papers and other Irish papers, to which the playwright later responded with a searing reply among the trenchant pieces contained in *The Green Crow*. Cusack himself played Codger Sleehaun, his wife, Maureen, played Keelin and Sheila Brennan played Foorawn. Manus was played by Denis Brennan and Father Boheroe by Patrick Layde. Others in the cast included Eddie Byrne, Seamus Kavanagh and Tony Quinn. Cusack described the playwright as 'a writer of deep religious feeling even if he happens to be anti-clerical'. Some English critics thought the play the author's best since *The Silver Tassie*.

London audiences had to wait until 1961, when Bernard Miles made his presentation at the Mermaid Theatre, directed by Frank Dunlop. Among the cast, Celia Salkeld played Foorawn, Annette Crosbie, Keelin and Davy Kaye, the Codger. Although some critics objected to what they termed 'preposterous melodrama', the playwright, in his mid-seventies, was judged as 'unquenchable as ever'. A successful French production was done at the Comédie de L'Est in 1965, directed by P. Lefevre, and an even more acclaimed version was put on in West Berlin's Schlosspark-Theater, directed by Wilfried Minks (later transferring to the wider, more popular Schiller-Theater). The play has also been presented on Soviet television and translations have appeared in French, German, Italian and Russian.

20 *The Drums of Father Ned* (1960): a Prefigurative Comedy

Sean O'Casey's last full-length play is a gay-spirited, triumphal comedy, sub-titled 'A Mickrocosm of Ireland'. The Sheridanesque motto preceding the printed text indicates that it is 'an idle, laughing play' about follies and failings 'encumbering Ireland's way', whose hallmark is to ensure

> That mobled minds may all new courage grow,
> And miser'd hearts be merry.

Its dominant mood, says Dr Robert Hogan, who staged the world *première* in America, 'is as gay as *The Bishop's Bonfire*'s was sad'. (The comment appears in *After the Irish Renaissance*, 1967.) Mixing realism and symbolism, says Trewin in a review, it is a play that 'whirls across the stage in sound and colour'. This inspired extravaganza is both a romp and a riposte. 'O'Casey's prepossession with youthful life-joy', says Professor Wilson Knight in *The Christian Renaissance*, unites 'two positive rival powers in our Western culture: Christ and Eros', prefiguring, in relation to Ireland – in a prophetic ending – the fusion of North and South and of Catholic and Protestant rites and ideals.

The play is as topical now as its early precursor, *The Shadow of a Gunman*. In the shadow of present-day terrorism and late twentieth-century violence, the play is as prognostic as any political solution or panacea. London managements would do well to cast a closer look at its phenomenalistic dramatic possibilities, its compassionate outlook and exuberant, rip-roaring fun, combining in billowing synthesis, all the colour, music, poetry, laughter, violence and tenderness, farce and satire, associated with the broader spectrum of theatre.

In this play of unquenchable spirit, O'Casey does not have to plead for tolerance and unity among his countrymen. They exist, he says, in embryo, in the hearts of those of the newer generations in Ulster and Eire. The young people in his play turn their backs on the violence and self-immolation of the past, and with unsimulated smiles shrug off the bigotries of priests and Orangemen and laugh them out of court, refusing to allow themselves to be labelled children of wrath, in place of children of God. 'Lasses an' lads', says one of them, Michael, at the end of the play, 'it's time to go, for more life, more laughter: a sturdier spirit and a stronger heart. Father Ned is on the march!' The descendants of the Children of Lir have now become, unashamedly and defiantly, the apostles and apprentices of tomorrow.

With a good deal of knockabout, both in words and action, O'Casey's high-spirited comedy shows how a little Irish town, named Doonavale, chooses to celebrate the national Spring Festival or An Tostal, by turning away from the paralysing pieties of its local priest and the parochial provincialism of its spiritual and temporal institutions – in league with each other, as they see it. They are fired, instead, by the life-force and latitudinarianism of the invisible, opposing, revitalising and omnipresent Father Ned who is symbolic of the few, hitherto lonely voices representing longsuffering, radical, social and religious beliefs (in Ireland), to whom the playwright (an intensely religious infidel himself) pays affectionate tribute, once again, in this his embattled quest for greater libertarianism of life.

Like Beckett's Godot, Father Ned never appears, and like Godot, he exerts a powerful influence upon the remaining characters in the play; but, unlike Beckett or Godot, he is firmly on the side of life. The elusive Father Ned is a pantheistic spirit: part myth (from Irish mythology, 'Nuard' or 'Nudd' of the Silver Hand, referred to by O'Killigain, in the first act of *Purple Dust*; accomplished in the arts of battle, eloquence and magic); part embodiment of Pan and Eros, with the trinitarian attribute of liberality and progressiveness, symptomatic of forward-looking forces everywhere. He is a seraphic symbol, a numinous force: an alternative religious influence, akin to Shaw's concept of anthropomorphic Deism – the motivation behind Fathers Boheroe, Peter Keegan, Walter McDonald and other reforming priests.

On the young he has the same inhibition-releasing influence as the Cock in *Cock-a-Doodle Dandy*. Belonging to the same superworld, his temporal manifestation is recognised by the sound of drums; and his drumming always indicates a march forward. Those who enquire his whereabouts are told: 'Here, but he might be anywhere, though some may think he's nowhere; again, he may be everywhere; but he's always with th' drums'. The drums of O'Casey's Father Ned are analogous to Hesione Hushabye's 'sort of splendid drumming in the sky' in *Heartbreak House*, or the mysterious sound in *The Cherry Orchard* like a snapping string dying away – foretelling the release of a new society from the ruination of the old.

A warrior against all philistinism and sectarianism, it is clear that he is identified with a beneficent authority; a prepotency as powerful as Prometheus in ancient mythology; or former Celtic gods and heroes themselves: in futuristic terms, he is analogous to an ideology, close to O'Casey's heart, whose symbol, as we have seen from *Purple Dust* and *The Star Turns Red*, is enshrined in the red or evening star. Outwardly, Father Ned is also identified with the mysterious Echo, heard at intervals throughout, recalling Webster's echo at the end of *The Duchess of Malfi*. (Elizabethan drama, like O'Casey's, belongs to the strange realms of suprareality, and both have the superb, unflagging vigour of youth.)

Father Ned is also emblemised as Angus the Young, the Platonic Eros of O'Casey's fable. (Angus was also the motivating force behind the Messenger in *Cock-a-Doodle Dandy*.) In the playwright's preoccupation with youthful life-joy, he sees an analogy with Oengus, the Cupid of Irish mythology, or 'Saint of love'. (Oengus' kisses, we recall, turn birds into singing love-songs, and the music he plays draws in his wake all who hear it.) Angus, Wilson Knight suggests, is also Apollo, god of art, with his harp. He embodies all O'Casey's poet-dreamers as well as his youthful lovers. The young lovers in *The Drums of Father Ned* (those in *Oak Leaves and Lavender*, too) seem to be aware of this:

MICHAEL: My God, an' we're tangled, too, in life's great glittering braid! . . . All the stars of heaven are close to me when you are near. Angus the Young is by our side; we hear his harp-music, and his brilliant birds are perching on our shoulders.

NORA: For a brief while, my Michael. The purple tint of love must fade, and its passion becomes a whisper from a night that's gone. May our love pass quietly into companionship, for that is the one consummation of united life.

MICHAEL: Yes, the Bard and his harp, with his birds, must go one day, leaving us to live our own light, and make our own music. So we shall; then take a kiss for what it's worth, and let the dream go by.

(Act Three)

Angus, or Eros-Apollo, says Wilson Knight, is a deity known only transiently, and though we cannot be always on a level where Olympian splendour exists, it is enough to have known, as O'Casey's dramas illustrate, that there is such a level and magnificence. The 'epiphanies' which surround *Red Roses for Me*, *Oak Leaves and Lavender* and *Cock-a-Doodle Dandy* are eloquent testimony, as are such golden passages which transmogrify the experience of Stephen Dedalus in Joyce's works. For O'Casey, as with Tennyson (whose poetry he so much admired), the constellations of the heavens are uppermost – the stars glittering (in Tennyson's words) 'like a swarm of fire-flies tangled in a silver braid'. O'Casey's path, too, was always from the plough to the stars; the superhuman endeavour, epitomised by Browning, in the celebrated lines:

> . . . a man's reach should exceed his grasp,
> Or what's a heaven for?

'The theatre is a place of magic', he told David Phethean, who directed the British *première* of *The Drums of Father Ned*. (The interview appears in *The Sting and the Twinkle*.) 'It should be full of colour and excitement and gaiety. That's what it's *there* for! To bring colour into people's lives!' (Angus' Bird, says Wilson Knight, 'has the colours of the various *aspirations* handled in O'Casey's dramas: black for the priesthood; red for Communism; green for Eire; gold, perhaps for Ulster, but for more too, since gold is O'Casey's highest colour'.)

The identification of Christ with Eros is the mystical union proposed in *The Drums of Father Ned*, as well as, by implication, the merging of Northern and Southern parts of Ireland, and all opposing ideologies that lead to bloodshed and war. Adapting Blake's contraries – reflected in the impasse between Christian and pagan cultures (witnessed to a sharp degree in *Within the Gates* and *Cock-a-Doodle Dandy*) – O'Casey, in *The Drums of Father Ned*, offers his own Marriage of Heaven and Hell, and expounds, in fuller terms, in an expressionistic conclusion, the unification of disparate elements (in Ireland, and elsewhere) as advocated in *Red Roses for Me*.

The summery quality of *The Drums of Father Ned* dispels any despair which lingers in the conclusion to *The Bishop's Bonfire*. A new mood of optimism is apparent. In *Blasts and Benedictions*, O'Casey proclaims: 'I try to show this awakening, this thrust forward in thought, this new resolution, in my latest play'. There are some who regard it as O'Casey's happiest play. He does not, as in *Cock-a-Doodle Dandy*, descend Jove-like, to give his life-fearers the lash of condemnation; this time, there are no villains or 'bog Savonarolas' to outrage. The devil's advocate, Father Fillifogue, is simply a figure of farce, and the play is in the nature of a benign frivolity.

Written in 1957 (six months after the death of his younger son, Niall) and published in 1960, the play was to have had its *première* in 1958 during the Irish Festival, An Tostal (meaning Hosting or Gathering), instituted in 1953 to give an added fillip to the tourist season. (After 1958, the Tostal, as such, was replaced by a series of local festivals, but the annual Theatre Festival continued to remain a national commemorative event.)

O'Casey's play – along with *Bloomsday*, a play by Allan McClelland based on Joyce's *Ulysses*, and three mime plays and a radio play by Beckett – was to have been the centrepiece of the Tostal programme, scheduled to be opened in May 1958. O'Casey was enthusiastic, both about the Tostal and the Dublin Theatre Festival, as his letter to the Festival director, Brendan Smith, recalls:

> As for the play of mine, it is a little curious, a frolic, more or less, with an odd serious line here and there, and the Tostal as the background. I am of the opinion that this Festival could be a Bringer of new life and activity to Ireland, replacing the lost enthusiasm of the old National Movement, which, in many ways, is now old-fashioned, and outworn. Ireland, if she is to live, must create a new Ireland from the old one, and, I think, that this is the spirit of the play I have tried to write. Well, there's your answer, and, though it may not please you, be heavens, it's better than none.

Lamentably, O'Casey's last throwaway line proved to be true. It did not please what the *Irish Times* (echoing Shaw) had termed the illiberal 'cohorts of comstockery' among the Tostal authorities, who, fearful of O'Casey's anti-clerical tirades of the past and, apparently, in awe of squeaks and strictures from Dublin's Archbishop, wrote demanding alterations, alleging the play's 'structural state made the play unproduceable . . .', at which, O'Casey, sensing this was an improvident attempt to get him to back down, withdrew his play, in retaliation, and henceforward slapped a ban on all performances of his works in Ireland, which remained in force until almost immediately prior to his death.

The forced withdrawal of *The Drums of Father Ned* from the Dublin Theatre Festival thus became a chauvinistic charade; an inane parody of the Abbey Theatre's previous refusal, for similar, specious reasons, of *The Silver Tassie*. Ironically, one of O'Casey's intentions had been to show that Ireland was maturing. If immediate events had proved his optimism to have been too near-sighted, ultimately, his allegory will be seen in an efficacious light, having a conclusion that is both joyful and futuristic. Consequently, his very last plays – the short *Behind the Green Curtains* and *Figuro in the Night* – are tinged with a searing bitterness and Swiftian irony which make the gaiety and optimism of his festival drama, in hindsight, a lacuna of temporarily misjudged hope, even though its apocalyptic conclusion is one of triumphal vision and of life growing into fuller consciousness from its own power.

The priestly and forward-looking spirit of the play is reflected in its long and soulful dedication:

> *The Memory be Green* Of Dr Walter McDonald, courageous theologian in Maynooth College for forty years; of Dr Morgan Sheedy, his lifelong friend, banished for venturing to defend a Parish Priest against a Bishop, and who sent me 'an old priest's blessing' from Pennsylvania to New York in 1934; of Father Yorke of San Francisco, who warned Irish Ireland of fond delusions many years ago, and who told Dr McDonald, his friend, that in the *Rerum Novarum* the Church was offering the workers no more than a string of platitudes; of Canon Hayes, Founder of Muintir na Tire, bringing a sense of community life and co-operation to rural Ireland, and brightness with them; and of Father O'Flanagan who, when his poor flock were shivering through a black winter, bade them go to a private-owned bog, and take from it all the turf they needed, led them there to do it,

and was, consequently, banished from his Parish and from County Sligo by his Bishop. Each in his time was a Drummer for Father Ned, and the echoes of their drumming sound in Ireland still.

The self-reliance of such opposing forces, in creating a new and active life, says O'Casey, in a letter written at the time of the controversy,

> clashed with business, parochialism, and out-dated clericalism (a humorous figure and kindly withal), all against the background of the work for the Tostal. This microcosm is meant . . . to portray the whole condition of Ireland as she is; for today, in confusion of politics, art, literature, and sex, Ireland is a colorless kaleidoscope; a kaleidoscope, twist it how you may, never shows a settled or colorful pattern; that is the technique which no one could seemingly accept . . .

O'Casey's effervescent extravaganza – with prophetic overtones – is a three-act drama, with a prologue, which the dramatist describes, characteristically, as a 'Prerumble'. Time is equated as 'the present day'. The play tells of a group of villagers who are preparing to celebrate the Tostal, the Irish Folk Festival. In the words of the English producer, David Phethean, in *The Sting and The Twinkle*:

> All is gaiety, laughter, singing and dancing. The parish priest – an outraged, umbrella-waving pillar of the Established Church – tries desperately to restrain the rumbustious spirits of his flock while they, in turn, excuse themselves by crying: "It's all Father Ned's work!"

Subsequently, events in the plot playfully forecast almost precisely the happenings and hostilities which the play ran into itself.

The parable of the short 'Prerumble' is, in itself, as relevant and biting as Shaw's 'Epilogue' in *Saint Joan*. In a flashback to the time of 'The Troubles', two Irishmen, McGilligan and Binnington, both Republicans – the one a Free Stater, the other a Diehard – are surrounded by an Officer of the Black and Tans and his four men, as the little town is burning to destruction; significantly, only the spire of a church and a Celtic Cross (twin symbols of Christianity and

Druidism) remaining unscathed against a shadowy background of darkness and belching, red flame. Estranged Sinn Feiners, in the wake of newly independent Ireland, are plunging the countryside into a wall of flame and skulking snipers are on the rampage in boreens and hills. Although, observes one of the Tan soldiers, everything is as quiet 'as a grave a generation old', he is reminded by his commanding officer that 'Quiet graves in his country have a habit sometimes of spitting out bullets'. Binnington and McGilligan, who are on opposite sides of the fence, politically, hate each other more than they hate the British.

When asked by the military to settle their grievances, they decline, even at gunpoint. The officer is jeeringly sarcastic at their expense: 'Mass in the morning and murder at night. Well, you can have a good look at what it has done for your town'. As the two remain scowling and cowering, at the moment of death, the Black and Tans' officer – in an ironic twist – decides not to shoot them, because, as he observes scathingly to the rest of his men, 'these two rats will do more harm to Ireland living than they'll ever do to Ireland dead'.

As the 'Prerumble' ends in the midst of further shooting and destruction, to a chorus of faint voices chanting woefully in the distant background – with the two opposing patriots crawling their curse-filled way to safety (instead of, in the words of Spenser the poet, 'like ghosts crying out of their graves') – the irony of their release is worked out with the utmost relish and exploitation for the remainder of the play, mingling farce and tragedy as the play cavorts to its romping conclusion.

More than just a 'Mickrocosm' of Irish life, it is, indeed, an allegory of modern Ireland.

As the main plot switches to scenes of the present, and, finally, to the future (the time-sequence is *Oak Leaves and Lavender* all over again), indoor settings replace the burning Main Street – a cameo-reflection of trouble-torn Ireland of 1922 – used in the Prologue. In the mainstream of the play, the escaped Irishmen, Binnington and McGilligan, emerge, ironically, as two important dignitaries of the New Republic. Binnington, who has become Mayor, is a solicitor, coroner and Commissioner for Oaths and owner of the town of Doonavale's general stores. His rival, McGilligan, who went to the same school and worships in the same church, is Deputy Mayor and chief building contractor for the town. Both, although married to sisters, remain implacably hostile to each other, and aloof, except on business, a formality which, to them, is just 'a quid pro quo' – as the effective Echo, offstage, reiterates to the audience, Webster-style, and, at strategic intervals throughout. The echo-device proves an amusing variant to Father Neds' distant drum-rolls. (The drumbeats in this play signify optimism and defiance, as opposed to the mournful beats, accompanying the down-and-outs, in *Within the Gates*, or the menacing ones preluding the entry of the fascists in *The Star Turns Red*.)

The settings for the first and last acts are the drawing-room and parlour belonging to the Mayor whilst the second act centres on the lounge of the Deputy Mayor in the home of the McGilligans. Both lounges are almost identical in their highly-polished, mahogany décor, with similar ostentatious palm-trees, window-boxes and grand pianos; only the colours of the curtains being contradistinctive. As in the final act of *The Star Turns Red*, the settings show the exalted world of mayoral drawing-rooms, forming an ironical background to and hunting-ground of veiled insurrection, with similar conjural expectations. (A total irony is apparent when the Tostal workers – and those helping with the pageant – invade the privacies of both lounges, and, as in similar circumstances in the final act of *Oak Leaves and Lavender*, adapt them to their immediate, pressing needs.)

Apart from the four Black and Tan British soldiers, and their officer, employed in the introductory sleight-of-hand – together with an expressionistic chorus of distant voices at the beginning and end of the sequence – fifteen characters (including the mysterious Echo) infiltrate the main action, augmented by a crowd of local villagers preparing for the Tostal play and pageant.

Binnington and McGilligan are the main cartoon capitalists in the same fanciful mould as Stoke and Poges in *Purple Dust*, Mahan and Marthraun in *Cock-a-Doodle Dandy*, or Reiligan in *The Bishop's Bonfire*. (All are variants of the same arrogant 'paycock' species.) They symbolise the realities of the world of business-sense and commonsense in a striking way or obliquely comment on them. As characters, they are ideal for comedy, retreating in the more harmless avenues of farce and fantasy.

Aided and abetted by the ridiculous clerical poltroon, the Reverend D. Fillifogue (his name suggests 'trickery'), parish priest of Doonavale ('town of the shut-mouth'), is a similar stalking-horse of absurdity – dominating the lives of those around him – as the Reverend Canon Burren in O'Casey's previous play. The

watchword of their sway (and downfall) is a progressive materialism, whose dialectical consequences spell havoc for them and the
tradition they represent. Although life-long social and political
enemies, the Mayor and his Deputy remain true business allies,
united in their detestation of newer, whimsical trends – such as
enlivening opportunities that the Tostal brings – which they
envision as threats to the rights and duties of employers such as
themselves, prompting the jibe from Binnington, referring to the
workforce, that will they ever realise 'that when they work for us
they're workin' for God?' In their absurd and unreal adulation of
civic ritual and pride – evidenced in Binnington's self-expressed
'dereliction of good taste for a Deputy Mayor to wear a more
gorgeous gown than the Mayor' – these self-important dignitaries
have encouraged their fully approving and snobbish wives into
taking lessons in deportment and etiquette, producing laughable
and indecorous results, in the knockabout style of *Purple Dust* and
Cock-a-Doodle Dandy.

Thackeray's comments in *The Book of Snobs* are underscored:

> Irish snobbishness develops itself not in pride so much as in
> servility and mean admirations, and trumpery imitations of their
> neighbours . . . indeed it is hard not to grin at some of their *naive*
> exhibitions . . . Twopenny magnificence, indeed, exists all over
> Ireland, and may be considered as the great characteristic of the
> Snobbishness of that country.

As the play proceeds, the Binningtons vie with the McGilligans in
their twopenny splendours, their small-town prosperity and sham
loyalties, and, in Thackeray's words, 'solemnly do honour to
humbug'.

Their shared maid, Bernadette Shillayley, a high-spirited, good-
looking young colleen, with more than an iota of Irish insouciance,
and an ardent supporter of the Tostal festivities and Father Ned's
new thinking, reminds her plutocrat-employers that they would not
have pianos at all if it were not for the dead who died for Ireland.
The exponents of mammon, along with the self-ridiculous Father
Fillifogue, an avid little plenipotentiary, a Quilp of clerical
expectation, are opposed to the Tostal because it threatens their
way of life. Bernadette lets it be known to her employer that 'Father
Ned says that through music, good books, an' good pictures, we may
get to know more about th' mystery of life'. Those nostrums spin

Alderman Aloysius Binnington into an ire of exasperated expediency as he rampages:

> Oh, doesn't this stuff make a body yell! Mysthery of life! There's no mysthery in it, girl. There's nothin' more than gettin' all you can, holdin' what you have, doin' justice to your religious duties, and actin' decent to a neighbour.

Binnington also shows his scorn when the actors for the Tostal pageant invade his mayoral lounge for the dress rehearsal; and one of them, dressed as a Man of the Pike, without fuss, brushes him aside, reminding him that he and his fellow-workers have to hurry along with 'th' work of resuscitatin' Ireland', which brings a contemptuous snort and cry of 'waste of money' from Binnington.

The irascible McGilligan and Binnington, along with the narrow-minded Father Fillifogue, are constantly taunted and thwarted by the town's youth and those who participate in the Tostal pageantries. These comprise Binnington's son, Michael, and McGilligan's daughter, Nora (who are lovers), Tom Killsallighan, McGilligan's foreman-carpenter (in love with Bernadette), together with Oscar McGunty and his fellow-actors in the historical pageant specified as Man of the Musket and Man of the Pike. The parish priest's rebellious church organist, an eccentric Victorian known as Mr Murray, an over-excited, whimsical character, with a Limerick lisp, given to gusto, and a continual thorn in the side of the elderly cleric, is a fanatical admirer of Mozart's music, displaying an equally fanatical antipathy towards Father Fillifogue's hymns. ('Dee hymns an dee prayer till Ireland sinks into a deep freeze of frosty piety an' sham', he retorts.) Ignoring the priest's ridiculous jibe that 'There's nothing apostolic or evangelical in the riddle-me-randy music of Mozart', he rejoices and exults in the fact that the Tostal will be a means of bringing Mozart, Bach – 'an' Angus, too' – to the town's festivities.

The town is later visited (in Act Two) by an eccentric Ulsterman, Alec Skerighan, down on business, to supply Doonavale with timber from the shipyards of the North, with commission, of course, (and connivance) from the business-duo, Binnington and McGilligan, later causing a great stir, as the wood has originated from the forests of 'Red' Siberia. Skerighan has a marvellous penchant for upsetting most of the local pillars of the establishment, including Father Fillifogue, who rebukes this self-important Cock o' the North for his carefree and capricious comments: 'our town, sir, is Christian an' cultured . . . and no skuttle-alley, as you call it!' Skerighan's risible asides annoy his business associates, but he is, in the end, like the youth of the town, infected with Tostal fever. Although he polarises arguments between Catholic and Protestant, he finally surrenders to the magic of the Tostal and Father Ned's influence, and, indeed, becomes, in the finish, the playwright's chosen instrument in the mystical union between North and South.

This roaring bull of a character from Portadown rouses many local passions and inhibitions, and provokes a furious debate in the mayoral lounge, in the final act, drowned by a chorus of dissidents, in richest O'Casey tradition:

> SKERIGHAN (*cautiously*): Mind ye, I'm fast tae th' Crown an' Constitution, but ma Ulsther heart longs tae see th' Republic of Ireland goin' strang; but watchin' on' lussenin', suttin' aside this mod Tosthal, most of your festeevities seem tae be around some grave here, or round anither grave yon.
>
> MICHAEL: You're right there, Ulsther; our hearts beat best to th' music of a dirge; our marching feet too often point th' way to a grave. But with Father Ned, th' young will let th' dead bury their dead, an' give their thought an' energy to th' revelry of life!
>
> BERNADETTE: An' near time, too!
>
> SKERIGHAN: A grond ombeetion, lad; but somewhere ye'll floundher on' fall. Howe'er far ye gae, ye'll ever be afeart on' feckless, sae lang as ye suffer – [*He hesitates*]
>
> MICHAEL (*prompting*): Suffer what?
>
> SKERIGHAN: So lang as ye suffer th' inseedious dumination of your Church, on' th' waefu' intherfurence of your clergy in what ye thry tae do.
>
> BINNINGTON (*trying to be conciliatory*): Now, Alec, that's a matter of diversified opinion. The Catholic Faith is never an obstacle to any man's advancement.
>
> SKERIGHAN (*somewhat warmly*): I'm tullin' you dufferent, Mr Binnington, on' wull ye know yoursel' it's thrue. There's one thing stuppin' ye doon here: th' clingin' tae what has no wurrant from th' mind o' mon, or th' plain ravelations of Holy Scrupture.
>
> MRS MCGILLIGAN: Shishto, oh, whish.

BINNINGTON (*a little less conciliatory*): That's a debatable question, Mr Skerighan; a highly debatable question.

SKERIGHAN (*warmly*): It's no' a debatable question, I'm tullin' you! It's th' pure on' prime truth! What ye call your releegion has put your thochts aswither, on' turned ye all intil tuttherah toddlem duves!

MCGILLIGAN (*explosively*): I strongly resent being called a tut- therah toddlem dove!

MRS MCGILLIGAN (*soothingly*): Mr Skerighan, I'm sure, is jokin', but he should ha' left th' tatterah out.

A fierce, fun-inspired altercation then breaks out, Skerighan asking Michael Binnington 'whether God is ipso a Protestant or a Roman Catholic'. Michael, reflecting the views of O'Casey (in turn, echoing Joyce's Stephen Dedalus), replies:

He's neither; but He is all, and above noticin' th' tinkle of an opinion. He may be more than He is even claimed to be; He may be but a shout in th' street . . .

which immediately causes an uproar of conversational bellicosity (with verbal ingenuity) releasing argumentative cats among the sparring pigeons and drawing-room 'tatterah' turtle-doves! The resurrectional spirit of Kathleen Ni Houlihan, as well as the invisible presence of Father Ned, become centres of controversy, as the stage-disputants hurl their opinions at each other in what turns out to be a Mad Hatter's tea-party of nonsensical invective – aimed at those viscerally critical Irish areas of blood, death, honour, love, loyalty, intemperance, friendship, damnation and redemption – culminating in the course of the finale in 'Th' thondher of th' dhrums!' (those inspired by Father Ned), which fill the stage, as in a Lewis Carroll dream-fantasy, drumming out of town, as well as offstage, any paucity of logic or excess of chauvinism stemming from ignorance, superstition and repression: qualities inherent in a weak bourgeoisie held together by the caprice of capitalism and clericalism.

Conflict between conservative old and creative young is high- lighted in Act Two, set, this time in McGilligan's lounge. (Despite their differences, Binnington and McGilligan are Doonavale's equivalent of Tweedledum and Tweedledee in the indistinguish- able world of the Republic's indigenous, bucolic establishment-figures in Eire's essentially rural fantasy-existence.) The slogan on the Tostal poster – 'We were DEAD and are ALIVE AGAIN!' (with its Biblical reminders) – sets the theme of liberalisation and the recognition of regenerative forces in the real Irish hangover from the past.

The resurgence is outlined in a significant conversation between Bernadette and Tom. Quoting Father Ned, Bernadette tells her lover that just as old fields can still bring forth new corn, 'wintry' minds, even in Doonavale, can be transfused with the reawakening of spring. The Tostal, or Spring Festival, will bring something of the liveliness of colour to the town of Doonavale, and 'within th' timid stir of this dim town' (in the words of Father Ned) 'would come laughter and a song or two', says the gay-hearted Bernadette; and constraints on love would disappear. Under Father Ned's banner, the aspirations of the Boheroes and Keegans and McDonalds would be realised, in the fertility-hopes raised within the expectant atmosphere and apocalyptic settings of *Within the Gates* and *Cock-a-Doodle Dandy*.

The point of the play is embedded in dialogue which constitutes the Tostal 'play' itself. The play-within-a-play sequence (Act One) has the same vital role and significance as that within the plot of *Hamlet*: it restates the play's message and resolve. The Irish Rebellion of 1798 – the theme of the Tostal 'play' – parallels the watchword of greater freedom, for Catholic, Protestant and Presbyterian alike, as outlined by United Irishmen under Wolfe Tone. The historical play – within the genesis of O'Casey's own play – points an unhistoric parable and principle: freedom to live a fuller and unfettered life; the freedom Milton declared essential in *Areopagitica*. As Michael, in his role as one of the leaders of the ninety-eight insurgents, declares:

> We have stood quiet in our fields, in our hills, in our valleys; we have sat quiet in our homes, trusting the power that held us down would show justice; but we have found neither security nor peace in submission; so we must strike for the liberty we all need, the liberty we must have to live.

Ideals of past heroes can be translated into meaningful, futuristic terms: 'the cloak of green', at youth's behest, says O'Casey, can shake off 'the sable shawl', and release the strangleholds of priest, politician and their gombeen allies. Michael Binnington and Nora

McGilligan oppose the candidatures of their parents: fighting what they see as 'the meanness their policies preach'; offering themselves, in a new crusade, as nominees for their fathers' posts in the forthcoming council elections. In a new mood of determined opportunism and defiant optimism, youth can overturn and outweigh the derisions and disasters of the past – the future pattern of ploughing and reaping being enlivened by greater jollities from a fuller participation in revived fairs, feasts and gay festivals. Doonavale, by means of the Tostal, can be revitalised in a spirit of regenerative application of combined concepts of revelries from the past, such as Dublin's Donnybrook Fair with its gay abandon, discontinued in the Victorian era, after centuries of celebration, and Lammas fairs, special to the North, celebrating harvest festivals in first-fruits of a wider and more joyous existence to come. By such reviviscent means, Doonavale can give a lead, which other O'Casey centres of villagery – Clune na Geera, Nyadnanave or Ballyoonagh – were unable to do.

The mood of the whole play is permeated by the feverish activities of those involved in Tostal preparations, and these blossom, to the sound of Father Ned's reverberating drums, into a roistering, farcical comedy, where pretence is reduced to absurdity and controversy sails along on a sea of slapstick. McGilligan warns Skerighan that 'a Protestant tune's no fit thing to be played on a Catholic piano', amid riotous hurly-burly; and, as the combatants rage in 'fearfu' animosity', the befooling playwright turns the pageant into a spectacle of playful absurdity and will-o'-the-wisp comedy.

The old hatred for the northern counties is used by Father Fillifogue to manipulate his Southern flock into doing his will. But, as the 'climmax' and Tostal celebrations get under way, the umbrella-waving tactics diminish into a pantomimic farce; and, as ritual and symbol merge into O'Casey's tide of farce, in an aura of Father Ned's utopia, the roar of the clerical lion transmutes into the squeak of a timid mouse. In the final moments of the last act, the once-powerful cleric can only chant pathetically and symbolically in a dazed, 'semistupified way': 'Oh, dear, what can the matter be?', only to be told by the life-savers and yea-sayers around him – in a chorus of comic approval – 'Ireland has gone to the fair!' In a bout of cosmopolitan frenzy, Father Fillifogue attributes all the confusion and rebelliousness resulting from the Tostal, and natural merry-making between village Jack and village Jill, to the direct results, as he quaintly puts it, of 'th' College lettin' th' students wear jeans', producing what he fears is 'a Communist tendency and influence'. The young rejoice in a different plutonomy as theocratic values and controls are superseded. O'Casey's preternatural vision triumphs in the end and *The Drums of Father Ned* lives up to its expectation of being 'an idle, laughing play' in hilarious, heroic style, in O'Casey's richest, cornucopian manner.

The play is farcical comedy to be done with spirit, but with the comedy element uppermost. The ending is a triumphant shout of colour, song, and drum-rolls. (The older generation has been repudiated; its hypocrisy exposed.) In a 'Note' prefacing the play, O'Casey suggests that the drum-roll, heard intermittently throughout, should be of the kind which Haydn uses in his Symphony No. 103 (known as the 'Drum Roll' symphony). The echo device is a successful piece of additional magic which provides an ironic commentary on the dialogue; as effective, in its way, as the dramatic asides in O'Neill's *Strange Interlude*, or the soliloquies in *Hamlet*; or even the repetitious dialogue of the Old Man and Old Woman in the opening scene of *The Star Turns Red*.

O'Casey's use of magic in this play occurs mostly offstage. The magical atmosphere centres around Father Ned, and even though he never appears, his presence is always wonderfully and widely felt. He is O'Casey's own version of the charisma of Holy Ghost and the living interiority of human inspiration. He appears to Skerighan, in a vision of 'fierce green eyes shinin' lak umeralds on fire in a white face that was careerin' aboot though stayin' stull as an evenin' star, starin' up from doon in th' valley below'. He represents, says Wilson Knight, 'a private theology'. (The image of 'evening star' analogy unites socio-political and religious ideals, and accords with the playwright's own cherished aspirations.)

The fun-fair of the final act develops into a high-spirited extravaganza, forming – in the opinion of one commentator – an 'Aristophanic' allegory, presaging an undivided Ireland where the politics of terrorism have been successfully outwitted and routed.

Robert Hogan, intimately associated with the play's first professional production, makes the revealing comment:

. . . This last act, which appears weak on the page, is on the stage one of the most energetic and magical scenes O'Casey wrote since

the stupendous third act of *Red Roses for Me*. His use of music –
with his Ulsterman roaring out "Lillibulero", with Bizet's March
from "The Maid of Perth Suite", with the offstage bugle
sounding a Forward, with the roll of drums, and the shout of the
Echo – proves what theatre can really be when all of its resources
are used by a master.

(Hogan, 'In Sean O'Casey's Golden Days', in Ayling (ed.),
Sean O'Casey: Modern Judgements)

The young, in O'Casey's vivacious comedy, are invested with the
important roles. Father Fillifogue and his mayoral cohorts –
representing mammon – are the dying forces, and, with dramatic
dexterity on O'Casey's part, fade into the role of subsidiary
characters.

The role of two pairs of lovers is significant: the politics of sex and
the politics of leadership are interchangeable. Tennyson's aspiration in *Locksley Hall* – 'Love took up the glass of Time, and turn'd it
in his glowing hands' – is O'Casey's, too. The new lead given to the
townspeople by Nora and Michael and Bernadette and Tom is
emblematic and significant. O'Casey recognises this, too, towards
the closure of *Sunset and Evening Star*:

The young were busy in the house of life that the old were leaving;
throwing out some of the musty stuff, bringing in the fresh and the
new; changing the very shape of the house itself (though there
were many young ones coming into life who were mouldier than
the older ones going out of it); placing new pictures on the walls;
knocking out walls separating one family from another; polishing
everything with a newer glow; opening the windows wider.

The younger ones coming into life, professes O'Casey, can never be
the same as the older ones going out (Tennysonian philosophy of the
Lotos-Eaters and *Locksley Hall* in transposed circumstances). And,
implies O'Casey, in *The Drums of Father Ned*, if the old do not make
allowances for this, they are doomed, and the young will harass
them (as the lesson of *King Lear* teaches). In stepping down, the old –
'Pilots of the purple twilight' (to use a Tennysonian phrase) – must
recognise no disgrace or humiliation is involved in their inability to
dominate a newer generation (the philosophy we encounter in
Purple Dust and expressed in most of the plays subsequently; and

reiterated, trumpetingly, as an important fanfare in *The Drums of Father Ned*).

The dream of Tennyson and the vision of O'Casey are one:

> Forward, forward let us range.
> Let the great world spin for ever down
> the ringing grooves of change.

In the spring setting of the play, to harmonise with Tostal activities, the role of the lovers is important. In spring, Tennyson reminds us again in *Locksley Hall*, 'a young man's fancy' turns 'to thoughts of love'. As love takes up 'the harp of Life', the fuller visions of spring and wider argosies of fulfilment become manifest.

The drumming optimism of O'Casey's last fully-developed play spells defeat for his particular species of lampooned humanity – the vainglorious peacock breed. As political 'paycocks' – and manifestations of local influence – Binnington and McGilligan merit the scorn meted out to them by the younger generation, including, of course, their own offspring, who have no personal quarrel with them, only, as they proclaim, 'the hate, the meanness their policies preach; and to make a way for th' young and thrusting'.

Binnington, who is tall, thin and wiry, sporting a close-cropped beard and moustache – older than his middle-aged wife – is a political 'paycock' of ultra-absurdity. (So, also, is his adversary, the Deputy Mayor.) Although dressed in a brown tweed suit, he is pompously bedecked in a red Mayoral robe, which he wears all the time, with green velvet piping, from which a stiff white collar obtrudes. In the words of the dramatist, he is 'Business-man, patriot, and pietist' and 'loves himself more than anything else living or dead, though he isn't really a bad chap'. McGilligan, who is stoutish, semi-bald, and clad in a dark-grey suit, also always wears a red municipal robe, bordered with gold braid – richer and more ostentatious than the Mayor's. Both are political Humpty Dumpties in the pocket of Father Fillifogue. Their wives are sisters, and both middle-aged women show traces of former good looks. Elena Binnington is more snobbish than her sister. Meeda McGilligan embraces the ideals of the Tostal, in practice; joins the Tostal parade, eventually even persuading her sister to join in. (The men, like those in *Cock-a-Doodle Dandy*, are completely irredeemable.)

Michael Binnington is a tall, slim, handsome twenty-four-year-old, shaped, says O'Casey, 'to the lines of a well-faced fox', sharing similar physical characteristics with Feelim and Drishogue O'Morrigun. He is dressed in historical costume – as one of the leaders of the ninety-eight insurgents – white frilled shirt and dark green tailed coat and white knee-breeches. He carries a sword hanging from a light-green shoulder-sash. Tom Killsallighan – foreman carpenter in the employ of McGilligan – is also in his twenties, but stouter and of more muscular build. He is dark-haired, pleasant-faced with humorous eyes. He is dressed in the uniform of an English eighteenth-century army captain, having a crimson cutaway coat and carrying a sword. He is shrewd as well as bucolic-looking.

Nora McGilligan, a pretty lass of nineteen, slim, with brown hair, is attired in eighteenth-century pageantry dress, as are the rest of the girls participating in the Tostal pageant. Bernadette Shillayley is also nineteen or twenty, pretty in a simple way, but with a knowing, saucy air. She is dressed in ordinary attire: black, short skirt and yellow jumper, partly hidden by a large blue apron. She is a romantic rebel and spokesman for aspiring youth – transplendent with Father Ned's radical ideals. (Her role is similar to Marion's in *Cock-a-Doodle Dandy*.)

Father Fillifogue is stout, balding, middle-aged, and – like Canon Burren in *The Bishop's Bonfire* – dressed in conventional clerical garb, which makes him seem baggy. He grips an umbrella fiercely, which he stamps with furious emphasis when roused to anger or sarcasm. He treats his parishioners as if they were benign sheep, who, in the light of Tostal rehabilitation, regard him as a lost shepherd. He is out-of-touch and out of breath for most of the time.

Mr Murray, his temperamental organist, is of middle height, plump, and easily agitated. He is dressed in black frock coat, waistcoat and trousers. He speaks excitedly with a lisp and wipes the occasional froth which accumulates on a grey moustache. He and Father Fillifogue are a pair of sparring cocks.

Alec Skerighan, the Ulsterman, is in his forties 'with the look of a Jersey bull'. He is dressed in well-tailored dark suit, stiff collar, and carries the emblematic bowler – symbol of the Orangeman. Like Brennan o' the Moor in *Red Roses for Me*, he is a volatile argufier and sufficient indication that a Protestant can always be expected to out-bigot a Catholic in O'Casey's world. When asked, in the ebullience of Tostal celebrations, to give a thumping rendition of 'Lillibulero' – the lilting Protestant marching tune and rousing anthem (earlier, he annoys McGilligan by tapping it out on the piano) – he confesses to the revellers that the march-theme is 'nae gude withoot th' dhrums!' The song, with its rousing, repetitive refrain – *Lero, lero, lillibullero* – grips, actors and audiences alike, as the festive spirit of the Tostal spreads from stage to auditorium. In transcendental moments before the final curtain, a roll of drums in the distance cascades into rousing intensity and spontaneous rapture as to general approval, the 'thonder of th' dhrums of th' North' mixes with those of the forward-sounding, onward-marching Father Ned. The dramatic effect is like the climax of a symphony.

Among the remaining actors who participate in the play and Tostal pageant, Oscar McGunty – a man of forthright, sturdy opinions, always culminating, in the swaggering terms of his own catchphrase, in 'McGunty's climmax' – is a worker in McGilligan's factory. He is ceremonially dressed as a sergeant of the British Army in the eighteenth century, and, with his unwavering trumpet-calls at the end – prompted by Mr Murray – heralds his fellow-workers and actors into the spirit of the pageantries, spurred on by the thunderous roll of Father Ned's drums, in resurgence of youth and music of life.

The Black and Tan soldiers in the 'Prerumble' – as befits an expressionistic opening – are clad, not in khaki, but dressed fancifully in vivid yellow and black, contrasting startlingly with the spouting red flames of destruction engulfing stage scenario. In the graphics employed in this Gaelic parable, O'Casey uses image, scenario, syndrome and confrontation, in gay and lavish profusion.

Following the collapse of the projected Dublin *première* in 1958, the world *première* was in America, on 25 April 1959, at Lafayette's Little Theatre, Indiana. Robert Hogan co-directed with Jeanne Orr, in sets by Michael Brown. In the words of the playwright, it was performed 'in a mettlesome and most meritorious manner'.

David Phethean, in *The Sting and the Twinkle*, has described how he directed the English *première* at Queen's Theatre, Hornchurch, in Essex, where the run opened on 8 November 1960, with a cast which included David Blake Kelly, Kevin Fitzgerald and Doreen Keogh. (The designer was David Jones.) H. A. L. Craig, in the *New Statesman*, praised the event as 'a liberation', but looked forward to a suitably lavish production whirling its way on to a broader stage, but, in the plaudits of Richard Findlater, Phethean had achieved wonders with necessarily limited civic resources. In London, it was left to the prerogative of a non-professional group, the enterprising Tavistock Repertory Company, to stage what, in the testimony of

The Times, was 'a bustling, spirited account of the play' by its director, Walter Kennedy, at Islington's Tower Theatre in 1965.

The play that Dublin did not see in 1958 had its Irish *première* in 1966, in the capital's Olympia Theatre, directed by Tomas MacAnna (with settings by Robert Heade). A crowning cast included Joe Lynch, Jim Norton, Anna Manahan and Martin Dempsey. In a triumph of equivocation, Irish critics, on the whole, would only admit to what one of them termed 'a good piece of theatre'.

Despite unsuccessful ventures in France at the Théâtre Quotidien de Marseille and Le Cothurne, Lyon, in 1962 and 1963 respectively, the play was chosen, in the centennial year of O'Casey's birth, by the Lyric Players Theatre, Belfast, as an incandescent tribute, celebrating, mystically, O'Casey's vision of a united Ireland in the apocalyptic years ahead. Separate translations have appeared in French, Czech, Italian and Russian.

21 *Behind the Green Curtains* (1961): a Tragi-Comedietta

O'Casey's final collection of three characteristic short plays – interweaving outrageous satire and farce with melodramatic symbolism and a thread of tragedy, laced with song and dance – includes a biting satire on what the elderly dramatist sees as a debased modern Ireland. In the first play, *Behind the Green Curtains*, the irony is Swiftian, though its craftsmanship is unmistakably O'Casey's own. The published collection appeared a year after O'Casey had celebrated his eightieth birthday in 1960.

The green curtains of the title-play, in the wording of the dust-jacket to the printed volume, 'symbolise the obscurantism and humbug of Irish Catholicism which the author attacks with his still glorious use of language'.

The theme is that nothing matters but life as it is, and making the most of it. Man must be his own saviour – his own god – a concept, in itself, thoroughly Shavian. It leads to the conclusion that theocentric values – those according to preacher and prelate – especially those practised inhumanly in Ireland, are divorced from reality and lead to abuse of happiness and stultification of free thought and progress. As proclaimed, also, in *The Bishop's Bonfire* and *The Drums of Father Ned*, man must learn, not by prayer, but by experience and world science. The play is a warning against intellectual and artistic sterility which a too intense concentration upon Gaelicism and Catholicism is liable to produce.

A bitter allegory on intellectual life in the Republic of Ireland in the second half of the twentieth century, O'Casey's three-scened triptych is essentially in the realm of the non-realistic (though with vital implications) in a wholly fantastic setting. It is a short play, with three secenes named 'The Jittering Gate', 'Behind the Green Curtains', and 'Day of the Marching Souls'. It is entertaining, and, in a high degree, moving, but, on the whole, too witheringly satirical to earn a permanent place in playgoers' hearts.

The intellectual leaders of Ireland – the journalist, poet, actor and senator – are shown to be intellectual dwarfs, cowed by their duplicity and public cowardice, yet, privately, behind the pulled curtains of their own sanctums, they voice their brave, independent but ineffectual thoughts. Publicly, they are seen to do homage to hypocrisy and humbug. (Many of them cannot speak Gaelic, yet profess it in the schools and press and flaunt it in public ceremonial.) The dramatist voices his disturbance at the literary void in Ireland, as clerical power tightens its grip; though within a decade after the death of Dublin's reactionary Archbishop John McQuaid, and as the humanistic aims of Pope John XXIII began to take universal effect, some warmer, outside air had filtered even through the 'green curtains' of Eire's Republic.

Throughout this short morality, the struggle between life and death forces continues, with exile as the inevitable conclusion, and the consoling belief, which O'Casey puts into the mouth of his young heroine, Reena Kilternan, in the final scene: 'As long as you have life, you can be exiled from nothing'.

In the wake of disturbances in Ireland caused by his own innocuous play, *The Drums of Father Ned*, and at the same time the cowardice shown by certain intellectuals, inspired by the refusal of some of them to attend even the funeral service of the Protestant dramatist and Abbey Theatre Director, Lennox Robinson, O'Casey, in *Behind the Green Curtains*, analyses some bovine reactions of a group of characters representing 'th' leaders of Ireland's thought', when faced with a similar occurrence, in the opening scene, of the public funeral of a Protestant benefactor and celebrated playwright, the fictional (Lionel) Robartes, the subject of inspiration, also, in some of the lengthier poems of Yeats. The scene is the forlorn locality of Ballybeedhust (literally, 'Bally be dust'), suggesting intellecutal and moral death, as the playwright sings a dirge of Ireland.

The first scene opens with a couple of one-time hawkers, Angela Carrigeen and Lizzie Latterly, sitting on a bench opposite a Protestant church in a residential district, on a hot summer's day, engaged in a tangle of cross-talk, staring up at a portrait of one of Ireland's past political heroes in the main window of a house adjacent to the church, whose porchway is open, in readiness for Robartes's funeral. The two old crones fail to recognise the portrait and speculate whether the likeness is of St Joseph or St Peter. When told by a bystander, one of those attending the funeral, the atheistic Martin Beoman – 'A betther man than either of them. PARNELL!' – one of them rebukes her companion for asking embarrassing question of positive strangers: 'them swagger-mouths is part of the scenery now'.

As the two cautiously wend their way down the street for a drink, the scene is set as the rest of the intelligentsia arrive at the church for the funeral – Wycherley McGeera, a dramatist, Leslie Horawn, a poet, Bunny Conneen, an actor, and Jack McGeelish, a gossip columnist – and, later, arriving breathless, as an afterthought, Senator Dennis Chatastray, their living patron. (Strains of the 'Dead March' in Saul can be heard on the organ from within.) While they are dithering at the gate, unsure whether to enter and attend, apprehensive of being watched and speculating whether to set foot inside 'a heretical church', a 'squinting prober' for *The Catholic Buzzer*, Christy Kornavaun, arrives with the welcome Archepiscopal advice that to attend would be a serious breach of their religious faith. (Before the close of the scene, Beoman, the communist, and Reena, the sodality worker – at this point of the play, she is a practising Legionary of Mary – are the only ones to attend). As Kornavaun counsels the others to pull themselves together, and as the church bell has begun tolling, the two coster-women return blind drunk and collapse in front of the church where the assembled group are vacillating. The scene closes, ironically, as one of the women repeats: 'For Jasus' sake, Angela, thry to pull yourself together'.

The second scene shows Chatastray behind the green curtains of his house in Ballybeedhust, where he lives with his maid, Noneen Melbayle. The same intellectuals, introduced to us briefly in the first scene, are foregathered in his sitting-room, squabbling among themselves and villifying less respectable members of the establishment. They are seen to be no better than the bigoted reporter, Kornavaun, whom they all despise and secretly fear and whom they see as an 'ill-omened crawleen . . . on the prowl'. The duplicity of their motives is searingly exposed, like those of their trade union counterparts in the second act of *The Star Turns Red*.

A visit from the probing reporter sends them nervously scuttling into Chatastray's office in the next room, while the maid is left to explain that the Senator cannot see him because of a trade conference. Kornavaun, whose suspicions are aroused, leaves word that his paper wants the Senator's reactions to a forthcoming anti-communist demonstration and the names of those writers he is likely to select to speak from the platform; but, before leaving, makes some insulting imputations to Noneen about her situation with Chatastray, to which she reacts by flinging a drink in his face.

Back in the sitting-room after the reporter has gone, the writers and Chatastray are jittering over the proposal, when a second ring at the bell sends them into another paroxysm of fear, but this is allayed when Beoman, Chatastray's engineering foreman, calls to tell the Senator that there is trouble at his factory, and that the factory-hands will probably strike if a Protestant engineer who is anxious to marry a Catholic forewoman is not dismissed. Beoman reveals that the prying Kornavaun has been largely instrumental in whipping up support at the factory for the intended strike. Despite antipathy towards Kornavaun among the writers, one of them, with typical ambivalence, alleges: 'He was only doin' his duty as a good Catholic'.

Whilst they are discussing among themselves how they can avoid joining the protest march (even behind a banner proclaiming 'Free Thought in a Free World'!), the Legion-of-Mary-lass, Reena, at the behest of Kornavaun, who suspects they are all 'wobblin', appears with Papal-coloured rosettes, which they all shame-facedly put on (except Beoman, who has already declared, amid abuse, his political faith).

When Kornavaun himself appears later with a deputation from the Senator's factory demanding the instant dismissal of those contemplating a mixed marriage, Chatastray argues that such a marriage is permitted by law. O'Casey here demonstrates that the Church is more reactionary than the capitalist State – an extension of the thesis propounded in *The Star Turns Red*.

The *coup de grace* comes in the final moments of the scene's macabre farce, as Noneen, after seeing the deputation out, is attacked at the door by a gang of masked vigilantes, who carry her away, protestingly, from the scene; in the words of one of them, 'She's been taken to be taught that this town doesn't allow a young unmarried girl to live with an unmarried man'. Beoman rushes at one of the thugs and seizes one of their sticks, but the writers and Chatastray stand aside and do not intervene. 'It's no use', Beoman is told. Reena's sympathies now are with Beoman's, as Chatastray, too, is taken away.

The third scene takes place on the day of the demonstration. The setting is the same as in the previous scene. Chatastray, covered in bandages, is back in his room. The dishevelled state of the sitting-room remains. Reena enters and tells him of Noneen's plight: stripped, and left out all night in a rough night-gown, tied to a telegraph-pole (figuratively tarred-and-feathered with unfounded suspicion). The incident, which is factual in origin, is mentioned in the second volume of O'Casey's letters, at about the time of the storm of press controversy over the reception in Ireland of the published version of *Cock-a-Doodle Dandy*. 'We are a huddled nation frightened undher th' hood of fear', Reena tells Chatastray. Tidying the disorder of the room, she reminds him what cowardice has brought.

Renouncing her pietistic activities, Reena has decided not to attend the demonstration rally, but Chatastray cannot make up his mind, though concedes he will go, despite Reena's persuasiveness and personal encouragement ('I imagined you had a heart that wanted to be brave, so I came to help you'). The scene reveals, as does the nature of the whole play, the progressive deterioration of those afflicted by cowardice.

After Reena has pulled back the green curtains (a symbolic gesture bringing its own ironical consequences), the procession is soon to pass his door. When he hears the band playing 'Faith of our Fathers', he suddenly seizes, in a moment of expiation, his sash and rosettes and marches with his former cronies. 'Poor frightened Denis!' exclaims Reena to Martin Beoman (who has joined her in the room). 'He saved his soul at the eleventh hour.' 'Let's go from this dead place', says her stormy Romeo; and, taking Noneen with them, follow the same path as Loreleen, Robin and Marion at the end of *Cock-a-Doodle Dandy*: to a community where the mind is given its due and the body not distrusted – away from the spiritually bankrupt climate of The Land of Scholars and Saints! Casting an equally cold eye upon Catholic and upon Protestant, we can imagine them chanting, in moments of sad self-reflection, the MacNeice-inspired verses from *Autumn Journal*:

> Why should I want to go back
> To you, Ireland, my Ireland?

wishing to forget 'the blots on the page' or the 'faggot of useless memories' (the school-children fumbling their sums 'in a half-dead language', says MacNeice; or the censor 'busy on the books' or the games played in Gaelic). *Odi atque amo.*

The play is a savage lampoon; a topical burlesque, as well-calculated as Sheridan's *The Critic*, where Sheridan amused himself at the expense of the literary foibles of the day. The piece depends on Reena, who must have personality. Her progress along the primrosed path, from sodality-worker to emancipated woman, is the epicurean parallel of Susie in *The Silver Tassie*. She needs to be played with spirit and conviction. In this playlet, she is O'Casey's version of Barbara Undershaft from Shaw's *Major Barbara*. Beoman is, on the whole, a rather faceless, revolutionary figure; likewise Noneen, his passive accomplice. Chatastray is a tortured soul, who should be played with understanding and consciousness of torment. The rebel in him is swamped by a timorous conformity and egregious respect for Establishment behaviour.

The writers are a cross-section of types. The two coster-women are a couple of character parts providing farcical relief. Both are described as middle-aged, living on meagre pensions, dressed in faded clothing. One has a blue straw-hat, the other a faded, black-and-red-patterned shawl. Beoman is thirty, dressed in workaday attire and dungarees, with a vivid handkerchief round his neck; Reena is an attractive young lass, dressed in a tailored suit.

Robert Hogan directed and designed the first production of the play in December 1962, at the University of Rochester, New York State. Its first professional staging was at the Theater der Stadt, Cottbus, in East Germany, on 20 November, 1965. In Dublin, it was produced in 1975 at the Project Arts Centre. Elsewhere, it awaits a more convincing production. Its biting satire must be tempered with golden-humoured direction and what Shaw once termed the 'phosphorescence of romance' to do justice to its full tragicomic vein. Translations exist in French and German.

22 *Figuro in the Night* (1961): a Farfetched Fantasy

This bravura piece, in two short scenes, is a comedietta, in gay satirical mood; as outrageous in style as its exuberant forerunner, *Cock-a-Doodle Dandy*. This prefigurative romancelet is the second play included in the author's final collection of plays, published under the general title of *Behind the Green Curtains*. The theme is the extended theme of the title-play: namely, the awakening of the soul. Like Shaw, in his prefacing comments to his own short *Fanny's First Play*, O'Casey endorses the Shavian philosophy that 'the young had better have their souls awakened by disgrace . . . than drift along from their cradles to their graves doing what other people do for no other reason than that other people do it'.

The 'Deadication' ridicules 'The Ferocious Chastity of Ireland', and the play shows the sterile plight of the country resulting from such steadfast adherence to sexual abstinence.

Dublin is the setting throughout, in one of the streets of the new outer districts, bounded at each end by a memorial obelisk and Celtic Cross, each commemorating the dead of World War I and struggles for independence. Ironic strains, in the opening chorus, offstage, of 'Love's Old Sweet Song' can be heard but soon fade out as a Young Girl opens the front-door of her house overlooking the dark deserted street (it is night and most of the blinds are drawn), plaintively singing, in an excess of forlorn longing, 'Oh Dear, What Can the Matter Be', in improvised lyrics supplied by the dramatist. An Old Woman walking slowly down the street in the direction of the memorial cross takes up the chant in a cracked voice, relating such sentiments to her own entrenched puritanism and to what she calls 'the mantelshelf of memory'. While she is sitting on the steps of the stone pedestal attached to the Celtic Cross, an Old Man, muttering to himself, joins her on the opposite side, and both

diffidently recall long-lost memories of unrequited love and un-
bridled occasions of sin afforded by notions of blue ribbons and bird-
song suggested by the lyrics of the Young Girl's song. Fear and
chastity have banished such thoughts from their minds.

The Young Girl, continuing her song, yearns for more than blue
ribbons: 'Johnny's so long at the fair', she bemoans. The old couple,
listening to her nostalgic notes, are far away from such yearnings;
they are firmly ensconced in their own purity of conduct. The Old
Man's bankrupt thinking enables him to declare: 'We all know
what happens when he ties up her bonnie brown hair! That's what'll
shatther the counthry and toss her soul to perdition!' But later the
Old Woman reminds him that 'Life with a Lover and his lass sits
singing on the tomb, and mocks the stone'.

Such comments, together with the tale of Adam and Eve, recalled
between them – and its everyday implications for Eire's Eden – plus
an Angelus of crow's caws heard offstage, all anticipate the
transformation-effects of the second scene, in a fantasised world
where – O'Casey suggests in his stage-comments – 'Everything
seems wonderful to eyes that see and ears that hear'. (An Arcadian
parable is to be unfolded.) The morality figures of the first scene are
superseded by others (with the exception of the Young Girl)
arguing cornucopially among themselves in richest O'Casey fashion, in a phantasmagorically conceived scene of extravagant
humour, colour, song and dance. The excitement in the capital
generated by a statue of a young figurine (in the wording of the
'Deadication') 'doing an Obscene and Most Indecent Action under
the Guise of an Innocent Fountain' produces a welter of boisterous
comedy, in fantastic style, as well as conjured magnificence, similar
to those episodes which heighten many passages in the autobiographies and *Cock-a-Doodle Dandy*.

The figurine – a sort of fictional Mannekin Pis – which has
suddenly appeared in the city-centre, in full glare of O'Connell
Street, causes a great stir among the populace, becoming more than
just a civic and national mascot: a potential danger in the eyes of the
old and puritanical; a statue-of-liberty and phallic-symbol in the
vision of the young.

Objurgatory comments between two old men, who address each
other as 'Mr Tynan' and 'Mr Murphy' – both in torn, bedraggled
clothing; the one wearing a cap, the other a bowler – condemn the
statue in forthright, flamboyant tones. A Young Man, his clothing

torn and his face scratched and bleeding, tells of the same plight, informing the old bystanders – and prognosticators – that he thought he would lose all virtue and his 'decent dangling accessory'! The elliptical comment from the Second Old Man is enshrined in the observation: 'We're gonners, Mr Murphy', and both together exclaim: 'It's the end, the end of all things here'.

Asked by two reporters in the crowd – one deaf, the other blind (prefigurative of their present and future mental collapse) – why the Civic Guards weren't able to contain the commotion, one of the old men weaves a ludicrously fantastic description of how the assembled guarda were set upon by thousands of marauding women, who tore at their uniforms and 'endangered the unfortunate men's erectitude of feelin's'. 'Near desthroyed them', says the other, 'but not a one of them yielded'. And, in punning reference to one of Thomas Moore's national airs – 'Oft in the Stilly Night' – one of the doom-watchers solemnly declares: 'Darkness has come upon the Light of Other Days'. As stage-effects mockingly reinforce the assumption (from the sounds of cuckoos and crows to the 'rasping rattles' of corncrakes, in a deeper display of fooling or foreboding than even Carroll's 'monstrous crow' in *Through the Looking Glass* or Coleridge's dreaded Albatross in *The Rime of the Ancient Mariner*), the 'unholy figaries' and 'sinuosities' of Figuro, in the eyes of the Ancients, spell prognostic doom; but to the young and forward-looking, such auguries of innocence herald Blakean bliss and Yeatsian visions, in 'The Song of Wandering Aengus', of 'golden apples of the Sun' and 'silver apples of the Moon'.

In the hyperbole of clowning and conversational 'chassis', the entrance of a mythical or Birdlike Lad informs the disputants that 'Figuro is an abounding joy everywhere at last', from Cork to Sligo, and Belfast to Portadown; the Bishops are even infected with its riotous spirit, seated round a table in Maynooth, singing not community-hymns but love songs ('Come and Kiss Me, Sweet and Twenty') in gleeful and full-throated unison. In the triumphal moments of the twilight ending, the spirit of 'Love's Old Sweet Song' prevails; the puritanical are defeated ('We're bet, Mr Murphy . . . this is the end!') and the Birdlike Lad announces 'the world outside is changing'. Ireland, too, must hurry to the Fair, is the implication, as the Young Man serenades the Young Girl outside her casement-window, in a harlequinade of fantasy, and a troupe of colourful lads and young maidens on centre-stage lead a processional dance of jubilation and joy, to the accompaniment of stirring music. The young, unlike their doomed elders, have discovered new joys of living before it is too late.

The entire playlet must be fantastically treated, for everything is absurd, nothing rational. The characters are types rather than particular human beings, though the Birdlike Lad is a prefigurative creation, whose function is prognostic: his role is Ariel-like. He is dressed, close-fittingly, in black and wears a tight-fitting, green peaked cap, and looks very much like a crow (resembling, perhaps, in a phantasmagoric way, O'Casey himself – as self-styled 'Green Crow').

Although satirical in theme, the dramatic conclusion of this short fantasy is strongly apocalyptic: taboos which inhibit new thinking will disappear, just as all serious-minded individuals who contribute to that process deserve humanity's blessing and encouragement. In O'Casey's boisterous satire Kathleen Ni Houlihan has been transformed into a fertility-symbol despite the excoriation of narrow minds.

The play's *première* was on 4 May 1962 at Hofstra University, New York. Director-designer was Mirim Tulin. Its first professional staging followed later the same year (together with *The Moon Shines on Kylenamoe*) at New York's Theatre de Lys. The director was John O'Shaughnessy and the designer was Robert L. Ramsey. Its Irish *première*, in the same double billing, in 1975, was at the Abbey's Peacock Theatre, Dublin, where Tomas MacAnna directed and Bronwen Casson was the designer.

The play is a talisman for the young and needs a correspondingly supportive production giving vent and enthusiasm to such ideals. The playwright's daughter, together with a group of young actors, in a company styling itself Theatre Group 20, toured American colleges and campuses giving their own performances of the play in 1965. Their director was Gordon Taylor.

Figuro, although translated into French (but unpublished), still awaits a cue from Paris or Brussels, where it could harness its own satiric fantasy with its superb erotic, Gallic humour.

23 *The Moon Shines on Kylenamoe* (1961): a Realistic Fantasy

Ireland's hypocritical piety, pilloried so rumbustiously in *Behind the Green Curtains* and *Figuro in the Night*, is again one of prime targets in the third of O'Casey's final volume of plays – the highly amusing one-act, *The Moon Shines on Kylenamoe*.

In essence, the playlet is a warm-hearted, timely warning against ridiculous, inward, God-fearing, Gaelic-orientated, agrarian society indifferent to world culture and opinion; carrying within its reach the threat of intellectual death and the seeds of social and economic decay.

Kylenamoe is no hallowed spot afar from human ken, or druidic inspiration from Yeats: rather, a barren, rural version of Ballybeedhust; a desolate village inhabited by the very old: 'th' lot o' them, man an' woman, if not there already, is on th' tip o' 70', says Sean Tomasheen, a railway signalman and 'Pro-Tem Stationmaster', in his mid-twenties, who is one of the locality's rare exceptions. Apart from a little general store and railway siding and platform (trains only halt, on average, once in the day), there is no sign of active community life in this 'ghost' hamlet.

The setting is the railway platform and adjacent goods hut, in what is familiarly known by the residents as the 'station', flanked by a small thatched cottage with a low half-door, occupied by a seventy-year-old railway worker and his wife – Cornelius and Martha Conway. The time is the bewitching hour of midnight.

The play is farcical comedy in light, naturalistic manner, with symbolic overtones. As indicated on the flyleaf to the printed version, it 'should be welcome wherever one-act plays are performed and Irish accents available'.

The lone passenger who steps off the train and takes the sparring locals by surprise is a stage Englishman rejoicing in the name of

Lord Leslieson of Ottery St Oswald; a burlesque transplant and incongruity-figure from Westminster parliamentary sources, partly hidden by attaché case and umbrella (O'Casey's version of the French-inspired Major Thompson), vainly seeking the where-abouts of his Prime Minister holidaying in a nearby manor in the vicinity. 'Never heard such a name whispered on the Four Winds of Eireann', is Martha Conroy's immediate reaction, capped by Tomasheen's 'Of all th' saints I heard tell of, I never heard of an Otthery St Oswald mentioned; not once'.

The contrast between English and Irish makes the delicious humour of the play. The Englishman is unmistakable, despite the Devonian ring to his name. The Irish types are straight from life. O'Casey knew a good cross-section of them from the period when he worked with the GNRI in Dublin at the beginning of the century, up till 1911.

In the midst of heated argument and a 'configuration of confusions' – contributed conjointly by the guard, Michael Mulehawn, and the engine-driver, Andy O'Hurrie, and Sean Tomasheen himself – after the train has come to an unexpected halt (leaving the bewildered Earl on the lonely platform prey to the vagaries and verbal dispensations of the moonshiners), the seventy-year-old crofter and his wife, roused from slumber by the disturb-ance, proceed to pour further troubled oil on the loquacities of a situation that distinguishes the Irish countryside from the bog-perimeters of the rest of the world.

The argumentation momentarily subsides as a lone courting couple invades the privacy of the night:

SEAN: . . . Jasus, will yous look at what's comin' towards us at this unholy time o' th' night!

GUARD: Patrick Dunphy's boy an' Mave Linanawn, arms round each other, lost to th' world at large! Musta been at a dance or somethin'.

SEAN (*excitedly*): There's no dance anywhere tonight, not one; an' if there was, it would be in another direction altogether. What are they doin' here on railway property? That pair has been up to no good.

GUARD: What else, an' they stealin' evil excitements within th' secret niches of th' night.

SEAN: All sense o' decency hidden away from th' undulations of forbidden thoughts.

L. LESLIESON (*impatiently*): Oh, nonsense! For heaven's sake, let's confine our attention to the problem of my getting where I want to go. [*Indicating with a gesture towards where the couple are*.] This is no unusual sight, men. Just another lover and his lass. They are to be seen everywhere.

GUARD: What, in Kylenamoe?

SEAN: At this time o' th' night?

L. LESLIESON (*losing his patience – loudly, almost a shout*): At any time of the night, fool!

SEAN (*to the Guard*): Hear that, Mick!

GUARD (*seriously*): In your counthry, yessir; not here; so th' sooner you get back there, th' betther an' safer for us!

L. LESLIESON (*still angry*): I'm not interested in your Dunphy's boy or the girl he's hooking with his arm. [*Explosively*] I want to get to the town!

Calling for the hire of a car, to the bemused surprise of the natives, he is told by Tomasheen: 'Car! I dunno if one o' them has ever seen one, even from a distance. Neither kid nor car!'

Eventually, through the prevarications and persuasions of the Conroys, who come to the ruritanian rescue, the bewildered Earl finally arrives at his destination in a donkey-drawn turf creel cart.

The lovers, like the young of Ireland, are threatened and ordered off the property for infringing the rules. As they fling back their final taunt: 'Let us leave these fools for God to help them!' they disappear into the night. Yeatsian aspirations, voiced in 'Sailing to Byzantium', are doubtless theirs, as well as O'Casey's: for Ireland, O'Casey reiterates, 'is no country for old men'. And, caught in the 'sensual music' of their own desires, the joys they seek are to be found elsewhere; in a Byzantium of their own. Thus, the play's true conclusion is tragicomic. In Yeats's appropriate words (from 'The Gyres' in *Last Poems*): 'we that look on but laugh in tragic joy'.

The characters are vignettes from the realms of past reality (though past, present and future are one in Ireland). Lord Leslieson is a pompous variation of Poges, a typical Englishman, as seen through Irish eyes: a John Bull in plus-fours, 'utterly unconscious of his comic aspect'.

Sean Tomasheen is a young Irish labourer, described by O'Casey as 'not bad-looking, but rather thin, tall, and a little ungainly'. He is accused by the guard, Mick Mulehawl, of being 'a bog-born ignoremus' and by the engine-driver of being a 'threatenin' jaytalker'. The disordered guard is older, and exerts, in a farcical overspecialisation of his authority (symbolised by the band of silver adorning his official peaked cap, in contrast to the wider green band of Sean's), a more pretentious sense of delaying tactics; and for most of his time, literally and figuratively, wanders off track. The engine-driver, Andy O'Hurrie, whose name belies his behaviour, is a parody of the one in the Percy French song:

> Are ye right there, Michael? are ye right?
> Do you think that we'll be there before the night?
> Ye've been so long in startin',
> That ye couldn't say for sartin' –
> Still ye might now, Michael, so ye might!

He and the stubborn guard, Mulehawl, are well-matched: while wobbling through the dark, they live in a permanent, semi-unreal world of 'to-morra'.

The septuagenarian Conways resemble the Old Man and Woman portrayed in *The Star Turns Red*, Martha forever repeating her husband's last words, the farcical flavour and refrain of which add to the comicality of their portrayal. The lovers are simply types: like most bucolic-looking young Irish, they are famously-shrewd in some of their whirling opinions and will-o-the wisp replies. (When it comes to opportune rejoinders their hearts are as hard as rock itself.) The Woman Passenger, who leaves the train to cajole the cross-talking officials back to their cabins and compartments, is a veritable jaytalker herself, though she is not of moonshining stuff. In Kylenamoe, she insists, they may dream the earth is standing still while everyone is asleep, but, elsewhere, life beats to a more urgent rhythm, away from the darkness and death-hour surrounding it.

The Moon Shines on Kylenamoe was first performed at the Theatre de Lys, New York, together with *Figuro in the Night*, as an O'Casey double-bill, on 30 October 1962. The director was John O'Shaughnessy. Edward Roth produced the playlet for Irish television on 4 November 1962. A strong cast included Dermot Kelly, Harry Brogan, Seamus Kavanagh and May Cluskey. There was much hilarity on the lines of the author's early one-act farces. The Abbey staged the Irish *première* at its Peacock Theatre in Dublin in 1975, directed by Tomas MacAnna. (The designer was

Bronwen Casson.) The cast included Bryan Murray, Gerry Walsh and Eamon Kelly.

In Berlin, in 1965, it was featured in a programme of the dramatist's three short plays (the others were *Hall of Healing* and *A Pound on Demand*) at the Kammerspiele des Deutschen Theaters, directed by Adolf Dresen. Other German versions have been done at Leipsig's Keller Theater in 1969, and at Cottbus the same year. Translations are known to exist in Danish, German and Persian.

Although over eighty when the playlet was written, the dramatist was still blazingly young in spirit, and it is to the young he is mainly addressing himself in the final phase of his work. Arise from sleep and shake off sloth is the play's absolute message. His words, as virile and vivid as ever, are directed against codes and conventions which threaten to straitjacket youthful minds. His final play is thus a trumpet-call to the energies of youth, corresponding to Longfellow's *Excelsior!*, implying 'Upward Hope' – the constant effort, in the overflow of endeavour, to achieve nobler things for humanity, if not in the present cycle of life, at least in the apocalypse of future fulfilment.

Select Bibliography

(Published in London unless otherwise stated)

Agate, James, '*Juno and the Paycock* and *The Plough and the Stars*', in R. Ayling (ed.), *Sean O'Casey: Modern Judgements* (Macmillan, 1969).
—— 'A masterpiece: *The Star Turns Red*' [play review], *The Sunday Times*, 17 Mar. 1940.
Armstrong, W. A., *Sean O'Casey* (*Writers and Their Work*, no. 198) (Longman, 1967).
——'Sean O'Casey, W. B. Yeats and the Dance of Life', in R. Ayling (ed.), *Sean O'Casey: Modern Judgements*.
Atkinson, Brooks, *Sean O'Casey*, ed. Robert G. Lowery (Macmillan, 1982).
Ayling, Ronald, (ed.), *Sean O'Casey: Modern Judgements*, Macmillan, 1969.
—— and Durkan, Michael J. *Sean O'Casey: A Bibliography* (Macmillan, 1978).
Beckett, Samuel, 'The Essential and the Incidental' [review of *Windfalls*], *The Bookman*, Christmas 1934.
Benstock, Bernard, *Paycocks and others: Sean O'Casey's World* (Dublin: Gill and Macmillan, 1976).
Bentley, Eric, *What is Theatre?* (Dobson, 1957).
Boas, Guy, 'Introduction', *Juno and the Paycock and The Plough and the Stars* (*The Scholar's Library*) (Macmillan, 1948).
Boucicault, Dion, *The Dolmen Boucicault*, ed. David Krause (Dublin: Dolmen Press, 1964).
Brophy, John and Partridge, Eric, *The Long Trail: Soldiers' songs and slang 1914–18* (Deutsch, 1965).
Fallon, Gabriel, *Sean O'Casey: The Man I Knew* (Routledge, 1965).
Gassner, John, *Masters of the Drama* (New York: Random House, 3rd ed., 1954).
—— (ed.), 'Genius Without Fetters', Introduction to *Selected Plays of Sean O'Casey* (New York: Braziller, 1954).
Gregory, Augusta, *Journals, 1916–1930*, ed. Lennox Robinson (Putnam, 1946).
Grene, Nicholas, *Synge: A Critical Study of the Plays* (Macmillan, 1975).
Heppner, Sam, '*Cockie*' [C. B. Cochran], with a foreword by Noel Coward (L. Frewin, 1969).
Hogan, Robert, *After the Irish Renaissance* (Macmillan, 1967).
—— 'In Sean O'Casey's Golden Days', Ayling (ed.), *Sean O'Casey: Modern Judgements*.
Hunt, Hugh, *The Abbey: Ireland's National Theatre 1904–1978* (Dublin: Gill and Macmillan, 1979).
Joyce, James, *Selected Letters of James Joyce*, ed. Richard Ellmann (Faber, 1975).
Kee, Robert, *The Green Flag: A History of Irish Nationalism* (Weidenfeld and Nicolson, 1972).

411

Kleiman, Carol, *Sean O'Casey's Bridge of Vision* (University of Toronto Press, 1982).
Knight, G. Wilson, *The Golden Labyrinth: A Study of British Drama* (Phoenix, 1962).
—— *The Christian Renaissance* (Methuen, 1962).
Krause, David, *Sean O'Casey: The Man and His Work* (New York: Macmillan, 2nd ed., 1975).
—— *The Profane Book of Irish Comedy* (Cornell University Press, 1982).
Larkin, Emmet, *Jim Larkin, Irish Labour Leader 1876–1947* (Routledge, 1965).
Leeson, R. A. (ed.), *Strike: A Live History 1887–1971* (Allen & Unwin, 1973).
Lowery, Robert G. (ed.), *Essays on Sean O'Casey's Autobiographies* (Macmillan, 1981).
—— *The Sean O'Casey Review* (New York, 1974–82).
—— the *O'Casey Annual*, Macmillan, 1982–.
MacDiarmid, Hugh (pseud.), *The Company I've Kept* (Hutchinson, 1966).
—— 'Sean O'Casey's new play: *Within the Gates*' [book review], *Scots Observer*, Edinburgh, 17 Feb. 1934.
McDonald, Walter, *Reminiscences of a Maynooth Professor* (Cape, 1925).
Malone, Maureen, *The Plays of Sean O'Casey* (Southern Illinois University Press, 1969).
Masefield, John, *The Old Front Line*, with an introduction on The Battle of the Somme by Col. Howard Green, Bourne End, Bucks (Spurbooks, 1972).
Mikhail, E. H., *Sean O'Casey: A Bibliography of Criticism*, with an introduction by Ronald Ayling (Macmillan, 1972, rev. ed. in progress).
—— and O'Riordan, John (eds), *The Sting and The Twinkle: Conversations with Sean O'Casey* (Macmillan, 1974).
Mitchell, Jack, *The Essential O'Casey: A Study of the Twelve Major Plays of Sean O'Casey* (Berlin: Seven Seas Publishing, 1980).
—— 'The Theatre of Sean O'Casey', *Zeitschrift für Anglistik und Amerikanistik*, no. 1, Berlin, 1978.
Morgan, Margery M., *The Shavian Playground: An Exploration of the Art of George Bernard Shaw* (Methuen, 1972).
Nathan, George Jean, *Encyclopaedia of the Theatre* (New York: Knopf, 1940).
—— (ed.) 'Foreword', *Five Great Modern Irish Plays* (New York: Random House, 1941).
Nicoll, Allardyce, *British Drama: An Historical Survey from the Beginnings to the Present Time* (Harrap, 1925; 4th ed., 1947).
O'Casey, Eileen, *Sean*, edited with an introduction by J. C. Trewin (Macmillan, 1971).
—— 'Red Roses for Sean', Mikhail & O'Riordan (eds), *The Sting and The Twinkle*.
O'Casey, Sean.
Plays: Separate edns (Macmillan 1925–61); Collected Plays 5 vols (Macmillan, 1984); *The Harvest Festival*, with a Foreword by Eileen O'Casey and Introduction by John O'Riordan (Gerrards Cross: C. Smythe, 1980).
Autobiographies: *I Knock at the Door, Pictures in the Hallway, Drums Under the Windows, Inishfallen, Fare Thee Well, Rose and Crown, Sunset and Evening Star*, 6 vols (Macmillan, 1939–54). Reissued as *Autobiographies*, 2 vols, with index and chronology by J. C. Trewin (Macmillan, 1981).
Prose: Separate edns. (Macmillan) *Windfalls*, 1934, *The Flying Wasp*, 1937, *Under a Colored Cap*, 1963; *The Green Crow* (New York: Braziller, 1956); *Feathers From The Green Crow*, ed. Robert Hogan (Macmillan, 1963), *Blasts and Benedictions*, ed.

Ronald Ayling (Macmillan, 1967). *The Letters of Sean O'Casey*, 3 vols, ed. David Krause (New York: Macmillan, 1975) – in progress.

O'Flaherty, Liam, *A Tourist's Guide to Ireland* (Mandrake, 2nd ed., 1930).

O'Riordan, John, 'Sean O'Casey: Colourful Quixote of the Drama', *Library Review*, 22, Glasgow, Spring 1970.

Priestley, J. B., *The Art of the Dramatist* (Heinemann, 1957).

—— 'O'Casey's Predicament: How Can one Dramatise the English?' [Book review of *Oak Leaves and Lavender*]. *Our Time*, June 1946.

Purdom, C. B., *A Guide to the Plays of Bernard Shaw* (Methuen, 1963).

Shaw, G. Bernard; *Everybody's Political What's What* (Constable, 1944).

—— *What I Really Wrote about The War* (Constable, 1931).

Sheaffer, Louis, *O'Neill: Son and Artist* (Elek, 1974).

Short, Ernest, *Theatrical Cavalcade* (Eyre & Spottiswoode, 1942).

Smith, B. L., *O'Casey's Satiric Vision* (Ohio Kent State University Press, 1978).

Stephens, James, *The Insurrection in Dublin* (Dublin & London: Maunsel, 1916).

—— 'Dublin Letter', *Dial*, Chicago, 1924, *Letters of James Stephens*, ed. Richard J. Finneran (Macmillan, 1974).

Stock, A. G., *W. B. Yeats: His Poetry and Thought* (Cambridge, 1961).

—— 'The Heroic Image: *Red Roses for Me*', in Ayling (ed.), *Sean O'Casey: Modern Judgements*.

Styan, J. L., *The Dramatic Experience: A Guide to the Reading of Plays* (Cambridge, 1965).

Trewin, J. C., *Dramatists of Today* (Staples, 1953).

—— *Going to Shakespeare* (Allen & Unwin, 1978).

—— (ed.) 'Introduction', *Three More Plays by Sean O'Casey* (Macmillan, 1965).

Weintraub, Stanley, *Bernard Shaw, 1914–1918: Journey to Heartbreak* (Routledge, 1973).

Williams, Raymond, *Drama from Ibsen to Brecht* (Chatto & Windus, 1968).

Worth, Katharine J., *Revolutions in Modern English Drama* (Bell, 1972).

—— 'O'Casey's Dramatic Symbolism', in Ayling (ed.), *Sean O'Casey: Modern Judgements*.

Index